THE ORIGINAL BOSTON COOKING-SCHOOL COOK BOOK 1896

BY

Fannie Merritt Farmer

A facsimile of the first edition of
THE BOSTON COOKING-SCHOOL COOK BOOK

WEATHERVANE BOOKS
NEW YORK

THE

BOSTON COOKING-SCHOOL

COOK BOOK.

BY

FANNIE MERRITT FARMER,

PRINCIPAL OF THE BOSTON COOKING-SCHOOL.

1896.

TO

MRS. WILLIAM B. SEWALL,

President of the Boston Cooking-School,

IN APPRECIATION OF HER HELPFUL ENCOURAGEMENT AND
UNTIRING EFFORTS IN PROMOTING THE WORK OF
SCIENTIFIC COOKERY, WHICH MEANS THE
ELEVATION OF THE HUMAN RACE,

THIS BOOK IS AFFECTIONATELY DEDICATED

BY THE AUTHOR.

Cookery means the knowledge of Medea and of Circe and of Helen and of the Queen of Sheba. It means the knowledge of all herbs and fruits and balms and spices, and all that is healing and sweet in the fields and groves and savory in meats. It means carefulness and inventiveness and willingness and readiness of appliances. It means the economy of your grandmothers and the science of the modern chemist; it means much testing and no wasting; it means English thoroughness and French art and Arabian hospitality; and, in fine, it means that you are to be perfectly and always ladies — loaf givers. — RUSKIN.

PREFACE.

"BUT for life the universe were nothing; and all that has life requires nourishment."

With the progress of knowledge the needs of the human body have not been forgotten. During the last decade much time has been given by scientists to the study of foods and their dietetic value, and it is a subject which rightfully should demand much consideration from all. I certainly feel that the time is not far distant when a knowledge of the principles of diet will be an essential part of one's education. Then mankind will eat to live, will be able to do better mental and physical work, and disease will be less frequent.

At the earnest solicitation of educators, pupils, and friends, I have been urged to prepare this book, and I trust it may be a help to many who need its aid. It is my wish that it may not only be looked upon as a compilation of tried and tested recipes, but that it may awaken an interest through its condensed scientific knowledge which will lead to deeper thought and broader study of what to eat.

F. M. F.

TABLE OF CONTENTS.

CHAPTER I.

FOOD 1

CHAPTER II.

COOKERY 17

CHAPTER III.

BEVERAGES 36

CHAPTER IV.

CHAPTER V.

CHAPTER VIII.

CHAPTER IX.

CHAPTER X.

CHAPTER XI.

CHAPTER XII.

CHAPTER XIII.

CHAPTER XVIII.

CHAPTER XIX.

CHAPTER XX.

CHAPTER XXI.

CHAPTER XXII.

CHAPTER XXIII.

CHAPTER XXIV.

CHAPTER XXV.

CHAPTER XXVI.

ICES, ICE CREAMS, AND OTHER FROZEN DESSERTS . . 365

CHAPTER XXVII.

CHAPTER XXVIII.

CHAPTER XXIX.

CHAPTER XXX.

CHAPTER XXXI.

CHAPTER XXXII.

CHAPTER XXXIII.

CHAPTER XXXVI.

COOKING, PRESERVING, AND CANNING FRUITS 473

JELLIES 477

JAMS 480

MARMALADES 480

CANNING AND PRESERVING 481

CHAPTER XXXVII.

CHAPTER XXXVIII.

CHAPTER XXXIX.

THE BOSTON COOKING-SCHOOL COOK BOOK.

CHAPTER I.

FOOD.

FOOD is anything which nourishes the body. Thirteen elements enter into the composition of the body: oxygen, $62\frac{1}{2}$%; carbon, $21\frac{1}{2}$%; hydrogen, 10%; nitrogen, 3%; calcium, phosphorus, potassium, sulphur, chlorine, sodium, magnesium, iron, and fluorine the remaining 3%. Others are found occasionally, but, as their uses are unknown, will not be considered.

Food is necessary for growth, repair, and energy; therefore the elements composing the body must be found in the food. The thirteen elements named are formed into chemical compounds by the vegetable and animal kingdoms to support the highest order of being, man. All food must undergo chemical change after being taken into the body, before it can be utilized by the body; this is the office of the digestive system.

Food is classified as follows: —

I. ORGANIC
{ 1. Proteid (nitrogenous or albuminous).
{ 2. Carbohydrates (sugar and starch).
{ 3. Fats and oils.

II. INORGANIC
{ 1. Mineral matter.
{ 2. Water.

The chief office of proteids is to build and repair tissues. They can furnish energy, but at greater cost than carbo-hydrates, fats, and oils. They contain nitrogen, carbon, oxygen, hydrogen, and sulphur or phosphorus, and include all forms of animal foods (excepting fats and glycogen) and some vegetable foods. Examples: milk, cheese, eggs, meat, fish, cereals, peas, beans, and lentils. The principal constituent of proteid food is albumen. Albumen as found in food takes different names, but has the same chemical composition; as, *albumen* in eggs, *fibrin* in meat, *casein* in milk and cheese, *vegetable casein* or *legumen* in peas, beans, and lentils; and *gluten* in wheat. To this same class belongs gelatine.

The chief office of the carbohydrates is to furnish energy and maintain heat. They contain carbon, hydrogen, and oxygen, and include foods containing starch and sugar. Examples: vegetables, fruits, cereals, sugars, and gums.

The chief office of fats and oils is to store energy and heat to be used as needed, and constitute the adipose tissues of the body. Examples: butter, cream, fat of meat, fish, cereals, nuts, and the berry of the olive-tree.

The chief office of mineral matter is to furnish the necessary salts which are found in all animal and vegetable foods. Examples: sodium chloride (common salt); carbonates, sulphates and phosphates of sodium, potassium, and magnesium; besides calcium phosphates and iron.

Water constitutes about two-thirds the weight of the body, and is in all tissues and fluids; therefore its abundant use is necessary. One of the greatest errors in diet is neglect to take enough water; while it is found in all animal and vegetable food, the amount is insufficient.

CORRECT PROPORTIONS OF FOOD.

Age, sex, occupation, climate, and season must determine the diet of a person in normal condition.

Liquid food (milk or milk in preparation with the various prepared foods on the market) should constitute the diet of a child for the first eighteen months. After the teeth appear, by which time ferments have been developed for the digestion of starchy foods, entire wheat bread, baked potatoes, cereals, meat broths, and occasionally boiled eggs may be given. If mothers would use Dr. Johnson's Educators in place of the various sweet crackers, children would be as well pleased and better nourished; with a glass of milk they form a supper suited to the needs of little ones, and experience has shown children seldom tire of them. The diet should be gradually increased by the addition of cooked fruits, vegetables, and simple desserts; the third or fourth year fish and meat may be introduced, if given sparingly. Always avoid salted meats, coarse vegetables (beets, carrots, and turnips), cheese, fried food, pastry, rich desserts, confections, condiments, tea, coffee, and iced water. For school children the diet should be varied and abundant, constantly bearing in mind that this is a period of great mental and physical growth. Where children have broken down, supposedly from over-work, the cause has often been traced to impoverished diet. It must not be forgotten that digestive processes go on so rapidly that the stomach is soon emptied. Thanks to the institutor of the school luncheon-counter!

The daily average ration of an adult requires

3½ oz. proteid.   10 oz. starch.
3 oz. fat.   1 oz. salt.
          5 pints water.

About one-third of the water is taken in our food, the remainder as a beverage. To keep in health and do the best mental and physical work, authorities agree that a mixed diet is suited for temperate climates, although sound arguments appear from the vegetarian. Women, even though they do the same amount of work as men, as a rule require less food. Brain workers should take their proteid in a form easily digested. In consideration of this fact, fish and eggs form desirable substitutes for meat. The working man needs quantity as well as quality, that the stomach may have something to act upon. Corned beef, cabbage, brown-bread, and pastry will not overtax his digestion. In old age the digestive organs lessen in activity, and diet should be almost as simple as that of a child, increasing the amount of carbohydrates and decreasing the amount of proteids and fat.

WATER (H_2O).

Water is a transparent, odorless, tasteless liquid. It is derived from five sources,— rains, rivers, surface-water or shallow wells, deep wells, and springs. Water is never found pure in nature; it is nearly pure when gathered in an open field, after a heavy rainfall, or from springs. For town and city supply, surface-water is furnished by some adjacent pond or lake. Samples of such water are carefully and frequently analyzed, to make sure that it is not polluted with disease germs.

The hardness of water depends upon the amount of salts of lime and magnesia which it contains. Soft water is free from objectionable salts, and is preferable for household purposes. Hard water may be softened by boiling, or by the addition of a small amount of bicarbonate of soda $(NaHCO_3)$.

Water freezes at a temperature of 32° F., boils at 212° F.; when bubbles appear on the surface and burst, the boiling-point is reached. In high altitudes water boils at a lower temperature. From 32° to 65° F. water is termed cold; from 65° to 92° F. tepid; 92° to 100° F. warm; over that temperature, hot. Boiled water is freed from all organic impurities, and salts of lime are precipitated; it does not ferment, and is a valuable antiseptic. Hot water is more stimulating than cold, and is of use taken on an empty stomach, while at a temperature of from 60° to 95° F. it is used as an emetic; 90° F. being the most favorable temperature.

Distilled water is chemically pure and is always used for medicinal purposes. It is flat and insipid to the taste, having been deprived of its atmospheric gases.

There are many charged, carbonized, and mineral spring waters bottled and put on the market; many of these are used as agreeable table beverages. Examples: Soda water, Apollinaris, Poland, Seltzer, and Vichy. Some contain minerals of medicinal value. Examples: Lithia, saline, and sulphur waters.

SALTS.

Of all salts found in the body, the most abundant and valuable is sodium chloride (NaCl), common salt; it exists in all tissues, secretions, and fluids of the body, with exception of enamel of the teeth. The amount found in food is not always sufficient; therefore salt is used as a condiment. It assists digestion, inasmuch as it furnishes chlorine for hydrochloric acid found in gastric juice.

Common salt is obtained from evaporation of spring and sea water, also from mines. Our supply of salt obtained by evaporation comes chiefly from Michigan and New York; mined salt from Louisiana and Kansas.

Salt is a great preservative; advantage is taken of this in salting meat and fish.

Other salts — lime, phosphorus, magnesia, potash, sulphur, and iron — are obtained in sufficient quantity from food we eat and water we drink. In young children, perfect formation of bones and teeth depends upon phosphorus and lime taken into the system; these are found in meat and fish, but abound in cereals.

STARCH ($C_6H_{10}O_5$).

Starch is a white, glistening powder; it is largely distributed throughout the vegetable kingdom, being found most abundantly in cereals and potatoes. Being a force-producer and heat-giver, it forms one of the most important foods.   Alone it cannot sustain life, but must be taken in combination with foods which build and repair tissues.

Test for Starch.   A weak solution of iodine added to cold cooked starch gives an intense blue color.

Starch is insoluble in cold water, almost soluble in boiling water.   Cold water separates starch-grains, boiling water causes them to swell and burst, thus forming a paste.

Starch subjected to heat is changed to *dextrine* ($C_6H_{10}O_5$), British gum.   Dextrine subjected to heat plus an acid or a ferment is changed to *dextrose* ($C_6H_{12}O_6$). Dextrose occurs in ripe fruit, honey, sweet wine, and as a manufactured product.   When grain is allowed to germinate for malting purposes, starch is changed to dextrine and dextrose.   In fermentation, dextrose is changed to alcohol (C_2H_5HO) and carbon-dioxide (CO_2).   Examples: Bread-making, vinegar, and distilled liquors.

Glycogen, animal starch, is found in many animal tissues and in some fungi.   Examples: In liver of meat and oysters.

Raw starch is not digestible; consequently all foods containing starch should be subjected to boiling water, and thoroughly cooked.   Starch is manufactured from wheat, corn, and potatoes.   **Corn-starch** is manufactured from Indian corn.   **Arrowroot,** the purest form of starch, is obtained from two or three species of the Maranta plant, which grows in the West Indies and other tropical countries.   Bermuda arrowroot is most highly esteemed. **Tapioca** is starch obtained from tuberous roots of the bitter cassava, native of South America.   **Sago** is starch obtained from sago palms, native of India.

SUGAR ($C_{12}H_{22}O_{11}$).

Sugar is a crystalline substance, differing from starch by its sweet taste and solubility in cold water.   As food, its uses are the same as starch; all starch must be converted into sugar before it can be assimilated.

The principal kinds of sugar are: Cane sugar or *sucrose*, grape sugar or *glucose* ($C_6H_{12}O_6$), milk sugar or *lactose* ($C_{12}H_{22}O_{11}$), and fruit sugar or *levulose* ($C_6H_{12}O_6$).

Cane sugar is obtained from sugar cane beets, and the palm and sugar-maple trees. Sugar cane is a grass supposed to be native to Southern Asia, but now grown throughout the tropics, a large amount coming from Cuba and Louisiana; it is the commonest and sweetest of all, and in all cases the manufacture is essentially the same. The products of manufacture are: Molasses, syrup, brown sugar, loaf, cut, granulated, powdered, and confectioners' sugar. Brown sugar is cheapest, but is not so pure or sweet as white grades; powdered and confectioners' sugars are fine grades, pulverized, and, although seeming less sweet to the taste, are equally pure. Confectioners' sugar when applied to the tongue will dissolve at once; powdered sugar is a little granular.

Cane sugar when added to fruits, and allowed to cook for some time, changes to grape sugar, losing one-third of its sweetness; therefore the reason for adding it when fruit is nearly cooked. Cane sugar is of great preservative value, hence its use in preserving fruits and milk; also, for the preparation of syrups.

Three changes take place in the cooking of sugar: First, barley sugar; second, caramel; third, carbon.

Grape sugar is found in honey and all sweet fruits. It appears on the outside of dried fruits such as raisins, dates, etc., and is only two-thirds as sweet as cane sugar. As a manufactured product it is obtained from the starch of corn.

Milk sugar is obtained from the milk of mammalia, but unlike cane sugar does not ferment.

Fruit sugar is obtained from sweet fruits, and is sold as *diabetin*, is sweeter than cane sugar, and is principally used by diabetic patients.

GUM, PECTOSE AND CELLULOSE.

These compounds found in food are closely allied to the carbohydrates, but are neither starchy, saccharine, nor oily. Gum exists in the juices of almost all plants, coming from the stems, branches, and fruits. Examples: Gum arabic, gum tragacanth, and mucilage. Pectose exists in the fleshy pulp of unripe fruit; during the process of ripening it changes to pectin; by cooking, pectin is changed to pectosic acid, and by longer cooking to pectic acid. Pectosic acid is jelly-like when cold; pectic acid is jelly-like when hot or cold. Cellulose constitutes the cell-walls of vegetable life; in very young vegetables it is possible that it can be acted upon by the digestive ferments; in older vegetables it becomes woody and completely indigestible.

FATS AND OILS.

Fats and oils are found in both the animal and vegetable kingdom. Fats are solid; oils are liquid; they may be converted into a liquid state by application of heat; they contain three substances, *stearin* (solid), *olein* (liquid), *palmitin* (semi-solid). Suet is an example where stearin is found in excess; lard where olein is in excess, and butter where palmitin is in excess. Margarin is a mixture of stearin and palmitin. The fatty acids are formed of stearin, olein, and palmitin, with glycerine as the base. Examples: stearic, palmitic, and oleic acid. Butyric acid is acid found in butter. These are not sour to the taste, but are called acids on account of their chemical composition.

Among animal fats cream and butter are of first importance as foods, on account of their easy assimilation. Other examples are: The fat of meats, bone-marrow, suet (the best found around the loin and kidneys of the beef creature), lard, cottolene, coto-suet, cocoanut butter, butterine and oleomargarine. The principal animal oils are cod liver oil and oil found in the yolk of egg; principal vegetable oils are olive, cotton-seed, poppy, and cocoanut oil, and oils obtained from various nuts.

Oils are divided into two classes, *essential* and *fixed*. Essential oils are volatile and soluble in alcohol. Examples : Clove, rose, nutmeg, and violet. Fixed oils are non-volatile and soluble in ether, oil or turpentine. Examples : Oil of nuts, corn-meal, mustard, and glycerine.

Fats may be heated to a high temperature, as considered in cookery they have no boiling-point. When appearing to boil, it is evident water has been added, and the temperature lowered to that of boiling water, 212° F.

MILK.

COMPOSITION.

Proteid, 3.4%.	Mineral matter, .7%.
Fat, 4%.	Water, 87%.
Lactose, 4.9%.	

Boston Chemist.

The value of milk as a food is obvious from the fact that it constitutes the natural food of all young mammalia during the period of their most rapid growth. There is some danger, however, of overestimating its value in the dietary of adults, as solid food is essential, and liquid taken should act as a stimulant and a solvent rather than as a nutrient. One obtains the greatest benefit from milk when taken alone at regular intervals between meals, or before retiring, and sipped, rather than drunk. Hot milk is often given to produce sleep.

When milk is allowed to stand for a few hours, the globules of fat, which have been held in suspension throughout the liquid, rise to the top in the form of *cream;* this is due to their lower specific gravity.

The difference in quality of milk depends chiefly on the quantity of fat therein : casein, lactose, and mineral mat-

ter being nearly constant, water varying but little unless
milk is adulterated.

Why Milk Sours. A germ found floating in the air
attacks a portion of the lactose in the milk, converting it
into lactic acid; this, in turn, acts upon the casein (proteid) and precipitates it, producing what is known as
curd and *whey*. Whey contains water, salts, and some
sugar.

Milk is preserved by sterilization, pasteurisation, and
evaporation. *Fresh condensed milk*, a form of evaporized milk, is sold in bulk, and is preferred by many to
serve with coffee. Various brands of condensed milk and
cream are on the market in tin cans, hermetically sealed.
Examples: Nestle's Swiss Condensed Milk, Eagle Condensed Milk, Daisy Condensed Milk, Highland Evaporated Cream, Borden's Peerless Evaporated Cream.
Malted milk — evaporized milk in combination with extracts of malted barley and wheat — is used to a considerable extent; it is sold in the form of powder.

Thin, or strawberry, and thick cream may be obtained
from almost all creameries. Devonshire, or clotted cream,
is cream which has been removed from milk allowed to
heat slowly to a temperature of about 150° F.

In feeding infants with milk, avoid all danger of infec-
tious germs by sterilization. By this process milk can be
kept for many days, and transported if necessary. To
prevent acidity of the stomach, add from one to two tea-
spoonfuls of lime water to each half pint of milk. Lime
water may be bought at any druggist's, or easily prepared
at home.

Lime Water. Pour two quarts boiling water over an
inch cube unslacked lime; stir thoroughly and stand over
night; in the morning pour off the liquid that is clear, and
bottle for use. Keep in a cool place.

MILK FOR THE SICK.

It is generally conceded that in typhoid fever and diphtheria, milk should constitute the diet in early stages of either disease. In cases where it cannot be taken alone, it may be taken in combination with soda, seltzer, Apollinaris, or Vichy water, bearing in mind that it should be given in small quantities, at frequent, regular intervals.

In cases of extreme weakness *peptonized milk* is often used which is partially pre-digested. *Koumiss* (fermented milk), which can be easily prepared at home, is much used in fevers and gastric troubles.

Where a larger amount of nutriment is required, *albumenized milk* is valuable.

Good reports come from the use of *modified milk*, prepared at the Walker-Gordon Laboratory, Boston, and from a similar laboratory in Philadelphia. Modified milk is put up by physicians' prescriptions; the milk is separated into its parts, and recombined in different proportions to better suit the needs of individual cases. The milk is always sterilized before it leaves the laboratory.

BUTTER.

COMPOSITION.

Fat, 93%.	Mineral matter, .95%.
Water, 5.34%.	Casein, .71%.

Pratt Institute.

Butter of commerce is made from cream of cow's milk. The quality depends upon the breed of cow, manner of, and care in feeding. Milk from Jersey and Guernsey cows yields the largest amount of butter.

Butter should be kept in a cool place, and well covered, otherwise it is liable to become rancid; this is due to the albuminous constituents of the milk, acting as a ferment, setting free the fatty acids. First-quality butter should

be used; this does not include pat butter or fancy grades.
Poor butter has not been as thoroughly worked during
manufacture, consequently more casein remains; therefore it is more apt to become rancid.   Fresh butter spoils
quickly; salt acts as a preservative.   Butter which has
become rancid by too long keeping may be greatly improved by melting, heating, and quickly chilling with ice-
water.   The butter will rise to the top, and may be easily
removed.

Where butter cannot be afforded, there are several
products on the market which have the same chemical
composition as butter, and are equally wholesome.   Examples: Butterine and oleomargarine.

Buttermilk is liquid remaining after butter "has come."
When taken fresh, it makes a wholesome beverage.

CHEESE.

COMPOSITION.

Proteid, 31.23%.	Water, 30.17%.
Fat, 34.39%.	Mineral matter, 4.31%.

Cheese is the solid part of sweet milk obtained by heating milk and coagulating it by means of rennet or an acid.
Rennet is an infusion made from prepared inner membrane of the fourth stomach of the calf.   The curd is
salted and subjected to pressure.   Cheese is made from
skim milk, milk plus cream, or cream.   Cheese is kept
for a longer or shorter time, according to the kind,
that fermentation or decomposition may take place.
This is called ripening.   Some cream cheeses are not
allowed to ripen.   Milk from Jersey and Guernsey cows
yields the largest amount of cheese.

Cheese is very valuable food; being rich in proteid, it
may be used as a substitute for meat.   A pound of cheese
is equal in proteid to two pounds of beef.   Cheese in the
raw state is difficult of digestion.   This is somewhat overcome by cooking and adding a small amount of bicar-

bonate of soda. A small piece of rich cheese is often eaten to assist digestion.

The various brands of cheese take their names from the places where made. Many foreign ones are now well imitated in this country. The favorite kinds of skim-milk cheese are: Edam, Gruyère, and Parmesan. Parmesan is very hard and used principally for grating. The holes in Gruyère are due to aeration.

The favorite kinds of milk cheese are: Gloucester, Cheshire, Cheddar, and Gorgonzola; Milk and cream cheese: Stilton and Double Gloucester; Cream cheese: Brie, Neufchâtel, and Camembert.

FRUITS.

The varieties of fruits consumed are numerous, and their uses important. They are chiefly valuable for their sugar, acids, and salts, and are cooling, refreshing, and stimulating. They act as a tonic, and assist in purifying the blood. Many contain a jelly-like substance, called pectin, and several contain starch, which during the ripening process is converted into glucose. Bananas, dates, figs, prunes, and grapes, owing to their large amount of sugar and small amount of water, are the most nutritious. Melons, oranges, lemons, and grapes contain the largest amount of water. Apples, lemons, and oranges are valuable for their potash salts, and oranges and lemons especially valuable for their citric acid. It is of importance to those who are obliged to exclude much sugar from their dietary, to know that plums, peaches, apricots, and raspberries have less sugar than other fruits; apples, sweet cherries, grapes, and pears contain the largest amount. Apples are obtainable nearly all the year, and on account of their variety, cheapness, and abundance are termed queen of fruits.

Thoroughly ripe fruits should be freely indulged in, and to many are more acceptable than desserts prepared in the kitchen. If possible, fruits should always appear on the breakfast-table. In cases where uncooked fruit cannot be freely eaten, many kinds may be cooked and prove valuable. Never eat unripe fruit, or that which is beginning to decay. Fruits should be wiped or rinsed before serving.

VEGETABLE ACIDS, AND WHERE FOUND.

The principal vegetable acids are:

I. Acetic ($HC_2H_3O_2$), found in wine and vinegar.

II. Tartaric ($H_2C_4H_4O_6$), found in grapes, pineapples, and tamarinds.

III. Malic, much like tartaric, found in apples, pears, peaches, apricots, gooseberries, and currants.

IV. Citric ($H_3C_6H_5O_7$), found in lemons, oranges, limes, and citron.

V. Oxalic ($H_2C_2O_4$), found in rhubarb and sorrel.

To these may be added tannic acid, obtained from gall nuts. Some fruits contain two or more acids. Malic and citric are found in strawberries, raspberries, gooseberries, and cherries; malic, citric, and oxalic in cranberries.

CONDIMENTS.

Condiments are not classed among foods, but are known as food adjuncts. They are used to stimulate the appetite by adding flavor to food. Among the most important are salt, spices, and various flavorings. Salt, according to some authorities, is called a food, being necessary to life.

Black pepper is ground peppercorns. Peppercorns are the dried berries of Piper nigrum, grown in the West Indies, Sumatra, and other Eastern countries.

White pepper is made from the same berry, the outer husk being removed before grinding. It is less irritating than black pepper to the coating of the stomach.

Cayenne pepper is the powdered pod of capsicum grown on the eastern coast of Africa and in Zanzibar.

Mustard is the ground seed of two species of the Brassica. Brassica alba yields white mustard seeds; Brassica nigra, black mustard seeds. Both species are grown in Europe and America.

Ginger is pulverized dried root of Zanzibar officinale, grown in Jamaica, China, and India. Commercially speaking, there are three grades, — Jamaica, best and strongest; Cochin, and African.

Cinnamon is ground inner bark of Cinnamomum zeylanicum, principally grown in Ceylon. The cinnamon of commerce (cassia) is powdered bark of different species of the same shrub, which is principally grown in China, and called Chinese cinnamon. It is cheaper than true cinnamon.

Clove is ground flower buds of Caryophyllus aromaticus, native to the Moluccas or Spice Islands, but now grown principally in Zanzibar, Pemba, and the West Indies.

Pimento (commonly called allspice) is ground fruit of the Eugenia pimenta, grown in Jamaica and the West Indies.

Nutmeg is the kernel of the fruit of the Myristica fragrans, grown in Banda Islands.

Mace. The fibrous network which envelops the nutmeg seed constitutes the mace of commerce.

Vinegar is made from apple cider, malt, and wine, and is the product of fermentation. It is a great preservative; hence its use in the making of pickles, sauces, and other condiments. The amount of acetic acid in vinegar varies from two to seven per cent.

Capers are flower buds of Capparis spinosa, grown in countries bordering the Mediterranean. They are preserved in vinegar, and bottled for importation.

Horse-radish is root of Cochliaria armoracia, — a plant native to Europe, but now grown in our own country. It is generally grated, mixed with vinegar, and bottled.

FLAVORING EXTRACTS.

Many flavoring extracts are on the market. Examples:
Almond, vanilla, lemon, orange, peach, and rose. These
are made from the flower, fruit, or seed from which they
are named. Strawberry, pineapple, and banana extracts
are manufactured from chemicals.

CHAPTER II.

COOKERY.

COOKERY is the art of preparing food for the nourishment of the body.

Prehistoric man may have lived on uncooked foods, but there are no savage races to-day who do not practice cookery in some way, however crude. Progress in civilization has been accompanied by progress in cookery.

Much time has been given in the last few years to the study of foods, their necessary proportions, and manner of cooking them. Educators have been shown by scientists that this knowledge should be disseminated; as a result, "Cookery" is found in the curriculum of public schools of many of our towns and cities.

Food is cooked to develop new flavors, and make it more palatable and digestible. For cooking there are three essentials (besides the material to be cooked), — heat, air, and moisture.

Heat is molecular motion, and is produced by combustion. Heat used for cookery is obtained by the combustion of inflammable substances — wood, coal, charcoal, coke, gas, gasoline, kerosene, and alcohol — called fuels. Heat for cookery is applied by radiation, conduction, and convection.

Air is composed of oxygen, nitrogen, and argon, and surrounds everything. Combustion cannot take place without it, the oxygen of the air being the only supporter of combustion.

Moisture, in the form of water, either found in the food or added to it.

The combined effect of heat and moisture swells and bursts starch-grains; hardens albumen in eggs, fish, and meat; softens fibrous portions of meat, and cellulose of vegetables.

Among fuels, kerosene oil is the cheapest; gas gives the greatest amount of heat in the shortest time. *Soft wood*, like pine, on account of its coarse fibre, burns quickly; therefore makes the best kindling. *Hard wood*, like oak and ash, having the fibres closely packed, burns slowly, and is used in addition to pine wood for kindling coal. Where only wood is used as a fuel, it is principally hard wood.

Charcoal for fuel is produced by the smothered combustion of wood. It gives an intense, even heat; therefore makes a good broiling fire. Its use for kindling is not infrequent.

There are two kinds of coal: *Anthracite*, or *hard coal*. Examples: Hard and free-burning White Ash, Shamokin, and Franklin. Nut is any kind of hard coal obtained from screenings. *Bituminous*, or *soft coal*. Example: Cannel coal.

Coke is the solid product of carbonized coal, and bears the same relation to coal that charcoal bears to wood.

Alcohol is employed as fuel when the chafing-dish is used.

FIRE.

Fire for cookery is confined in a stove or range, so that heat may be utilized and regulated. Flame-heat is obtained from kerosene, gas, or alcohol, as used in oil-stoves, gas-stoves or gas-ranges, and chafing-dishes.

A **cooking-stove** is a large iron box set on legs. It has a fire-box in the front, the sides of which are lined with fire-proof material similar to that of which bricks are made. The bottom is furnished with a movable iron grate. Underneath the fire-box is a space which extends from the grate to a pan for receiving ashes. At the back of fire-box is a compartment called the oven, accessible on each side of the stove by a door. Between the oven and the top of the stove is a space for the circulation of air.

Stoves are connected with chimney-flues by means of a stove-pipe, and have dampers to regulate the supply of air and heat, and as an outlet for smoke and gases.

The damper below the fire-box is known as the *front damper*, by means of which the air supply is regulated, thus regulating the heat.

The oven is heated by a circulation of hot air. This is accomplished by closing the *oven-damper*, which is situated near the oven. When this damper is left open, the hot air rushes up the chimney. The damper near the chimney is known as the *chimney-damper*. When open it gives a free outlet for the escape of smoke and gas. When partially closed, as is usually the case in most ranges, except when the fire is started, it serves as a saver of heat. There is also a *check*, which, when open, cools the fire and saves heat, but should always be closed except when used for this purpose.

Stoves are but seldom used, portable ranges having taken their places.

A portable range is a cooking-stove with one door; it often has an under oven, of use for warming dishes and keeping food hot.

A set range is built in a fireplace. It usually has two ovens, one on each side of the fire-box, or two above it at the back. Set ranges, as they consume so large an amount of fuel, are being replaced by portable ones.

HOW TO BUILD A FIRE.

Before starting to build a fire, free the grate from ashes. To do this, put on covers, close front and back dampers, and open oven-damper; turn grate, and ashes will fall into the ash receiver. If these rules are not followed, ashes will fly over the room. Turn grate back into place, remove the covers over fire-box, and cover grate with pieces of paper (twisted in centre and left loose at the ends). Cover paper with small sticks, or pieces of pine wood, being sure that the wood reaches the ends of fire-box, and so arranged that it will admit air. Over pine wood arrange hard wood; then sprinkle with two shovelfuls of coal. Put on covers, open closed dampers, strike a match, — sufficient friction is formed to burn the phosphorus, this in turn lights the sulphur, and the sulphur the wood, — then apply the lighted match under the grate, and you have a fire.

Now blacken the stove. Begin at front of range, and work towards the back; as the iron heats, a good polish may be obtained. When the wood is thoroughly kindled, add more coal. A blue flame will soon appear, which is the gas (CO) in the coal burning to carbon deoxide (CO_2), when the blue flame changes to a white flame; then the oven-damper should be closed. In a few moments the front damper may be nearly closed, leaving space to admit sufficient oxygen to feed the fire. It is sometimes forgotten that oxygen is necessary to keep a fire burning. As soon as the coal is well ignited, half close the chimney-damper, unless the draft be very poor.

Never allow the fire-box to be more than three-fourths filled. When full, the draft is checked, a larger amount of fuel is consumed, and much heat is lost. This is a point that should be impressed on the mind of the cook.

Ashes must be removed and sifted daily; pick over and save good coals, — which are known as cinders, — throwing out useless pieces, known as clinkers.

If a fire is used constantly during the day, replenish coal frequently, but in small quantities. If for any length of time the fire is not needed, open check, the dampers being closed; when again wanted for use, close check, open front damper, and with a poker rake out ashes from under fire, and wait for fire to burn brightly before adding new coal.

Coal when red hot has parted with most of its heat. Some refuse to believe this, and insist upon keeping dampers open until most of the heat has escaped into the chimney.

To keep a fire over night, remove the ashes from under the fire, put on enough coal to fill the box, close the dampers, and lift the back covers enough to admit air. This is better than lifting the covers over the fire-box, and prevents poisonous gases entering the room.

WAYS OF COOKING.

The principal ways of cooking are boiling, broiling, stewing, roasting, baking, frying, sautéing, braising, and fricasseeing.

Boiling is cooking in boiling water. Solid food so cooked is called boiled food, though literally this expression is incorrect. Examples: Boiled eggs, potatoes, mutton, etc.

Water boils at 212° F. (sea level), and simmers at 185° F. Rapidly boiling water has the same temperature as slowly boiling water, consequently is able to do the same work, — a fact often forgotten by the cook, who is too apt "to wood" the fire that water may boil vigorously.

Watery vapor and steam pass off from boiling water. Steam is invisible; watery vapor is visible, and is often miscalled steam. Cooking utensils commonly used admit the escape of watery vapor and steam; thereby much heat is lost if food is cooked in rapidly boiling water.

Water is boiled for two purposes: First, cooking of itself to destroy organic impurities; second, for cooking foods. Boiling water toughens and hardens albumen in eggs; toughens fibrin and dissolves tissues in meat; bursts starch-grains and softens cellulose in cereals and vegetables. Milk should never be allowed to boil. At boiling temperature (214° F.) the casein is slightly hardened, and the fat is rendered more difficult of digestion. Milk heated over boiling water, as in a double boiler, is called *scalded milk*, and reaches a temperature of 196° F. When foods are cooked over hot water the process is called steaming.

Stewing is cooking in a small amount of hot water for a long time at low temperature; it is the most economical way of cooking meats, as all nutriment is retained, and the ordinary way of cooking cheaper cuts. Thus fibre and connective tissues are softened, and the whole is made tender and palatable.

Broiling is cooking over or in front of a clear fire. The food to be cooked is usually placed in a greased broiler or on a gridiron held near the coals, turned often at first to sear the outside,— thus preventing escape of inner juices, — afterwards turned occasionally. Tender meats and fish may be cooked in this way. The flavor obtained by broiling is particularly fine; there is, however, a greater loss of weight in this than in any other way of cooking, as the food thus cooked is exposed to free circulation of air. When coal is not used, or a fire is not in condition for broiling, a plan for *pan broiling* has been adopted. This is done by placing food to be cooked in a hissing hot frying-pan, turning often as in broiling.

Roasting is cooking before a clear fire, with a reflector to concentrate the heat. Heat is applied in the same way as for broiling, the difference being that the meat for roasting is placed on a spit and allowed to revolve, thicker pieces always being employed. Tin-kitchens are now but seldom used. Meats cooked in a range oven, though really baked, are said to be roasted. Meats so cooked are pleasing to the sight and agreeable to the palate, although, according to Mr. Edward Atkinson, not so easily digested as when cooked at a lower temperature in the Aladdin oven.

Baking is cooking in a range oven.

Frying is cooking by means of immersion in deep fat raised to a temperature of 350° to 400° F. For frying purposes olive oil, lard, beef drippings, cottolene, coto-suet, and cocoanut butter are used. A combination of two-thirds lard and one-third beef suet (tried out and clarified) is better than lard alone. Cottolene, coto-suet, and cocoanut butter are economical, inasmuch as they may be heated to a high temperature without discoloring, therefore may be used for a larger number of fryings. Cod fat obtained from beef is often used by *chefs* for frying.

Great care should be taken in frying that fat is of the right temperature; otherwise food so cooked will absorb fat.

Nearly all foods which do not contain eggs are dipped in flour or crumbs, egg, and crumbs, before frying. The intense heat of fat hardens the albumen, thus forming a coating which prevents food from " soaking fat."

When meat or fish is to be fried, it should be kept in a warm room for some time previous to cooking, and wiped as dry as possible. If cold, it decreases the temperature of the fat to such extent that a coating is not formed quickly enough to prevent fat from penetrating the food. The ebullition of fat is due to water found in food to be cooked.

Great care must be taken that too much is not put into the fat at one time, not only because it lowers the temperature of the fat, but because it causes it to bubble and go over the sides of the kettle. It is not fat that boils, but water which fat has received from food.

All fried food on removal from fat should be drained on brown paper.

Rules for Testing Fat for Frying. 1. When the fat begins to smoke, drop in an inch cube of bread, from soft part of loaf, and if in forty seconds it is golden brown, the fat is then of right temperature for frying any cooked mixture.

2. Use same test for uncooked mixtures, allowing one minute for bread to brown.

Many kinds of food may be fried in the same fat; new fat should be used for batter and dough mixtures, potatoes, and fish-balls; after these, fish, meat, and croquettes. Fat should be frequently clarified.

To Clarify Fat. Melt fat, add raw potato cut in quarter-inch slices, and allow fat to heat gradually; when fat ceases to bubble and potatoes are well browned, strain through double cheese-cloth, placed over wire strainer, into a pan. The potato absorbs any odors or gases, and collects to itself some of the sediment, remainder settling to bottom of kettle.

When small amount of fat is to be clarified, add to cold fat boiling water, stir vigorously, and set aside to cool; the fat will form a cake on top, which may be easily removed; on bottom of the cake will be found sediment, which may be readily scraped off with a knife.

Remnants of fat, either cooked or uncooked, should be saved and tried out, and when necessary clarified.

Fat from beef, poultry, chicken, and pork, may be used for shortening or frying purposes; fat from mutton and smoked meats may be used for making hard and soft soap; fat removed from soup stock, the water in which corned beef has been cooked, and drippings from roast beef, may be tried out, clarified, and used for shortening or frying purposes.

To Try out Fat. Cut in small pieces and melt in top of a double boiler; in this way it will require less watching than if placed in kettle on the back of range. Leaf lard is tried out in the same way; in cutting the leaf, remove membrane. After straining lard, that which remains may be salted, pressed, and eaten as a relish, and is called scraps.

Sautéing is frying in a small quantity of fat. Food so cooked is much more difficult of digestion than when fried in deep fat; it is impossible to cook in this way without the food absorbing fat. A frying-pan or griddle is used; the food is cooked on one side, then turned, and cooked on the other.

Braising is stewing and baking (meat). Meat to be braised is frequently first sautéd to prevent escape of much juice in the gravy. The meat is placed in a pan with a small quantity of stock or water, vegetables (carrot, turnip, celery, and onion) cut in pieces, salt, pepper, and sweet herbs. The pan should have a tight-fitting cover.   Meat so prepared should be cooked in an oven at low uniform temperature for a long time.   This is an economical way of cooking, and the only way besides stewing or boiling of making a large piece of tough meat palatable and digestible.

Fricasseeing is sautéing and serving with a sauce. Tender meat is fricasseed without previous cooking; less tender meat requires cooking in hot water before fricasseeing.   Although veal is obtained from a young creature, it requires long cooking; it is usually sautéd, and then cooked in a sauce at low temperature for a long time.

Various Ways of Preparing Food for Cooking.

Egging and Crumbing.   Use for crumbing dried bread crumbs which have been rolled and sifted, or soft stale bread broken in pieces and forced through a colander. An ingenious machine on the market, "The Bread Crumber," does this work.   Egg used for crumbing should be broken into a shallow plate and beaten with a silver fork to blend yolk and white; dilute each egg with two tablespoons water.   The crumbs should be taken on a board; food to be fried should be first rolled in crumbs (care being taken that all parts are covered with crumbs), then dipped in egg mixture (equal care being taken to cover all parts), then rolled in crumbs again; after the last crumbing remove food to a place on the board where there are no crumbs, and shake off some of the outer ones which make coating too thick.   A broad-bladed knife with short handle — the Teller knife — is the most convenient utensil for lifting food to be crumbed from egg mixture.   Small scallops, oysters, and crabs are more easily crumbed by putting crumbs and fish in paper and shaking paper until the fish is covered with crumbs.   The object of first crumbing is to dry the surface that egg may cling to it; and where a thin coating is desired flour is often used in place of crumbs.

Larding is introducing small pieces of fat salt pork or bacon through the surface of uncooked meat. The flavor of lean and dry meat is much improved by larding; tenderloin of beef (fillet), grouse, partridge, pigeon, and liver are often prepared in this way. Pig pork being firm, is best for larding. Pork should be kept in a cold place that it may be well chilled. Remove rind and use the part of pork which lies between rind and vein. With sharp knife (which is sure to make a clean cut) remove slices a little less than one-fourth inch thick; cut the slices into strips a little less than one-fourth inch wide; these strips should be two and one-fourth inches long, and are called *lardoons*. Lardoons for small birds — quail, for example — should be cut smaller and not quite so long. To lard, insert one end of lardoon into larding-needle, hold needle firmly, and with pointed end take up a stitch one-third inch deep and three-fourths inch wide; draw needle through, care being taken that lardoon is left in meat and its ends project to equal lengths. Arrange lardoons in parallel rows, one inch apart, stitches in the alternate rows being directly underneath each other. Lard the upper surface of cuts of meat with the grain, never across it. In birds, insert lardoons parallel to breast-bone on either side. When large lardoons are forced through meat from surface to surface, the process is called daubing. Example: Beef à la mode. Thin slices of fat salt pork placed over meat may be substituted for larding, but flavor is not the same as when pork is drawn through flesh, and the dish is far less sightly.

Boning is removing bones from meat or fish, leaving the flesh nearly in its original shape. For boning, a small sharp knife with pointed blade is essential. Legs of mutton and veal and loins of beef may be ordered boned at market, no extra charge being made.

Whoever wishes to learn how to bone should first be taught boning of a small bird; when this is accomplished, larger birds, chickens, and turkeys may easily be done, the processes varying but little. In large birds, tendons are drawn from legs, and the wings are left on and boned.

How to Bone a Bird.

In buying birds for boning, select those which have been fresh killed, dry picked and not drawn. Singe, remove pinfeathers, head, and feet, and cut off wings close to body. Lay bird on a board, breast down.

Begin at neck and with sharp knife cut through the skin the entire length of body. Scrape the flesh from backbone until end of one shoulder-blade is found; scrape flesh from shoulder-blade and continue around wing-joint, cutting through tendonous portions which are encountered; then bone other side. Scrape skin from backbone the entire length of body, working across the ribs. Free wish-bone and collar-bones, at same time removing crop and windpipe; continue down breast-bone, particular care being taken not to break the skin as it lies very near bone. or to cut the delicate membranes which enclose entrails. Scrape flesh from second joints and drumsticks, laying it back and drawing off as a glove may be drawn from the hand. Withdraw carcass and put flesh back in its original shape. In large birds where wings are boned, scrape flesh to middle joint, where bone should be broken, leaving bone at tip end to assist in preserving shape.

How to Measure.

Correct measurements are absolutely necessary to insure the best results. Good judgment, with experience, has taught some to measure by sight; but the majority need definite guides.

Tin measuring-cups, divided in quarters or thirds, holding one half-pint, and tea and table spoons of regulation sizes,—which may be bought at any store where kitchen furnishings are sold, —and a case knife, are essentials for correct measurement.   Mixing-spoons, which are little larger than tablespoons, should not be confounded with the latter.

1. Measuring-cup divided in thirds, with tablespoon, illustrating the measuring of dry ingredients.

2. Measuring-cup divided in quarters, with teaspoon one-half full of dry ingredients.

Measuring Ingredients.   Flour, meal, powdered and confectioners' sugar, and soda should be sifted before measuring.   Mustard and baking-powder, from standing in boxes, settle, therefore should be stirred to lighten; salt frequently lumps, and these lumps should be broken. *A cupful* is measured level.   To measure a cupful, put in the ingredient by spoonfuls or from a scoop, round slightly, and level with a case knife, care being taken not to shake the cup.   *A tablespoonful is measured level. A teaspoonful is measured level.*

To measure tea or table spoonfuls, dip the spoon in the ingredient, fill, lift, and level with a knife, the sharp edge of knife being toward tip of spoon.   Divide with knife lengthwise of spoon, for a half-spoonful; divide halves crosswise for quarters, and quarters crosswise for eighths. Less than one-eighth of a teaspoonful is considered a few grains.

Measuring Liquids. A cupful of liquid is all the cup will hold.

A tea or table spoonful is all the spoon will hold.

Measuring Butter, Lard, etc. To measure butter, lard, and other solid fats, pack solidly into cup or spoon, and level with a knife.

When dry ingredients, liquids, and fats are called for in the same recipe, measure in the order given, thereby using but one cup.

How to Combine Ingredients.

Next to measuring comes care in combining, — a fact not always recognized by the inexperienced. Three ways are considered, — stirring, beating, cutting and folding.

To stir, mix by using circular motion, widening the circles until all is blended. Stirring is the motion ordinarily employed in all cookery, alone or in combination with beating.

To beat, turn ingredient or ingredients over and over, continually bringing the under part to the surface, thus allowing the utensil used for beating to be constantly brought in contact with bottom of the dish and throughout the mixture.

To cut and fold, introduce one ingredient into another ingredient or mixture by two motions : with a spoon, a repeated vertical downward motion, known as cutting; and a turning over and over of mixture, allowing bowl of spoon each time to come in contact with bottom of dish, is called folding. These repeated motions are alternated until thorough blending is accomplished.

By stirring, ingredients are mixed; *by beating*, a large amount of air is inclosed; *by cutting and folding*, air already introduced is prevented from escaping.

1. Steel fork.	8. Vegetable knife.
2. Teaspoon.	9. Double boiler.
3. Tablespoon.	10. Potato ricer.
4. Mixing-spoon.	11. Wire whisk in small granite
5. Cake spoon.	saucepan.
6. Small wooden spoon.	12. Dover egg-beater.
7. Case knife.	

Ways of Preserving.

1. By Freezing. Foods which spoil readily are frozen for transportation, and must be kept packed in ice until used. Examples: Fish and poultry.

2. By Refrigeration. Foods so preserved are kept in cold storage. The cooling is accomplished by means of ice, or by a machine where compressed gas is cooled and then permitted to expand. Examples: Meat, milk, butter, eggs, etc.

3. By Canning. Which is preserving in air-tight glass jars, or tin cans hermetically sealed. When fruit is canned, sugar is usually added.

4. By Sugar. Examples: Fruit-juices and condensed milk.

5. By Exclusion of Air. Foods are preserved by exclusion of air in other ways than canning. Examples: Grapes in bran, eggs in lime-water, etc.

6. By Drying. Drying consists in evaporation of nearly all moisture, and is generally with salting, except in vegetables and fruits.

7. By Evaporation. There are examples where considerable moisture remains, though much is driven off. Example: Beef extract.

8. By Salting. There are two kinds of salting,— dry, and corning or salting in brine. Examples: Salt codfish, beef, pork, tripe, etc.

9. By Smoking. Some foods, after being salted, are hung in a closed room for several hours, where hickory wood is allowed to smother. Examples: Ham, beef, and fish.

10. By Pickling. Vinegar, to which salt is added, and sometimes sugar and spices, is scalded; and cucumbers, onions, and various kinds of fruit are allowed to remain in it.

11. By Oil. Examples: Sardines, anchovies, etc.

12. By Antiseptics. The least wholesome way is by the use of antiseptics. Borax and salicilic acid, when employed, should be used sparingly.

TABLE OF MEASURES AND WEIGHTS.

2	cups butter (packed solidly) . . .	= 1 pound.
2	" flour (pastry)	= 1 "
2	" granulated sugar	= 1 "
2⅔	" powdered "	= 1 "
3½	" confectioners' sugar	= 1 "
2⅔	" brown sugar	= 1 "
2⅔	" oatmeal	= 1 "
4¾	" rolled oats	= 1 "
2⅔	" granulated corn meal	= 1 "
4⅓	" rye meal	= 1 "
1⅞	" rice	= 1 "
4½	" Graham flour	= 1 "
3⅞	" entire wheat flour	= 1 "
4⅓	" coffee	= 1 "
2	" finely chopped meat	= 1 "
9 large eggs		= 1 "
1 square Baker's chocolate		= 1 ounce
⅓ cup almonds blanched and chopped .		= 1 "

A few grains is less than one-eighth teaspoon.

3 teaspoons	= 1 tablespoon.
16 tablespoons	= 1 cup.
2 tablespoons butter	= 1 ounce.
4 tablespoons flour	= 1 ounce.

TIME TABLES FOR COOKING.

Boiling.

ARTICLES.	TIME.	
	Hours.	Minutes.
Coffee		1 to 3
Eggs, soft cooked		6 to 8
" hard "		35 to 45
Mutton, leg	2 to 3	
Ham, weight 12 to 14 lbs.	4 to 5	
Corned Beef or Tongue	3 to 4	
Turkey, weight 9 lbs.	2 to 3	
Fowl, " 4 to 5 lbs.	2 to 3	
Chicken, " 3 lbs.	1 to 1¼	

Articles.	Time. Hours.	Minutes
Lobster		25 to 30
Cod and Haddock, weight 3 to 5 lbs.		20 to 30
Halibut, thick piece, " 2 to 3 lbs.		30
Bluefish and Bass, " 4 to 5 lbs.		40 to 45
Salmon, weight, 2 to 3 lbs.		30 to 35
Small Fish		6 to 10
Potatoes, white		20 to 30
" sweet		15 to 25
Asparagus		20 to 30
Peas		20 to 60
String Beans	1 to 2½	
Lima and other Shell Beans	1 to 1¼	
Beets, young		45
" old	3 to 4	
Cabbage		35 to 60
Oyster Plant		45 to 60
Turnips		30 to 45
Onions		45 to 60
Parsnips		30 to 45
Spinach		25 to 30
Green Corn		12 to 20
Cauliflower		20 to 25
Brussels Sprouts		15 to 20
Tomatoes, stewed		15 to 20
Rice		20 to 30
Macaroni		20 to 25

Broiling.

Steak, one inch thick	4 to 6
" one and one-half inch thick	8 to 10
Lamb or Mutton Chops	6 to 8
" " " in paper cases	10
Quails or Squabs	8
" " in paper cases	10 to 12
Chickens	20
Shad, Bluefish, and Whitefish	15 to 20
Slices of Fish, Halibut, Salmon, and Swordfish	12 to 15
Small, thin Fish	5 to 8
Liver and Tripe	4 to 5

Baking.

ARTICLES.	TIME. Hours.	Minutes.
Bread (white loaf)		45 to 60
" (Graham loaf)		35 to 45
" (sticks)		10 to 15
Biscuits or Rolls (raised)		12 to 20
" (baking powder)		12 to 15
Gems		25 to 30
Muffins (raised)		30
" (baking powder)		20 to 25
Corn Cake (thin)		15 to 20
" (thick)		30 to 35
Gingerbread		20 to 30
Cookies		6 to 10
Sponge Cake		45 to 60
Cake (layer)		20 to 30
" (loaf)		40 to 60
" (pound)	1¼ to 1½	
" (fruit)	1¼ to 2	
" (wedding)	3	
or steam 2 hours and bake 1½		
Baked batter puddings		35 to 45
Bread puddings	1	
Tapioca or Rice Pudding	1	
Rice Pudding (poor man's)	2 to 3	
Indian "	2 to 3	
Plum "	2 to 3	
Custard "		30 to 45
" (baked in cups)		20 to 25
Pies		30 to 50
Tarts		15 to 20
Patties		20 to 25
Vol-au-vent		50 to 60
Cheese Straws		8 to 10
Scalloped Oysters		25 to 30
Scalloped dishes of cooked mixtures		12 to 15
Baked Beans	6 to 8	
Braised Beef	3½ to 4½	
Beef, sirloin or rib, rare, weight 5 lbs.	1	5
" " " " " 10 "	1	30
" " " well done, weight 5 lbs.	1	20
" " " " " 10 "	1	50

ARTICLES.	TIME.	
	Hours.	Minutes.
Beef, rump, rare, weight 10 lbs. . . .	1	35
" " well done, weight 10 lbs. . .	1	55
" (fillet)		20 to 30
Mutton (saddle)	1¼ to 1½	
Lamb (leg)	1¼ to 1¾	
" (forequarter)	1 to 1¼	
" (chops) in paper cases		15 to 20
Veal (leg)	3½ to 4	
" (loin)	2 to 3	
Pork (chine or sparerib)	3 to 3½	
Chicken, weight 3 to 4 lbs.	1 to 1½	
Turkey, weight 9 lbs.	2½ to 3	
Goose, weight 9 lbs.	2	
Duck (domestic)	1 to 1¼	
" (wild)		20 to 30
Grouse		25 to 30
Partridge		45 to 50
Pigeons (potted)	2	
Fish (thick), weight 3 to 4 lbs.		15 to 60
" (small)		20 to 30

Frying.

Muffins, Fritters, and Doughnuts	3 to 5
Croquettes and Fishballs	1
Potatoes, raw	4 to 8
Breaded Chops	5 to 8
Fillets of Fish	4 to 6
Smelts, Trout, and other small Fish	3 to 5

NOTE. — Length of time for cooking fish and meat does not depend so much on the number of pounds to be cooked as the extent of surface exposed to the heat.

CHAPTER III.

BEVERAGES.

A BEVERAGE is any drink. Water is the beverage provided for man by Nature. Water is an essential to life. All beverages contain a large percentage of water, therefore their uses should be considered : —

I.   To quench thirst.
II.   To introduce water into the circulatory system.
III.   To regulate body temperature.
IV.   To assist in carrying off waste.
V.   To nourish.
VI.   To stimulate the nervous system and various organs.
VII.   For medicinal purposes.

Freshly boiled water should be used for making hot beverages; freshly drawn water for making cold beverages.

TEA.

Tea is used by more than one-half the human race; and, although the United States is not a tea-drinking country, one and one-half pounds are consumed per capita per annum.

All tea is grown from one species of shrub, *Thea*, the leaves of which constitute the tea of commerce. Climate, elevation, soil, cultivation, and care in picking and curing all go to make up the differences. First-quality tea is made from young, whole leaves. Two kinds of tea are considered : —

Black tea, made from leaves which have been allowed to ferment before curing.

Green tea, made from unfermented leaves artificially colored.

The best black tea comes from India and Ceylon. Some familiar brands are Oolong, Formosa, English Breakfast, Orange Pekoe, and Flowery Pekoe. The last two named, often employed at the "five o'clock tea," command high prices; they are made from the youngest leaves. Orange Pekoe is scented with orange leaves. The best green tea comes from Japan. Some familiar brands are Hyson, Japan, and Gunpowder.

From analysis, it has been found that tea is rich in proteid, but taken as an infusion acts as a stimulant rather than as a nutrient. The nutriment is gained from sugar and milk served with it. The stimulating property of tea is due to the alkaloid, *theine*, together with an essential oil; it contains an astringent, tannin. Black tea contains less theine, essential oil, and tannin, than green tea. The tannic acid, developed from the tannin by infusion, injures the coating of the stomach.

Although tea is not a substitute for food, it appears so for a considerable period of time, as its stimulating effect is immediate. It is certain that less food is required where much tea is taken, for by its use there is less wear of the tissues, consequently less need of repair. When taken to excess, it so acts on the nervous system as to produce sleeplessness and insomnia, and finally makes a complete wreck of its victim. Taken in moderation, it acts as a mild stimulant, and ingests a considerable amount of water into the system; it heats the body in winter, and cools the body in summer.

Freshly boiled water should be used for making tea. Boiled, because below the boiling-point the stimulating property, theine, would not be extracted. Freshly boiled, because long cooking renders it flat and insipid to taste on account of escape of its atmospheric gases. Tea should always be infused, never boiled. Long steeping destroys the delicate flavor by developing a larger amount of tannic acid.

How to make Tea.

3 teaspoons tea.   2 cups boiling water.

Scald an earthen or china teapot.

Put in tea, and pour on boiling water. Let stand on back of range or in a warm place five minutes. Strain and serve immediately, with or without sugar and milk. Avoid second steeping of leaves with addition of a few fresh ones. If this is done, so large an amount of tannin is extracted that various ills are apt to follow.

Five o'Clock Tea.

When tea is made in dining or drawing room, a " Five o'Clock Teakettle " (Samovar), and tea-ball or teapot are used.

Russian Tea.

Follow recipe for making tea. Russian tea may be served hot or cold, but always without milk. A thin slice of lemon, from which seeds have been removed, or a few drops of lemon-juice, is allowed for each cup. Sugar is added according to taste. In Russia a preserved strawberry to each cup is considered an improvement. We imitate our Russian friends by garnishing with a candied cherry.

Iced Tea.

4 teaspoons tea.   2 cups boiling water.

Follow recipe for making tea. Strain into glasses one-third full of cracked ice. Sweeten to taste. The flavor is much finer by chilling the infusion quickly.

COFFEE.

The coffee-tree is native to Abyssinia, but is now grown in all tropical countries. It belongs to the genus *Coffea*, of which there are about twenty-two species. The seeds of berries of coffee-trees constitute the coffee of commerce. Each berry contains two seeds, with exception of maleberry, which is a single round seed. In their natural state they are almost tasteless; therefore color, shape, and size determine value. Formerly, coffee was cured by exposure to the sun; but on account of warm climate and sudden rainfalls, coffee was often injured. By the new method coffee is washed, and then dried by steam heat.

In coffee plantations, trees are planted in parallel rows, from six to eight feet apart, and are pruned so as never to exceed six feet in height. Banana-trees are often grown in coffee plantations, advantage being taken of their outspreading leaves, which protect coffee-trees from direct rays of the sun. Brazil produces about two-thirds the coffee used. Central America, Java, and Arabia are also coffee centres.

Tea comes to us ready for use; coffee needs roasting. In process of roasting the seeds increase in size, but lose fifteen per cent in weight. Roasting is necessary to develop the delightful aroma and flavor. Java coffee is considered finest. Mocha commands a higher price, owing to certain acidity and sparkle, which alone is not desirable; but when combined with Java, in proportion of two parts Java to one part Mocha, the coffee best suited to average taste is made. Some people prefer Maleberry Java; so especial care is taken to have male berries separated, that they may be sold for higher price. Old Government Java has deservedly gained a good reputation, as it is carefully inspected, and its sale controlled by Dutch government. Strange as it may seem to the consumer, all coffee sold as Java does not come from the island of Java. Any coffee, wherever grown, having same characteristics and flavor, is sold as Java. The same is true of other kinds of coffee.

The stimulating property of coffee is due to the alkaloid *caffeine*, together with an essential oil. Like tea, it contains an astringent. Coffee is more stimulating than tea, although, weight for weight, tea contains about twice as much *theine* as coffee contains *caffeine*. The smaller proportion of tea used, accounts for the difference. A cup of coffee with breakfast, and a cup of tea with supper, serve as a mild stimulant for an adult, and form a valuable food adjunct, but should never be found in the dietary of a child or dyspeptic. Coffee taken in moderation quickens action of the heart, acts directly upon the nervous system, and assists gastric digestion. Fatigue of body and mind are much lessened by moderate use of coffee; severe exposure to cold can be better endured by the coffee drinker. In times of war, coffee has proved more valuable than alcoholic stimulants to keep up the enduring power of soldiers. Coffee acts as an antidote for opium and alcoholic poisoning. Tea and coffee are much more readily absorbed when taken on an empty stomach; therefore this should be avoided except when used for medicinal purposes. Coffee must be taken in moderation; its excessive use means palpitation of the heart, tremor, insomnia, and nervous prostration.

Coffee is often adulterated with chiccory, beans, peas, and various cereals, which are colored, roasted, and ground. By many, a small amount of chiccory is considered an improvement, owing to the bitter principle and volatile oil which it contains. Chiccory is void of caffeine. The addition of chiccory may be detected by adding cold water to supposed coffee; if chiccory is present, the liquid will be quickly discolored, and chiccory will sink; pure coffee will float.

Buying of Coffee. Coffee should be bought for family use in small quantities, freshly roasted and ground; or, if one has a coffee-mill, it may be ground at home as needed. After being ground, unless kept air tight, it quickly deteriorates. If not bought in air-tight cans, with tight-fitting cover, or glass jar, it should be emptied into canister as soon as brought from grocer's.

Coffee may be served as filtered coffee, infusion of coffee, or decoction of coffee. Commonly speaking, boiled coffee is preferred, and is more economical for the consumer. Coffee is ground fine, coarse, and medium; and the grinding depends on the way in which it is to be made. For filtered coffee have it finely ground; for boiled, coarse or medium.

Filtered Coffee.

(*French or Percolated.*)

1 cup coffee (finely ground). 6 cups boiling water.

Various kinds of coffee-pots are on the market for making filtered coffee. They all contain a strainer to hold coffee without allowing grounds to mix with infusion. Some have additional vessel to hold boiling water, upon which coffee-pot may rest.

Place coffee in strainer, strainer in coffee-pot, and pot on the range. Add gradually boiling water, and allow it to filter. Cover between additions of water. If desired stronger, re-filter. Serve at once with cut sugar and cream.

Put sugar and cream in cup before hot coffee. There will be perceptible difference if cream is added last. If cream is not obtainable, scalded milk may be substituted, or part milk and part cream may be used, if a diluted cup of coffee is desired.

Boiled Coffee.

1 cup coffee.	1 cup cold water.
1 egg.	6 cups boiling water.

Scald a *granite-ware* coffee-pot. Wash egg, break, and beat slightly. Dilute with one-half the cold water, add crushed shell, and mix with coffee. Turn into coffee-pot, pour on boiling water, and stir thoroughly. Place on front of range, and boil three minutes. If not boiled, coffee is cloudy; if boiled too long, too much tannic acid is developed. The spout of pot should be covered or stuffed with soft paper to prevent escape of fragrant aroma. Stir and pour some in a cup to be sure that spout is free from grounds. Return to coffee-pot and repeat. Add remaining cold water, which perfects clearing. Cold water being heavier than hot water sinks to the bottom, carrying grounds with it. Place on back of range for ten minutes, where coffee will not boil. Serve at once. If any is left over, drain from grounds, and reserve for making of jelly or other dessert.

Egg shells may be saved and used for clearing coffee. Three egg shells are sufficient to effect clearing where one cup of ground coffee is used. The shell performs no office in clearing except for the albumen which clings to it. Burnett's Crystal Coffee Settler, or salt fish skin, washed, dried, and cut in inch pieces, is used for same purpose.

Coffee made with an egg has a rich flavor which egg alone can give. Where strict economy is necessary, if great care is taken, egg may be omitted. Coffee so made should be served from range, as much motion causes it to become roiled.

Tin is an undesirable material for a coffee-pot, as tannic acid acts on such metal and is apt to form a poisonous compound.

When coffee and scalded milk are served in equal proportions, it is called *Café au lait*. Coffee served with whipped cream is called *Vienna Coffee.*

To Make a Small Pot of Coffee. Mix one cup ground coffee with one egg slightly beaten and crushed shell. To one-third of this amount add one-third cup cold water. Turn into a scalded coffee-pot, add one pint boiling water, and boil three minutes. Let stand on back of range ten minutes; serve. Keep remaining coffee and egg closely covered, in a cool place, to use two successive mornings.

To Make Coffee for One. Allow two tablespoons ground coffee to one cup cold water. Add coffee to cold water, cover closely, and let stand over night. In the morning bring to boiling point. If carefully poured, a clear cup of coffee may be served.

After-Dinner Coffee.

(Black Coffee, or Café Noir.)

For after-dinner coffee use twice the quantity of coffee, or half the amount of liquid, given in previous recipes. Filtered coffee is often preferred where milk or cream is not used, as is always the case with black coffee. Serve in after-dinner coffee cups, with or without cut sugar.

After-dinner coffee retards gastric digestion; but where the stomach has been overtaxed by a hearty meal, it may prove beneficial, so great are its stimulating effects.

KOLA.

The preparations on the market made from the kola nut have much the same effect upon the system as coffee and chocolate, inasmuch as they contain caffeine and theobromine; they are also valuable for their diastase and a milk-digesting ferment.

COCOA AND CHOCOLATE.

The cacao tree (*Theobroma cacao*) is native to Mexico. Although successfully cultivated between the twentieth parallels of latitude, its industry is chiefly confined to Mexico, South America, and the West Indies. Cocoa and chocolate are both prepared from seeds of the cocoa bean. The bean pod is from seven to ten inches long, and three to four and one-half inches in diameter. Each pod contains from twenty to forty seeds, imbedded in mucilaginous material. Cocoa beans are dried previous to importation. Like coffee, they need roasting to develop flavor. After roasting, outer covering of bean is removed; this covering makes what is known as *cocoa shells*, which have little nutritive value. The beans are broken and sold as *cocoa nibs*.

The various preparations of cocoa on the market are made from ground cocoa nibs, from which, by means of hydraulic pressure, a large amount of fat is expressed, leaving a solid cake. This in turn is pulverized and mixed with sugar, and frequently a small amount of cornstarch or arrowroot. To some preparations cinnamon or vanilla is added. Broma contains both arrowroot and cinnamon.

Chocolate is made from cocoa nibs, but contains a much larger proportion of fat than cocoa preparations. Bitter, sweet, or flavored chocolate is always sold in cakes.

The fat obtained from cocoa bean is *cocoa butter*, which gives to cocoa its principal nutrient.

Cocoa and chocolate differ from tea and coffee inasmuch as they contain nutriment as well as stimulant. *Theobromine*, the active principle, is almost identical with theine and caffeine in its composition and effects.

Many people who abstain from the use of tea and coffee find cocoa indispensable. Not only is it valuable for its own nutriment, but for the large amount of milk added to it. Cocoa may well be placed in the dietary of a child after his third year, while chocolate should be avoided as a beverage, but may be given as a confection. Invalids and those of weak digestion can take cocoa where chocolate would prove too rich.

Cocoa shells.

1 cup cocoa shells.   6 cups boiling water.

Boil shells and water three hours; as water boils away it will be necessary to add more. Strain and serve with milk and sugar. By adding one-third cup cocoa nibs, a much more satisfactory drink is obtained.

Cracked Cocoa.

½ cup cracked cocoa.   3 pints boiling water.

Boil cracked cocoa and water two hours. Strain, and serve with milk and sugar. If cocoa is pounded in a mortar and soaked over night in three pints water, it will require but one hour's boiling.

Breakfast Cocoa.

1½ tablespoons prepared cocoa.   2 cups boiling water.
2 tablespoons sugar.   2 cups milk.
                        Few grains salt.

Scald milk. Mix cocoa, sugar, and salt, dilute with
one-half cup boiling water to make smooth paste, add
remaining water and boil one minute; turn into scalded
milk and beat two minutes, using Dover egg-beater.

Reception Cocoa.

3 tablespoons cocoa.   A few grains salt.
⅓ cup sugar.   4 cups milk.
                   ¾ cup boiling water.

Scald milk. Mix cocoa, sugar, and salt, adding enough
boiling water to make a smooth paste; add remaining
water and boil one minute; pour into scalded milk. Beat
two minutes, using Dover egg-beater, when froth will
form, preventing scum, which is so unsightly; this is
known as *milling*.

Brandy Cocoa.

2 tablespoons cocoa.   1½ cups boiling water.
⅓ cup sugar.   4 cups milk.
                 3 teaspoons cooking brandy.

Prepare as Reception Cocoa, and add brandy just before milling.

Chocolate.

1½ squares Baker's chocolate.   Few grains salt.
4 tablespoons sugar.   1 cup boiling water.
                     3 cups milk.

Scald milk. Melt chocolate in small saucepan placed
over hot water, add sugar, salt, and gradually boiling
water; when smooth, place on range and boil one minute;
add to scalded milk, mill, and serve in chocolate cups with
whipped cream. One and one-half ounces vanilla choco-

late may be substituted for Baker's chocolate; being sweetened, less sugar is required.

FRUIT DRINKS.

Lemonade.

1 cup sugar.	⅓ cup lemon juice.

1 pint water.

Make syrup by boiling sugar and water twelve minutes; add fruit juice, cool, and dilute with ice water to suit individual tastes. Lemon syrup may be bottled and kept on hand to use as needed.

Pineapple Lemonade.

1 pint water.	1 quart ice water.
1 cup sugar.	1 can grated pineapple.

Juice 3 lemons.

Make syrup by boiling water and sugar ten minutes; add pineapple and lemon juice, cool, strain, and add ice water.

Orangeade.

Make syrup as for Lemonade. Sweeten orange juice with syrup, and dilute by pouring over crushed ice.

Mint Julep.

1 quart water.	1 cup orange juice.
2 cups sugar.	Juice 8 lemons.
1 pint claret wine.	1½ cups boiling water.
1 cup strawberry juice.	12 sprigs fresh mint.

Make syrup by boiling quart of water and sugar twenty minutes. Separate mint in pieces, add to the boiling water, cover, and let stand in warm place five minutes, strain, and add to syrup; add fruit juices, and cool. Pour into punch-bowl, add claret, and chill with a large piece of ice; dilute with water. Garnish with fresh mint leaves and whole strawberries.

Claret Punch.

1 quart cold water.	Few shavings lemon rind.
½ cup raisins.	1⅓ cups orange juice.
2 cups sugar.	⅓ cup lemon juice.
2 inch piece stick cinnamon.	1 pint claret wine.

Put raisins in cold water, bring slowly to boiling point, and boil twenty minutes; strain, add sugar, cinnamon, lemon rind, and boil five minutes. Add fruit juice, cool, strain, pour in claret, and dilute with ice water.

Fruit Punch I.

1 quart cold water.	½ cup lemon juice.
2 cups sugar.	2 cups chopped pineapple.
1 cup orange juice.	

Boil water, sugar, and pineapple twenty minutes; add fruit juice, cool, strain, and dilute with ice water.

Fruit Punch II.

1 cup water.	2 cups strawberry syrup.
2 cups sugar.	Juice 5 lemons.
1 cup tea infusion.	Juice 5 oranges.
1 quart Apollinaris.	1 can grated pineapple.
1 cup Maraschino cherries.	

Make syrup by boiling water and sugar ten minutes; add tea, strawberry syrup, lemon juice, orange juice, and pineapple; let stand thirty minutes, strain, and add ice water to make one and one-half gallons of liquid. Add cherries and Apollinaris. Serve in punch-bowl, with large piece of ice. This quantity will serve fifty.

Ginger Punch.

1 quart cold water.	½ lb. Canton ginger.
1 cup sugar.	½ cup orange juice.
½ cup lemon juice.	

Chop ginger, add to water and sugar, boil fifteen minutes; add fruit juice, cool, strain, and dilute with crushed ice.

Unfermented Grape Juice.

10 lbs. grapes.   1 cup water.

3 lbs. sugar.

Put grapes and water in granite stew-pan.   Heat until stones and pulp separate; then strain through jelly-bag, add sugar, heat to boiling-point, and bottle.   This will make one gallon.   When served, it should be diluted one-half with water.

CHAPTER IV.

BREAD AND BREAD MAKING.

BREAD is the most important article of food, and history tells of its use thousands of years before the Christian era. Many processes have been employed in making and baking; and as a result, from the first flat cake has come the perfect loaf. The study of bread making is of no slight importance, and deserves more attention than it receives.

Considering its great value, it seems unnecessary and wrong to find poor bread on the table; and would that our standard might be raised as high as that of our friends across the water! Who does not appreciate the loaf produced by the French baker, who has worked months to learn the art of bread making!

Bread is made from flour of wheat, or other cereals, by addition of water, salt, and a ferment. Wheat flour is best adapted for bread making, as it contains gluten in the right proportion to make the spongy loaf. But for its slight deficiency in fat, wheat bread is a perfect food; hence arose the custom of spreading it with butter. It should be remembered, in speaking of wheat bread as perfect food, that it must be made of entire wheat flour. Next to wheat flour ranks rye in importance for bread making; but it is best used in combination with wheat, for alone it makes heavy, sticky, moist bread. Corn also needs to be used in combination with wheat for bread making, for if used alone the bread will be crumbly.

The miller, in order to produce flour (which will make the white loaf, so sightly to many), in the process of grinding wheat has been forced to remove the inner bran coats, so rich in mineral matter, and much of the gluten intimately connected with them.

To better understand the details of bread making, wheat, from which bread is principally made, should be considered.

A grain of wheat consists of (1) an outer covering or husk, which is always removed before milling; (2) bran coats, which contain mineral matter; (3) gluten, the proteid matter and fat; and (4) starch, the centre and largest part of the grain. Wheat is distinguished as *white* and *hard*, or *red* and *soft*. The former is known as *winter wheat*, having been sown in the fall, and living through the winter; the latter is known as *spring wheat*, having been sown in the spring. From winter wheat, pastry flour, sometimes called St. Louis, is made; from spring wheat, bread flour, also called Haxall. St. Louis flour takes its name from the old process of grinding; Haxall, from the name of the inventor of the new process. All flours are now milled by the same process. For difference in composition of wheat flours, consult table in Chapter VI. on Cereals.

Wheat is milled for converting into flour by processes producing essentially the same results, all requiring cleansing, grinding, and bolting. Entire wheat flour has only the outer husk removed, the remainder of the kernel being finely ground. *Graham flour*, confounded with entire wheat, is too often found to be an inferior flour, mixed with coarse bran.

Grinding is accomplished by one of four systems: (1) Low milling; (2) Hungarian system, or high milling; (3) Roller milling; and (4) By a machine known as disintegrator.

In low milling process, grooved stones are employed for grinding. The stones are inclosed in a metal case, and provision is made within case for passage of air to prevent wheat from becoming overheated. The lower stone being permanently fixed, the upper stone being so balanced above it that grooves may exactly correspond, when upper stone rotates, sharp edges of grooves meet each other, and operate like a pair of scissors. By this process flour is made ready for bolting by one grinding.

In high milling process, grooved stones are employed, but are kept so far apart that at first the wheat is only bruised, and a series of grindings and siftings is necessary. This process is applicable only to the hardest wheats, and is partially supplanted by roller-milling.

In roller milling, wheat is subjected to action of a pair of steel or chilled-iron horizontal rollers, having toothed surfaces. They revolve in opposite directions, at different rates of speed, and have a cutting action.

Porcelain rollers, with rough surfaces, are sometimes employed. In this system, grinding is accomplished by cutting rather than crushing.

" The disintegrator consists of a pair of circular metal disks, set face to face, studded with circles of projecting bars so arranged that circles of bars on one disk alternate with those of the other. The disks are mounted on the same centre, and so closely set to one another that projecting bars of one disk come quite close to plane surface of the other. They are inclosed within an external casing. The disks are caused to rotate in opposite directions with great rapidity, and the grain is almost instantaneously reduced to a powder."

After grinding comes bolting, by which process the different grades of flour are obtained. The ground wheat is placed in octagonal cylinders (covered with silk or linen bolting-cloth of different degrees of fineness), which are allowed to rotate, thus forcing the wheat through. The flour from first siftings contains the largest percentage of gluten.

Flour is branded under different names to suit manufacturer or dealer. In consequence, the same wheat, milled by the same process, makes flour which is sold under different names.

In buying flour, whether bread or pastry, select the best kept by the grocer with whom you trade. Some of the

well-known brands of bread flour are Swan's Down, Bridal
Veil, Columbia, Washburn's Extra, and Pillsbury's Best;
of pastry, Best St. Louis.   Bread flour should be used
in all cases where yeast is called for, with few exceptions; in other cases, pastry flour.   The difference between bread and pastry flour may be readily determined.
Take bread flour in the hand, close hand tightly, then
open, and flour will not keep in shape; if allowed to
pass through fingers it will feel slightly granular.   Take
pastry flour in the hand, close hand tightly, open, and
flour will be in shape, having impression of the lines of
the hand, and feeling soft and velvety to touch.   Flour
should always be sifted before measuring.

Entire wheat flour differs from ordinary flour, inasmuch as it contains all the gluten found in wheat, the
outer husk of kernels only being removed, the remainder
ground to different degrees of fineness and left unbolted.
Such flours are sold by the different health-food compa-
nies, who have agencies in the large cities.   Franklin
Mills flour is included in this class.

Gluten, the proteid of wheat, is a gray, tough, elastic
substance, insoluble in water.   On account of its great
power of expansion, it holds the gas developed in bread
dough by fermentation, which otherwise would escape.

Yeast.

Yeast is a microscopic plant of fungous growth, and is
the lowest form of vegetable life.   It consists of spores,
or germs, found floating in air, and belongs to a family
of which there are many species.   These spores grow
by budding and division, and multiply very rapidly under
favorable conditions, and produce fermentation.

Fermentation is the process by which, under influence
of air, warmth, moisture, and some ferment, sugar (or
dextrose, starch converted into sugar) is changed into
alcohol (C_2H_5HO) and carbon-dioxide (CO_2).   The product of all fermentation is the same.   Three kinds are

considered, — alcoholic, acetic, and lactic. Where bread dough is allowed to ferment by addition of yeast, the fermentation is *alcoholic;* where alcoholic fermentation continues too long, *acetic* fermentation sets in, which is a continuation of alcoholic. *Lactic* fermentation is fermentation which takes place when milk sours.

Liquid, dry or compressed yeast, may be used for raising bread. The compressed yeast cakes done up in tin foil have long proved satisfactory, and are now almost universally used, having replaced the home-made liquid yeast. Never use a yeast cake unless perfectly fresh, which may be determined by its light color and absence of dark streaks.

The *yeast plant* is killed at 212° F. ; life is suspended, but not entirely destroyed, at 32° F. The temperature best suited for its growth is from 65° to 68° F. The most favorable conditions for the growth of yeast are a warm, moist, sweet, nitrogenous soil. These must be especially considered in bread making.

Bread Making.

Fermented bread is made by mixing to a dough, flour, with a definite quantity of water, milk, or water and milk, salt, and a ferment. Sugar is usually added to hasten fermentation. Dough is then kneaded that the ingredients may be thoroughly incorporated, covered, and allowed to rise in a temperature of 68° F., until dough has doubled its bulk. This change has been caused by action of the ferment, which attacks some of the starch in flour, and changes it to sugar, and sugar in turn to alcohol and carbon dioxide, thus lightening the whole mass. Dough is then kneaded a second time to break bubbles and distribute evenly the carbon dioxide. It is shaped in loaves, put in greased bread pans (they being half filled), covered, allowed to rise in temperature same as for first rising, to double its bulk. If risen too long, it will be full of large holes; if not risen long enough, it will be heavy and soggy. If pans containing loaves are put in too hot a place while rising, a heavy streak will be found near bottom of loaf.

How to Shape Loaves and Biscuits. To shape bread dough in loaves, divide dough in parts, each part large enough for a loaf, knead until smooth, and if possible avoid seams in under part of loaf. If baked in brick pan, place two loaves in one pan, brushed between with a little melted butter. If baked in long shallow pan, when well kneaded, roll with both hands to lengthen, care being taken that it is smooth and of uniform thickness. Where long loaves are baked on sheets, shape and roll loosely in a towel sprinkled with corn meal for last rising.

To shape bread dough in biscuits, pull or cut off as many small pieces (having them of uniform size) as there are to be biscuits. Flour palms of hands slightly; take up each piece and shape separately, lifting, with thumb and first two fingers of right hand, and placing in palm of left hand, constantly moving dough round and round, while folding towards the centre; when smooth, turn it over and roll between palms of hands. Place in greased pans near together, brushed between with a little melted butter, which will cause biscuits to separate easily after baking. For finger rolls, shape biscuits and roll with one hand on part of board where there is no flour, until of desired length, care being taken to make smooth, of uniform size, and round at ends.

Biscuits may be shaped in a great variety of ways, but they should always be small. Large biscuits, though equally good, never tempt one by their daintiness.

Bread is often brushed over with milk before baking, to make a darker crust.

Where bread is allowed to rise over night, a small piece of yeast cake must be used; one-fourth yeast cake to one pint liquid is sufficient, one-third yeast cake to one quart liquid. Bread mixed and baked during the day requires a larger quantity of yeast; one yeast cake, or sometimes even more, to one pint of liquid. Bread dough mixed with a large quantity of yeast should be watched during rising, and cut down as soon as mixture doubles its bulk. If proper care is taken, the bread will be found most satisfactory, having neither " yeasty" nor sour taste.

Fermented bread was formerly raised by means of leaven.

Baking of Bread.

Bread is baked: (1) To kill ferment, (2) to make soluble the starch, (3) to drive off alcohol and carbon dioxide, and (4) to form brown crust of pleasant flavor. Bread should be baked in a hot oven. If the oven be too hot the crust will brown quickly before the heat has reached the centre, and prevent further rising; loaf should continue rising for first fifteen minutes of baking, when it should begin to brown, and continue browning for the next twenty minutes. The last fifteen minutes it should finish baking, when the heat may be reduced. When bread is done, it will not cling to sides of pan, and may be easily removed. Biscuits require more heat than loaf bread, should continue rising the first five minutes, and begin to brown in eight minutes. Experience is the best guide for testing temperature of oven. Various oven thermometers have been made, but none have proved practical. Bread may be brushed over with melted butter, three minutes before removal from oven, if a more tender crust is desired.

Care of Bread after Baking.

Remove loaves at once from pans, and place side down on a wire bread or cake cooler. If crisp crust is desired, allow bread to cool without covering; if soft crust, cover with a towel during cooling. When cool, put in tin box or stone jar, and cover closely.

Never keep bread wrapped in cloth, as the cloth will absorb moisture and transmit an unpleasant taste to bread.

Bread tins or jars should be washed and scalded twice a week in winter, and every other day in summer; otherwise bread is apt to mould. As there are so many ways of using small and stale pieces of bread, care should be taken that none is wasted.

Unfermented Bread is raised without a ferment, the carbon dioxide being produced by the use of soda (alkaline salt, and an acid). Soda, employed in combination with cream of tartar, for raising mixtures, in proportion of one-third soda to two-thirds cream of tartar, was formerly used to a great extent, but has been generally superseded by baking powder.

Soda bicarbonate ($NaHCO_3$) is manufactured from sodium chloride ($NaCl$), common salt.

Baking powder is composed of soda and cream of tartar in definite, correct proportions, mixed with small quantity of dry material (flour or corn-starch) to keep action from taking place. If found to contain alum or ammonia, it is impure. In using baking powder, allow two teaspoons baking powder to each cup of flour, when eggs are not used; to egg mixtures allow one and one-half teaspoons baking powder. When a recipe calls for soda and cream of tartar, in substituting baking powder use double amount of cream of tartar given.

These rules apply to the various soda and cream of tartar baking powders on the market. Horsford's Baking Powder, the only mineral one, requires one-third less than others.

Soda and cream of tartar, or baking powder mixtures, are made light by liberation of gas in mixture; the gas in soda is set free by the acid in cream of tartar; in order to accomplish this, moisture and heat are both required. As soon as moisture is added to baking powder mixtures, the gas will begin to escape; hence the necessity of baking as soon as possible. If baking powder only is used for raising, put mixture to be cooked in a hot oven.

Cream of tartar ($HKC_4O_6H_4$) is obtained from argols found adhering to bottom and sides of wine casks, which are ninety per cent. cream of tartar. The argols are ground and dissolved in boiling water, coloring matter removed by filtering through animal charcoal, and by a process of recrystallization the cream of tartar of commerce is obtained.

The acid found in molasses, sour milk, and lemon juice, will liberate gas in soda, but the action is much quicker than when cream of tartar is used.

Fermented and unfermented breads are raised to be made light and porous, that they may be easily acted upon by the digestive ferments. Some mixtures are made light by beating sufficiently to enclose a large amount of air, and when baked in a hot oven air is forced to expand.

Aërated bread is made light by carbon dioxide forced into dough under pressure. The carbon dioxide is generated from sulphuric acid and lime. Aërated bread is of close texture, and has a flavor peculiar to itself. It is a product of the baker's skill, but has found little favor except in few localities.

Water Bread.

2 cups boiling water.	1½ teaspoons salt.
1 tablespoon butter.	¼ yeast cake dissolved in
1 tablespoon lard.	¼ cup lukewarm water.
1 tablespoon sugar.	6 cups sifted flour.

Put butter, lard, sugar, and salt in bread raiser, or large bowl without a lip; pour on boiling water; when lukewarm, add dissolved yeast cake and five cups of flour; then stir until thoroughly mixed, using a knife or mixing-spoon. Add remaining flour, mix, and turn on a floured board, leaving a clean bowl; knead until mixture is smooth, elastic to touch, and bubbles may be seen under the surface. Some practice is required to knead quickly, but the motion once acquired will never be forgotten. Return to bowl, cover with a clean cloth kept for the purpose, and board or tin cover; let rise over night in temperature of 65° F. In morning cut down: this is accomplished by cutting through and turning over dough several times with a case knife, and checks fermentation for a short time; dough may be again raised, and recut down if it is not convenient to shape into loaves or biscuits after first cutting. When properly cared for, bread need never sour. Toss on board slightly floured, knead, shape into loaves or biscuits, place in greased pans, having pans nearly half full. Cover, let rise again to double its bulk, and bake in hot oven. (See Baking of Bread and Time Table for Baking.) This recipe will make a double loaf of bread and pan of biscuit. Cottolene, coto-suet, or beef drippings may be used for shortening, one-third less being required. Bread shortened with butter has a good flavor, but is not as white as when lard is used.

Milk and Water Bread.

1 cup scalded milk.	1½ teaspoons salt.
1 cup boiling water.	¼ yeast cake dissolved in
1 tablespoon lard.	¼ cup lukewarm water.
1 tablespoon butter.	6 cups sifted flour.

Prepare and bake as Water Bread. Bread may be mixed, raised, and baked in five hours, by using one yeast cake. Bread made in this way has proved most satisfactory. It is usually mixed in the morning, and the cook is able to watch the dough while rising and keep it at uniform temperature. It is often desirable to place bowl containing dough in pan of water, keeping water at uniform temperature of from 95° to 100° F.

Entire Wheat Bread.

2 cups scalded milk.	1 teaspoon salt.
¼ cup sugar or	¼ yeast cake dissolved in
⅓ cup molasses.	¼ cup lukewarm water.

4⅓ cups entire wheat flour.

Add sweetening and salt to milk, cool, and when lukewarm add dissolved yeast cake and flour; beat well, cover, and let rise to double its bulk. Again beat, and turn into greased bread pans, having pans one-half full; let rise, and bake. Entire Wheat Bread should not quite double its bulk during last rising. This mixture may be baked in gem pans.

Entire Wheat and Flour Bread.

Use same ingredients as for Entire Wheat Bread, with exception of flour. For flour use three and one-fourth cups entire wheat and two and three-fourths cups white flour. The dough should be slightly kneaded, and if handled quickly will not stick to board. Loaves and biscuit should be shaped with hands instead of pouring into pans as in Entire Wheat Bread.

Graham Bread.

2½ cups hot liquid (water, or milk and water).   ¼ yeast cake dissolved in ¼ cup lukewarm water.
⅓ cup molasses.   3 cups flour.
1½ teaspoons salt.   3 cups Graham flour.

Prepare and bake as Entire Wheat Bread. The bran remaining in sieve after sifting Graham flour should be discarded.

Third Bread.

2 cups lukewarm water.   1 cup rye flour
1 yeast cake.   1 cup granulated corn meal.
½ tablespoon salt.
½ cup molasses.   3 cups flour.

Dissolve yeast cake in water, add remaining ingredients, and mix thoroughly. Let rise, shape, and bake as Entire Wheat Bread.

Quaker Oats Bread.

2 cups boiling water.   ½ yeast cake dissolved in ½ cup lukewarm water.
½ cup molasses.
½ tablespoon salt.   1 cup Quaker Rolled Oats.
4¾ cups flour.

Add boiling water to oats and let stand one hour; add molasses, salt, dissolved yeast cake, and flour; let rise.

beat thoroughly, turn into buttered bread pans, let rise
again, and bake. By using one-half cup less flour, the
dough is better suited for biscuits, but, being soft, is difficult to handle. To make shaping of biscuits easy, take
up mixture by spoonfuls, drop into plate of flour, and
have palms of hands well covered with flour before attempting to shape.

Rye Bread.

1 cup scalded milk.   1½ teaspoons salt.
1 cup boiling water.   ¼ yeast cake dissolved in
1 tablespoon lard.   ¼ cup lukewarm water.
1 tablespoon butter.   3 cups flour.
⅓ cup brown sugar.   Rye meal.

To milk and water add lard, butter, sugar, and salt;
when lukewarm, add dissolved yeast cake and flour, beat
thoroughly, cover, and let rise until light. Add rye meal
until dough is stiff enough to knead; knead thoroughly,
let rise, shape in loaves, let rise again, and bake.

Boston Brown Bread.

1 cup rye-meal.   ¾ tablespoon soda.
1 cup granulated corn-meal.   1 teaspoon salt.
1 cup Graham flour.   ¾ cup molasses.
2 cups sour milk, or 1¾ cups sweet milk or water.

Mix and sift dry ingredients, add molasses and milk,
stir until well mixed, turn into a well-buttered mould, and
steam three and one-half hours. The cover should be
buttered before being placed on mould, and then tied down
with string; otherwise the bread in rising might force
off cover. Mould should never be filled more than two-
thirds full. A melon-mould or one-pound baking powder
boxes make the most attractive-shaped loaves, but a five-
pound lard pail answers the purpose. For steaming,
place mould on a trivet in kettle containing boiling water,
allowing water to come half-way up around mould, cover
closely, and steam, adding, as needed, more boiling water.

Indian Bread.

1½ cups Graham flour.
1 cup Indian meal.
½ tablespoon soda.

1 teaspoon salt.
½ cup molasses.
1⅔ cups milk.

Mix and steam as Boston Brown Bread.

Steamed Graham Bread.

3 cups Arlington meal.
1 cup flour.
3½ teaspoons soda.

1 teaspoon salt.
1 cup molasses (scant).
2½ cups sour milk.

Mix as Boston Brown Bread, and steam four hours. This bread may often be eaten when bread containing corn-meal could not be digested.

Parker House Rolls.

2 cups scalded milk.
3 tablespoons butter.
2 tablespoons sugar.

1 teaspoon salt.
1 yeast cake dissolved in
¼ cup lukewarm water.
Flour.

Add butter, sugar, and salt to milk; when lukewarm, add dissolved yeast cake and three cups of flour. Beat thoroughly, cover, and let rise until light; cut down, and add enough flour to knead (it will take about two and one-half cups). Let rise again, toss on slightly floured board, knead, pat, and roll out to one-third inch thickness. Shape with biscuit-cutter, first dipped in flour. Dip the handle of a case knife in flour, and with it make a crease through the middle of each piece; brush over one-half of each piece with melted butter, fold, and press edges together. Place in greased pan, one inch apart, cover, let rise, and bake in hot oven twelve to fifteen minutes. As rolls rise they will part slightly, and if hastened in rising are apt to lose their shape.

Parker House Rolls may be shaped by cutting or tearing off small pieces of dough, and shaping round like a biscuit; place in rows on floured board, cover, and let rise fifteen minutes. With handle of large wooden spoon, or toy rolling-pin, roll through centre of each biscuit, brush edge of lower halves with melted butter, fold, press lightly, place in buttered pan one inch apart, cover, let rise, and bake.

Salad or Dinner Rolls.

Use same ingredients as for Parker House Rolls, allowing one-fourth cup butter. Shape in small biscuits, place in rows on a floured board, cover with cloth and pan, and let rise until light and well puffed. Flour handle of wooden spoon and make a deep crease in middle of each biscuit, take up, and press edges together. Place closely in buttered pan, cover, let rise, and bake twelve to fifteen minutes in hot oven. From this same mixture crescents, braids, twists, bow-knots, and other fancy shapes may be made.

Sticks.

1 cup scalded milk.	1 yeast cake dissolved in
¼ cup butter.	¼ cup lukewarm water.
1½ tablespoons sugar.	White 1 egg.
½ teaspoon salt.	3¾ cups flour.

Add butter, sugar, and salt to milk; when lukewarm, add dissolved yeast cake, white of egg well beaten, and flour. Knead, let rise, shape, let rise again, and start baking in a hot oven, reducing heat, that sticks may be crisp and dry. To shape sticks, first shape as small biscuits, roll on board (where there is no flour) with hands until eight inches in length, keeping of uniform size and rounded ends, which may be done by bringing fingers close to, but not over, ends of sticks.

Swedish Rolls.

Use recipe for Salad Rolls. Roll to one-fourth inch thickness, spread with butter, and sprinkle with two tablespoons sugar mixed with one-third teaspoon cinnamon, one-third cup stoned raisins finely chopped, and two table-spoons chopped citron; roll up like jelly roll, and cut in three-fourths inch pieces. Place pieces in pan close together, flat side down. When rolls are taken from oven, brush over with white of egg slightly beaten, diluted with one-half tablespoon water; return to oven to dry egg, and thus glaze top.

Sweet French Rolls.

1 cup milk.	1 teaspoon salt.
1 yeast cake dissolved in	1 egg.
¼ cup lukewarm water.	Yolk 1 egg.
Flour.	⅛ teaspoon mace.
¼ cup sugar.	¼ cup melted butter.

Scald milk; when lukewarm, add dissolved yeast cake and one and one-half cups flour; beat well, cover, and let rise until light. Add sugar, salt, eggs well beaten, mace, and butter, and enough more flour to knead; knead, let rise again, shape, and bake as Salad Rolls. This same mixture may be rolled in a long strip to one-fourth inch thickness, spread with butter, rolled up like a jelly roll, and cut in one inch pieces. Place pieces in pan close together, flat side down.

Luncheon Rolls.

½ cup scalded milk.	2 tablespoons melted butter.
2 tablespoons sugar.	1 egg.
¼ teaspoon salt.	Few gratings from rind of
½ yeast cake dissolved in	lemon.
2 tablespoons lukewarm water.	Flour.

Add sugar and salt to milk; when lukewarm, add dissolved yeast cake and three-fourths cup flour. Cover and let rise; then add butter, egg well beaten, grated rind of lemon, and enough flour to knead. Let rise again, roll to one-half inch thickness, shape with small biscuit-cutter, place in buttered pan close together, let rise again, and bake.

French Rusks.

$\frac{1}{2}$

2 cups scalded milk.	Flour.
¼ cup butter.	1 egg.
¼ cup sugar.	Yolks 2 eggs.
1 teaspoon salt.	Whites 2 eggs.
1 yeast cake dissolved in	¾ teaspoon vanilla.
¼ cup lukewarm water.	

Add butter, sugar, and salt to scalded milk; when luke-warm, add dissolved yeast cake and three cups flour. Cover and let rise; add egg and egg yolks well beaten, and enough flour to knead. Let rise again, and shape as Parker House Rolls. Before baking, make three parallel creases on top of each roll. When nearly done, brush over with whites of eggs beaten slightly, diluted with one tablespoon cold water and vanilla. Sprinkle with sugar.

Rusks (Zwieback).

½ cup scalded milk.	¼ cup sugar.
½ teaspoon salt.	¼ cup melted butter.
2 yeast cakes.	3 eggs.
Flour.	

Dissolve yeast cakes in milk; when lukewarm, add salt and one cup flour; cover, and let rise until very light; then add sugar, butter, eggs unbeaten, and flour enough to handle. Shape as finger rolls, and place close together on a buttered sheet in parallel rows, two inches apart; let rise again and bake twenty minutes. When cold, cut diagonally in one-half inch slices, and brown evenly in oven.

German Coffee Bread.

1 cup scalded milk.	1 egg.
⅓ cup butter, or butter and lard.	⅓ yeast cake dissolved in ¼ cup lukewarm milk.
¼ cup sugar.	½ cup raisins stoned and cut in pieces.
½ teaspoon salt.	

Add butter, sugar, and salt to milk; when lukewarm, add dissolved yeast cake, egg well beaten, flour to make stiff batter, and raisins ; cover, and let rise over night; in morning spread in buttered dripping-pan one-half inch thick. Cover and let rise again. Before baking, brush over with beaten egg, and cover with following mixture : Melt three tablespoons butter, add one-third cup sugar and one teaspoon cinnamon. When sugar is partially melted, add three tablespoons flour.

Coffee Cakes (Brioche).

1 cup scalded milk.   ½ cup sugar.

~~¼ cup yolks of eggs.~~   2 yeast cakes.

3 ~~½ cup~~ whole eggs.   ½ teaspoon extract lemon, or

⅔ cup butter.   2 pounded cardamom seeds.

4⅔ cups flour.

French Confectioner.

Cool milk ; when lukewarm, add yeast cakes, and when they are dissolved add remaining ingredients, and beat thoroughly with hand ten minutes ; let rise six hours. Keep in ice-box over night; in morning turn on floured board, roll in long rectangular piece one-fourth inch thick ; spread with softened butter, fold from sides toward centre to make three layers. Cut off pieces three-fourths inch wide ; cover and let rise. Take each piece separately in hands and twist from ends in opposite directions, coil and bring ends together at top of cake. Let rise in pans and bake twenty minutes in a moderate oven; cool and brush over with confectioners' sugar, moistened with enough boiling water to spread.

Buns.

1 cup scalded milk.   ½ teaspoon salt.

⅓ cup butter.   ½ cup raisins stoned and

1 cup sugar.   cut in quarters.

1 yeast cake dissolved in   1 teaspoon extract lemon.

¼ cup lukewarm water.   Flour.

Add one-half sugar and salt to milk ; when lukewarm, add dissolved yeast cake and one and one-half cups flour ; cover, and let rise until light; add butter, remaining sugar, raisins, lemon, and enough flour to knead ; let rise, shape like biscuits, let rise again, and bake.   If wanted glazed, brush over with beaten egg before baking.

Hot Cross Buns.

1 cup scalded milk.	¾ teaspoon cinnamon.
¼ cup sugar.	3 cups flour.
2 tablespoons butter.	1 egg.
½ teaspoon salt.	¼ cup raisins stoned and
½ yeast cake dissolved in	quartered, or
¼ cup lukewarm water.	¼ cup currants.

Add butter, sugar, and salt to milk ; when lukewarm, add dissolved yeast cake, cinnamon, flour, and egg well beaten ; when thoroughly mixed, add raisins, cover, and let rise over night.   In morning, shape in forms of large biscuits, place in pan one inch apart, let rise, brush over with beaten egg, and bake twenty minutes ; cool, and with ornamental frosting make a cross on top of each bun.

Raised Muffins.

1 cup scalded milk.	¾ teaspoon salt.
1 cup boiling water.	¼ yeast cake dissolved in
2 tablespoons butter.	¼ cup lukewarm water.
¼ cup sugar.	1 egg.

4 cups flour.

Add butter, sugar, and salt to milk and water ; when lukewarm, add dissolved yeast cake, egg well beaten, and flour ; beat thoroughly, cover, and let rise over night.   In morning, fill buttered muffin rings two-thirds full ; let rise until rings are full, and bake thirty minutes in hot oven.

Grilled Muffins.

Put buttered muffin rings on a hot greased griddle.   Fill one-half full with raised muffin mixture, and cook slowly until well risen and browned underneath ; turn muffins and rings and brown the other side.   This is a convenient way of cooking muffins when oven is not in condition for baking.

Raised Oatmeal Muffins.

¾ cup scalded milk.
¼ cup sugar.
½ teaspoon salt.

¼ yeast cake dissolved in
¼ cup lukewarm milk.
1 cup cold cooked oatmeal.

2½ cups flour.

Add sugar and salt to scalded milk; when lukewarm, add dissolved yeast cake. Work oatmeal into flour with tips of fingers, and add to first mixture; beat thoroughly, cover, and let rise over night. In morning, fill buttered iron gem pans two-thirds full, let rise on back of range that pan may gradually heat and mixture rise to fill pan. Bake in moderate oven twenty-five to thirty minutes.

Squash Biscuits.

½ cup squash (steamed and sifted).
¼ cup sugar.
⅛ teaspoon salt.
½ cup scalded milk.

¼ yeast cake dissolved in
¼ cup lukewarm water.
¼ cup butter.
2½ cups flour.

Add squash, sugar, salt, and butter to milk; when lukewarm, add dissolved yeast cake and flour; cover, and let rise over night. In morning shape into biscuits, let rise, and bake.

Dry Toast.

Cut stale bread in one-fourth inch slices. Crust may or may not be removed. Put slices on wire toaster, lock toaster and place over clear fire to dry, holding some distance from coals; turn and dry other side. Hold nearer to coals and color a golden brown on each side. Toast, if piled compactly and allowed to stand, will soon become moist. Toast may be buttered at table or before sending to table.

Water Toast.

Dip slices of dry toast quickly in boiling salted water, allowing one-half teaspoon salt to one cup boiling water. Spread slices with butter, and serve at once.

Milk Toast I.

1 pint scalded milk.	½ teaspoon salt.
2 tablespoons butter.	1 cup milk.
1½ tablespoons bread flour.	Cold water.

6 slices dry toast.

Add cold water gradually to flour to make a smooth, thin paste. Add to milk, stirring constantly until thickened, cover, and cook twenty minutes; then add salt and butter in small pieces. Dip slices of toast separately in sauce; when soft, remove to serving dish. Pour remaining sauce over all.

Milk Toast II.

Use ingredients given in Milk Toast I., omitting cold water, and make as Thin White Sauce. Dip toast in sauce.

Brown Bread Milk Toast.

Make same as Milk Toast, using slices of toasted brown bread in place of white bread. Brown bread is better toasted by first drying slices in oven.

Cream Toast.

Substitute cream for milk, and omit butter in recipe for Milk Toast I. or II.

Tomato Cream Toast.

1½ cups stewed and strained tomato.	3 tablespoons butter.
½ cup scalded cream.	3 tablespoons flour.
¼ teaspoon soda.	½ teaspoon salt.

6 slices toast.

Put butter in saucepan; when melted and bubbling, add flour, mixed with salt, and stir in gradually tomato, to which soda has been added, then cream and butter. Dip slices of toast in sauce. Serve as soon as made.

German Toast.

3 eggs. 2 tablespoons sugar.
½ teaspoon salt. 1 cup milk.
6 slices stale bread.

Beat eggs slightly, add salt, sugar, and milk; strain into a shallow dish. Soak bread in mixture until soft. Cook on a hot, well-greased griddle; brown on one side, turn and brown other side. Serve for breakfast or luncheon, or with a sauce for dessert.

Brewis.

Break stale bits or slices of brown and white bread in small pieces, allowing one and one-half cups brown bread to one-half cup white bread. Butter a hot frying-pan, put in bread, and cover with equal parts milk and water. Cook until soft; add butter and salt to taste.

Bread for Garnishing.

Dry toast is often used for garnishing, cut in various shapes. Always shape before toasting. Cubes of bread, toast points, and small oblong pieces are most common. Cubes of stale bread, from which centres are removed, are fried in deep fat and called croûstades; half-inch cubes, browned in butter, or fried in deep fat, are called croûtons.

Uses for Stale Bread.

All pieces of bread should be saved and utilized. Large pieces are best for toast. Soft stale bread, from which crust is removed, when crumbed, is called stale bread crumbs, or raspings, and is used for puddings, griddle-cakes, omelets, scalloped dishes, and dipping food to be fried. Remnants of bread, from which crusts have not been removed, are dried in oven, rolled, and sifted. These are called dry bread crumbs, and are useful for crumbing croquettes, cutlets, fish, meat, etc.

CHAPTER V.

BISCUITS, BREAKFAST CAKES, AND SHORTCAKES.

Batters, Sponges, and Doughs.

BATTER is a mixture of flour and some liquid (usually combined with other ingredients, as sugar, salt, eggs, etc.), of consistency to pour easily, or to drop from a spoon.

Batters are termed thin or thick, according to their consistency.

Sponge is a batter to which yeast is added.

Dough differs from batter inasmuch as it is stiff enough to be handled.

Baking Powder Biscuit I.

2 cups flour.	1 tablespoon lard.
4 teaspoons baking powder.	¾ cup milk and water
1 teaspoon salt.	in equal parts.
1 tablespoon butter.	

Mix dry ingredients, and sift twice.

Work in butter and lard with tips of fingers; add gradually the liquid, mixing with knife to a soft dough. It is impossible to determine the exact amount of liquid, owing to differences in flour. Toss on a floured board, pat, and roll lightly to one-half inch in thickness. Shape with a biscuit-cutter. Place on buttered pan, and bake in hot oven twelve to fifteen minutes. If baked in too slow an oven, the gas will escape before it has done its work.

Baking Powder Biscuit II.

2 cups flour.   2 tablespoons butter.
4 teaspoons baking powder.   ¾ cup milk.
½ teaspoon salt.

Mix and bake as Baking Powder Biscuit I.

Emergency Biscuit.

Use recipe for Baking Powder Biscuit I. or II., with the addition of more milk, that mixture may be dropped from spoon without spreading. Drop by spoonfuls on a buttered pan, one-half inch apart. Brush over with milk, and bake in hot oven eight minutes.

Fruit Rolls (Pin Wheel Biscuit).

2 cups flour.   ⅔ cup milk.
4 teaspoons baking powder.   ⅓ cup stoned raisins
½ teaspoon salt.   (finely chopped).
2 tablespoons sugar.   2 tablespoons citron
2 tablespoons butter.   (finely chopped).
⅓ teaspoon cinnamon.

Mix as Baking Powder Biscuit II. Roll to one-fourth inch thickness, brush over with melted butter, and sprinkle with fruit, sugar, and cinnamon. Roll like a jelly roll; cut off pieces three-fourths inch in thickness. Place on buttered tin, and bake in hot oven fifteen minutes. Currants may be used in place of raisins and citron.

One Egg Muffins I.

3½ cups flour.   1¾ cups milk.
5 teaspoons baking powder.   3 tablespoons melted butter.
1 teaspoon salt.   1 egg.
3 tablespoons sugar.

Mix and sift dry ingredients; add gradually milk, egg well beaten, and melted butter. Bake in buttered gem pans twenty-five minutes. If iron pans are used they must be previously heated. This recipe makes thirty muffins. Use half the proportions given and a small egg, if half the number is required.

One Egg Muffins II.

2½ cups flour.	2 tablespoons sugar.
3½ teaspoons baking powder.	1 cup milk.
½ teaspoon salt.	2 tablespoons melted butter.

1 egg.

Mix and bake as One Egg Muffin I.

Twin Mountain Muffins.

¼ cup butter.	¾ cup milk.
¼ cup sugar.	2 cups flour.
1 egg.	3 teaspoons baking powder.

Cream the butter; add sugar and egg well beaten; sift baking powder with flour, and add to the first mixture, alternating with milk. Bake in buttered tin gem pans twenty-five minutes.

Queen of Muffins.

¼ cup butter.	½ cup milk (scant).
⅓ cup sugar.	1½ cups flour.
1 egg.	2½ teaspoons baking powder.

Mix and bake as Twin Mountain Muffins.

Berry Muffins I.   (Without eggs.)

2 cups flour.	2 tablespoons butter.
¼ cup sugar.	1 cup milk (scant).
4 teaspoons baking powder.	1 cup berries.

½ teaspoon salt.

Mix and sift dry ingredients; work in butter with tips of fingers; add milk and berries.

Berry Muffins II.

¼ cup butter.
⅓ cup sugar.
1 egg.
2⅔ cups flour.

4 teaspoons baking powder.
½ teaspoon salt.
1 cup milk.
1 cup berries.

Cream the butter; add gradually sugar and egg well beaten; mix and sift flour, baking powder, and salt, reserving ¼ cup flour to be mixed with berries and added last; add the remainder alternately with milk.

Rice Muffins.

2½ cups flour.
1 cup cooked rice.
4 teaspoons baking powder.

1 cup milk.
1 egg.
¼ cup melted butter.

½ teaspoon salt.

Mix and sift flour, salt, and baking powder; work in rice with tips of fingers; add gradually milk, egg well beaten, and butter; bake in buttered muffin rings placed in buttered pan or buttered gem pans.

Oatmeal Muffins.

1 cup cooked oatmeal.
1½ cups flour.
2 tablespoons sugar.
3 teaspoons baking powder.

½ teaspoon salt.
½ cup milk.
1 egg.
1 tablespoon melted butter.

Mix and bake as Rice Muffins.

Quaker Muffins.

⅔ cup rolled oats.
1⅓ cups flour.
3 tablespoons sugar.
3 tablespoons baking powder.

½ teaspoon salt.
1 cup scalded milk.
1 egg.
1 tablespoon melted butter.

Turn scalded milk on rolled oats, let stand five minutes; add sugar, salt, and melted butter; sift in flour and baking powder, mix thoroughly, and add egg well beaten.

Graham Muffins I.

1¼ cups graham flour. ⅓ cup molasses.
1 cup flour. ¾ teaspoon soda.
1 cup sour milk. 1 teaspoon salt.

Mix and sift dry ingredients; add milk to molasses, and combine mixtures.

Graham Muffins II.

1 cup graham or entire wheat 1 teaspoon salt.
  flour. 1 cup milk.
1 cup flour. 1 egg.
¼ cup sugar. 1 tablespoon melted butter.
3½ teaspoons baking powder.

Mix and sift dry ingredients; add milk gradually, egg well beaten, and melted butter; bake in hot oven in buttered gem pans twenty-five minutes.

Rye Muffins I.

Make as Graham Muffins II., substituting rye meal for graham flour.

Rye Muffins II.

1¼ cups rye meal. ¼ cup molasses.
1¼ cups flour. 1¼ cups milk.
4 teaspoons baking powder. 1 egg.
1 teaspoon salt. 1 tablespoon melted butter.

Mix and bake as Graham Muffins II., adding molasses with milk.

Corn Meal Gems.

½ cup corn meal. 1 tablespoon melted butter.
1 cup flour. ½ teaspoon salt.
3 teaspoons baking powder. ¾ cup milk.
1 tablespoon sugar. 1 egg.

Mix and bake as Graham Muffins II.

Berkshire Muffins.

½ cup corn meal.	½ teaspoon salt.
½ cup flour.	⅔ cup scalded milk (scant).
½ cup cooked rice.	1 egg.
2 tablespoons sugar.	1 tablespoon melted butter.

3 teaspoons baking powder.

Turn scalded milk on meal, let stand five minutes; add rice, and flour mixed and sifted with remaining dry ingredients. Add yolk of egg well beaten, butter, and white of egg beaten stiff and dry.

Golden Corn Cake.

¾ cup corn meal.	½ teaspoon salt.
1¼ cups flour.	1 cup milk.
¼ cup sugar.	1 egg.
4 teaspoons baking powder.	1 tablespoon melted butter.

Mix and sift dry ingredients; add milk, egg well beaten, and butter; bake in shallow buttered pan in hot oven twenty minutes.

Corn Cake (sweetened with Molasses).

1 cup corn meal.	¼ cup molasses.
¾ cup flour.	¾ cup milk.
3½ teaspoons baking powder.	1 egg.
1 teaspoon salt.	1 tablespoon melted butter.

Mix and bake as Golden Corn Cake, adding molasses to milk.

White Corn Cake.

¼ cup butter.	1¼ cups white corn meal.
½ cup sugar.	1¼ cups flour.
1⅓ cups milk.	4 teaspoons baking powder.
Whites 3 eggs.	1 teaspoon salt.

Cream the butter; add sugar gradually; add milk, alternating with dry ingredients, mixed and sifted. Beat thoroughly; add whites of eggs beaten stiff. Bake in buttered cake pan thirty minutes.

Susie's Spider Corn Cake.

1½ cups corn meal.	1 teaspoon salt.
2 cups sour milk.	2 eggs.
1 teaspoon soda.	2 tablespoons butter.

Mix soda, salt, and corn meal; gradually add eggs well beaten and milk. Heat frying-pan, grease sides and bottom of pan with butter, turn in the mixture, place on middle grate in hot oven, and cook twenty minutes.

Pop-overs.

1 cup flour.	⅞ cup milk.
¼ teaspoon salt.	1 egg.
½ teaspoon melted butter.	

Mix salt and flour; add milk gradually, in order to obtain a smooth batter. Add egg, beaten until light, and butter; beat two minutes,— using Dover egg-beater, — turn into hissing hot buttered iron gem pans, and bake thirty to thirty-five minutes in a hot oven. They may be baked in buttered earthen cups, when the bottom will have a glazed appearance. Small round iron gem pans are best for Pop-overs.

Graham Pop-overs.

⅔ cup entire wheat flour.	⅞ cup milk.
⅓ cup flour.	1 egg.
¼ teaspoon salt.	½ teaspoon melted butter.

Prepare and bake as Pop-overs.

Breakfast Puffs.

1 cup flour.	½ cup milk.
½ cup water.	

Mix milk and water; add gradually to flour, and beat with Dover egg-beater until very light. Bake as Pop-overs.

Fadges.

1 cup entire wheat flour.   1 cup cold water.

Add water gradually to flour, and beat with Dover egg-beater until very light. Bake as Pop-overs.

Maryland Biscuit.

1 pint flour.   1 teaspoon salt.
⅓ cup lard.   Milk and water in equal quantities.

Southern Pupil.

Mix flour and salt; work in lard with tips of fingers, and moisten to a stiff dough. Toss on slightly floured board, and beat with rolling-pin thirty minutes, continually folding over the dough. Roll one-third inch in thickness, shape with small round cutter, prick with fork, and place on a buttered tin. Bake twenty minutes in hot oven.

GRIDDLE-CAKES.

Sour Milk Griddle-Cakes.

2½ cups flour.   2 cups sour milk.
½ teaspoon salt.   ½ teaspoon soda.
1 egg.

Mix and sift flour, salt, and soda; add sour milk, and egg well beaten. Drop by spoonfuls on a greased hot griddle; cook on one side. When puffed, full of bubbles, and cooked on edges, turn, and cook other side. Serve with butter and maple syrup.

Sweet Milk Griddle-Cakes.

3½ cups flour.   ¼ cup sugar.
1½ tablespoons baking powder.   2 cups milk.
1 teaspoon salt.   1 egg.
2 tablespoons melted butter.

Mix and sift dry ingredients; beat egg, add milk, and pour slowly on first mixture. Beat thoroughly, and add butter. Cook as Sour Milk Griddle-Cakes.

Entire Wheat Griddle-Cakes.

½ cup entire wheat flour.	3 tablespoons sugar.
1 cup flour.	1 egg.
3 teaspoons baking powder.	1¼ cups milk.
½ teaspoon salt.	1 tablespoon melted butter.

Prepare and cook as Sweet Milk Griddle-Cakes.

Corn Griddle-Cakes.

2¼ cups flour.	⅓ cup sugar.
½ cup corn meal.	1½ cups boiling water.
1¼ tablespoons baking powder.	1 cup milk.
1½ teaspoons salt.	1 egg.
2 tablespoons melted butter.	

Add meal to boiling water, and boil five minutes; turn into bowl, add milk, and remaining dry ingredients mixed and sifted, then the egg well beaten, and butter. Cook as other griddle-cakes.

Rice Griddle-Cakes I.

2½ cups flour.	¼ cup sugar.
½ cup cold cooked rice.	1½ cups milk.
1 tablespoon baking powder.	1 egg.
½ teaspoon salt.	2 tablespoons melted butter.

Mix and sift dry ingredients. Work in rice with tips of fingers; add egg well beaten, milk, and butter. Cook as other griddle-cakes.

Rice Griddle-Cakes II.

1 cup milk.	Yolks 2 eggs.
1 cup warm boiled rice.	Whites 2 eggs.
½ teaspoon salt.	1 tablespoon melted butter.
⅞ cup flour.	

Pour milk over rice and salt, add yolks of eggs beaten until thick and lemon color, butter, flour, and fold in whites of eggs beaten until stiff and dry.

Bread Griddle-Cakes.

1½ cups fine stale bread crumbs.   2 eggs.
1½ cups scalded milk.   ½ cup flour.
2 tablespoons butter.   ½ teaspoon salt.
3½ teaspoons baking powder.

Add milk and butter to crumbs, and soak until crumbs are soft; add eggs well beaten, then flour, salt, and baking powder mixed and sifted. Cook as other griddle-cakes.

Buckwheat Cakes.

⅓ cup fine bread crumbs.   ¼ yeast cake.
2 cups scalded milk.   ½ cup lukewarm water.
½ teaspoon salt.   Buckwheat flour.
1 tablespoon molasses.

Pour milk over crumbs, and soak thirty minutes; add salt, yeast cake dissolved in lukewarm water, and buckwheat to make a batter thin enough to pour. Let rise over night; in the morning, stir well, add molasses, and cook as griddle-cakes. Save enough batter to raise another mixing, instead of using yeast cake; it will require one-half cup.

Waffles.

2 cups flour.   1 cup milk.
3 teaspoons baking powder.   Yolks 2 eggs.
½ teaspoon salt.   Whites 2 eggs.
1 tablespoon melted butter.

Mix and sift dry ingredients; add milk gradually, yolks of eggs well beaten, butter, and whites of eggs beaten stiff; cook on a greased hot waffle iron. Serve with maple syrup.

A waffle iron should fit closely on range, be well heated on one side, turned, heated on other side, and thoroughly greased before iron is filled. In filling, put a tablespoonful of mixture in each compartment near centre of iron, cover, and mixture will spread to just fill iron. If sufficiently heated, it should be turned almost as soon as filled and covered. In using a new iron, special care must be taken in greasing, or waffles will stick.

Rice Waffles.

1¾ cups flour.	3 teaspoons baking powder.
⅔ cup cold cooked rice.	¼ teaspoon salt.
1½ cups milk.	1 tablespoon melted butter.
2 tablespoons sugar.	1 egg.

Mix and sift dry ingredients; work in rice with tips of fingers; add milk, yolk of egg well beaten, butter, and white of egg beaten stiff. Cook as Waffles.

Virginia Waffles.

1½ cups boiling water.	1¼ tablespoons baking powder.
½ cup white corn meal.	1½ teaspoons salt.
1½ cups milk.	Yolks 2 eggs.
2 cups flour.	Whites 2 eggs.
3 tablespoons sugar.	2 tablespoons melted butter.

Cook meal in boiling water twenty minutes; add milk, dry ingredients mixed and sifted, yolks of eggs well beaten, butter, and whites of eggs beaten stiff. Cook as Waffles.

Raised Waffles.

1¾ cups milk.	¼ cup lukewarm water.
1 teaspoon salt.	2 cups flour.
1 tablespoon butter.	Yolks 2 eggs.
¼ yeast cake.	Whites 2 eggs.

Scald milk; add salt and butter, and when lukewarm, add yeast cake dissolved in water, and flour. Beat well; let rise over night; add yolks of eggs well beaten, and whites of eggs beaten stiff. Cook as Waffles. By using a whole yeast cake, the mixture will rise in one and one-half hours.

Fried Drop Cakes.

1⅓ cups flour.   ⅓ cup sugar.
2½ teaspoons baking powder.   ½ cup milk.
¼ teaspoon salt.   1 egg.
           1 teaspoon melted butter.

Beat egg until light; add milk, dry ingredients mixed and sifted, and melted butter. Drop by spoonfuls in hot, new, deep fat; fry until light brown and cooked through, which must at first be determined by piercing with a skewer, or breaking apart. Remove with a skimmer, and drain on brown paper.

Rye Drop Cakes.

⅔ cup rye meal.   ½ teaspoon salt.
⅔ cup flour.   2 tablespoons molasses.
2½ teaspoons baking powder.   ½ cup milk.
                1 egg.

Mix and sift dry ingredients; add milk gradually, molasses, and egg well beaten. Cook as Fried Drop Cakes.

Doughnuts I.

1 cup sugar.   3½ teaspoons baking powder.
2½ tablespoons butter.   ¼ teaspoon cinnamon.
2 eggs.   ¼ teaspoon grated nutmeg.
1 cup milk.   1½ teaspoons salt.
                Flour to roll.

Cream the butter, and add one-half sugar. Beat egg until light, add remaining sugar, and combine mixtures. Add three and one-half cups flour, mixed and sifted with baking powder, salt, and spices; then enough more flour to make dough stiff enough to roll. Toss one-third of mixture on floured board, knead slightly, pat, and roll out to one-fourth inch thickness. Shape with a doughnut cutter, fry in deep fat, take up on a skewer, and drain on brown paper. Add trimmings to one-half remaining mixture, roll, shape, and fry as before; repeat. Doughnuts should come quickly to top of fat, brown on one side, then be turned to brown on the other; avoid turning more than once.   The fat must be kept at a uniform temperature.   If too cold, doughnuts will absorb fat; if too hot, doughnuts will brown before sufficiently risen.   See rule for testing fat.

Doughnuts II.

4 cups flour.	¼ teaspoon cinnamon.
1½ teaspoons salt.	½ tablespoon butter.
1¾ teaspoons soda.	1 cup sugar.
1¾ teaspoons cream tartar.	1 cup sour milk.
¼ teaspoon grated nutmeg.	1 egg.

Put flour in shallow pan; add salt, soda, cream tartar, and spices.   Work in butter with tips of fingers; add sugar, egg well beaten, and sour milk.   Stir thoroughly, and toss on board thickly dredged with flour; knead slightly, using more flour if necessary.   Pat and roll out to one-fourth inch thickness; shape, fry, and drain. Sour milk doughnuts may be turned as soon as they come to top of fat, and frequently afterwards.

Raised Doughnuts.

1 cup milk.	⅓ cup butter and lard mixed.
¼ yeast cake.	1 cup light brown sugar.
¼ cup lukewarm water.	2 eggs.
1 teaspoon salt.	½ grated nutmeg.
	Flour.

Scald and cool milk; when lukewarm, add yeast cake dissolved in water, salt, and flour enough to make a stiff batter; let rise over night.   In morning add shortening melted, sugar, eggs well beaten, nutmeg, and enough flour to make a stiff dough; let rise again, and if too soft to handle, add more flour.   Toss on floured board, pat, and roll to three-fourths inch thickness.   Shape with cutter, and work between hands until round.   Place on floured board, let rise one hour, turn, and let rise again; fry in deep fat, and drain on brown paper.   Cool, and roll in powdered sugar.

Crullers.

¼ cup butter.   4 cups flour.
1 cup sugar.   ¼ teaspoon grated nutmeg.
Yolks 2 eggs.   3½ teaspoons baking powder.
Whites 2 eggs.   1 cup milk.
Powdered sugar and cinnamon.

Cream the butter, add sugar gradually, yolks of eggs well beaten, and whites of eggs beaten stiff. Mix flour, nutmeg, and baking powder; add alternately with milk to first mixture; toss on floured board, roll thin, and cut in pieces three inches long by two inches wide; make four one inch gashes at equal intervals. Take up by running finger in and out of gashes, and lower into deep fat. Fry same as Doughnuts I.

Strawberry Short Cake I.

2 cups flour.   2 teaspoons sugar.
4 teaspoons baking powder.   ¾ cup milk.
½ teaspoon salt.   ¼ cup butter.

Mix dry ingredients, sift twice, work in butter with tips of fingers, and add milk gradually. Toss on floured board, divide in two parts. Pat, roll out, and bake twelve minutes in a hot oven in buttered Washington pie or round layer cake tins. Split and spread with butter. Sweeten strawberries to taste, place on back of range until warmed, crush slightly, and put between and on top of Short Cakes; cover top with Cream Sauce I. Allow from one to one and one-half boxes berries to each Short Cake.

Strawberry Short Cake II.

2 cups flour.   1 tablespoon sugar.
4 teaspoons baking powder.   ¾ cup milk.
½ teaspoon salt.   ⅓ cup butter.

Mix as Strawberry Short Cake I. Toss and roll on floured board. Put in round buttered tin, and shape with back of hand to fit pan.

Rich Strawberry Short Cake.

2 cups flour.
¼ cup sugar.
4 teaspoons baking powder.
½ teaspoon salt.

Few grains nutmeg.
1 egg.
⅓ cup butter.
1¼ tablespoons lard.

⅔ cup milk.

Hotel Pastry Cook.

Mix dry ingredients and sift twice, work in shortening with tips of fingers, add egg well beaten, and milk. Bake as Strawberry Short Cake II. Split cake and spread under layer with Cream Sauce II. Cover with strawberries which have been sprinkled with powdered sugar; again spread with sauce, and cover with upper layer.

Fruit Short Cake.

¼ cup butter.
½ cup sugar.
1 egg.

¼ cup milk.
1 cup flour.
2 teaspoons baking powder.

¼ teaspoon salt.

Cream the butter, add sugar gradually, and egg well beaten. Mix and sift flour, baking powder, and salt, adding alternately with milk to first mixture. Beat thoroughly, and bake in a buttered round tin. Cool, spread thickly with sweetened fruit, and cover with Cream Sauce I. or II. Fresh strawberries, peaches, apricots, raspberries, or canned quince or pineapple may be used. When canned goods are used, drain fruit from syrup and cut in pieces. Dilute cream for Cream Sauce with fruit syrup in place of milk.

CHAPTER VI.

CEREALS.

CEREALS (cultivated grasses) rank first among vegetable foods; being of hardy growth and easy cultivation, they are more widely diffused over the globe than any of the flowering plants. They include wheat, oats, rye, barley, maize (Indian corn), and rice; some authorities place buckwheat among them. Wheat probably is the most largely consumed; next to wheat, comes rice.

TABLE SHOWING COMPOSITION.

	Proteid.	Fat.	Starch.	Mineral matter.	Water.
Oatmeal	15.6	7.3	68.0	1.9	7.2
Corn meal	8.9	2.2	75.1	0.9	12.9
Wheat flour (spring) .	11.8	1.1	75.0	0.5	11.6
Wheat flour (winter) .	10.4	1.0	75.6	0.5	12.5
Entire wheat flour . .	14.2	1.9	70.6	1.2	12.1
Graham flour . . .	13.7	2.2	70.3	2.0	11.8
Pearl barley	9.3	1.0	77.6	1.3	10.8
Rye meal	7.1	0.9	78.5	0.8	12.7
Rice	7.8	0.4	79.4	0.4	12.4
Buckwheat flour . .	6.1	1.0	77.2	1.4	14.3
Macaroni	11.7	1.6	72.9	3.0	10.8

Department of Agriculture, Washington, D. C.

Macaroni, spaghetti, and *vermicelli* are made from wheaten flour, rich in gluten, moistened to a stiff dough with water, and forced through small apertures in an iron plate by means of a screw press. Various Italian pastes are made from the same mixture. Macaroni is manufactured to some extent in this country, but the best comes from Italy, Lagana and Pejero, being the favorite brand. When macaroni is colored, it is done by the use of saffron, not by eggs, as is generally supposed. The only egg macaroni is manufactured in strips, and comes from Minneapolis.

Macaroni is valuable food, as it is very cheap and nutritious; but being deficient in fat, it should be combined with cream, butter, or cheese, to make a perfect food.

From cereals many preparations are made, used alone, or in combination with other food products. From rice is made rice flour; from oats, oatmeal, and oats steam-cooked and rolled, — as Rolled Avena, Quaker Rolled Oats, H-O, etc. There are many species of corn, the principal varieties being white, yellow, and red. From corn is made corn meal, — both white and yellow, — corn-starch, hominy, maizena, cerealine, samp, and hulled corn; from wheat, wheaten or white flour, Wheatena, Wheatlet, Wheat Grits, Pettijohns, etc. Rye is principally used for meal and flour; barley, for flour and pearl barley. Buckwheat, throughout the United States, is used only when made into flour for buckwheat cakes.

For family use, cereals should be bought in small quantities, and kept in glass jars, tightly covered. Many cereal preparations are on the market for making breakfast mushes, put up in one and two pound packages, with directions for cooking. In nearly all cases, time allowed for cooking is not sufficient, unless dish containing cereal is brought in direct contact with fire, which is not the best way. Mushes should be cooked over hot water after the first five minutes; if a double boiler is not procurable, improvise one. Boiling water and salt should always be added to cereals, allowing one teaspoon salt to each cup of cereal, — boiled to soften cellulose and swell starch grains, salted to give flavor. Indian meal and finely ground preparations should be mixed with cold water before adding boiling water, to prevent lumping.

TABLE FOR COOKING CEREALS.

Kind.	Quantity.	Water.	Time.
Steam-cooked and rolled oats, Rolled Avena, Quaker Rolled Oats.	1 cup.	1¾ cups.	30 minutes.
Steam-cooked and rolled wheats, H–O, Pettijohns, etc.	1 cup.	1¼ cups.	20 minutes.
Rice (steamed) . .	1 cup.	2¾–3¼ cups (according to age of rice).	45–60 minutes.
Indian meal . . .	1 cup.	3½ cups.	3 hours.
Wheatlet, Wheatena, Wheat Germ, Germea, etc.	1 cup.	3¾ cups.	30 minutes.
Oatmeal (coarse) .	1 cup.	4 cups.	3 hours.
Hominy (fine) .	1 cup.	4 cups.	1 hour.

Oatmeal Mush with Apples.

Core apples, leaving large cavities; pare, and cook until soft in syrup made by boiling sugar and water together. Fill cavities with oatmeal mush; serve with sugar and cream. The syrup should be saved and re-used.

Cereal with Fruit.

¾ cup Wheat Germ.
¾ cup cold water.
2½ cups boiling water.
1 teaspoon salt.
½ lb. dates, stoned, and cut in pieces.

Mix cereal, salt, and cold water; add to boiling water placed on front of range. Boil five minutes, steam in double boiler thirty minutes; stir in dates, and serve with cream. To serve for breakfast, or as a simple dessert.

Fried Mushes.

Mush left over from breakfast may be packed in greased, one pound baking-powder box, and covered, which will prevent crust from forming. The next morning remove from box, slice thinly, dip in flour, and sauté. Serve with maple syrup.

Fried Corn Meal Mush, or Fried Hominy.

Pack corn meal or hominy mush in greased, one pound baking-powder boxes, or small bread pan, cool, and cover. Cut in thin slices, and sauté; cook slowly, if preferred crisp and dry. Where mushes are cooked to fry, use less water in steaming.

Boiled Rice.

1 cup rice.   2 quarts boiling water
              1 tablespoon salt.

French Chef.

Pick over rice; add slowly to boiling, salted water, so as not to check boiling of water. Boil thirty minutes, or until soft, which may be determined by testing kernels. Old rice absorbs much more water than new rice, and takes longer for cooking. Drain in coarse strainer, and pour over one quart hot water; return to kettle in which it was cooked; cover, place on back of range, and let stand to dry off, when kernels are distinct. When stirring rice, always use a fork to avoid breaking kernels.

Steamed Rice.

1 cup rice.   2¾ to 3¼ cups boiling water
1 teaspoon salt.   (according to age of rice).

Put salt and water in top of double boiler, place on range, and add gradually well-washed rice, stirring with a fork to prevent adhering to boiler. Boil five minutes, cover, place over under part double boiler, and steam forty-five minutes, or until kernels are soft; uncover, that steam may escape. When rice is steamed for a simple dessert, use one-half quantity of water given in recipe, and steam until rice has absorbed water; then add scalded milk for remaining liquid.

To wash rice. Put rice in strainer, place strainer over bowl nearly full of cold water; rub rice between hands, lift strainer from bowl, and change water. Repeat process three or four times, until water is quite clear.

Rice with Cheese.

Steam one cup rice, allowing one tablespoon salt; cover bottom of buttered pudding-dish with rice, dot over with three-fourths tablespoon butter, sprinkle with thin shavings mild cheese and a few grains cayenne; repeat until rice and one-fourth pound cheese are used. Add milk to half the depth of contents of dish, cover with buttered cracker crumbs, and bake until cheese melts.

Rice à la Riston.

Finely chop two thin slices bacon, add to one-half raw medium sized cabbage, finely chopped; cover, and cook slowly thirty minutes. Add one-fourth cup rice, boiled, one-half teaspoon chopped parsley, and salt and pepper to taste. Moisten with one-half cup White Stock, and cook fifteen minutes.

Turkish Pilaf I.

Wash and drain one-half cup rice, cook in one tablespoon butter until brown, add one cup boiling water, and steam until water is absorbed. Add one and three-fourths cups hot stewed tomatoes, cook until rice is tender, and season with salt and pepper.

Turkish Pilaf II.

½ cup washed rice.
¾ cup tomatoes, stewed and
strained.

1 cup Brown Stock, highly
seasoned.
3 tablespoons butter.

Add tomato to stock, and heat to boiling point; add rice, and steam until rice is soft; stir in butter with a fork, and keep uncovered that steam may escape. Serve in place of a vegetable, or as border for curried or fricasseed meat.

Boiled Macaroni.

¾ cup macaroni, broken in
inch pieces.

2 quarts boiling water.
1 tablespoon salt.

½ cup cream.

Cook macaroni in boiling salted water twenty minutes or until soft, drain in strainer, pour over it cold water to prevent pieces from adhering; add cream, reheat, and season with salt.

Macaroni with White Sauce.

¾ cup macaroni broken in
inch pieces.

2 quarts boiling water.
1 tablespoon salt.

1½ cups white sauce.

Cook as for Boiled Macaroni, and reheat in white sauce.

White Sauce. Melt two tablespoons butter, add two tablespoons flour with one-half teaspoon salt, and pour on slowly one and one-half cups scalded milk.

Baked Macaroni.

Put macaroni with White Sauce in buttered baking dish, cover with buttered crumbs, and bake until crumbs are brown.

Baked Macaroni with Cheese.

Put a layer of boiled macaroni in buttered baking dish, sprinkle with grated cheese; repeat, pour over White

Sauce, cover with buttered crumbs, and bake until crumbs are brown.

Macaroni with Tomato Sauce.

Reheat Boiled Macaroni in one and one-half cups Tomato Sauce I., sprinkle with grated cheese, and serve; or prepare as Baked Macaroni, using Tomato in place of White Sauce.

Macaroni à l'Italienne.

¾ cup macaroni.	1½ cups Tomato Sauce II.
2 quarts boiling salted water.	½ cup grated cheese.
½ onion.	2 tablespoons wine.
2 cloves.	½ tablespoon butter.

Cook macaroni in boiling salted water, with butter, and onion stuck with cloves; drain, remove onion, reheat in tomato sauce, add cheese and wine.

Macaroni à la Milanaise.

Cook macaroni as for Macaroni à l'Italienne, reheat in Tomato Sauce II., add six sliced mushrooms, two slices cooked smoked beef tongue cut in strips, and one-half cup grated cheese.

Spaghetti.

Spaghetti may be cooked in any way in which macaroni is cooked, but is usually served with tomato sauce.

It is cooked in long strips rather than broken in pieces; to accomplish this, hold quantity to be cooked in the hand, and dip ends in boiling salted water; as spaghetti softens it will bend, and may be coiled under water.

CHAPTER VII.

EGGS.

COMPOSITION.

Proteid, 14.9%.	Mineral matter, 1%.
Fat, 10.6%.	Water, 73.5%.

EGGS, like milk, form a typical food, inasmuch as they contain all the elements, in the right proportion, necessary for support of the body. Their highly concentrated, nutritive value renders it necessary to use them in combination with other foods, rich in starch (bread, potatoes, etc.). In order that the stomach may have enough to act upon, a certain amount of bulk must be furnished.

A pound of eggs (nine) is equivalent in nutritive value to a pound of beef. From this it may be seen that eggs, at even twenty-five cents per dozen, should not be freely used by the strict economist. Eggs being rich in proteid, serve as a valuable substitute for meat. In most families, their use in the making of cake, custard, puddings, etc., renders them almost indispensable. It is surprising how many intelligent women, who look well to the affairs of the kitchen, are satisfied to use what are termed " cooking eggs; " this shows poor judgment from an economical standpoint. Strictly fresh eggs should always be used, if obtainable. An egg after the first twenty-four hours steadily deteriorates. If exposed to air, owing to the porous structure of the shell, there is an evaporation of water, air rushes in, and decomposition takes place.

White of egg contains albumen in its purest form. Albumen coagulates at a temperature of from 134° to 160° F. Herein lies the importance of cooking eggs at a low temperature, thus rendering them easy of digestion. Eggs cooked in boiling water are tough and horny, difficult of digestion, and should never be served.

When eggs come from the market, they should be washed, and put away in a cold place.

Ways of Determining Freshness of Eggs. I. Hold in front of candle flame in dark room, and the centre should look clear.

II. Place in basin of cold water, and they should sink.

III. Place large end to the cheek, and a warmth should be felt.

Ways of Keeping Eggs. I. Pack in sawdust, small end down.

II. Keep in lime water.

III. From July to September a large number of eggs are packed, small ends down, in cases having compartments, one for each egg, and kept in cold storage. Eggs are often kept in cold storage six months, and then sold as cooking eggs

Boiled Eggs.

Have ready a saucepan containing boiling water. Carefully put in with a spoon the number of eggs desired, covering them with water. Remove saucepan to back of range, where water will not boil. Cook from six to eight minutes if liked " soft boiled," forty to forty-five if liked "hard boiled." Eggs may be cooked by placing in cold water and allowing water to heat gradually until the boiling point is reached, when they will be "soft boiled." In using hard-boiled eggs for making other dishes, when taken from the hot water they should be plunged into cold water to prevent, if possible, discoloration of yolks.

Eggs perfectly cooked should be placed and kept in water at a uniform temperature of 175° F.

Dropped Eggs (Poached).

Have ready a shallow pan two-thirds full of boiling salted water, allowing one-half tablespoon salt to one quart of water. Put two or three buttered muffin rings in the water. Break each egg separately into a cup, and carefully slip into a muffin ring. The water should cover the eggs. When there is a film over the top, and the white is firm, carefully remove with a buttered skimmer to circular pieces of buttered toast, and let each person season his own egg with butter, salt, and pepper. If cooked for an invalid, garnish with four toast-points and a bit of parsley. An egg-poacher may be used instead of muffin rings.

Eggs à la Finnoise.

Dropped Eggs, served with Tomato Sauce I.

Eggs à la Suisse.

4 eggs.	Salt.
½ cup cream.	Pepper.
1 tablespoon butter.	Cayenne.
2 tablespoons grated cheese.	

Heat a small omelet pan, put in butter, and when melted, add cream. Slip in the eggs one at a time, sprinkle with salt, pepper, and a few grains of cayenne. When whites are nearly firm, sprinkle with cheese. Finish cooking, and serve on buttered toast. Strain cream over the toast.

Baked or Shirred Eggs.

Butter an egg-shirrer. Cover bottom and sides with fine cracker crumbs. Break an egg into a cup, and carefully slip into shirrer. Cover with seasoned buttered crumbs, and bake in moderate oven until white is firm and crumbs brown. The shirrers should be placed on a tin plate, that they may be easily removed from the oven.

Eggs may be baked in small tomatoes. Cut a slice from stem end of tomato, scoop out the pulp, slip in an egg, sprinkle with salt and pepper, cover with buttered crumbs, and bake.

Scrambled Eggs.

5 eggs.	½ teaspoon salt.
½ cup milk.	⅛ teaspoon pepper.

2 tablespoons butter.

Beat eggs slightly with silver fork; add salt, pepper, and milk. Heat omelet pan, put in butter, and when melted, turn in the mixture. Cook until of creamy consistency, stirring and scraping from bottom of the pan.

Scrambled Eggs with Tomato Sauce.

6 eggs.	4 tablespoons butter.
1¾ cups tomatoes.	1 slice onion.
2 teaspoons sugar.	½ teaspoon salt.

⅛ teaspoon pepper.

Simmer tomatoes and sugar five minutes; fry butter and onion three minutes; remove onion, and add tomatoes, seasonings, and eggs slightly beaten. Cook as Scrambled Eggs. Serve with entire wheat bread or brown bread toast.

Scrambled Eggs with Anchovy Toast.

Spread thin slices of buttered toast with Anchovy Paste. Arrange on platter, and cover with scrambled eggs.

Eggs à la Buckingham.

Make five slices milk toast, and arrange on platter. Use recipe for Scrambled Eggs, having the eggs slightly under done. Pour eggs over toast, sprinkle with four tablespoons grated mild cheese. Put in oven to melt cheese, and finish cooking eggs.

Buttered Eggs.

Heat omelet pan. Put in one tablespoon butter; when melted, slip in an egg, and cook until the white is firm. Turn it over once while cooking. Add more butter as needed, using just enough to keep egg from sticking.

Buttered Eggs with Tomatoes.

Cut tomatoes in one-third inch slices. Sprinkle with salt and pepper, dredge with flour, and sauté in butter. Serve a buttered egg on each slice of tomato.

Fried Eggs.

Fried eggs are cooked as Buttered Eggs, without being turned. In this case the fat is taken by spoonfuls and poured over the eggs. Lard, pork, ham, or bacon fat, are usually employed, — a considerable amount being used.

Eggs à la Goldenrod.

3 hard boiled eggs.	½ teaspoon salt.
1 tablespoon butter.	⅛ teaspoon pepper.
1 tablespoon flour.	5 slices toast.
1 cup milk.	Parsley.

Make a thin white sauce with butter, flour, milk, and seasonings. Separate yolks from whites of eggs. Chop whites finely, and add them to the sauce. Cut four slices of toast in halves lengthwise. Arrange on platter, and pour over the sauce. Force the yolks through a potato ricer or strainer, sprinkling over the top. Garnish with parsley and remaining toast, cut in points.

Eggs au Gratin.

Arrange Dropped Eggs on a shallow buttered dish. Sprinkle with grated Parmesan cheese. Pour over eggs one pint Yellow Béchamel Sauce. Cover with stale bread crumbs, and sprinkle with grated cheese. Brown in oven. Tomato or White Sauce may be used.

Eggs in Batter.

1 egg.	2 tablespoons fine stale
1½ tablespoons thick cream.	bread crumbs.
¼ teaspoon salt.	

Mix cream, bread crumbs, and salt. Put one-half tablespoon of mixture in egg-shirrer. Slip in egg, and cover with remaining mixture. Bake six minutes in moderate oven.

Curried Eggs.

3 hard boiled eggs.	¼ teaspoon salt.
2 tablespoons butter.	½ teaspoon curry powder.
2 tablespoons flour.	⅛ teaspoon pepper.
1 cup hot milk.	

Melt butter, add flour and seasonings, and gradually hot milk. Cut eggs in eighths lengthwise, and re-heat in sauce.

Scalloped Eggs.

6 hard boiled eggs.	¾ cup chopped cold meat. ¼ lb. hame
1 pint White Sauce I.	¾ cup buttered cracker crumbs.

Chop eggs finely. Sprinkle bottom of a buttered baking dish with crumbs, cover with one-half the eggs, eggs with sauce, and sauce with meat; repeat. Cover with remaining crumbs. Place in oven on centre grate, and bake until crumbs are brown. Ham is the best meat to use for this dish. Chicken, veal, or fish may be used.

Stuffed Eggs in a Nest.

Cut hard boiled eggs in halves, lengthwise. Remove yolks, and put whites aside in pairs. Mash yolks, and add half the amount of devilled ham and enough melted butter to make of consistency to shape. Make in balls size of original yolks, and refill whites. Form remainder of mixture into a nest. Arrange eggs in the nest, and pour over one cup White Sauce I. Sprinkle with buttered crumbs, and bake until crumbs are brown.

Egg Farci.

Cut hard boiled eggs in halves, crosswise. Remove yolks, and put whites aside in pairs. Mash yolks, and add equal amount of cold cooked chicken or veal, finely chopped. Moisten with melted butter or Mayonnaise.

Season to taste with salt, pepper, lemon juice, mustard, and cayenne. Shape, and refill whites.

Omelets.

For omelets select large eggs, allowing one egg for each person, and one tablespoon liquid for each egg. Keep an omelet pan especially for omelets, and see that it is kept clean and smooth. A frying-pan may be used in place of omelet pan.

Plain Omelet.

4 eggs.	4 tablespoons hot water.
½ teaspoon salt.	1 tablespoon butter.
Few grains pepper.	1½ cups Thin White Sauce.

Separate yolks from whites. Beat yolks until thick and lemon colored; add salt, pepper, and hot water. Beat whites until stiff and dry, cutting and folding them into first mixture until they have taken up mixture. Heat omelet pan, and butter sides and bottom. Turn in mixture, spread evenly, place on range where it will cook slowly, occasionally turning the pan that omelet may brown evenly. When well " puffed " and delicately browned underneath, place pan on centre grate of oven to finish cooking the top. The omelet is cooked if it is firm to the touch when pressed by the finger. If it clings to the finger like the beaten white of egg, it needs longer cooking. Fold and turn on hot platter, and pour around one and one-half cups Thin White Sauce.

Milk is sometimes used in place of hot water, but hot water makes a more tender omelet.

To Fold and Turn an Omelet.

Hold omelet pan by handle with the left hand. With a case knife make two one-half inch incisions opposite each other at right angles to handle. Place knife under the part of omelet nearest handle, tip pan to nearly a vertical position; by carefully coaxing the omelet with knife, it will fold and turn without breaking.

Omelet with Meat or Vegetables.

Mix and cook Plain Omelet. Fold in remnants of finely chopped cooked chicken, veal, or ham. Remnants of fish may be flaked and added to White Sauce; or cooked peas, asparagus, or cauliflower may be added.

Oyster Omelet.

Mix and cook Plain Omelet. Fold in one pint oysters, parboiled, drained from their liquor, and cut in halves. Turn on platter, and pour around Thin White Sauce.

Orange Omelet.

3 eggs.	1 teaspoon lemon juice.
2 tablespoons powdered sugar.	2 oranges.
Few grains salt.	½ tablespoon butter.
2½ tablespoons orange juice.	

Follow directions for Plain Omelet. Remove skin from oranges and cut in slices, lengthwise. Fold in one-third of the slices of orange, well sprinkled with powdered sugar; put remaining slices around omelet, and sprinkle with sugar.

Jelly Omelet.

Mix and cook Plain Omelet, omitting pepper and one-half the salt, and adding one tablespoon sugar. Spread before folding with jam, jelly, or marmalade. Fold, turn, and sprinkle with sugar.

Bread Omelet.

4 eggs.	¾ teaspoon salt.
½ cup milk.	⅛ teaspoon pepper.
½ cup stale bread crumbs.	1 tablespoon butter.

Soak bread crumbs fifteen minutes in milk, add beaten yolks and seasonings. fold in whites. Cook and serve as Plain Omelet.

French Omelet.

4 eggs.   ½ teaspoon salt.
4 tablespoons milk.   ⅛ teaspoon pepper.
                2 tablespoons butter.

Beat eggs slightly, just enough to blend yolks and whites, add the milk and seasonings. Put butter in hot omelet pan ; when melted, turn in the mixture ; as it cooks, prick and pick up with a fork until the whole is of creamy consistency. Place on hotter part of range that it may brown quickly underneath. Fold and turn on hot platter.

Spanish Omelet.

Mix and cook a French Omelet. Serve with Tomato Sauce in the centre and around omelet.

Tomato Sauce. Cook two tablespoons of butter with one tablespoon of finely chopped onion, until yellow. Add one and three-fourths cups tomatoes, and cook until moisture has nearly evaporated. Add one tablespoon sliced mushroom, one-fourth teaspoon salt, and few grains cayenne. This is improved by a small piece of red or green pepper, finely chopped, cooked with butter and onion.

Rich Omelet.

2¼ tablespoons flour.   1 cup milk.
¾ teaspoon salt.   3 eggs.
                3 tablespoons butter.

Mrs. E. A. Dwinell.

Mix salt and flour, add gradually milk. Beat eggs until thick and lemon colored, then add to first mixture. Heat frying-pan and put in two-thirds of the butter ; when butter is melted, pour in mixture. As it cooks, lift with a griddle-cake turner so that uncooked part may run underneath ; add remaining butter as needed, and continue lifting the cooked part until it is firm throughout. Place on hotter part of range to brown ; roll, and turn on hot platter.

CHAPTER VIII.

SOUPS.

IT cannot be denied that the French excel all nations in the excellence of their cuisine, and to their soups and sauces belong the greatest praise. It would be well to follow their example, and it is the duty of every housekeeper to learn the art of soup making. How may a hearty dinner be better begun than with a thin soup? The hot liquid, taken into an empty stomach, is easily assimilated, acts as a stimulant rather than as a nutrient (as is the popular opinion), and prepares the way for the meal which is to follow. The cream soups and purées are so nutritious that, with bread and butter, they furnish a satisfactory meal.

Soups are divided into two great classes: Soups with stock; soups without stock.

Soups with stock have, for their basis, beef, veal, mutton, fish, poultry, or game, separately or in combination. They are classified as: —

Bouillon, made from lean beef, delicately seasoned, and usually cleared. Exception, — clam bouillon.

Brown Soup Stock, made from beef (two-thirds lean meat, and remainder bone and fat), highly seasoned with vegetables, spices, and sweet herbs.

White Soup Stock, made from chicken or veal, with delicate seasonings.

Consommé, usually made from two or three kinds of meat (beef, veal, and fowl being employed), highly seasoned with vegetables, spices, and sweet herbs. Always served clear.

Lamb Stock, delicately seasoned, is served as mutton broth.

Soups without stock are classified as : —

Cream Soups, made of vegetables or fish, with milk, and a small amount of cream and seasonings.   Always thickened.

Purées, made from vegetables or fish, forced through a strainer, and retained in soup, milk, and seasonings. Generally thicker than cream soup.   Sometimes white stock is added.

Bisques, generally made from shell fish, milk, and seasonings, and served with fish dice; made similarly to purées.   They may be made of meat, game, or vegetables, with small dice of the same.

Various names have been given to soups, according to their flavorings, chief ingredients, the people who use them, etc.   To the Scotch belongs Scotch Broth; to the French, Pot-au-feu; to the Indo, Mulligatawny; and to the Spanish, Olla Podrida.

SOUP MAKING.

The art of soup making is more easily mastered than at first appears.   The young housekeeper is startled at the amazingly large number of ingredients the recipe calls for, and often is discouraged.   One may, with but little expense, keep at hand what is essential for the making of a good soup.   Winter vegetables — turnips, carrots, celery, and onions — may be bought in large or small quantities.   The outer stalks of celery, often not suitable for serving, should be saved for soups.   At seasons when celery is a luxury, the tips and roots should be saved and dried.   Sweet herbs, including thyme, savory, and marjoram, are dried and put up in packages, retailing from five to ten cents.   Bay leaves, which should be used sparingly, may be obtained at first class grocers' or druggists'; seeming never to lose strength, they may be kept indefinitely.   Spices, including whole cloves, allspice berries, peppercorns, and stick cinnamon, should be kept on hand.   These seasonings, with the addition of salt, pepper, and parsley, are the essential flavorings for stock soups. Flour, corn-starch, arrowroot, fine tapioca, sago, pearl barley, rice, bread or eggs are added to give consistency and nourishment.

In small families, where there are few left-overs, fresh meat must be bought for the making of soup stock, as a good soup cannot be made from a small amount of poor material. On the other hand, large families need seldom buy fresh meat, providing all left-overs are properly cared for. The soup kettle should receive small pieces of beef (roasted, broiled, or stewed), veal, carcasses of fowl or chicken, chop bones, bones left from lamb roast, and all trimmings and bones, which a careful housewife should see are sent from the market with her order. Avoid the use of smoked or corned meats, or large pieces of raw mutton or lamb, surrounded by fat, on account of the strong flavor so disagreeable to many. A small piece of bacon or lean ham is sometimes cooked with vegetables for flavor.

Beef ranks first as regards utility and economy in soup making. It should be cut from the fore or hind shin (which cuts contain marrow-bone), the middle cuts being most desirable. If the lower part of shin is used, the soup, although rich in gelatin, lacks flavor, unless a cheap piece of lean meat is used with it, which frequently is done. It must be remembered that meat, bone, and fat in the right proportions are all necessary; allow two-thirds lean meat, the remaining one-third bone and fat. From the meat the soluble juices, salts, extractives (which give color and flavor), and a small quantity of gelatin are extracted; from the bone, gelatin (which gives the stock when cold a jelly-like consistency) and mineral matter. Gelatin is also obtained from cartilage, skin, tendons, and ligaments. Some of the fat is absorbed, the remainder rises to the top and should be removed.

Soup-stock making is rendered easier by use of proper utensils. Sharp meat knives, hard-wood board, two purée strainers having meshes of different size, and a soup digester (a porcelain-lined iron pot, having tight-fitting cover, with valve in the top), or covered granite kettle, are essentials.   An iron kettle, which formerly constituted one of the furnishings of a range, may be used if perfectly smooth.   A saw, cleaver, and scales, although not necessary, are useful, and lighten labor.

When meat comes from market, remove from paper and put in cool place.   When ready to start stock, if scales are at hand, weigh meat and bone to see if correct proportions have been sent.   Wipe meat with clean cheese cloth, wrung out of cold water.   Cut lean meat in one-inch cubes; by so doing, a large amount of surface is exposed to the water, and juices are more easily drawn out.   Heat frying-pan hissing hot; remove marrow from marrow-bone, and use enough to brown one-third of the lean meat, stirring constantly, that all parts of surface may be seared, thus preventing escape of juices, — sacrificing a certain amount of goodness in the stock, to give additional color and flavor, which is obtained by caramelization.   Put fat, bone, and remaining lean meat in soup kettle; cover with cold water, allowing one pint to each pound of meat, bone, and fat.   Let stand one hour, that cold water may draw out juices from meat.   Add browned meat, taking water from soup kettle to rinse out frying-pan, that none of the coloring may be lost.   Heat gradually to boiling point, and cook six or seven hours at low temperature.   A scum will rise on the top, which contains coagulated albuminous juices; these give to soup its chief nutritive value; many, however, prefer a clear soup, and have them removed.   If allowed to remain, when straining, a large part will pass through strainer.   Vegetables, spices, and salt should be added the last hour of cooking.   Strain and cool quickly; by so doing stock is less apt to ferment.   A knuckle of veal is often used for making white soup stock.   Fowl should be used for stock in preference to chicken, as it is cheaper, and contains a larger amount of nutriment.   A cake of fat forms on stock when cold, which excludes air, and should not be removed until stock is used. To remove fat, run a knife around edge of bowl and carefully remove the same. A small quantity will remain, which should be removed by passing a cloth wrung out of hot water around edge and over top of stock. This fat should be clarified and used for drippings. If time cannot be allowed for stock to cool before using, take off as much fat as possible with a spoon, and remove the remainder by passing tissue or any absorbent paper over the surface.

How to Clear Soup Stock.

Whites of eggs slightly beaten, or raw, lean beef finely chopped, are employed for clearing soup stock. The albumen found in each effects the clearing by drawing to itself some of the juices which have been extracted from the meat, and by action of heat have been coagulated. Some rise to the top and form a scum, others are precipitated.

Remove fat from stock, and put quantity to be cleared in stew-pan, allowing white and shell of one egg to each quart of stock. Beat egg slightly, break shell in small pieces and add to stock. Place on front of range, and stir constantly until boiling point is reached; boil two minutes. Set back where it may simmer twenty minutes; remove scum, and strain through double thickness of cheese cloth placed over a fine strainer. If stock to be cleared is not sufficiently seasoned, additional seasoning must be added as soon as stock has lost its jelly-like consistency; not after clearing is effected. Many think the flavor obtained from a few shavings of lemon rind an agreeable addition.

How to Bind Soups.

Cream soups and purées, if allowed to stand, separate, unless bound together. To bind a soup, melt butter, and when bubbling add an equal quantity of flour; when well mixed add to boiling soup, stirring constantly. If recipe calls for more flour than butter, or soup is one that should be made in double boiler, add gradually a portion of hot mixture to butter and flour until of such consistency that it may be poured into the mixture remaining in double boiler.

SOUPS WITH MEAT STOCK.

† Brown Soup Stock.

6 lbs. shin of beef.	1 sprig marjoram.
3 quarts cold water.	2 sprigs parsley.
½ teaspoon peppercorns.	Carrot, ⎫
6 cloves.	Turnip, ⎬ ½ cup each,
½ bay leaf.	Onion, ⎪ cut in dice.
3 sprigs thyme.	Celery, ⎭
1 tablespoon salt.	

Wipe beef, and cut the lean meat in inch cubes. Brown one-third of meat in hot frying-pan in marrow from a marrow-bone. Put remaining two-thirds with bone and fat in soup kettle, add water, and let stand for thirty minutes. Place on back of range, add browned meat, and heat gradually to boiling point. As scum rises it should be removed. Cover and cook slowly six hours, keeping below boiling point during cooking. Add vegetables and seasonings, cook one and one-half hours, strain, and cool as quickly as possible.

Bouillon.

5 lbs. lean beef from middle of round.	1 tablespoon salt.
	Carrot, ⎫
2 lbs. marrow-bone.	Turnip, ⎬ ⅓ cup each,
3 quarts cold water.	Onion, ⎪ cut in dice.
1 teaspoon peppercorns.	Celery, ⎭

Wipe, and cut meat in inch cubes. Put two-thirds of meat in soup kettle, and soak in water thirty minutes. Brown remainder in hot frying-pan with marrow from marrow-bone. Put browned meat and bone in kettle.

† a meat extract dissolved in boiling water.

Heat to boiling point; skim thoroughly, and cook at temperature below boiling point five hours. Add seasonings and vegetables, cook one hour, strain and cool. Remove fat and clear. Serve in bouillon cups.

Macaroni Soup.

1 quart Brown Soup Stock.	Salt.
¼ cup macaroni, broken in half inch pieces.	Pepper.

Cook macaroni in boiling salted water until soft. Drain, and add to stock, heated to boiling point. Season with salt and pepper. Spaghetti or other Italian pastes may be substituted for macaroni.

Julienne Soup.

To one quart clear Brown Soup Stock, add one-fourth cup each carrot and turnip, cut in thin strips one and one-half inches long, previously cooked in boiling salted water, and two tablespoons each cooked peas and string beans. Heat to boiling point.

Tomato Soup with Stock.

1 quart Brown Soup Stock.	¼ cup flour.
1 can tomatoes.	Onion,
½ teaspoon peppercorns.	Carrot, ¼ cup each,
1 small bay leaf.	Celery. cut in dice.
3 cloves.	Raw ham,
3 sprigs thyme.	Salt.
4 tablespoons butter.	Pepper.

Cook onion, carrot, celery, and ham in butter five minutes, add flour, peppercorns, bay leaf, cloves, and thyme, and cook three minutes; then add tomatoes, cover, and cook slowly one hour. When cooked in oven it requires less watching. Rub through a strainer, add hot stock, and season with salt and pepper.

Turkish Soup.

5 cups Brown Soup Stock.
1/8 ¼ cup rice.
1½ cups stewed and strained
  tomatoes.
Bit of bay leaf.
1 tsp. Sugar

2 slices onion.
10 peppercorns.
¼ teaspoon celery salt.
2 tablespoons butter.
1½ tablespoons flour.
½ tbsp. Salt

Cook rice in Brown Stock until soft. Cook bay leaf,
onion, peppercorns, and celery salt with tomatoes thirty
minutes. Combine mixtures, rub through sieve, and bind
with butter and flour cooked together. Season with salt
and pepper if needed.

Crecy Soup.

3 pints Brown Soup Stock.
2 cups chopped carrots.
Blade of mace.

4 tablespoons butter.
4 tablespoons flour.
1¼ tsp. Salt and pepper. *⅛ tsp.*

Wash and scrape carrots; cut off the darker part, and
chop fine or force through meat-chopper. Cook with one-
half the butter fifteen minutes. Add stock and mace,
and cook slowly forty-five minutes. Strain, and rub carrots through sieve. Melt remaining butter, add flour,
and pour on gradually hot stock. If a more delicate soup
is desired, substitute White Stock and cream for Brown
Stock, using one quart stock and one cup cream or milk.

Ox-tail Soup.

1 small oxtail.
6 cups Brown Stock.
Carrot, } 1 cup each, cut in
Turnip, }   fancy shapes.
Onion, } 1 cup each, cut in
Celery, }   small pieces.

½ teaspoon salt.
Few grains cayenne.
¼ cup Madeira wine.
1 teaspoon Worcestershire
  Sauce.
1 teaspoon lemon juice.

Cut ox-tail in small pieces, wash, drain, sprinkle with
salt and pepper, dredge with flour, and fry in butter ten
minutes. Add to Brown Stock, and simmer one hour.
Then add vegetables, which have been parboiled twenty

minutes; simmer until vegetables are soft, add salt, cayenne, wine, Worcestershire Sauce, and lemon juice.

White Soup Stock I.

3 lbs. knuckle of veal.	1 large stalk celery.
1 lb. lean beef.	½ teaspoon peppercorns.
3 quarts boiling water.	½ bay leaf.
1 onion.	2 sprigs thyme.
6 slices carrot.	2 cloves. *French Chef.*

Wipe veal, remove from bone, and cut in small pieces; cut beef in pieces, put bone and meat in soup kettle, cover with cold water, and bring quickly to boiling point; drain, throw away the water. Wash thoroughly bones and meat in cold water; return to kettle, add vegetables, seasonings, and three quarts boiling water. Boil three or four hours; the stock should be reduced one-half.

White Soup Stock II.

4 lbs. knuckle of veal.	½ teaspoon peppercorns.
2 quarts boiling water.	1 onion.
1 tablespoon salt.	2 stalks celery.

Blade of mace.

Wipe meat, remove from bone, and cut in small pieces. Put meat, bone, water, and seasonings in kettle. Heat gradually to boiling point, skimming frequently. Simmer four or five hours, and strain. If scum has been carefully removed, and soup is strained through double thickness of cheese cloth, stock will be quite clear.

White Soup Stock III.

The water in which a fowl or chicken is cooked makes White Stock.

White Soup.

5 cups White Stock III.	1 stalk celery.
½ tablespoon salt.	2 cups scalded milk.
½ teaspoon peppercorns.	3 tablespoons butter.
1 slice onion.	4 tablespoons flour.

Yolks 2 eggs.

Add seasonings to stock, and simmer thirty minutes; strain, and thicken with butter and flour cooked together; add scalded milk. Dilute eggs, slightly beaten, with hot soup, and add to remaining soup; strain, add salt and pepper if needed.

Chicken Soup.

6 cups White Stock III.	2 stalks celery.
1 tablespoon lean raw ham,	½ bay leaf.
finely chopped.	¼ teaspoon peppercorns.
6 slices carrot, cut in cubes.	1 sliced onion.

⅓ cup hot boiled rice.

Add seasonings to stock, heat gradually to boiling point, and boil thirty minutes; strain, and add rice.

Turkey Soup.

Break turkey carcass in pieces, removing all stuffing; put in kettle with any bits of meat that may have been left over. Cover with cold water, bring slowly to boiling point, and simmer two hours. Strain, remove fat, and season with salt and pepper. One or two outer stalks of celery may be cooked with carcass to give additional flavor.

Hygienic Soup.

6 cups White Stock III.	2 tablespoons butter.
¼ cup oatmeal.	2 tablespoons flour.
2 cups scalded milk.	Salt and pepper.

Heat stock to boiling point, add oatmeal, and boil one hour; rub through sieve, add milk, and thicken with butter and flour cooked together. Season with salt and pepper.

Farina Soup.

4 cups White Stock III.	1 cup cream.
¼ cup farina.	Few gratings of nutmeg.
2 cups scalded milk.	Salt and pepper.

Heat stock to boiling point, add farina, and boil fifteen minutes; then add milk, cream, and seasonings.

Spring Soup.

1 quart White Stock I. or II.	1 cup milk.
1 large onion, sliced thin.	1 cup cream.
3 tablespoons butter.	2 tablespoons flour.
1/4 baker's small stale loaf.	Salt and pepper.

Cook onion fifteen minutes in one tablespoon butter; add to stock, with bread broken in pieces. Simmer one hour; rub through sieve. Add milk, and bind with remaining butter and flour cooked together; add cream, and season with salt and pepper. Serve with small pieces toasted bread.

Duchess Soup.

4 cups White Stock III.	1/3 cup butter.
2 slices carrot, cut in cubes.	1/4 cup flour.
2 slices onion.	1 teaspoon salt.
2 blades mace.	1/8 teaspoon pepper.

1/4 X cup grated mild cheese. *2 c. hot milk*

Cook vegetables three minutes in one and one-half tablespoons butter, then add stock and mace; boil fifteen minutes, strain, and add milk. Thicken with remaining butter and flour cooked together; add salt and pepper. Stir in cheese, and serve as soon as cheese is melted.

Potage à la Reine.

4 cups White Stock III.	1/3 cup cracker crumbs.
1/2 teaspoon peppercorns.	Breast meat from a boiled
1 stalk celery.	chicken.
1 slice onion.	2 cups scalded milk.
1/2 tablespoon salt.	1/2 cup cold milk.
Yolks 3 hard boiled eggs.	3 tablespoons butter.
3 tablespoons flour.	

Cook stock with seasonings twenty minutes. Rub yolks of eggs through sieve. Soak cracker crumbs in cold milk until soft; add to eggs. Chop meat and rub through sieve; add to egg and cracker mixture. Then pour milk on slowly, and add to strained stock; boil three minutes. Bind with butter and flour cooked together.

St. Germain Soup.

3 cups White Stock I., II., or III.	Blade of mace.
1 can Marrowfat peas.	2 teaspoons sugar.
1 cup cold water.	1 teaspoon salt.
½ onion.	⅛ teaspoon pepper.
Bit of bay leaf.	2 tablespoons butter.
Sprig of parsley.	2 tablespoons corn-starch.

1 cup milk.

Drain and rinse peas, reserving one-third cup; put remainder in cold water with seasonings, and simmer one-half hour; rub through sieve and add stock. Bind with butter and corn-starch cooked together; boil five minutes. Add milk and reserved peas.

Imperial Soup.

4 cups White Stock III.	½ teaspoon peppercorns.
2 cups stale bread crumbs.	Bit of bay leaf.
2 stalks celery, broken in pieces.	Blade of mace.
2 slices carrot, cut in cubes.	1 teaspoon salt.
1 small onion.	½ breast boiled chicken.
3 tablespoons butter.	⅓ cup blanched almonds.
Sprig of parsley.	1 cup cream.
2 cloves.	½ cup milk.

2 tablespoons flour.

Cook celery, carrot, and onion in one tablespoon butter, five minutes; tie in cheese cloth with parsley, cloves, peppercorns, bay leaf, and mace; add to stock with salt and bread crumbs, simmer one hour, remove seasonings, and rub through a sieve. Chop chicken meat and rub through sieve; pound almonds to a paste, add to chicken, then add cream. Combine mixtures, add milk, reheat, and bind with remaining butter and flour cooked together.

Veal and Sago Soup.

2½ lbs. lean veal.	2 cups scalded milk.
3 quarts cold water.	Yolks 4 eggs.
¼ lb. pearl sago.	Salt and pepper.

Order meat from market, very finely chopped. Pick over, and remove particles of fat. Cover meat with water, bring slowly to boiling point, and simmer two hours, skimming occasionally; strain and reheat. Soak sago one-half hour in enough water to cover, stir into hot stock, boil thirty minutes, and add milk; then pour mixture slowly on yolks of eggs, slightly beaten. Season with salt and pepper.

Asparagus Soup.

3 cups White Stock II. or III.	¼ cup butter.
1 can asparagus.	¼ cup flour.
2 cups cold water.	2 cups scalded milk.
1 slice onion.	Salt and pepper.

Drain and rinse asparagus, reserve tips, and add stalks to cold water; boil five minutes, drain, add stock, and onion; boil thirty minutes, rub through sieve, and bind with butter and flour cooked together. Add salt, pepper, milk, and tips.

Cream of Celery Soup.

2 cups White Stock II. or III.	3 tablespoons flour.
3 cups celery, cut in inch pieces.	2 cups milk.
2 cups boiling water.	1 cup cream.
1 slice onion.	Salt.
2 tablespoons butter.	Pepper.

Parboil celery in water ten minutes; drain, add stock, cook until celery is soft, and rub through sieve. Scald onion in milk, remove onion, add milk to stock, bind, add cream, and season with salt and pepper.

Spinach Soup.

4 cups White Stock II. or III.	¼ cup butter.
2 quarts spinach.	⅓ cup flour.
3 cups boiling water.	Salt.
2 cups milk.	Pepper.

Cook spinach thirty minutes in boiling water; drain, chop, and rub through sieve; add stock, heat to boiling point, bind, add milk, and season with salt and pepper.

Cream of Lettuce Soup.

2½ cups White Stock II. or III.   1 tablespoon butter.
2 heads lettuce finely cut.   Yolk 1 egg.
2 tablespoons rice.   Few grains nutmeg.
½ cup cream.   Salt.
¼ tablespoon onion, finely chopped. Pepper.

Cook onion five minutes in butter, add lettuce, rice, and stock. Cook until rice is soft, then add cream, yolk of egg slightly beaten, nutmeg, salt, and pepper. Remove outer leaves from lettuce, using only tender part for soup.

Cream of Watercress Soup.

2 cups White Stock I., II., or III.   ½ cup milk.
2 bunches watercress.   Yolk 1 egg.
3 tablespoons butter.   Salt.
2 tablespoons flour.   Pepper.

Cut finely leaves of watercress; cook five minutes in two tablespoons butter, add stock, and boil five minutes. Thicken with butter and flour cooked together, add salt and pepper. Just before serving, add milk and egg yolk, slightly beaten. Serve with slices of French bread, browned in oven.

Cream of Cauliflower Soup.

4 cups hot White Stock II. or III.   ½ bay leaf.
1 cauliflower.   ¼ cup flour.
¼ cup butter.   2 cups milk.
1 slice onion.   Salt.
1 stalk celery, cut in inch pieces.   Pepper.

Soak cauliflower, head down, one hour in cold water to cover; cook in boiling salted water twenty minutes. Reserve one-half flowerets, and rub remaining cauliflower through sieve. Cook onion, celery, and bay leaf in butter five minutes. Remove bay leaf, then add flour, and stir into hot stock; add cauliflower and milk. Season with salt and pepper; then strain, add flowerets, and reheat.

String Bean Soup.

4 cups White Stock I., II., or III. ¼ cup flour.
2 quarts string beans. ¼ cup butter.
2 cups scalded milk. Salt and pepper.

Cook beans until soft in boiling salted water to cover; drain, and rub through sieve. Add pulp to White Stock, then milk; bind, and season with salt and pepper. Garnish with Fritter Beans.

Chestnut Purée.

4 cups White Stock II. or III. 2 cups scalded milk.
2 cups French chestnuts, ¼ cup butter.
  boiled and mashed. ¼ cup flour.
1 slice onion. Salt.
¼ teaspoon celery salt. Pepper.

Cook stock, chestnuts, onion, and celery salt ten minutes; rub through sieve, add milk, and bind. Season with salt and pepper.

Mulligatawny Soup.

5 cups White Stock II. ¼ cup butter.
1 cup tomatoes. ⅓ cup flour.
Onion, cut in slices, 1 teaspoon curry
Carrot, cut in cubes, } ¼ cup each. powder.
Celery, cut in cubes, Blade of mace.
1 pepper, finely chopped. 2 cloves.
1 apple, sliced. Sprig of parsley.
1 cup raw chicken, cut in dice. Salt and pepper.

French Chef.

Cook vegetables and chicken in butter until brown; add flour, curry powder, mace. cloves, parsley, stock, and tomato, and simmer one hour. Strain, reserve chicken, and rub vegetables through sieve. Add chicken to strained soup, season with salt and pepper, and serve with boiled rice.

Mock Turtle Soup.

1 calf's head.	2 cups brown stock.
6 cloves.	¼ cup butter.
½ teaspoon peppercorns.	½ cup flour.
6 allspice berries.	1 cup stewed and strained
2 sprigs thyme.	tomatoes.
⅓ cup sliced onion.	Juice ½ lemon.
⅓ cup carrot, cut in dice.	Madeira wine.

Clean and wash calf's head; soak one hour in cold water to cover. Cook until tender in three quarts boiling salted water (to which seasoning and vegetables have been added). Remove head; boil stock until reduced to one quart. Strain and cool. Melt and brown butter, add flour, and stir until well browned; then pour on slowly brown stock. Add head-stock, tomato, one cup face meat cut in dice, and lemon juice. Simmer five minutes; add Royal Custard cut in dice, and Egg Balls, or Force-meat Balls. Add Madeira wine, salt, and pepper to taste.

Consommé.

3 lbs. beef, poorer part of round.	2 tablespoons butter.
1 lb. marrow-bone.	1 tablespoon salt.
3 lbs. knuckle of veal.	1 teaspooon peppercorns.
1 quart chicken stock.	4 cloves.
Carrot, Turnip, Celery, } ⅓ cup each, cut in dice.	3 sprigs thyme.
	1 sprig marjoram.
	2 sprigs parsley.
⅓ cup sliced onion.	½ bay leaf.

Cut beef in one and one-half inch cubes, and brown one-half in some of the marrow from marrow-bone; put remaining half in kettle with cold water, add veal cut in pieces, browned meat, and bones. Let stand one-half hour. Heat slowly to boiling point, and let simmer three hours, removing scum as it forms on top of kettle. Add one quart liquor in which a fowl was cooked, and simmer two hours. Cook carrot, turnip, onion, and celery in butter five minutes; then add to soup, with remaining seasonings. Cook one and one-half hours, strain, cool quickly, remove fat, and clear.

Consommé à la Royale.

Consommé, served with Royal Custard.

Consommé au Parmesan

Consommé, served with Parmesan Pâte à Chou.

Consommé aux Pâtes.

Consommé, served with noodles, macaroni, spaghetti, or any Italian pastes, first cooked in boiling salted water.

Consommé Colbert.

To six cups Consommé add one-third cup each of cooked green peas, flageolets, carrots cut in small cubes, and celery cut in small pieces. Serve a poached egg in each plate of soup.

Consommé with Vegetables.

Consommé, served with French string beans, and cooked carrots cut in fancy shapes with French vegetable cutters.

Consommé Princess.

Consommé, served with green peas and cooked chicken meat cut in small dice.

SOUPS WITH FISH STOCK.

Clam Bouillon.

Wash and scrub with a brush one-half peck clams, changing the water several times. Put in kettle with three cups cold water, cover tightly, and steam until shells are well opened. Strain liquor, cool, and clear.

Oyster Stew.

1 quart oysters.	¼ cup butter.
4 cups scalded milk.	½ tablespoon salt.

⅛ teaspoon pepper.

Clean oysters by placing in a colander and pouring over them three-fourths cup cold water. Carefully pick over oysters, reserve liquor, and heat it to boiling point; strain through double cheese cloth, add oysters, and cook until oysters are plump and edges begin to curl. Remove oysters with skimmer, and put in tureen with butter, salt, and pepper. Add oyster liquor, strained a second time, and milk. Serve with oyster crackers.

Scallop Stew.

Make as Oyster Stew, using one quart scallops in place of oysters.

Oyster Soup.

1 quart oysters.	Sprig of parsley.
4 cups milk.	Bit of bay leaf.
1 slice onion.	⅓ cup butter.
2 stalks celery.	⅓ cup flour.
2 blades mace.	Salt and pepper.

Clean and pick over oysters as for Oyster Stew; reserve liquor, add oysters slightly chopped, and heat slowly to boiling point. Strain through cheese cloth, reheat liquor, and thicken with butter and flour cooked together. Scald milk with onion, celery, mace, parsley, and bay leaf; remove seasonings, and add to oyster liquor. Season with salt and pepper.

French Oyster Soup.

1 quart oysters.	⅓ cup butter.
4 cups milk.	⅓ cup flour.
1 slice onion.	Yolks 2 eggs.
2 blades mace.	Salt and pepper.

Make as Oyster Soup, adding yolks of eggs, slightly beaten, just before serving. Garnish with Fish Quenelles.

Oyster Gumbo.

1 pint oysters.	½ can okra.
4 cups fish stock.	⅓ can tomatoes.
¼ cup butter.	Salt.
1 tablespoon chopped onion.	Pepper.

Clean, pick over, and parboil oysters, drain, and add oyster liquor to fish stock. Cook onion five minutes in one-half the butter; add to stock. Then add okra, tomatoes heated and drained from some of their liquor, oysters, and remaining butter. Season with salt and pepper.

Fish Stock is the liquor obtained by covering the head, tail, skin, bones, and small quantity of flesh adhering to bones of fish, with cold water, bringing slowly to boiling point, simmering thirty minutes, and straining.

Clam Soup with Poached Eggs.

1 quart clams.	⅓ cup flour.
4 cups milk.	1½ teaspoons salt.
1 slice onion.	⅛ teaspoon pepper.
⅓ cup butter.	Few gratings nutmeg.

Whites 2 eggs.

Clean and pick over clams, using three-fourths cup cold water; reserve liquor. Put aside soft part of clams; finely chop hard part, add to liquor, bring gradually to boiling point, strain, then thicken with butter and flour cooked together. Scald milk with onion, remove onion, add milk and soft part of clams to stock; cook two minutes. Add seasonings, and pour over whites of eggs beaten stiff.

Clam and Oyster Soup.

1 pint clams.	Sprig of parsley.
1 pint oysters.	Bit of bay leaf.
4 cups milk.	⅓ cup butter.
1 slice onion.	⅓ cup flour.
2 blades mace.	Salt and pepper.

Clean and pick over oysters, using one-third cup cold water; reserve liquor, and add oysters slightly chopped.

Clean and pick over clams, reserve liquor, and add to hard part of clams, finely chopped; put aside soft part of clams. Heat slowly to boiling point clams and oysters with liquor from both, strain through cheese cloth. Scald milk with onion, mace, parsley, and bay leaf; remove seasonings, and add milk to stock. Thicken with butter and flour cooked together, add soft part of clams, and cook two minutes. Season with salt and pepper.

Cream of Clam Soup.

Make as French Oyster Soup, using clams in place of oysters.

Lobster Bisque.

2 lb. lobster.	¼ cup butter.
2 cups cold water.	¼ cup flour.
4 cups milk.	1½ teaspoons salt.

Few grains of cayenne.

Remove meat from lobster shell. Add cold water to body bones and tough end of claws, cut in pieces; bring slowly to boiling point, and cook twenty minutes. Drain, reserve liquor, and thicken with butter and flour cooked together. Scald milk with tail meat of lobster, finely chopped; strain, and add to liquor. Season with salt and cayenne; then add tender claw meat, cut in dice, and body meat. When coral is found in lobster, wash, wipe, force through fine strainer, put in a mortar with butter, work until well blended, then add flour, and stir into soup. If a richer soup is desired, White Stock may be used in place of water.

1. Saucepan, with purée strainer and potato masher.
2. Purée strainer.
3. Soup kettle.

CHAPTER IX.

SOUPS WITHOUT STOCK.

Black Bean Soup.

1 pint black beans.	⅛ teaspoon pepper.
2 quarts cold water.	¼ teaspoon mustard.
1 small onion.	Few grains cayenne.
2 stalks celery, or	3 tablespoons butter.
¼ teaspoon celery salt.	1½ tablespoons flour.
½ tablespoon salt.	2 hard boiled eggs.

1 lemon.

Soak beans over night; in the morning drain and add cold water. Slice onion, and cook five minutes with half the butter, adding to beans, with celery stalks broken in pieces. Simmer three or four hours, or until beans are soft; add more water as water boils away. Rub through a sieve, reheat to the boiling point, and add salt, pepper, mustard, and cayenne well mixed. Bind with remaining butter and flour cooked together. Cut eggs in thin slices, and lemon in thin slices, removing seeds. Put in tureen, and strain the soup over them.

Baked Bean Soup.

3 cups cold baked beans.
3 pints water.
2 slices onion.
2 stalks celery.
1½ cups stewed and strained
    tomatoes.

2 tablespoons butter.
2 tablespoons flour.
1 tablespoon Chili sauce.
Salt.
Pepper.

Put the first four ingredients in saucepan; simmer thirty minutes. Rub through a sieve, add tomato and Chili sauce, season to taste with salt and pepper, and bind with the butter and flour cooked together.

Cream of Lima Bean Soup.

1 cup dried lima beans.
3 pints cold water.
2 slices onion.
4 slices carrot.

1 cup cream or milk.
4 tablespoons butter.
2 tablespoons flour.
1 teaspoon salt.

½ teaspoon pepper.

Soak beans over night; in the morning drain and add cold water; cook until soft, and rub through a sieve. Cut vegetables in small cubes, and cook five minutes in half the butter; remove vegetables, add flour, salt, and pepper, and stir into boiling soup. Add cream, reheat, strain, and add remaining butter in small pieces.

Celery Soup.

3 cups celery (in one-half inch
    pieces).
1 pint boiling water.
2½ cups milk.

1 slice onion.
3 tablespoons butter.
¼ cup flour.
Salt and pepper.

Wash and scrape celery before cutting in pieces, cook in boiling water until soft, rub through a sieve. Scald milk with the onion, remove onion, and add milk to celery. Bind with butter and flour cooked together. Season with salt and pepper. Outer and old stalks of celery may be utilized for soups.

Corn Soup.

1 can corn.	2 tablespoons butter.
1 pint boiling water.	2 tablespoons flour.
1 pint milk.	1 teaspoon salt.
1 slice onion.	Few grains pepper.

Chop the corn, add water, and simmer twenty minutes; rub through a sieve. Scald milk with onion, remove onion, and add milk to corn. Bind with butter and flour cooked together. Add salt and pepper.

Halibut Soup.

¾ cup cold boiled halibut.	3 tablespoons butter.
1 pint milk.	1½ tablespoons flour.
1 slice onion.	½ teaspoon salt.
Blade of mace.	Few grains pepper.

Rub fish through a sieve. Scald milk with onion and mace. Remove seasonings, and add fish. Bind with half the butter, and flour, cooked together. Add salt, pepper, and the remaining butter in small pieces.

Pea Soup.

1 can Marrowfat peas.	1 slice onion.
2 teaspoons sugar.	2 tablespoons butter.
1 quart cold water.	2 tablespoons flour.
1 pint mik.	1 teaspoon salt.

⅛ teaspoon pepper.

Drain peas from their liquor, add sugar and cold water, and simmer twenty minutes. Rub through a sieve, reheat, and thicken with butter and flour cooked together. Scald milk with onion, remove onion, and add milk to pea mixture, season with salt and pepper. Peas too old to serve as a vegetable may be utilized for soups.

Split Pea Soup.

1 cup dried split peas.	3 tablespoons butter.
2½ quarts cold water.	2 tablespoons flour.
1 pint milk.	1½ teaspoons salt.
½ onion.	⅛ teaspoon pepper.

Pick over peas and soak several hours, drain, add cold water and onion. Simmer three or four hours, or until soft; rub through a sieve. Add butter and flour cooked together, salt, and pepper. Dilute with milk, adding more if necessary. The water in which a ham has been cooked may be used; in such case omit salt.

Kornlet Soup.

1 can kornlet.	1 tablespoon chopped onion.
1 pint cold water.	4 tablespoons flour.
1 quart milk, scalded.	1½ teaspoons salt.
4 tablespoons butter.	Few grains pepper.

Cook kornlet in cold water twenty minutes, rub through a sieve, and add milk. Fry butter and onion three minutes; remove onion, add flour, salt, and pepper, and stir into boiling soup.

Potato Soup.

3 potatoes.	1½ teaspoons salt.
1 quart milk.	¼ teaspoon celery salt.
2 slices onion.	⅛ teaspoon pepper.
4 tablespoons butter.	Few grains cayenne.
2 tablespoons flour.	1 teaspoon chopped parsley.

Cook potatoes in boiling salted water; when soft, rub through a strainer. Scald milk with onion, remove onion, and add milk slowly to potatoes. Melt half the butter, add dry ingredients, stir until well mixed, then stir into boiling soup; cook one minute, strain, add remaining butter, and sprinkle with parsley.

Swiss Potato Soup.

4 small potatoes.
1 large flat white turnip.
3 cups boiling water.
1 quart scalded milk.
½ onion.
4 tablespoons butter.
⅓ cup flour.
1½ teaspoons salt.
⅛ teaspoon pepper.

Wash, pare, and cut potatoes in halves. Wash, pare, and cut turnips in one-quarter inch slices. Parboil together ten minutes, drain, add onion cut in slices, and three cups boiling water. Cook until vegetables are soft; drain, reserving the water to add to vegetables after rubbing them through a sieve. Add milk, reheat, and bind with butter and flour cooked together. Season with salt and pepper.

Salmon Soup.

⅓ can salmon.
1 quart scalded milk.
2 tablespoons butter.
4 tablespoons flour.
1½ teaspoons salt.
Few grains pepper.

Drain oil from salmon, remove skin and bones, rub through a sieve. Add gradually the milk, season and bind.

Squash Soup.

¾ cup cooked squash.
1 quart milk.
1 slice onion.
2 tablespoons butter.
3 tablespoons flour.
1 teaspoon salt.
Few grains pepper.
¼ teaspoon celery salt.

Rub squash through a sieve before measuring. Scald milk with onion, remove onion, and add milk to squash, season and bind.

Tomato Soup.

1 can tomatoes.
1 pint water.
12 peppercorns.
Bit of bay leaf.
4 cloves.
2 teaspoons sugar.
1 teaspoon salt.
⅛ teaspoon soda.
2 tablespoons butter.
3 tablespoons flour.

Cook the first six ingredients twenty minutes; strain, add salt and soda; bind, and strain into tureen.

Cream of Tomato Soup.   (Mock Bisque.)

½ can tomatoes.
2 teaspoons sugar.
¼ teaspoon soda.
1 quart milk.

1 slice onion.
4 tablespoons flour.
1 teaspoon salt.
⅛ teaspoon pepper.

⅓ cup butter.

Scald milk with onion, remove onion, and thicken milk with flour diluted with cold water until thin enough to pour, being careful that the mixture is free from lumps; cook twenty minutes, stirring constantly at first. Cook tomatoes with sugar fifteen minutes, add soda, and rub through a sieve; combine mixtures, and strain into tureen over butter, salt, and pepper.

Vegetable Soup.   *2 tbsp - flour.*

⅓ cup carrot.
⅓ cup turnip.
½ cup celery.
1½ cups potato.
½ onion.

1 quart water.
4 5 tablespoons butter.
½ tablespoon finely
    chopped parsley.
Salt and pepper.

Wash and scrape a small carrot; cut in quarters lengthwise; cut quarters in thirds lengthwise; cut strips thus made in thin slices crosswise. Wash and pare half a turnip, and cut and slice same as carrot. Wash, pare, and cut potatoes in small pieces. Wash and scrape celery and cut in quarter-inch pieces. Prepare vegetables before measuring. Cut onion in thin slices. Mix vegetables (except potatoes), and cook ten minutes, in four tablespoons butter, stirring constantly. Add potatoes, cover, and cook two minutes. Add water, and boil one hour. Beat with spoon or fork to break vegetables. Add remaining butter and parsley. Season with salt and pepper.

CHOWDERS.

Corn Chowder.

1 can corn.	1 sliced onion.
4 cups potatoes, cut in ¼ inch slices.	4 cups scalded milk.
	8 common crackers.
1½ inch cube fat salt pork.	3 tablespoons butter.

Salt and pepper.

Cut pork in small pieces and try out; add onion and cook five minutes, stirring often that onion may not burn; strain fat into a stewpan. Parboil potatoes five minutes in boiling water to cover; drain, and add potatoes to fat; then add ~~two~~ 15 cups boiling water; cook until potatoes are soft, add corn and milk, then heat to boiling point. Season with salt and pepper; add butter, and crackers ~~split and soaked in enough cold milk to moisten. Remove~~ *when* crackers, turn chowder into a tureen; and ~~put crackers on top.~~ *are hot* *serve.*

Fish Chowder.

4 lb. cod or haddock.	1½ inch cube fat salt pork.
6 cups potatoes cut in ¼ inch slices, or	1 tablespoon salt.
	⅛ teaspoon pepper.
4 cups potatoes cut in ¾ inch cubes.	3 tablespoons butter.
	4 cups scalded milk.
1 sliced onion.	8 common crackers.

Order the fish skinned, but head and tail left on. Cut off head and tail and remove fish from backbone. Cut fish in two-inch pieces and set aside. Put head, tail, and backbone broken in pieces, in stewpan; add two cups cold water and bring slowly to boiling point; cook twenty minutes. Cut salt pork in small pieces and try out, add onion, and fry five minutes; strain fat into stewpan. Parboil potatoes five minutes in boiling water to cover; drain, and add potatoes to fat; then add two cups boiling

water and cook five minutes. Add liquor drained from bones and fish; cover, and simmer ten minutes. Add milk, salt, pepper, butter, and crackers split and soaked in enough cold milk to moisten. Pilot bread is sometimes used in place of common crackers.

Connecticut Chowder.

4 lb. cod or haddock.
4 cups potatoes cut in ¾ inch cubes.
1½ inch cube fat salt pork.
1 sliced onion.

2½ cups stewed and strained tomatoes.
3 tablespoons butter.
⅔ cup cracker crumbs.
Salt and pepper.

Prepare as Fish Chowder, using liquor drained from bones for cooking potatoes, instead of additional water. Use tomatoes in place of milk and add cracker crumbs just before serving.

Clam Chowder.

1 quart clams.
4 cups potatoes cut in ¾ inch dice.
1½ inch cube fat salt pork.
1 sliced onion.

1 tablespoon salt.
⅛ teaspoon pepper.
4 tablespoons butter.
4 cups scalded milk.
8 common crackers.

Clean and pick over clams, using one cup cold water; drain, reserve liquor, heat to boiling point, and strain. Chop finely hard part of clams; cut pork in small pieces and try out; add onion, fry five minutes, and strain into a stewpan. Parboil potatoes five minutes in boiling water to cover; drain and put a layer in bottom of stewpan, add chopped clams, sprinkle with salt and pepper, and dredge generously with flour; add remaining potatoes, again sprinkle with salt and pepper, dredge with flour, and add two and one-half cups boiling water. Cook ten minutes, add milk, soft part of clams, and butter; boil three minutes, and add crackers split and soaked in enough cold milk to moisten. Reheat clam water to boiling point,

and thicken with one tablespoon butter and flour cooked together. Add to chowder just before serving.

The clam water has a tendency to cause the milk to separate, hence is added at the last.

Lobster Chowder.

2 lb. lobster.	4 cups milk.
3 tablespoons butter.	1 slice onion.
2 common crackers,	1 cup cold water.
finely pounded.	Salt.
Paprika or cayenne.	

Remove meat from lobster shell and cut in small dice. Cream two tablespoons butter, add liver of lobster (green part), and crackers; scald milk with onion, remove onion and add milk to mixture. Cook body bones ten minutes in cold water to cover, strain, and add to mixture with lobster dice. Season with salt and paprika.

CHAPTER X.

SOUP GARNISHINGS AND FORCE-MEATS.

Crisp Crackers.

Split common crackers and spread thinly with butter, allowing one-fourth teaspoon butter to each half cracker; put in pan and bake until delicately browned.

Croûtons (Duchess Crusts).

Cut stale bread in one-third inch slices, remove crusts, and spread thinly with butter. Cut slices in one-third inch cubes, put in pan and bake until delicately browned, or fry in deep fat.

Imperial Sticks.

Cut stale bread in one-third inch slices, remove crusts, spread thinly with butter, and cut slices in one-third inch strips; put in pan and bake until delicately browned.

Egg Balls.

Yolks 2 hard boiled eggs.	Few grains cayenne.
⅛ teaspoon salt.	½ teaspoon melted butter.

Rub yolks through sieve, add seasonings, and moisten with raw egg yolk to make of consistency to handle. Shape in small balls, roll in flour, and sauté in butter. Serve in Brown Soup Stock, Consommé, or Mock Turtle Soup.

Egg Custard.

Yolks 2 eggs.   Few grains salt.
2 tablespoons milk.

Beat eggs slightly, add milk and salt. Pour into small buttered cup, place in pan of hot water and bake until firm; cool, remove from cup, and cut in fancy shapes with French vegetable cutters.

Royal Custard.

Yolks 3 eggs.   ⅛ teaspoon salt.
1 egg.   Slight grating nutmeg.
½ cup Consommé.   Few grains cayenne.

Beat eggs slightly, add Consommé and seasonings. Pour into a small buttered tin mould, place in pan of hot water and bake until firm; cool, remove from mould, and cut in fancy shapes.

Noodles.

1 egg.   ½ teaspoon salt.
Flour.

Beat egg slightly, add salt, and flour enough to make very stiff dough; knead, toss on slightly floured board, and roll thinly as possible, which may be as thin as paper. Cover with towel, and set aside for twenty minutes; then cut in fancy shapes, using sharp knife or French vegetable cutter: or the thin sheet may be rolled like jelly-roll, cut in slices as thinly as possible, and pieces unrolled. Dry, and when needed cook twenty minutes in boiling salted water; drain, and add to soup.

Noodles may be served as a vegetable.

Fritter Beans.

1 egg.   ¾ teaspoon salt.
2 tablespoons milk.   ½ cup flour.

Beat egg until light, add milk, salt, and flour. Put through colander or pastry tube into deep fat, and fry until brown; drain on brown paper.

Pâte au Chou.

2½ tablespoons milk.   ⅛ teaspoon salt.
½ teaspoon lard.   ¼ cup flour.
½ teaspoon butter.   1 egg.

Heat butter, lard, and milk to boiling point, add flour and salt, and stir vigorously. Remove from fire, add egg unbeaten, and stir until well mixed. Cool, and drop small pieces from tip of teaspoon into deep fat. Fry until brown and crisp, and drain on brown paper.

Parmesan Pâte au Chou.

To Pâte au Chou mixture add two tablespoons grated Parmesan cheese.

White Bait Garnish.

Roll trimmings of puff paste, and cut in pieces three-fourths inch long and one-eighth inch wide; fry in deep fat until well browned, and drain on brown paper. Serve on folded napkin, to be passed with soup.

Fish Force-meat.

¼ cup fine stale bread crumbs.   1 egg.
¼ cup milk.   ⅔ cup raw fish.
Salt.

Cook bread and milk to a paste, add egg well beaten, and fish pounded and forced through a purée strainer. Season with salt. A meat chopper is of great assistance in making force-meats, as raw fish or meat may be easily forced through it. Bass, halibut, or pickerel are the best fish to use for force-meat. Force-meat is often shaped into small balls.

Clam Force-meat.

Follow recipe for Oyster Force-meat, using soft part of clams in place of oysters.

Salmon Force-meat.

½ cup milk.
½ cup soft stale bread crumbs.
½ cup cold flaked salmon.
2 tablespoons cream.

1 egg.
2 tablespoons melted butter.
½ teaspoon salt.
Few grains pepper.

Cook milk and bread crumbs ten minutes, add salmon chopped and rubbed through a sieve; then add cream, egg slightly beaten, melted butter, salt, and pepper.

Oyster Force-meat.

To Fish Force-meat add one-fourth small onion, finely chopped, and fried five minutes in one-half tablespoon butter; then add one-third cup soft part of oysters, par-boiled and finely chopped, one-third cup mushrooms finely chopped, and one-third cup Thick White Sauce. Season with salt, cayenne, and one teaspoon finely chopped parsley.

Chicken Force-meat I.

½ cup fine stale bread crumbs.
½ cup milk.
2 tablespoons butter.
White 1 egg.

⅔ cup breast raw chicken.
Salt.
Few grains cayenne.
Slight grating nutmeg.

Cook bread and milk to a paste, add butter, white of egg beaten stiff, and seasonings; then add chicken pounded and forced through purée strainer.

Chicken Force-meat II.

½ breast raw chicken.
White 1 egg.
Salt.

Pepper.
Slight grating nutmeg.
Heavy cream.

Chop chicken finely, or force through a meat chopper. Pound in mortar, add gradually white of egg, and work until smooth; then add heavy cream slowly until of right consistency, which can only be determined by cooking a small ball in boiling salted water. Add seasonings, and rub through sieve.

Quenelles.

Quenelles are made from any kind of force-meat, shaped in small balls or between tablespoons, making an oval, or by forcing mixture through pastry bag on buttered paper. They are cooked in boiling salted water or stock, and are served as garnish to soups or other dishes; when served with sauce, they are an entrée.

CHAPTER XI.

FISH.

THE meat of fish is the animal food next in importance to that of birds and mammals. Fish meat, with but few exceptions, is less stimulating and nourishing than meat of other animals, but is usually easier of digestion. Salmon, mackerel, and eels are exceptions to these rules, and should not be eaten by those of weak digestion. White-blooded fish, on account of their easy digestibility, are especially desirable for those of sedentary habits. Fish is not recommended for brain-workers on account of the large amount of phosphorus (an element abounding largely in nerve tissue) which it contains, but because of its easy digestibility. It is a conceded fact that many fish contain less of this element than meat.

Fish meat is generally considered cheaper than meat of other animals. This is true when compared with the better cuts of meat, but not so when compared with cheaper cuts.

To obtain from fish its greatest value and flavor, it should be eaten fresh, and in season. Turbot, which is improved by keeping, is the only exception to this rule.

To Determine Freshness of Fish. Examine the flesh, and it should be firm; the eyes and gills, and they should be bright.

Broiling and baking are best methods for cooking fish. White-blooded fish may often be fried, but red-blooded rarely. Frozen fish are undesirable; but if used, should be thawed in cold water just before cooking.

On account of its strong odor, fish should never be put in an ice-box with other food, unless closely covered. A tin lard pail will be found useful for this purpose.

White and Red Blooded Fish.

White-blooded fish have fat secreted in the liver. Examples: Cod, haddock, trout, flounder, smelt, perch, etc.

Red-blooded fish have fat distributed throughout the flesh. Examples: Salmon, eels, mackerel, blue-fish, sword-fish, shad, herring, etc.

Cod belongs to one of the most prolific fish families (Gadidoe), and is widely distributed throughout the northern and temperate seas of both hemispheres. On account of its abundance, cheapness, and easy procurability, it forms, from an economical standpoint, one of the most important fish foods. Cod have been caught weighing over a hundred pounds, but average market cod weigh from six to ten pounds; a six-pound cod measures about twenty-three inches in length. Large cod are cut into steaks. The skin of cod is white, heavily mottled with gray, with a white line running the entire length of fish on either side. Cod is caught in shallow or deep waters. Shallow-water cod (caught off rocks) is called rock cod; deep-water cod is called off-shore cod. Rock cod are apt to be wormy. Cod obtained off George's Banks, Newfoundland, are called George's cod, and are commercially known as the best fish. Quantities of cod are preserved by drying and salting. Salted George's cod is the best brand on the market. Cod is in season throughout the year.

Cod Liver Oil is obtained from cods' livers, and has great therapeutic value. Isinglass, made from swimming bladder of cod, nearly equals in quality that made from bladder of sturgeon.

Haddock is more closely allied to cod than any other fish. It is smaller (its average weight being about four pounds), and differently mottled. The distinguishing mark of the haddock is a black line running the entire length of fish on either side. Haddock is found in the same water and in company with cod, but not so abundantly. Like cod, haddock is cheap, and in season throughout the year. Haddock, when dried, smoked, and salted, is known as *Finnan Haddie*.

Halibut is the largest of the flatfish family (Pleuronectidæ), specimens having been caught weighing from three to four hundred pounds. Small, or chicken, halibut is the kind usually found in market, and weighs from fifteen to twenty-five pounds. Halibut are distinctively cold-water fish, being caught in water at from 32° to 45° F. They are found in the North Atlantic and North Pacific Oceans, where they are nearly identical. The halibut has a compressed body, the skin on one side being white, on the other light, or dark gray, and both eyes are found on the dark side of head. Halibut is in season throughout the year.

Turbot (called little halibut) is a species of the flatfish family, being smaller than halibut, and of more delicate flavor. Turbot are in season from January to March.

Flounder is a small flatfish, which closely resembles the sole which is caught in English waters, and is often served under that name.

Trout are generally fresh-water fish, varying much in size and skin-coloring. Lake trout, which are the largest, reach their greatest perfection in Lakes Huron, Michigan, and Superior, but are found in many lakes. Salmon trout is the name applied to trout caught in New York lakes. Brook trout, caught in brooks and small lakes, are superior eating. Trout are in season from April to August, but a few are found later.

Whitefish is the finest fish found in the Great Lakes.

Smelts are small salt-water fish, and are usually caught in temperate waters at the mouths of rivers. New Brunswick and Maine send large quantities of smelts to market. Selected smelts are the largest in size, and command higher price. The Massachusetts Fish and Game Protective Law forbids their sale from March 15th to June 1st. Smelts are always sold by the pound.

Bluefish belongs to the Pomatomidæ family. It is widely distributed in temperate waters, taking different names in different localities.   In New England and the Middle States it is generally called Bluefish, although in some parts called Snappers, or Snapping Mackerel.   In the Southern States it is called Greenfish.   It is in season in our markets from May to October; as it is frozen and kept in cold storage from six to nine months, it may be obtained throughout the year.   The heavier the fish, the better its quality.   Bluefish weigh from one to eight pounds, and are from fourteen to twenty-nine inches in length.

Mackerel is one of the best-known food fishes, and is caught in North Atlantic waters.   Its skin is lustrous dark blue above, with wavy blackish lines, and silvery below.   It sometimes attains a length of eighteen inches, but is usually less.   Mackerel weigh from three-fourths of a pound to two pounds, and are sold by the piece. They are in season from May 1st to September 1st. Mackerel, when first in market, contain less fat than later in the season, therefore are easier of digestion.   The supply of mackerel varies greatly from year to year, and some years is very small.   *Spanish mackerel* are found in waters farther south than common mackerel, and in our markets command higher price.

Salmon live in both fresh and salt waters, always going inland, usually to the head of rivers, during the spawning season.   The young after a time seek salt water, but generally return to fresh water.   Penobscot River Salmon are the best, and come from Maine and St. John, New Brunswick.   The average weight of salmon is from fifteen to twenty-five pounds, and the flesh is of pinkish orange color.   Salmon are in season from May to September, but frozen salmon may be obtained the greater part of the year.   In the Columbia River and its tributaries salmon are so abundant that extensive canneries are built along the banks.

Shad, like salmon, are found in both salt and fresh water, always ascending rivers for spawning.   Shad is caught on the Atlantic coast of the United States, and its capture constitutes one of the most important fisheries.

Shad have a silvery hue, which becomes bluish on the back; they vary in length from eighteen to twenty-eight inches, and are always sold by the piece, price being irrespective of size. *Jack shad* are usually cheaper than *roe shad*. The roe of shad is highly esteemed. Shad are in season from January to June. First shad in market come from Florida, and retail from one and one-half to two dollars each. The finest come from New Brunswick, and appear in market about the first of May.

Caviare is the salted roe of the sturgeon.

Herring are usually smoked, or smoked and salted, and, being very cheap, are a most economical food.

SHELLFISH.

I. Bivalve Mollusks.

Oysters are mollusks, having two shells. The shells are on the right and left side of the oyster, and are called right and left valves. The one upon which the oyster rests, grows faster, becomes deeper, and is known as the left valve. The valves are fastened by a ligament, which, on account of its elasticity, admits of opening and closing of the shells. The oyster contains a tough muscle, by which it is attached to the shell; the body is made up largely of the liver (which contains *glycogen*, animal starch), and is partially surrounded by fluted layers, which are the gills. Natural oyster beds (or banks) are found in shallow salt water having stony bottom, along the entire Atlantic coast. The oyster industry of the world is chiefly in the United States and France, and on account of its increase many artificial beds have been prepared for oyster culture. Oysters are five years old before suitable for eating. Blue Points, which are small, plump oysters, take their name from Blue Point, Long Island, from which place they originally came. Their popularity grew so rapidly that the supply became inadequate for the demand,

and any small, plump oysters were soon sold for Blue Points. During the oyster season they form the first course of a dinner, served raw on the half-shell. In our markets, selected oysters (which are extremely large and used for broiling), Providence River, and Norfolk oysters are familiarly known, and, taken out of the shells, are sold by the quart. Farther south, they are sold by count.

Oysters are obtainable all the year, but are in season from September to May. During the summer months they are flabby and of poor flavor, although when fresh they are perfectly wholesome. *Mussels*, eaten in England and other parts of Europe, are similar to oysters, though of inferior quality. Oysters are nutritious and of easy digestibility, especially when eaten raw.

To Open Oysters. Put a thin, flat knife under the back end of the right valve, and push forward until it cuts the strong muscle which holds the shells together. As soon as this is done, the right valve may be raised and separated from the left.

To Clean Oysters. Put oysters in a strainer placed over a bowl. Pour over oysters cold water, allowing one-half cup water to each quart oysters. Carefully pick over oysters, taking each one separately in the fingers, to remove any particles of shell which adhere to tough muscle.

Clams, among bivalve mollusks, rank in value next to oysters. They are found just below the surface of sand and mud, above low-water mark, and are easily dug with shovel or rake. Clams have hard or soft shells. Soft-shell clams are dear to the New Englander. From New York to Florida are found hard-shelled clams (quahaugs). *Small quahaugs* are called *Little Neck Clams* and take the place of Blue Points at dinner, when Blue Points are out of season.

Scallops are bivalve mollusks, the best being found in Long Island Sound and Narragansett Bay. The central muscle forms the edible portion, and is the only part sent to market. Scallops are in season from October first to April first.

II. Crustaceans.

Lobsters belong to the highest order of Crustaceans, live exclusively in sea-water, generally near rocky coasts, and are caught in pots set on gravelly bottoms. The largest and best species are found in Atlantic waters from Maine to New Jersey, being most abundant on Maine and Massachusetts coasts. Lobsters have been found weighing from sixteen to twenty-five pounds, but such have been exterminated from our coast. The average weight is two pounds, and the length from ten to fifteen inches. Lobsters are largest and most abundant from June to September, but are obtainable all the year. When taken from the water, shells are of mottled dark green color, except when found on sandy bottoms, when they are quite red. Lobsters are generally boiled, causing the shell to turn red.

A lobster consists of body, tail, two large claws, and four pairs of small claws. On lower side of body, in front of large claws, are various small organs which surround the mouth, and a long and short pair of feelers. Under the tail are found several pairs of appendages. In the female lobster, also called hen lobster, is found, during the breeding season, the spawn, known as *coral*. Sex is determined by the pair of appendages in the tail which lie nearest the body; in the female they are soft and pliable, in the male hard and stiff. At one time small lobsters were taken in such quantities that it was feared, if the practice was long continued, they would be exterminated. To protect the continuance of lobster fisheries, a law has been passed in many states prohibiting their sale unless at least ten inches long.

Lobsters shed their shells at irregular intervals, when old ones are outgrown. The new ones begin to form and take on distinctive characteristics before the old ones are discarded. New shells after twenty-four hours' exposure to the water are quite hard.

Lobsters, being coarse feeders (taking almost any animal substance attainable), are difficult of digestion, and with some create great gastric disturbance; notwithstanding, they are seldom found diseased.

To Select a Lobster. Take in the hand, and if heavy in proportion to its size, the lobster is fresh. Straighten the tail, and if it springs into place the lobster was alive (as it should have been) when put into the pot for boiling. There is greater shrinkage in lobsters than in any other fish.

To Open Lobsters. Take off large claws, small claws, and separate tail from body. Tail meat may sometimes be drawn out whole with a fork; more often it is necessary to cut the thin shell portion (using scissors or a can-opener) in under part of the tail, then the tail meat may always be removed whole. Separate tail meat through centre, and remove the small intestinal vein which runs its entire length; although generally darker than the meat, it is sometimes found of the same color. Hold body shell firmly in left hand, and with first two fingers and thumb of right hand draw out the body, leaving in shell the stomach (known as *the lady*), which is not edible, and also some of the green part, the *liver*. The liver may be removed by shaking the shell. The sides of the body are covered with the *lungs;* these are always discarded. Break body through the middle and separate body bones, picking out meat that lies between them, which is some of the sweetest and tenderest to be found. Separate large claws at joints. If shells are thin, with a knife cut off a strip down the sharp edge, so that shell may be broken apart and meat removed whole. Where shell is thick, it must be broken with a. mallet or hammer. Small claws are used for garnishing. The shell of body, tail, and lower part of large claws, if not broken, may be washed, dried, and used for serving of lobster meat after it has been prepared. The portions of lobsters which are not edible are *lungs, stomach* (lady), and *intestinal vein.*

Crabs among Crustaceans are next in importance to lobsters, commercially speaking. They are about two and one-half inches long by five inches wide, and are found along the Atlantic coast from Massachusetts to Florida, and in the Gulf of Mexico. Crabs, like lobsters, change their shells. *Soft-shell crabs* are those which have recently shed their old shells, and the new shells have not had time to harden; these are considered by many a great luxury. *Oyster crabs* (very small crabs found in shells with oysters), are a delicacy not often indulged in. Crabs are in season during the spring and summer.

Shrimps are found largely in our Southern waters, the largest and best coming from Lake Pontchartrain. They are about two inches long, covered with a thin shell, and are boiled and sent to market with heads removed. Their grayish color is changed to pink by boiling. Shrimps are in season from May first to October first, and are generally used for salads. Canned shrimps are much used and favorably known.

Reptiles. Frogs and terrapin belong to a lower order of animals than fish, — reptiles. They are both table delicacies, and are eaten by the few.

Only the hind legs of frogs are eaten, and have much the same flavor as chicken.

Terrapin, although sold in our large cities, specially belong to Philadelphia, Baltimore, and Washington, where they are cooked and served at their best. They are shipped from the South, packed in seaweed, and may be kept for some time in a dark place. Terrapin are found in both fresh and salt water. The Diamond Back, salt water terrapin, coming from Chesapeake Bay, are considered the best, and command a very high price. Terrapin closely resembling Diamond Back, coming from Texas and Florida, are principally sold in our markets. Terrapin are in season from November to April, but are best in January, February, and March. They should always be cooked alive.

TO PREPARE FISH FOR COOKING.

To Clean a Fish. Fish are cleaned and dressed at market as ordered, but need additional cleaning before cooking. Remove scales which have not been taken off. This is done by drawing a knife over fish, beginning at tail and working towards head, occasionally wiping knife and scales from fish. Incline knife slightly towards you to prevent scales from flying. The largest number of scales will be found on the flank. Wipe thoroughly inside and out with cloth wrung out of cold water, removing any clotted blood which may be found adhering to backbone.

Head and tail may or may not be removed, according to size of fish and manner of cooking. Small fish are generally served with head and tail left on.

To Skin a Fish. With sharp knife remove fins along the back and cut off a narrow strip of skin the entire length of back. Loosen skin on one side from bony part of gills, and being once started, if fish is fresh, it may be readily drawn off; if flesh is soft do not work too quickly, as it will be badly torn. By allowing knife to closely follow skin this may be avoided. After removing skin from one side, turn fish and skin the other side.

To Bone a Fish. Clean and skin before boning. Beginning at the tail, run a sharp knife under flesh close to backbone, and with knife follow bone (making as clean a cut as possible) its entire length, thus accomplishing the removal of one-half the flesh; turn and remove flesh from other side. Pick out with fingers any small bones that may remain. Cod, haddock, halibut, and whitefish are easily and frequently boned; flounders and smelts, occasionally.

To Fillet Fish. Clean, skin, and bone. A piece of fish large or small, freed from skin and bones, is known as a fillet. Halibut, cut in three-fourths inch slices, is more often cut in fillets than any kind of fish, and fillets are frequently rolled. When flounder is cut in fillets it is served under the name of *fillet of sole*. Sole found in English waters is much esteemed, and flounder is our nearest approach to it.

To fillet a slice of fish, and to roll and skewer a fillet.

WAYS OF COOKING FISH.

To Cook Fish in Boiling Water. Small cod, haddock, or cusk are cooked whole in enough boiling water to cover, to which is added salt and lemon juice or vinegar. Salt gives flavor; lemon juice or vinegar keeps the flesh white. A long fish-kettle containing a rack on which to place fish is useful but rather expensive. In place of fish-kettle, if the fish is not too large to be coiled in it, a frying-basket may be used placed in any kettle.

Large fish are cut in thick pieces for boiling, containing the number of pounds required. Examples: Salmon and halibut.

Pieces cut from large fish for boiling should be cleaned and tied in a piece of cheese cloth to prevent scum being deposited on the fish. If skin is not removed before serving, scald the dark skin and scrape to remove coloring: this may be easily accomplished by holding fish on two forks, and lowering into boiling water the part covered with black skin; then remove and scrape. Time required for boiling fish depends on extent of surface exposed to water. Consult Time Table for Boiling, which will serve as a guide. The fish is cooked when flesh leaves the bone, no matter how long the time.

To Broil Fish. Cod, haddock, bluefish, and mackerel are split down the back and broiled whole, removing head and tail or not, as desired. Salmon, chicken halibut, and swordfish are cut in inch slices for broiling. Smelts and other small fish are broiled whole, without splitting. Clean and wipe fish as dry as possible, sprinkle with salt and pepper, and place in well greased wire broiler. Slices of fish should be turned often while broiling; whole fish should be first broiled on flesh side, then turned and broiled on skin side just long enough to make skin brown and crisp.

To remove from broiler, loosen fish on one side, turn and loosen on other side; otherwise flesh will cling to broiler. Slip from broiler to hot platter, or place platter over fish and invert platter and broiler together.

To Bake Fish. Clean, and bake on a greased fish-sheet placed in a dripping-pan. If a fish-sheet is not at hand, place strips of cotton cloth under fish, by which it may be lifted from pan.

To Fry Fish. Clean fish and wipe as dry as possible. Sprinkle with salt, dip in flour or crumbs, egg, and crumbs, and fry in deep fat.

To Sauté Fish. Prepare as for frying, and cook in frying-pan with small amount of fat; or, if preferred, dip in granulated corn meal. Cod steak and smelts are often cooked in this way.

TABLE SHOWING COMPOSITION OF THE VARIOUS FISH USED FOR FOOD.

Articles.	Refuse.	Proteid.	Fat.	Mineral matter.	Water.
Bass, black . . .	54.8	9.3	.8	.5	34.6
Bluefish	55.7	8.3	.5	.5	35.
Butterfish	42.8	10.2	6.3	.6	40.1
Cod, fresh	52.5	8.	.2	.6	38.7
Cod, salt, boneless .		22.2	.3	23.1	54.4
Cusk	40.3	10.1	.1	.5	49.
Eels	20.2	14.6	7.2	.8	57.2
Flounder	61.5	5.6	.3	.5	32.1
Haddock	51.	8.2	.2	.6	40.
Halibut, sections .	17.7	15.1	4.4	.9	61.9
Herring	42.6	10.0	3.0	.0	41.7
Mackerel	44.6	10.	4.3	.7	40.4
Mackerel, Spanish .	34.6	13.7	6.2	1.	44.5
Perch, white . . .	62.5	7.2	1.5	.4	28.4
Pickerel	47.1	9.8	.2	.7	42.2
Pompano	45.5	10.2	4.3	.5	39.5
Red Snapper . . .	46.1	10.6	.6	.7	42.
Salmon	39.2	12.4	8.1	.9	39.4
Shad	50.1	9.2	4.8	.7	35.2

	Carbo-hydrates.				
Shad, roe	2.6	20.9	3.8	1.5	71.2

	Refuse.				
Sheepshead . . .	66.	6.4	.2	.5	26.9
Smelts	41.9	10.	1.	1.	46.1
Trout	48.1	9.8	1.1	.6	40.4
Turbot	47.7	6.8	7.5	.7	37.3
Whitefish	53.5	10.3	3.	.7	32.5

				Carbo-hydrates.	
Lobsters	61.7	5.9	.7	.8	.2	30.7
Clams, out of shell .		10.6	1.1	2.3	5.2	80.8
Oysters, solid . .		6.1	1.4	.9	3.3	88.3
Crabs, soft shell . .		15.8	1.5	2.	.7	80.

W. O. Atwater, Ph.D.

Boiled Haddock.

Clean and boil as directed in Ways of Cooking Fish. Remove to a hot platter, garnish with slices of hard boiled eggs and parsley, and serve with Egg Sauce. A thick piece of halibut may be boiled and served in the same way.

Boiled Salmon.

Clean and boil as directed in Ways of Cooking Fish. Place on a hot platter, remove skin, and garnish with slices of lemon and parsley. Serve with Egg Sauce I. or II., or Hollandaise Sauce.

Broiled Scrod.

A young cod, split down the back, and backbone removed, except a small portion near the tail, is called a scrod. Scrod are always broiled, spread with butter, and sprinkled with salt and pepper. Haddock is also so dressed.

Broiled Chicken Halibut.

Clean and broil as directed in Ways of Cooking Fish. Spread with butter, and sprinkle with salt and pepper.

Broiled Swordfish.

Clean and broil fish, spread with butter, sprinkle with salt and pepper, and serve with Cucumber or Horseradish Sauce.

Broiled Shad Roe.

Wipe, sprinkle with salt and pepper, put on greased wire broiler, and broil five minutes on each side. Serve with Maître d'Hôtel Butter. Mackerel roe are delicious cooked in this way.

Baked Halibut with Stuffing.

Clean a four-pound haddock, sprinkle with salt inside and out, stuff and sew. Cut five diagonal gashes on each

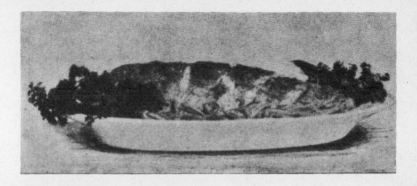

Baked Stuffed Fish.

side of backbone and insert narrow strips of fat salt pork, having gashes on one side come between gashes on other side. Shape with skewers in form of letter S, and fasten skewers with small twine. Place on greased fish-sheet in a dripping-pan, sprinkle with salt and pepper, brush over with melted butter, dredge with flour, and place around fish small pieces of fat salt pork. Bake one hour in hot oven, basting as soon as fat is tried out, and continue basting every ten minutes. Serve with Drawn Butter, Egg or Hollandaise Sauce.

Fish Stuffing I.

½ cup cracker crumbs.　　¼ teaspoon salt.
½ cup stale bread crumbs.　⅛ teaspoon pepper.
¼ cup melted butter.　　　Few drops onion juice.
　　　　¼ cup hot water.

Mix ingredients in order given.

Fish Stuffing II.

1 cup cracker crumbs.　　　Few drops onion juice.
¼ cup melted butter.　　　Parsley,⎫
¼ teaspoon salt.　　　　　Capers, ⎬ 1 teaspoon each,
⅛ teaspoon pepper.　　　　Pickles,⎭ finely chopped.

Mix ingredients in order given. This makes a dry, crumbly stuffing.

Baked Bluefish.

Clean a four-pound bluefish, stuff, sew, and bake as Baked Halibut with Stuffing, omitting to cut gashes on sides, as the fish is rich enough without addition of pork. Baste often with one-third cup butter melted in two-thirds cup boiling water. Serve with Shrimp Sauce.

Bluefish à l'Italienne.

Clean a four-pound bluefish, sprinkle with salt and pepper, and put side down on buttered fish-sheet in a dripping-pan. Add three tablespoons white wine, three tablespoons mushroom liquor, one-half onion finely chopped, eight mushrooms finely chopped, and enough water to allow sufficient liquor in pan for basting. Bake forty-five minutes in hot oven, basting five times. Serve with Sauce à l'Italienne.

Baked Cod with Oyster Stuffing.

Clean a four-pound cod, sprinkle with salt and pepper, brush over with lemon juice, stuff, and sew. Gash, skewer, and bake as Baked Halibut with Stuffing. Serve with Oyster Sauce.

Oyster Stuffing.

1 cup cracker crumbs.	1½ teaspoons lemon juice.
¼ cup melted butter.	½ tablespoon finely chopped
½ teaspoon salt.	parsley.
⅛ teaspoon pepper.	1 cup oysters.

Add seasonings and butter to cracker crumbs. Clean oysters, and remove tough muscles; add soft parts to mixture, with enough oyster liquor to moisten.

Baked Haddock with Oyster Stuffing.

Remove skin, head, and tail from a four-pound haddock. Bone, leaving in large bones near head, to keep fillets in shape of the original fish. Sprinkle with salt, and brush over with lemon juice. Lay one fillet on greased fish-sheet in a dripping-pan, cover thickly with oysters, cleaned, and dipped in buttered cracker crumbs, seasoned with salt and pepper. Cover oysters with other fillet, brush with egg slightly beaten, cover with buttered crumbs, and bake fifty minutes in a moderate oven. Serve with Hollandaise Sauce I. Allow one pint oysters and one cup cracker crumbs.

Baked Halibut with Tomato Sauce.

2 lbs. halibut.	$\frac{1}{2}$ tablespoon sugar.
2 cups tomatoes.	3 tablespoons butter.
1 cup water.	3 tablespoons flour.
1 slice onion.	$\frac{3}{4}$ teaspoon salt.
3 cloves.	$\frac{1}{8}$ teaspoon pepper.

Cook twenty minutes tomatoes, water, onion, cloves, and sugar. Melt butter, add flour, and stir into hot mixture. Add salt and pepper, cook ten minutes, and strain. Clean fish, put in baking-pan, pour around half the sauce, and bake thirty-five minutes, basting often. Remove to hot platter, pour around remaining sauce, and garnish with parsley.

Baked Halibut with Lobster Sauce.

Clean a piece of halibut weighing three pounds. Cut gashes in top, and insert a narrow strip of fat salt pork in each gash. Place in dripping-pan on fish-sheet, sprinkle with salt and pepper, and dredge with flour. Cover bottom of pan with water, add sprig of parsley, slice of onion, two slices carrot cut in pieces, and bit of bay leaf. Bake one hour, basting with one-fourth cup butter, and the liquor in pan. Serve with Lobster Sauce.

Baked Mackerel.

Split fish, clean, and remove head and tail. Put in buttered dripping-pan, sprinkle with salt and pepper, and dot over with butter (allowing one tablespoon to a medium-sized fish), and pour over two-thirds cup milk. Bake twenty-five minutes in hot oven.

Planked Shad or Whitefish.

Clean and split a three-pound shad.   Put skin side down on an oak plank one inch thick, and a little longer and wider than the fish, sprinkle with salt and pepper, and brush over with melted butter.   Bake twenty-five minutes in hot oven.   Remove from oven, spread with butter, and garnish with parsley and lemon.   The fish should be sent to the table on plank.   Planked Shad is well cooked in a gas range having the flame over the fish.

The Planked Whitefish of the Great Lakes has gained much favor.

Baked Stuffed Smelts.

Clean and wipe as dry as possible twelve selected smelts. Stuff, sprinkle with salt and pepper, and brush over with lemon juice.   Place in buttered shallow plate, cover with buttered paper, and bake five minutes in hot oven.   Remove from oven, sprinkle with buttered crumbs, and bake until crumbs are brown.   Serve with Sauce Béarnaise.

Stuffing.   Cook one tablespoon finely chopped onion with one tablespoon butter three minutes.   Add one-fourth cup finely chopped mushrooms, one-fourth cup soft part of oysters (parboiled, drained, and chopped), one-half teaspoon chopped parsley, three tablespoons Thick White Sauce, and one-half cup Fish Force-meat.

Baked Shad Roe with Tomato Sauce.

Cook shad roe fifteen minutes in boiling salted water to cover, with one-half tablespoon vinegar; drain, cover with cold water, and let stand five minutes.   Remove from cold water, and place on buttered pan with three-fourths cup Tomato Sauce I. or II.   Bake twenty minutes in hot oven, basting every five minutes.   Remove to a platter, and pour around three-fourths cup Tomato Sauce.

Baked Fillets of Bass or Halibut.

Cut bass or halibut into small fillets, sprinkle with salt and pepper, put into a shallow pan, cover with buttered paper, and bake twelve minutes in hot oven. Arrange on a rice border, garnish with parsley, and serve with Hollandaise Sauce II.

Fillets of Halibut with Brown Sauce.

Cut a slice of halibut weighing one and one-half pounds in eight short fillets, sprinkle with salt and pepper, put in greased pan, and bake five minutes; drain off water, pour over one and one-half cups Brown Sauce I., cover with one-half cup buttered cracker crumbs, and bake until crumbs are brown.

Halibut à la Poulette.

Halibut à la Poulette.

A slice of halibut, weighing
   1½ lbs.
¼ cup melted butter.
⅛ teaspoon pepper.
2 teaspoons lemon juice.
Few drops onion juice.
¼ teaspoon salt.

Clean fish and cut in eight fillets. Add seasonings to melted butter, and put dish containing butter in saucepan of hot water to keep butter melted. Take up each fillet separately with a fork, dip in butter, roll, and fasten with a small wooden skewer. Put in shallow pan, dredge with flour, and bake twelve minutes in hot oven. Remove skewers, arrange on platter for serving, pour around one and one-half cups Béchamel Sauce, and garnish with yolks of two hard boiled eggs rubbed through a strainer, whites of hard boiled eggs cut in strips, lemon cut fan-shaped, and parsley.

Halibut à la Rarebit.

Sprinkle two small slices halibut with salt and pepper, brush over with melted butter, place in dripping-pan on greased fish-sheet, and bake twelve minutes. Remove to hot platter for serving, and pour over it a Welsh Rarebit.

Sandwiches of Chicken Halibut.

Cut chicken halibut in thin fillets. Put together in pairs, with Fish or Chicken Force-meat between, first dipping fillets in melted butter seasoned with salt and pepper and brushing over with lemon juice. Place in shallow pan with one-fourth cup white wine. Bake twenty minutes in hot oven. Arrange on hot platter for serving, sprinkle with finely chopped parsley, garnish with Tomato Jelly, and serve with Hollandaise Sauce.

Fried Cod Steaks.

Clean steaks, sprinkle with salt and pepper, and dip in granulated corn meal. Try out slices of fat salt pork in frying-pan, remove scraps, and sauté steaks in fat.

Fried Smelts.

Clean smelts, leaving on heads and tails. Sprinkle with salt and pepper, dip in flour, egg, and crumbs, and fry three to four minutes in deep fat. As soon as smelts are put into fat, remove fat to back of range so that they may not become too brown before cooked through. Arrange on hot platter, garnish with parsley, lemon, and fried gelatine. Serve with Sauce Tartare.

Various ways of skewering smelts.

Smelts are fried without being skewered, but often are skewered in variety of shapes.

To fry gelatine. Take up a handful and drop in hot, deep fat; it will immediately swell and become white; it should at once be removed with a skimmer, then drained.

Phosphated or granulated gelatine cannot be used for frying.

Fried Fillets of Halibut or Flounder.

Clean fish and cut in long or short fillets. If cut in long fillets, roll and fasten with skewers. Sprinkle fillets with salt and pepper, dip in crumbs, egg, and crumbs, fry in deep fat, and drain. Serve with Sauce Tartare.

Fried Eels.

Clean eels, and cut in two-inch pieces. Sprinkle with salt and pepper, dip in corn meal, and sauté in pork fat.

Fried Stuffed Smelts.

Smelts are stuffed as for Baked Stuffed Smelts, dipped in crumbs, egg, and crumbs, fried in deep fat, and served with Sauce Tartare.

Fried Shad Roe.

Parboil and cook shad roe as for Baked Shad Roe. Cut in pieces, sprinkle with salt and pepper, and brush over with lemon juice. Dip in crumbs, egg, and crumbs, fry in deep fat, and drain.

Soft-shell Crabs.

Clean crabs, sprinkle with salt and pepper, dip in crumbs, egg, and crumbs, fry in deep fat, and drain. Being light they will rise to top of fat, and should be turned while frying. Soft-shell crabs are usually fried.

To Clean a Crab. Lift and fold back the tapering points which are found on each side of the back shell, and remove spongy substance that lies under them. Turn crab on its back, and with a pointed knife remove the small piece at lower part of shell, which terminates in a point; this is called the apron.

Frogs' Hind Legs.

Trim and clean. Sprinkle with salt and pepper, dip in crumbs, egg, and crumbs again, then fry three minutes in deep fat, and drain. If used as an entrée, serve with Sauce Tartare.

Terrapin.

To prepare terrapin for cooking, plunge into boiling water and boil five minutes. Lift out of water with skimmer, and remove skin from feet and tail by rubbing with a towel. Draw out head with a skewer and rub off skin.

To Cook Terrapin. Put in a kettle, cover with boiling salted water, add two slices each of carrot and onion, and a stalk of celery. Cook until meat is tender, which may be determined by pressing feet-meat between thumb and finger. The time required will be from thirty-five to forty minutes. Remove from water, cool, draw out nails from feet, cut under shell close to upper shell and remove.

Empty upper shell and carefully remove and discard gall-bladder, sand-bags, and thick, heavy part of intestines. Any of the gall-bladder would give bitter flavor to the dish. The liver, small intestines, and eggs are used with the meat.

Washington Terrapin.

1 terrapin.	½ cup chopped mushrooms.
1½ tablespoons butter.	Salt.
1½ tablespoons flour.	Few grains cayenne.
1 cup cream.	2 eggs.

2 tablespoons Sherry wine.

Melt the butter, add flour, and pour on slowly the cream. Add terrapin meat with bones cut in pieces, entrails cut smaller, liver separated in pieces, eggs of terrapin, and mushrooms. Season with salt and cayenne. Just before serving, add eggs slightly beaten and two tablespoons Sherry wine.

Terrapin à la Baltimore.

1 terrapin.	Cayenne.
¾ cup Chicken Stock.	1½ tablespoons butter.
1½ tablespoons wine.	Salt and pepper.

Yolks 2 eggs.

To stock and wine add terrapin meat, with bones cut in pieces and entrails cut in smaller pieces; then cook slowly until liquor is reduced one-half. Add liver separated in pieces, eggs, butter, salt, pepper, and cayenne.

Terrapin à la Maryland.

Add to Terrapin à la Baltimore one tablespoon each butter and flour creamed together, one-half cup cream, yolks two eggs slightly beaten, and one teaspoon lemon juice; then add, just before serving, one tablespoon Sherry wine. Pour in a deep dish and garnish with toast or puff paste points.

WAYS OF USING REMNANTS OF COOKED FISH.

Fish à la Crême.

1¾ cups cold flaked fish (cod,
    haddock, halibut, or cusk).
1 cup White Sauce I.
Bit of bay leaf.
Sprig of parsley.

½ slice onion.
Salt and pepper.
½ cup buttered cracker
    crumbs.

Scald milk, for the making of White Sauce, with bay leaf, parsley, and onion. Cover the bottom of small buttered platter with one-half of the fish, sprinkle with salt and pepper, and pour over one-half the sauce; repeat. Cover with crumbs, and bake in hot oven until crumbs are brown. Fish à la Crême, baked in scallop shells, makes an attractive luncheon dish, or may be served for a fish course at dinner.

Turban of Fish.

2½ cups cold flaked fish (cod,
    haddock, halibut, or cusk).
1½ cups milk.
1 slice onion.
Blade of mace.
Sprig of parsley.

¼ cup butter.
¼ cup flour.
½ teaspoon salt.
⅛ teaspoon pepper.
Lemon juice.
Yolks 2 eggs.

⅔ cup buttered cracker crumbs.

Scald milk with onion, mace, and parsley; remove seasonings. Melt butter, add flour, salt, pepper, and gradually the milk; then add eggs, slightly beaten. Put a layer of fish on buttered dish, sprinkle with salt and pepper, and add a few drops of lemon juice. Cover with sauce, continuing until fish and sauce are used, shaping in pyramid form. Cover with crumbs, and bake in hot oven until crumbs are brown.

Fish Hash.

Take equal parts of cold flaked fish and cold boiled potatoes finely chopped. Season with salt and pepper.

Try out fat salt pork, remove scraps, leaving enough fat in pan to moisten fish and potatoes. Put in fish and potatoes, stir until heated, then cook until well browned underneath; fold and turn like an omelet.

Fish Croquettes.

To two cups cold flaked halibut or salmon add one cup Thick White Sauce. Season with salt and pepper, and spread on a plate to cool. Shape, roll in crumbs, egg, and crumbs, and fry in deep fat; drain, arrange on hot dish for serving, and garnish with parsley. If salmon is used, add lemon juice and finely chopped parsley.

Scalloped Cod.

Line a buttered baking-dish with cold flaked cod, sprinkle with salt and pepper, cover with a layer of oysters (first dipped in melted butter, seasoned with onion juice, lemon juice, and a few grains of cayenne, and then in cracker crumbs), add two tablespoons oyster liquor; repeat, and cover with buttered cracker crumbs. Bake twenty minutes in hot oven. Serve with Egg or Hollandaise Sauce I.

Salmon Box.

Line a bread pan, slightly buttered, with warm steamed rice. Fill the centre with cold boiled salmon, flaked, and seasoned with salt, pepper, and a slight grating of nutmeg. Cover with rice, and steam one hour. Turn on a hot platter for serving, and pour around Egg Sauce II.

WAYS OF COOKING SALT FISH.

Creamed Salt Codfish.

Pick salt codfish in pieces, and soak in lukewarm water, the time depending upon hardness and saltness of the fish. Drain, and add one cup Thin White Sauce. Add one beaten egg just before sending to table. Garnish with slices of hard boiled eggs.   Creamed Codfish is better made with cream slightly thickened in place of Thin White Sauce.

Fish Balls.

1 cup salt codfish. 1 egg.
2 heaping cups potatoes. ½ tablespoon butter.
⅛ teaspoon pepper.

Wash fish in cold water, and pick in very small pieces. or cut, using scissors.   Wash, pare, and soak potatoes, cutting in pieces of uniform size before measuring.   Cook fish and potatoes in boiling water to cover until potatoes are soft.   Drain through strainer, return to kettle in which they were cooked, mash thoroughly (being sure there are no lumps left in potato), add butter, egg well beaten, and pepper.   Beat with a fork two minutes.   Add salt if necessary.   Take up by spoonfuls, put in frying-basket, and fry one minute in deep fat, allowing six fish balls for each frying; drain on brown paper.   Reheat the fat after each frying.

Salted Codfish Hash.

Prepare as for Fish Balls, omitting egg.   Try out fat salt pork, remove scraps, leaving enough fat in pan to moisten fish and potatoes.   Put in fish and potatoes, stir until heated, then cook until well browned underneath; fold, and turn like an omelet.

Toasted Salt Fish.

Pick salt codfish in long thin strips.   If very salt, it may need to be freshened by standing for a short time in lukewarm water.   Place on a greased wire broiler, and broil until brown on one side; turn, and brown the other. Remove to platter, and spread with butter.

Baked Finnan Haddie.

Put fish in dripping-pan, surround with milk and water in equal proportions, place on back of range where it will heat slowly. Let stand twenty-five minutes; pour off liquid, spread with butter, and bake twenty-five minutes.

Broiled Finnan Haddie.

Broil in a greased broiler until brown on both sides. Remove to a pan, and cover with hot water; let stand ten minutes, drain, and place on a platter. Spread with butter, and sprinkle with pepper.

WAYS OF COOKING SHELLFISH.

Oysters on the Half Shell.

Serve oysters on deep halves of the shells, allowing six to each person. Arrange on plates of crushed ice, with one-fourth of a lemon in the centre of each plate.

Raw Oysters.

Raw oysters are served on oyster plates, or in a block of ice. Place block of ice on a folded napkin on platter, and garnish the base with parsley and quarters of lemon, or ferns and lemon.

To Block Ice for Oysters. Use a rectangular piece of clear ice, and with hot flatirons melt a cavity large enough to hold the oysters. Pour water from cavity as rapidly as it forms.

Panned Oysters.

Clean one pint large oysters. Place in dripping-pan small oblong pieces of toast, put an oyster on each piece, sprinkle with salt and pepper, and bake until oysters are plump. Serve with Lemon Butter.

Lemon Butter. Cream three tablespoons butter, add one-half teaspoon salt, one tablespoon lemon juice, and a few grains of cayenne.

Fancy Roast.

Clean one pint oysters and drain from their liquor. Put in a stewpan and cook until oysters are plump and edges begin to curl. Shake pan to prevent oysters from adhering to pan, or stir with a fork. Season with salt, pepper, and two tablespoons butter, and pour over four small slices of toast. Garnish with toast points and parsley.

Oyster Fricassee.

1 pint oysters.	¼ teaspoon salt.
Milk or cream.	Few grains cayenne.
2 tablespoons butter.	1 teaspoon finely chopped
2 tablespoons flour.	parsley.
1 egg.	

Clean oysters, heat oyster liquor to boiling point and strain through double thickness of cheese cloth; add oysters to liquor and cook until plump. Remove oysters with skimmer and add enough cream to liquor to make a cupful. Melt butter, add flour, and pour on gradually hot liquid; add salt, cayenne, parsley, oysters, and egg slightly beaten.

Creamed Oysters.

1 pint oysters.	1½ cups White Sauce II.
⅛ teaspoon celery salt.	

Clean, and cook oysters until plump and edges begin to curl; drain, and add to White Sauce seasoned with celery salt. Serve on toast, in timbale cases, patty shells, or vol-au-vents. One-fourth cup sliced mushrooms are often added to Creamed Oysters.

Oysters in Brown Sauce.

1 pint oysters.	½ cup milk.
¼ cup butter.	½ teaspoon salt.
¼ cup flour.	1 teaspoon Anchovy essence.
1 cup oyster liquor.	⅛ teaspoon pepper.

Parboil and drain oysters, reserve liquor, heat, strain, and set aside for sauce. Brown butter, add flour, and stir until well browned; then add oyster liquor, milk, seasonings, and oysters. For filling patty cases or vol-au-vents.

Broiled Oysters.

1 pint selected oysters.   ¼ cup melted butter.
⅔ cup seasoned cracker crumbs.

Clean oysters and dry between towels.   Lift with plated fork by the tough muscle and dip in butter, then in cracker crumbs which have been seasoned with salt and pepper. Place in a buttered wire broiler and broil over a clear fire until juices flow, turning while broiling.   Serve with or without Maître d'Hôtel Butter.

Oyster Toast.

Serve Broiled Oysters on small pieces of Milk Toast. Sprinkle with finely chopped celery.

Oysters and Macaroni.

1 pint oysters.   Salt and pepper.
¾ cups macaroni broken in   Flour.
   1 inch pieces.   ½ cup buttered crumbs.
        ¼ cup butter.

Cook macaroni in boiling salted water until soft; drain, and rinse with cold water.   Put a layer in bottom of a buttered pudding-dish, cover with oysters, sprinkle with salt and pepper, dredge with flour, and dot over with one-half of the butter; repeat, and cover with buttered crumbs. Bake twenty minutes in hot oven.

Scalloped Oysters.

1 pint oysters.   1 cup cracker crumbs.
4 tablespoons oyster liquor.   ½ cup melted butter.
2 tablespoons milk or cream.   Salt.
½ cup stale bread crumbs.   Pepper.

Mix bread and cracker crumbs, and stir in butter.   Put a thin layer in bottom of a buttered shallow baking-dish, cover with oysters, and sprinkle with salt and pepper; add one-half each of oyster liquor and cream.   Repeat, and cover top with remaining crumbs.   Bake thirty minutes in hot oven.   Never allow more than two layers of oysters for Scalloped Oysters; if three layers are used, the middle layer will be underdone, while others are properly cooked. A sprinkling of mace or grated nutmeg to each layer is considered by many an improvement.   Sherry wine may be used in place of cream.

Sautéd Oysters.

Clean one pint oysters, sprinkle on both sides with salt and pepper.   Take up by the tough muscle with plated fork and dip in cracker crumbs.   Put two tablespoons butter in hot frying-pan, add oysters, brown on one side, then turn and brown on the other.

Fried Oysters.

Clean, and dry between towels, selected oysters.   Season with salt and pepper, dip in flour, egg, and cracker or stale bread crumbs, and fry in deep fat.   Drain on brown paper and serve on a folded napkin.   Garnish with parsley and serve with or without Sauce Tyrolienne.

Fried Oysters in Batter.

Clean, and dry between towels, selected oysters.   Dip in batter, fry in deep fat, drain, and serve on a folded napkin; garnish with lemon and parsley.

Batter.

2 eggs.	⅛ teaspoon pepper.
1 teaspoon salt.	1 cup bread flour.

¾ cup milk.

Beat eggs until light, add salt and pepper.   Add milk slowly to flour, stir until smooth and well mixed.   Combine mixtures.

Little Neck Clams.

Little Neck Clams are served raw on the half shell, in same manner as raw oysters.

Steamed Clams.

Clams for steaming should be bought in the shell and always be alive. Wash clams thoroughly, scrubbing with a brush, changing the water several times. Put into a large kettle, allowing one-half cup hot water to four quarts clams; cover closely and steam until shells partially open, care being taken that they are not overdone. Serve with individual dishes of melted butter. Some prefer a few drops of lemon juice or vinegar added to the butter. If a small quantity of boiling water is put into the dishes, the melted butter will float on top and remain hot much longer.

Roasted Clams.

Roasted clams are served at Clam Bakes. Clams are washed in sea-water, placed on stones which have been previously heated by burning wood on them, ashes removed, and stones sprinkled with thin layer of seaweed. Clams are piled on stones, covered with seaweed, and a piece of canvas thrown over them to retain the steam.

Fried Scallops.

Clean one quart scallops, add one and one-half cups boiling water, and let stand two minutes; drain, and dry between towels. Season with salt and pepper, roll in fine cracker crumbs, dip in egg, again in crumbs, and fry two minutes in deep fat; then drain on brown paper.

Plain Lobster.

Remove lobster meat from shell, arrange on platter, and garnish with small claws. If two lobsters are opened, stand tail shells (put together) in centre of platter, and arrange meat around them.

Fried Lobster.

Remove lobster meat from shell. Use tail meat, divided in fourths, and large pieces of claw meat. Sprinkle with salt, pepper, and lemon juice; dip in crumbs, egg, and again in crumbs; fry in deep fat, drain, and serve with Sauce Tartare.

Buttered Lobster.

2 lb. lobster.	Salt and pepper.
3 tablespoons butter.	Lemon juice.

Remove lobster meat from shell and chop slightly. Melt butter, add lobster, and when heated, season and serve garnished with lobster claws.

Scalloped Lobster.

Scalloped Lobster.

2 lb. lobster.	½ teaspoon salt.
1½ cups White Sauce II.	Few grains cayenne.
2 teaspoons lemon juice.	

Remove lobster meat from shell and cut in cubes. Heat in White Sauce and add seasonings. Refill lobster shells, cover with buttered crumbs, and bake until crumbs are brown. To prevent lobster shells from curling over lobster while baking, insert small wooden skewers of sufficient length to keep shell in its original shape. To assist in preserving color of shell, brush over with olive oil before putting into oven. Scalloped lobster may be baked in buttered scallop shells, or in a buttered baking-dish.

Devilled Lobster.

Scalloped lobster highly seasoned is served as Devilled Lobster. Use larger proportions of same seasonings, with the addition of mustard.

Curried Lobster.

Prepare as Scalloped Lobster, adding to flour one-half teaspoon curry powder when making White Sauce.

Lobster Farci.

1 cup chopped lobster meat.	Slight grating nutmeg.
Yolks 2 hard boiled eggs.	⅓ cup buttered crumbs.
½ tablespoon chopped parsley.	Salt.
1 cup White Sauce I.	Pepper.

To lobster meat add yolks of eggs rubbed to a paste, parsley, sauce, and seasonings to taste. Fill lobster shells, cover with buttered crumbs, and bake until crumbs are brown.

Stuffed Lobster à la Béchamel.

2 lb. lobster.	Few grains cayenne.
1½ cups milk.	Slight grating nutmeg.
Bit of bay leaf.	1 teaspoon chopped parsley.
3 tablespoons butter.	1 teaspoon lemon juice.
3 tablespoons flour.	Yolks 2 eggs.
½ teaspoon salt.	½ cup buttered crumbs.

Remove lobster meat from shell and cut in dice. Scald milk with bay leaf, remove bay leaf and make a White Sauce of butter, flour, and milk; add salt, cayenne, nutmeg, parsley, yolks of eggs slightly beaten, and lemon juice. Add lobster dice, refill shells, cover with buttered crumbs, and bake until crumbs are brown. One-half chicken stock and one-half cream may be used for sauce if a richer dish is desired.

Broiled Live Lobster.

Live lobsters may be dressed for broiling at market, or may be done at home.   Clean lobster and place in a buttered wire broiler.   Broil eight minutes on flesh side, turn and broil six minutes on shell side.   Serve with melted butter.   Lobsters taste nearly the same when placed in dripping-pan and baked fifteen minutes in hot oven, and are much easier cooked.

To Split a Live Lobster.   Cross large claws and hold firmly with left hand.   With sharp-pointed knife, held in right hand, begin at the mouth and make a deep incision, and, with a sharp cut, draw the knife quickly through body and entire length of tail.   Open lobster, remove intestinal vein, liver, and stomach, and crack claw shells with a mallet.

Lobster à l'Américaine.

Split a live lobster and put in a large omelet pan, sprinkle with one-fourth onion finely chopped and a few grains of cayenne, and cook five minutes.   Add one-half cup Tomato Sauce II. and cook three minutes ; then add two tablespoons sherry wine, cover, and cook in oven seven minutes.   To the liver add one tablespoon wine, two tablespoons Tomato Sauce, and one-half tablespoon melted butter ; heat in pan after lobster has been removed.   As soon as sauce is heated, strain, and pour over lobster.

CHAPTER XII.

BEEF.

MEAT is the name applied to the flesh of all animals used for food. Beef is the meat of steer, ox, or cow, and is the most nutritious and largely consumed of all animal foods. Meat is chiefly composed of the albuminoids (fibrin, albumen, gelatin), fat, mineral matter, and water.

Fibrin is that substance in blood which causes it to coagulate when shed. It consists of innumerable delicate fibrils which entangle the blood corpuscles, and form with them a mass called blood clot. Fibrin is insoluble in both cold and hot water.

Albumen is a substance found in the blood and muscle. It is soluble in cold water, and is coagulated by hot water or heat. It begins to coagulate at 134° F. and becomes solid at 160° F. Here lies the necessity of cooking meat in hot water at a low temperature; of broiling meat at a high temperature, to quickly sear surface.

Gelatin in its raw state is termed *collagen*. It is a transparent, tasteless substance, obtained by boiling with water, muscle, skin, cartilage, bone, tendon, ligament, or membrane of animals. By this process, collagen of connective tissues is dissolved and converted into gelatin. Gelatin is insoluble in cold water, soluble in hot water, but in boiling water is decomposed, and by much boiling will not solidify on cooling. When subjected to cold water it swells, and is called hydrated gelatin. Myosin is the albuminoid of muscle, collagen of tendons, ossein of bones, and chondrin of cartilage and gristle.

Gelatin, although highly nitrogenous, does not act in the system as other nitrogenous foods, as a large quantity passes out unchanged. In combination with albumen it has a food value.

Fat is the white or yellowish oily solid substance forming the chief part of the adipose tissue. Fat is found in thick layers directly under the skin, in other parts of the body, in bone, and is intermingled throughout the flesh. Fat as food is a great heat-giver and force-producer. *Suet* is the name given to fat which lies about the loins and kidneys. Beef suet tried out and clarified is much used in cookery for shortening and frying.

Mineral Matter. The largest amount of mineral matter is found in bone. It is principally calcium phosphate (phosphate of lime). Sodium chloride (common salt) is found in the blood and throughout the tissues.

Water abounds in all animals, constituting a large percentage of their weight.

The color of meat is due to the coloring matter (hæmoglobin) which abounds in the red corpuscles of the blood.

The distinctive flavor of meat is principally due to peptones and allied substances, and is intensified by the presence of sodium chloride and other salts.

The beef creature is divided by splitting through the backbone in two parts, each part being called *a side of beef*. Four hundred and fifty pounds is good market weight for a side of beef.

The most expensive cuts come from that part of the creature where muscles are but litle used, which makes the meat finer grained and consequently more tender, taking less time for cooking. Many of the cheapest cuts, though equally nutritious, need long, slow cooking to render them tender enough to digest easily. Tough meat which has long and coarse fibres is often found to be very juicy, on account of the greater motion of that part of the creature, which causes the juices to flow freely. Roasting and broiling, which develop so fine a flavor, can only be applied to the more expensive cuts. The liver, kidneys, and heart are of firm, close texture, and difficult of digestion. Tripe, which is the first stomach of the ox, is easy of digestion, but on account of the large amount of fat which it contains, it is undesirable for those of weak digestion.

1. First cut of rib.   2. Tip of sirloin.   3. First five ribs.

The quality of beef depends on age of the creature and manner of feeding. The best beef is obtained from a steer of four or five years. Good beef should be firm and of fine-grained texture, bright red in color, and well mottled and coated with fat. The fat should be firm, and of a yellowish color. Suet should be dry, and crumble easily. Beef should not be eaten as soon as killed, but allowed to hang and ripen, — from two to three weeks in winter, and two weeks in summer.

Meat should be removed from paper as soon as it comes from market, otherwise paper absorbs some of the juices.

Meat should be kept in a cool place. In winter, beef may be bought in large quantities and cut as needed. If one chooses, a loin or rump may be bought and kept by the butcher, who sends cuts as ordered.

Always wipe beef, before cooking, with a cheese cloth wrung out of cold water, but never allow it to stand in a pan of cold water, as juices will be drawn out.

DIVISION AND WAYS OF COOKING A SIDE OF BEEF.

HIND-QUARTER.

DIVISIONS.		WAYS OF COOKING.
Flank (thick and boneless) . .		Stuffed, rolled and braised, or corned and boiled.
Round . .	Aitchbone . .	Cheap roast, beef stew, or braised.
	Top	Steaks, best cuts for beef tea.
	Lower Part . .	Hamburg steaks, curry of beef, and cecils.
	Vein	Steaks.
Rump. . .	Back	Choicest large roasts and cross-cut steaks.
	Middle . . .	Roasts.
	Face	Inferior roasts and stews.
Loin . . .	Tip	Extra fine roasts.
	Middle . . .	Sirloin and porterhouse steaks.
	First Cut . . .	Steaks and roast.
The Tenderloin	Sold as a Fillet or cut in Steaks	Larded and roasted, or broiled.
Hind-shin		Cheap stew or soup stock.

FORE-QUARTER.

Five Prime Ribs		Good roast
Five Chuck Ribs		Small steaks and stews.
Neck		Hamburg steaks.
Sticking-Piece		Mincemeat.
Rattle Rand	Thick End Second Cut Thin End	Corned for boiling.
Brisket . .	Navel End Butt End or Fancy Brisket	Finest pieces for corning.
Fore-shin		Soup stock and stews.

Other Parts of Beef Creature used for Food.

BRAINS . . . . . Stewed, scalloped dishes, or croquettes.
TONGUE . . . . . Boiled or braised, fresh or corned.
HEART . . . . . Stuffed and braised.
LIVER . . . . . Broiled or fried.
KIDNEYS . . . . . Stewed or sautéd.
TAIL . . . . . Soup.
SUET (kidney suet is the best).
TRIPE . . . . . Lyonnaise, broiled, or fried in batter.

1. Aitchbone.
2. A rump from which cross-cut steaks have been cut.
3. A loin from which to cut porterhouse steaks.
a. Sirloin. *b.* Tenderloin. *c.* Kidney-suet.

The Effect of Different Temperatures on the Cooking of Meat.

By putting meat in cold water and allowing water to heat gradually, a large amount of juice is extracted and meat is tasteless; and by long cooking the connective tissues are softened and dissolved, which gives to the stock when cold a jelly-like consistency. This principle applies to soup-making.

By putting meat in boiling water, allowing the water to boil for a few minutes, then lowering the temperature, juices in the outer surface are quickly coagulated, and the inner juices are prevented from escaping. This principle applies where nutriment and flavor is desired in meat. Examples : Boiled mutton, fowl.

By putting in cold water, bringing quickly to the boiling point, then lowering the temperature and cooking slowly until meat is tender, some of the goodness will be in the stock, but a large portion left in the meat. Examples: Fowl, when cooked to use for made-over dishes, Scotch Broth.

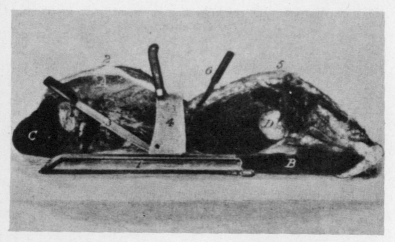

1. Butcher's saw.
2. Round of beef from which slices have been removed.
3. Butcher's large knife.
4. Cleaver.
5. Round of beef.

6. Butcher's boning knife.
a. Top of round.
b. Lower part of round.
c. Vein.
d. Marrow-bone.

TABLE SHOWING COMPOSITION OF MEATS.

Articles.	Refuse.	Proteid.	Fat.	Mineral matter.	Water.
BEEF.					
Fore-quarter .	19.8	14.1	16.1	.7	49.3
Hind-quarter .	16.3	15.3	15.6	.8	52.
Round . . .	8.5	18.7	8.8	1.	63.
Rump . . .	18.5	14.4	19.	.8	47.3
Loin . . .	12.6	15.9	17.3	.9	53.3
Ribs . . .	20.2	13.6	20.6	.7	44.9
Chuck ribs .	13.3	15.	20.8	.8	50.1
Tongue . .	15.1	14.8	15.3	.9	53.9
Heart . . .		16.	20.4	1.	62.6
	Carbo- hydrates.				
Kidney . . .	.4	16.9	4.8	1.2	76.7
Liver . . .	1.8	21.6	5.4	1.4	69.8
MUTTON.					
Hind-quarter .	16.7	13.5	23.5	.7	45.6
Fore-quarter .	21.1	11.9	25.7	.7	40.6
Leg	17.4	15.1	14.5	.8	52.2
Loin . . .	14.2	12.8	31.9	.6	40.5
VEAL.					
Fore-quarter .	24.5	14.6	6.	.7	54.2
Hind-quarter .	20.7	15.7	6.6	.8	56.2
Leg	10.5	18.5	5.	1.	65.
Sweetbreads .		15.4	12.1	1.6	70.9
PORK.					
Loin of pork .	16.	13.5	27.5	.7	42.3
Ham, smoked .	12.7	14.1	33.2	4.1	35.9
Salt pork . .	8.1	6.5	66.8	2.7	15.9
Bacon . . .	8.1	9.6	60.2	4.3	17.8
POULTRY.					
Chicken . .	34.8	14.8	1.1	.8	48.5
Fowl . . .	30.	13.4	10.2	.8	45.6
Turkey . . .	22.7	15.7	18.4	.8	42.4
Goose . . .	22.2	10.3	33.8	.6	33.1

W. O. Atwater, Ph.D.

Broiled Beefsteak.

The best cuts of beef for broiling are, porterhouse, sirloin, cross-cut of rump steaks, and second and third cuts from top of round. Porterhouse and sirloin cuts are the most expensive, on account of the great loss in bone and fat, although price per pound is about the same as for cross-cut of rump. Round steak is very juicy, but, having coarser fibre, is not as tender. Steaks should be cut at least an inch thick, and from that to one and one-

1. Rump cut next to round.
2. Rump cut next to loin.

half inches. The flank end of sirloin steak should be removed before cooking. It may be put in soup kettle, or lean part may be chopped and utilized for meat cakes; fat tried out and clarified for shortening.

To Broil Steak. Wipe with a cloth wrung out of cold water, and trim off superfluous fat. With some of the fat grease a wire broiler, place meat in broiler (having fat edge next to handle), and broil over a clear fire, turning every ten seconds for the first minute, that surface may be well seared, thus preventing escape of juices. After the first minute, turn occasionally until well cooked on both sides. Steak cut one inch thick will take five minutes, if liked rare; six minutes, if well done. Remove to hot platter, spread with butter, and sprinkle with salt and pepper.

Beefsteak with Maître d'Hôtel Butter.

Serve Broiled Steak with Maître d'Hôtel Butter.

Porterhouse Steak with Mushroom Sauce.

Serve broiled Porterhouse Steak with Mushroom Sauce.

Porterhouse Steak with Tomato and Mushroom Sauce.

Serve broiled Porterhouse Steak with Tomato and Mushroom Sauce.

Beefsteak with Oyster Blanket.

Wipe a sirloin steak, cut one and one-half inches thick, broil five minutes, and then remove to platter. Spread with butter and sprinkle with salt and pepper. Clean one pint oysters, cover steak with same, sprinkle oysters with salt and pepper and dot over with butter. Place on grate in hot oven, and cook until oysters are plump.

Broiled Fillets of Beef.

Slices cut from the tenderloin are called sliced fillets of beef. Wipe sliced fillets, place in greased broiler, and broil four or five minutes over a clear fire. These may be served with Maître d'Hôtel Butter or Mushroom Sauce.

Cutlets of Tenderloin with Chestnut Purée.

Shape slices of tenderloin, one inch thick, in circular pieces. Broil five minutes. Spread with butter, sprinkle with salt and pepper. Arrange on platter around a mound of Chestnut Purée.

Sautéd Mignon Fillets of Beef with Sauce Figaro.

Wipe and sauté small fillets in hot omelet pan. Arrange in a circle on platter with cock's-comb shaped croûtons between, and pour sauce in the centre. Serve as a luncheon dish with Brussels Sprouts or String Beans.

Sautéd Mignon Fillets of Beef with Sauce Trianon.

Wipe and sauté small fillets in hot omelet pan.   Arrange in a circle around a mound of fried potato balls sprinkled with parsley.   Put Sauce Trianon on each fillet.

Broiled Meat Cakes.

Chop finely lean raw beef, season with salt and pepper, shape in small flat cakes, and broil in a greased broiler or frying-pan.   Spread with butter, or serve with Maître d'Hôtel Butter.   In forming the cakes, handle as little as possible; for if pressed too compactly, cakes will be found solid.

Hamburg Steaks.

Chop finely one pound lean raw beef; season highly with salt, pepper, and a few drops onion juice or one-half shallot finely chopped.   Shape, cook, and serve as Meat Cakes.   A few gratings of nutmeg and one egg slightly beaten may be added.

Cannelon of Beef.

2 lbs. lean beef, cut from round.	½ teaspoon onion juice.
Grated rind ½ lemon.	2 tablespoons melted butter.
1 tablespoon finely chopped parsley.	Few gratings nutmeg.
	1 teaspoon salt.
1 egg.	¼ teaspoon pepper.

Chop meat finely, and add remaining ingredients in order given.   Shape in a roll six inches long, wrap in buttered paper, place on rack in dripping-pan, and bake thirty minutes.   Baste every five minutes with one-fourth cup butter, melted in one cup boiling water.   Serve with Brown Mushroom Sauce I.

Roast Beef.

The best cuts of beef for roasting are: tip or middle of sirloin, back of rump, or first three ribs.   Tip of sirloin roast is desirable for a small family. Back of rump makes a superior roast for a large family, and is more economical than sirloin. It is especially desirable where a large quantity of dish gravy is liked, for in carving, the meat juices follow the knife. Rib roasts contain more fat than either of the others, and are somewhat cheaper.

To Roast Beef. Wipe, put on a rack in dripping-pan, skin side down, rub over with salt, and dredge meat and pan with flour. Place in hot oven, that the surface may be quickly seared, thus preventing escape of inner juices. After flour in pan is browned, reduce heat, and baste with fat which has tried out; if meat is quite lean, it may be necessary to put trimmings of fat in pan. Baste every ten minutes; if this rule is followed, meat will be found more juicy. When meat is about half done, turn it over and dredge with flour, that skin side may be uppermost for final browning. For roasting, consult Time Table for Baking Meats, page 34.

If there is danger of flour burning in pan, add a small quantity of water; this, however, is not desirable, and seldom need be done if size of pan is adapted to size of roast. Beef to be well roasted should be started in hot oven and heat decreased, so that when carved the slices will be red throughout, with a crisp layer of golden brown fat on the top. Beef roasted when temperature is so high that surface is hardened before heat can penetrate to the centre is most unsatisfactory.

Sirloin or rib roasts may have the bones removed, and be rolled, skewered, and tied in shape. Chicago Butt is cut from the most tender part of back of rump. They are shipped from Chicago, our greatest beef centre, and if fresh and from a heavy creature, make excellent roasts at a small price.

Roast Beef Gravy. Remove some of the fat from pan, leaving three tablespoonfuls. Place on front of range, add three tablespoons flour, and stir until well browned. The flour, dredged and browned in pan, should give additional color to gravy. Add gradually one and one-half cups boiling water, cook five minutes, season with salt and pepper, and strain. If flour should burn in pan, gravy will be full of black particles.

To Carve a Roast of Beef. Have roast placed on platter, skin side up; with a pointed, thin-bladed, sharp knife cut a sirloin or rib roast in thin slices parallel to the ribs, and cut slices from ribs. If there is tenderloin, remove it from under the bone, and cut in thin slices across grain of meat. Carve back of rump in thin slices with the grain of meat; by so doing, some of the least tender muscle will be served with that which is tender. By cutting across grain of meat, the tenderest portion is sliced by itself, as is the less tender portion.

Yorkshire Pudding.

1 cup milk.	2 eggs.
1 cup flour.	¼ teaspoon salt.

Miss C. J. Wills.

Mix salt and flour, and add milk gradually to form a smooth paste; then add eggs beaten until very light. Cover bottom of hot pan with some of beef fat tried out from roast, pour mixture in pan one-half inch deep. Bake twenty minutes in hot oven, basting after well risen, with some of the fat from pan in which meat is roasting. Cut in squares for serving. Bake, if preferred, in greased, hissing hot iron gem pans.

Larded Fillet of Beef.

The tenderloin of beef which lies under the loin and rump is called fillet of beef. The fillet under the loin is known as the long fillet, and when removed no porterhouse steaks can be cut; therefore it commands a higher price than the short fillet lying under rump. Two short fillets are often skewered together, and served in place of a long fillet.

Wipe, remove fat, veins, and any tendinous portions;

skewer in shape, and lard upper side with grain of meat, following directions for larding on page 26. Place on a rack in small pan, sprinkle with salt and pepper, dredge with flour, and put in bottom of pan small pieces of pork. Bake twenty to thirty minutes in hot oven, basting three times. Serve with Mushroom, Figaro, or Horseradish Sauce I.

Braised Beef.

3 lbs. beef from lower part of round or face of rump.	Carrot, Turnip, ⎱ ¼ cup each, cut Onion, ⎰ in dice. Celery,
2 thin slices fat salt pork.	
½ teaspoon peppercorns.	Salt and pepper.

Try out pork and remove scraps. Wipe meat, sprinkle with salt and pepper, dredge with flour, and brown entire surface in pork fat. When turning meat, avoid piercing with fork or skewer, which allows the inner juices to escape. Place on trivet in deep granite pan or in earthen pudding-dish, and surround with vegetables, peppercorns, and three cups boiling water; cover closely, and bake four hours in very slow oven, basting every half-hour, and turn after second hour. Throughout the cooking, the liquid should be kept below the boiling point Serve with Horseradish Sauce or with brown sauce made from liquor in pan.

Beef à la Mode.

Insert twelve large lardoons in a four-pound piece of beef cut from the round. Make incisions for lardoons by running through the meat a large skewer. Season with salt and pepper, dredge with flour, and brown the entire surface in pork fat. Put on a trivet in kettle, surround with one-third cup each carrot, turnip, celery, and onion cut in dice, sprig of parsley, bit of bay leaf, and water to half cover meat. Cover closely and cook slowly four hours, keeping liquor below the boiling point. Remove to hot platter. Strain liquor, thicken and season to serve as a gravy. When beef is similarly prepared (with exception of lardoons and vegetables), and cooked in smaller amount of water, it is called Smothered Beef, or Pot Roast.

A bean pot (covered with a piece of buttered paper, tied firmly down) is the best utensil to use for a Pot Roast.

Dumplings.

2 cups flour.	½ teaspoon salt.
4 teaspoons baking powder.	2 teaspoons butter.
¾ cup milk.	

Mix and sift dry ingredients. Work in butter with tips of fingers, add milk gradually, using a knife for mixing. Toss on a floured board, pat, and roll out to one-half inch in thickness. Shape with biscuit cutter, first dipped in flour. Place closely together in a buttered steamer, put over kettle of boiling water, cover closely, and steam twelve minutes. A perforated tin pie plate may be used in place of steamer. A little more milk may be used in the mixture, when it may be taken up by spoonfuls, dropped and cooked on top of stew. In this case some of the liquid must be removed, that dumplings may rest on meat and potato, and not settle into liquid.

Beef Stew with Dumplings.

Aitchbone, weighing 5 lbs.	½ small onion, cut in thin slices.
4 cups potatoes, cut in ¼ inch slices.	¼ cup flour.
Turnip, ⎱ ⅔ cup each, cut in	Salt.
Carrot, ⎰ half-inch cubes.	Pepper.

Wipe meat, remove from bone, cut in one and one-half inch cubes, sprinkle with salt and pepper, and dredge with flour. Cut some of the fat in small pieces and try out in frying-pan. Add meat and stir constantly, that the surface may be quickly seared; when well browned, put in kettle, and rinse frying-pan with boiling water, that none of the goodness may be lost. Add to meat remaining fat, and bone sawed in pieces; cover with boiling water and boil five minutes, then cook at a lower temperature until meat is tender (time required being about three hours). Add carrot, turnip, and onion, with salt and pepper the last hour of cooking. Parboil potatoes five minutes, and add to stew fifteen minutes before taking from fire. Remove bones, large pieces of fat, and then skim. Thicken with one-fourth cup flour, diluted with enough cold water to pour easily. Pour in deep hot platter, and surround with dumplings. Remnants of roast beef are usually made into a beef stew; the meat having been once cooked, there is no necessity of browning it. If gravy is left, it should be added to the stew.

Corned Beef.

Corned beef has but little nutritive value. It is used to give variety to our diet in summer, when fresh meats prove too stimulating. It is eaten by the workingman to give bulk to his food. The best pieces of corned beef are the rattle rand and fancy brisket. The fancy brisket commands a higher price and may be easily told from the rattle rand by the selvage on lower side and the absence of bones. The upper end of brisket (butt end) is thick and composed mostly of lean meat, the middle cut has more fat but is not well mixed, while the lower (navel end) has a large quantity of fat. The rattle rand contains a thick lean end; the second cut contains three distinct layers of meat and fat, and is considered the best cut by those who prefer meat well streaked with fat. The rattle rand has a thin end, which contains but one layer of lean meat and much fat, consequently is not a desirable piece.

To Boil Corned Beef. Wipe the meat and tie securely in shape, if this has not been already done at market. Put in kettle, cover with cold water, and bring slowly to boiling point. Boil five minutes, remove scum, and cook at a lower temperature until tender. Cool slightly in water in which it was cooked, remove to a dish, cover, and place on cover a weight, that meat may be well pressed. The lean meat and fat may be separated and put in alternate layers in a bread pan, then covered and pressed.

Boiled Dinner.

A boiled dinner consists of warm unpressed corned beef, served with cabbage, beets, turnips. carrots, and potatoes. After removing meat from water, skim off fat and cook vegetables (with exception of beets, which require a long time for cooking) in this water. Carrots require a longer time for cooking than cabbage or turnips. Carrots and turnips, if small, may be cooked whole; if large, cut in pieces. Cabbage and beets are served in separate dishes, other vegetables on same dish with meat.

Boiled Tongue.

A boiled corned tongue is cooked the same as Boiled-Corned Beef. If very salt, it should be soaked in cold water several hours, or over night, before cooking. Take from water when slightly cooled and remove skin.

Braised Tongue.

A fresh tongue is necessary for braising. Put tongue in kettle, cover with boiling water, and cook slowly two hours. Take tongue from water and remove skin and roots. Place in deep pan and surround with one-third cup each carrot, onion, and celery, cut in dice, and one sprig parsley; then pour over four cups sauce. Cover closely, and bake two hours, turning after the first hour. Serve on platter and strain around the sauce.

Sauce for Tongue. Brown one-fourth cup butter, add one-fourth cup flour and stir together until well browned. Add gradually four cups of water in which tongue was cooked. Season with salt and pepper and add one tea-spoon Worcestershire Sauce. One and one-half cups stewed and strained tomatoes may be used in place of some of the water.

Broiled Liver.

Cover with boiling water slices of liver cut one-half inch thick, let stand five minutes to draw out the blood; drain, wipe, and remove the thin outside skin and veins. Sprinkle with salt and pepper, place in a greased wire broiler and broil five minutes, turning often. Remove to a hot platter, spread with butter, and sprinkle with salt and pepper.

Liver and Bacon.

Prepare as for Broiled Liver, cut in pieces for serving, sprinkle with salt and pepper, dredge with flour, and fry in bacon fat. Serve with bacon.

Bacon.

Place thin slices of bacon (from which the rind has been removed) closely together in a fine wire broiler; place broiler over dripping-pan and bake in a hot oven until bacon is crisp and brown, turning once. Drain on brown paper. This is the nicest way of cooking bacon. Fat which has dripped into the pan should be poured out and used for frying liver, eggs, potatoes, etc.

Braised Liver.

Skewer, tie in shape, and lard upper side of calf's liver. Place in deep pan, with trimmings from lardoons; surround with one-fourth cup each, carrot, onion, and celery, cut in dice; one-fourth teaspoon peppercorns, two cloves, bit of bay leaf, and two cups Brown Stock or water. Cover closely and bake slowly two hours, uncovering the last twenty minutes. Remove from pan, strain liquor, and use liquor for the making of a Brown Sauce with one and one-half tablespoons butter and two tablespoons flour. Pour sauce around liver for serving.

Broiled Tripe.

Fresh honeycomb tripe is best for broiling. Wipe tripe as dry as possible, dip in fine cracker dust and olive oil or melted butter, draining off all fat that is possible, and again dip in cracker dust. Place in a greased broiler and broil five minutes, cooking smooth side of tripe the first three minutes. Place on a hot platter, honeycomb side up, spread with butter and sprinkle with salt and pepper. Broiled tripe is at its best when cooked over a charcoal fire.

Tripe in Batter.

Wipe tripe and cut in pieces for serving. Sprinkle with salt and pepper, dip in batter, fry in a small quantity of hot fat, and drain.

Tripe Batter. Mix one cup flour with one-fourth teaspoon salt; add gradually one-half cup cold water, and when perfectly smooth add one egg well beaten, one-half tablespoon vinegar and one teaspoon olive oil or melted butter.

Lyonnaise Tripe.

Cut honeycomb tripe in pieces two inches long by one-half inch wide, having three cupfuls. Put on a pan and place in oven that water may be drawn out. Cook one tablespoon finely chopped onion in two tablespoons butter until slightly browned, add tripe drained from water, and cook five minutes. Sprinkle with salt and pepper and finely chopped parsley.

Tripe à la Creole.

Cut, bake, and drain tripe as for Lyonnaise Tripe. Cook same quantity of butter and onion, add one-eighth green pepper finely chopped, one tablespoon flour, one-half cup stock, one-fourth cup drained tomatoes, and one fresh mushroom cut in slices; then add tripe and cook five minutes. Season with salt and pepper.

Tripe à la Provençale.

Add to Lyonnaise Tripe one tablespoon white wine. Cook until quite dry, add one-third cup Tomato Sauce, cook two minutes, season with salt and pepper, and serve.

Calf's Head à la Terrapin.

Wash and clean a calf's head, and cook until tender in boiling water to cover. Cool and cut meat from cheek in small cubes. To two cups meat dice add one cup sauce made of two tablespoons butter, two tablespoons flour, and one cup White Stock, seasoned with one-half teaspoon salt, one-eighth teaspoon pepper, and few grains cayenne. Add one-half cup cream and yolks of two eggs slightly beaten; cook two minutes and add two tablespoons Madeira wine.

Calf's Heart.

Wash a calf's heart, remove veins, arteries, and clotted blood. Stuff (using half quantity of Fish Stuffing I. on page 149, seasoned highly with sage) and sew. Sprinkle with salt and pepper, roll in flour, and brown in hot fat. Place in small deep baking-pan, half cover it with boiling water, cover closely, and bake slowly two hours, basting every fifteen minutes. It may be necessary to add more water. Remove heart from pan and thicken the liquor with flour diluted with a small quantity of cold water. Season with salt and pepper, and pour around the heart before serving.

WAYS OF WARMING OVER BEEF.

Roast Beef with Gravy.

Cut cold roast beef in thin slices, place on a warm platter, and pour over some of the gravy reheated to the boiling point. If meat is allowed to stand in gravy on the range, it becomes hard and tough.

Cottage Pie.

Cover bottom of a small greased baking-dish with hot mashed potato, add a thick layer of roast beef, chopped or cut in small pieces (seasoned with salt, pepper, and a few drops of onion juice) and moistened with some of the gravy; cover with a thin layer of mashed potato, and bake in a hot oven long enough to heat through.

Beefsteak Pie.

Cut remnants of cold broiled steak or roast beef in one-inch cubes. Cover with boiling water, add one-half onion, and cook slowly one hour. Remove onion, thicken gravy with flour diluted with cold water, and season with salt and pepper. Add potatoes cut in one-fourth-inch slices, which have been parboiled eight minutes in boiling salted water. Put in a buttered pudding-dish, cool, cover with baking-powder biscuit mixture or pie crust. Bake in a hot oven. If covered with pie crust, make several incisions in crust that gases may escape.

Cecils with Tomato Sauce.

1 cup cold roast beef or rare steak finely chopped.	Onion juice.
	Worcestershire Sauce.
Salt.	2 tablespoons bread crumbs.
Pepper.	1 tablespoon melted butter.

Yolk 1 egg slightly beaten.

Season beef with salt, pepper, onion juice, and Worcestershire Sauce; add remaining ingredients, shape after the form of small croquettes, pointed at ends. Roll in flour, egg, and crumbs, fry in deep fat, drain, and serve with Tomato Sauce.

Corned Beef Hash.

Remove skin and gristle from cooked corned beef, then chop the meat. When meat is very fat, discard most of the fat. To chopped meat add an equal quantity of cold boiled chopped potatoes. Season with salt and pepper, put into a hot buttered frying-pan, moisten with milk or cream, stir until well mixed, spread evenly, then place on a part of the range where it may slowly brown underneath. Turn, and fold on a hot platter. Garnish with sprig of parsley in the middle.

Corned Beef Hash with Beets.

When preparing Corned Beef Hash, add one-half as much finely chopped cooked beets as potatoes. Cold roast beef or one-half roast beef and one-half corned beef may be used.

Dried Beef with Cream.

¼ lb. smoked dried beef, thinly sliced.	1 cup scalded cream.
	1½ tablespoons flour.

Remove skin and separate meat in pieces, cover with hot water, let stand ten minutes, and drain. Dilute flour with enough cold water to pour easily, making a smooth paste; add to cream, and cook in double boiler ten minutes. Add beef, and reheat. One cup White Sauce I. may be used in place of cream.

CHAPTER XIII.

LAMB AND MUTTON.

LAMB is the name given to the meat of lambs; mutton, to the meat of sheep. Lamb, coming as it does from the young creature, is immature, and less nutritious than mutton. The flesh of mutton ranks with the flesh of beef in nutritive value and digestibility. The fat of mutton, on account of its larger percentage of stearic acid, is more difficult of digestion than the fat of beef.

Lamb may be eaten soon after the animal is killed and dressed; mutton must hang to ripen. Good mutton comes from a sheep about three years old, and should hang from two to three weeks. The English South Down Mutton is cut from creatures even older than three years. Young lamb, when killed from six weeks to three months old, is called spring lamb, and appears in the market as early as the last of January, but is very scarce until March. Lamb one year old is called a yearling. Many object to the strong flavor of mutton; this is greatly overcome by removing the pink skin and trimming off superfluous fat.

Lamb and mutton are divided into two parts by cutting through entire length of backbone; then subdivided into fore and hind quarter, eight ribs being left on hind-quarter, — while in beef but three ribs are left on hind-quarter. These eight ribs are cut into chops and are known as *rib chops*. The meat which lies between these ribs and the leg, cut into chops, is known as *loin* or *kidney chops*.

Lamb and mutton chops cut from loin have a small piece of tenderloin on one side of bone, and correspond to porter-house steaks in the beef creature. Rib chops which have

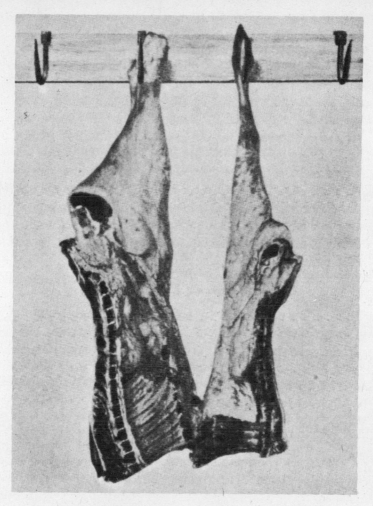

1. Hind-quarter of veal.   2. Hind-quarter of lamb.

the bone cut short and scraped clean, nearly to the lean meat, are called *French chops*.

The leg is sold whole for boiling or roasting. The fore-quarter may be boned, stuffed, rolled, and roasted, but is more often used for broth, stew, or fricassee.

For *a saddle of mutton* the loin is removed whole before splitting the creature. Some of bones are removed and the flank ends are rolled, fastened with wooden skewers, and securely tied to keep skewers in place.

Good quality mutton should be fine-grained and of bright pink color; the fat white, hard, and flaky. If the outside skin comes off easily, mutton is sure to be good. Lamb chops may be easily distinguished from mutton chops by the red color of bone. As lamb grows older, blood recedes from bones; therefore in mutton the bone is white. In *leg of lamb* the bone at joint is serrated, while in leg of mutton the bone at joint is smooth and rounded. Good mutton contains a larger proportion of fat than good beef. Poor mutton is often told by the relatively small proportion of fat and lean as compared to bone.

Lamb is usually preferred well done; mutton is often cooked rare.

Broiled Lamb or Mutton Chops.

Wipe chops, remove superfluous fat, and place in a broiler greased with some of mutton fat. In loin chops, flank may be rolled and fastened with a small wooden skewer. Follow directions for Broiling Beefsteak on page 176.

Pan-broiled Chops.

Chops for pan broiling should have flank and most of fat removed. Wipe chops and put in hissing hot frying-pan. Turn as soon as under surface is seared, and sear other side. Turn often, using knife and fork that the surface may not be pierced, as would be liable if fork alone were used. Cook six minutes if liked rare, eight to ten minutes if liked well done. Let stand around edge of frying-pan to brown the outside fat. When half cooked, sprinkle with salt. Drain on brown paper, put on hot platter, and spread with butter or serve with Tomato or Soubise Sauce.

Breaded Mutton Chops.

Wipe and trim chops, sprinkle with salt and pepper, dip in crumbs, egg, and crumbs, fry in deep fat from five to eight minutes, and drain. Serve with Tomato Sauce, or stack around a mound of mashed potatoes, fried potato balls, or green peas. Never fry but four at a time, and allow fat to reheat between fryings. After testing fat for temperature, put in chops and place kettle on back of range, that surface of chops may not be too brown while the inside is still underdone.

1. Loin Chop.   2. French Chop.   3. Rib Chop.

Chops à la Signora.

Gash French Chops on outer edge, extending cut halfway through lean meat. Insert in each gash a slice of truffle, sprinkle with salt and pepper, wrap in calf's caul. Roll in flour, dip in egg, then in stale bread crumbs, and sauté in butter eight minutes, turning often. Place in oven four minutes to finish cooking. Arrange on hot platter for serving, and place on top of each a fresh broiled mushroom or mushroom baked in cream. To fat in pan add small quantity of boiling water and pour around chops. This is a delicious way of cooking chops for a dinner party.

Chops en Papillote.

Finely chop the whites of three hard boiled eggs and force yolks through potato ricer, mix, and add to three common crackers, rolled and sifted; then add three table-spoons melted butter, salt, pepper, and onion juice, to taste. Add enough cream to make of right consistency to spread. Cover chops thinly with mixture and wrap in buttered paper cases. Bake twenty-five minutes in hot oven. Remove from cases, place on hot platter, and garnish with parsley.

Mutton Cutlets à la Maintenon.

Wipe six French Chops, cut one and one-half inches thick. Split meat in halves, cutting to bone. Cook two and one-half tablespoons butter and one tablespoon onion five minutes; remove onion, add one-half cup chopped mushrooms, and cook five minutes; then add two table-spoons flour, three tablespoons stock, one teaspoon finely chopped parsley, one-fourth teaspoon salt, and few grains of cayenne. Spread mixture between layers of chops, press together lightly, wrap in buttered paper cases, and broil ten minutes. Serve with Spanish Sauce.

Boiled Leg of Mutton.

Wipe meat, place in a kettle, and cover with boiling water. Bring quickly to boiling point, boil five minutes, and skim. Set on back of range and simmer until meat is tender. When half done, add one tablespoon salt. Serve with Caper Sauce, or add to two cups White Sauce (made of one-half milk and one-half Mutton Stock), two hard boiled eggs cut in slices.

Braised Leg of Mutton.

Order a leg of mutton boned. Wipe, stuff, sew, and place in deep pan. Cook five minutes in one-fourth cup butter, a slice each of onion, carrot and turnip cut in dice, one-half bay leaf, and a sprig each of thyme and parsley. Add three cups hot water, one and one-half teaspoons salt, and twelve peppercorns; pour over mutton. Cover closely, and cook slowly three hours, uncovering for the last half-hour. Remove from pan to hot platter. Brown three tablespoons butter, add four tablespoons flour and stir until well browned, pour on slowly the strained liquor; there should be one and three-fourths cups.

Stuffing.

1 cup cracker crumbs. ⅛ teaspoon pepper.
¼ cup melted butter. ½ tablespoon Poultry
¼ teaspoon salt. Seasoning.
¼ cup boiling water.

Roast Lamb.

A leg of lamb is usually sent from market wrapped in caul; remove caul, wipe meat, sprinkle with salt and pepper, place on rack in dripping-pan, and dredge meat and bottom of pan with flour. Place in hot oven, and baste as soon as flour in pan is brown, and every fifteen minutes afterwards until meat is done, which will take about one and three-fourths hours. It may be necessary to put a small quantity of water in pan while meat is cooking. Leg of lamb may be boned and stuffed for roasting. See Stuffing, under Braised Mutton.

Make gravy, following directions for Roast Beef Gravy on page 179, or serve with Currant Jelly Sauce.

To Carve a Leg of Lamb. Cut in thin slices across grain of meat, to the bone, beginning at top of the leg.

Saddle of Mutton.

Mutton for a saddle should always be dressed at market. Wipe meat, sprinkle with salt and pepper, place on rack in dripping-pan, and dredge meat and bottom of pan with flour. Bake in hot oven one and one-fourth hours, basting every fifteen minutes. Serve with Currant Jelly Sauce.

To Carve a Saddle of Mutton, cut thin slices parallel with backbone, then slip the knife under and separate slices from ribs.

Crown of Lamb.

Select parts from two loins containing ribs, scrape flesh from bone between ribs, as far as lean meat, and trim off backbone.   Shape each piece in a semicircle, having ribs outside, and sew pieces together to form a crown.   Trim ends of bones evenly, care being taken that they are not left too long, and wrap each bone in a thin strip of fat salt pork to prevent bone from burning.   Roast one and one-fourth hours, covering bones with buttered paper. Remove pork from bones before serving, and fill centre with Purée of Chestnuts.

Mutton Curry.

Wipe and cut meat from fore-quarter of mutton in one-inch pieces; there should be three cupfuls.   Put in kettle, cover with cold water, and bring quickly to boiling point; drain in colander and pour over one quart cold water. Return meat to kettle, cover with one quart boiling water, add three onions cut in slices, one-half teaspoon pepper-corns, and a sprig each of thyme and parsley.   Simmer until meat is tender, remove meat, strain liquor, and thicken with one-fourth cup each of butter and flour cooked together; to the flour add one-half tablespoon curry powder, one-half teaspoon salt, and one-eighth teaspoon pepper.   Add meat to gravy, reheat, and serve with border of steamed rice.

Fricassee of Lamb with Brown Gravy.

Order three pounds lamb from the fore-quarter, cut in pieces for serving.   Wipe meat, put in kettle, cover with boiling water, and cook slowly until meat is tender. Remove from water, cool, sprinkle with salt and pepper, dredge with flour, and sauté in butter or mutton fat. Arrange on platter, and pour around one and one-half cups Brown Sauce made from liquor in which meat was cooked after removing all fat. It is better to cook meat the day before serving, as then fat may be more easily removed.

Irish Stew with Dumplings.

Wipe and cut in pieces three pounds lamb from the fore-quarter. Put in kettle, cover with boiling water, and cook slowly two hours or until tender. After cooking one hour, add one-half cup each carrot and turnip cut in one-half inch cubes, and one onion cut in slices. Fifteen minutes before serving add four cups potatoes cut in one-fourth inch slices, previously parboiled five minutes in boiling water. Thicken with one-fourth cup flour, diluted with enough cold water to form a thin smooth paste. Season with salt and pepper, serve with Dumplings.

Scotch Broth.

Wipe three pounds mutton cut from fore-quarter. Cut lean meat in one-inch cubes, put in kettle, cover with three pints cold water, bring quickly to boiling point, skim, and add one-half cup barley which has been soaked in cold water over night; simmer one and one-half hours, or until meat is tender. Put bones in a second kettle, cover with cold water, heat slowly to boiling point, skim, and boil one and one-half hours. Strain water from bones and add to meat. Fry five minutes in two tablespoons butter, one-fourth cup each of carrot, turnip, onion, and celery, cut in one-half inch dice, add to soup with salt and pepper to taste, and cook until vegetables are soft. Thicken with two tablespoons each of butter and flour cooked together. Add one-half tablespoon finely chopped parsley just before serving. Rice may be used in place of barley.

Lambs' Kidneys I.

Pare and cut in slices six kidneys, and sprinkle with salt and pepper. Melt two tablespoons butter in hot frying-pan, put in kidneys, and cook five minutes; dredge thoroughly with flour, and add two-thirds cup boiling water or hot Brown Stock. Cook five minutes, add more salt and pepper if needed. Lemon juice, onion juice, or Madeira wine may be used for additional flavor. Kidneys must be cooked a short time, or for several hours; they are tender after a few minutes' cooking, but soon toughen, and need hours of cooking to again make them tender.

Lambs' Kidneys II.

Pare, trim, and slice six kidneys. Sprinkle with salt and pepper, sauté in butter, and remove to a hot dish. Cook one-half tablespoon finely chopped onion in two tablespoons butter until brown; add three tablespoons flour, and pour on slowly one and one-half cups hot stock. Season with salt and pepper, strain, add kidneys, and one tablespoon Madeira wine.

WAYS OF WARMING OVER MUTTON AND LAMB.

Minced Lamb on Toast.

Remove dry pieces of skin and gristle from remnants of cold roast lamb, then chop meat. Heat in well buttered frying-pan, season with salt, pepper, and celery salt, and moisten with a little hot water or stock; or, after seasoning, dredge well with flour, stir, and add enough stock to make thin gravy. Pour over small slices of buttered toast.

Scalloped Lamb.

Remove skin and fat from thin slices of cold roast lamb, and sprinkle with salt and pepper. Cover bottom of a buttered baking-dish with buttered cracker crumbs; cover crumbs with meat, cover meat with boiled macaroni, and add another layer of meat and macaroni. Pour over Tomato Sauce, and cover with buttered cracker crumbs. Bake in hot oven until crumbs are brown. Cold boiled rice may be used in place of macaroni.

Blanquette of Lamb.

Cut remnants of cooked lamb in cubes or strips. Reheat two cups meat in two cups sauce, — sauce made of one-fourth cup each of butter and flour, one cup White Stock, and one cup of milk which has been scalded with two blades of mace. Season with salt and pepper, and add one tablespoon Mushroom Catsup, or any other suitable table sauce. Garnish with large croutons, serve around green peas, or in a potato border, sprinkled with finely chopped parsley.

Salmi of Lamb.

Cut cold roast lamb in thin slices. Cook five minutes two tablespoons butter with one-half tablespoon finely chopped onion. Add lamb, sprinkle with salt and pepper, and cover with one cup Brown Sauce, or one cup cold lamb gravy seasoned with Worcestershire, Harvey, or Elizabeth Sauce. Cook until thoroughly heated. Arrange slices overlapping one another lengthwise of platter, pour around sauce, and garnish with toast points. A few sliced mushrooms or stoned olives improve this sauce.

Casserole of Rice and Meat.

Line a mould, slightly greased, with steamed rice. Fill the centre with two cups cold, finely chopped, cooked mutton, highly seasoned with salt, pepper, cayenne, celery salt, onion juice, and lemon juice; then add one-fourth cup cracker crumbs, one egg slightly beaten, and enough hot stock or water to moisten. Cover meat with rice, cover rice with buttered paper to keep out moisture while steaming, and steam forty-five minutes. Serve on a platter surrounded with Tomato Sauce. Veal may be used in place of mutton.

Breast of Lamb.

Wipe a breast of lamb, put in kettle with bouquet of sweet herbs, a small onion stuck with six cloves, one-half tablespoon salt, one-half teaspoon peppercorns, and one-fourth cup each carrot and turnip cut in dice. Cover with boiling water, and simmer until bones will slip out easily. Take meat from water, remove bones, and press under weight. When cool, trim in shape, dip in crumbs, egg, and crumbs, fry in deep fat, and drain. Serve with Spanish Sauce. Small pieces of cold lamb may be sprinkled with salt and pepper, dipped in crumbs, egg, and crumbs, and fried in deep fat.

CHAPTER XIV.

VEAL.

VEAL is the meat obtained from a young calf killed when six to eight weeks old. Veal from a younger animal is very unwholesome, and is liable to provoke serious gastric disturbances. Veal contains a much smaller percentage of fat than beef or mutton, is less nutritious and (though from a young creature) more difficult of digestion. Like lamb, it is not improved by long hang-

1. Saddle of Mutton.   2. Pork for Larding.
3. Leg of Veal from which Cutlets are cut.

ing, but should be soon eaten after killing and dressing. It should always be remembered that the flesh of young animals does not keep fresh as long as that of older ones. Veal is divided in same manner as lamb, into fore and hind quarters. The fore-quarter is subdivided into breast, shoulder, and neck; the hind-quarter into loin, leg, and knuckle. Cutlets, fillets (cushion), and fricandeau are cut from the thick part of leg.

Good veal may be known by its pinkish-colored flesh and white fat; when the flesh lacks color, it has been taken from a creature which was too young to kill for

food, or, if of the right age, was bled before killing.
Veal may be obtained throughout the year, but is in
season during the spring. Veal should be thoroughly
cooked; being deficient in fat and having but little flavor,
pork or butter should be added while cooking, and more
seasoning is required than for other meats.

Veal Cutlets.

Use slices of veal from leg cut one-half inch thick.
Wipe, remove bone and skin, then cut in pieces for serving. The long, irregular-shaped pieces may be rolled, and
fastened with small wooden skewers. Sprinkle with salt
and pepper; dip in flour, egg, and crumbs; fry slowly,
until well browned, in salt pork fat or butter; then
remove cutlets to stewpan and pour over one and one-
half cups Brown Sauce. Place on back of range and
cook slowly forty minutes, or until cutlets are tender.
Arrange on hot platter, strain sauce and pour around
cutlets, and garnish with parsley.

Brown Sauce. Brown three tablespoons butter, add
three tablespoons flour, and stir until well browned. Add
gradually one and one-half cups stock or water, or half
stock and half stewed and strained tomatoes. Season
with salt, pepper, lemon juice, and Worcestershire Sauce.
The trimmings from veal (including skin and bones) may
be covered with one and one-half cups cold water, allowed to heat slowly to boiling point, then cooked,
strained, and used for sauce.

Fricassee of Veal.

Wipe two pounds sliced veal, cut from loin, and cover
with boiling water; add one small onion, two stalks celery,
and six slices carrot. Cook slowly until meat is tender.
Remove meat, sprinkle with salt and pepper, dredge with
flour, and sauté in pork fat. Strain liquor and use in
making a Brown Sauce to pour around veal; there should
be two cups of the sauce.

Loin of Veal à la Jardinière.

Wipe four pounds loin of veal, sprinkle with salt and pepper, and dredge with flour. Put one-fourth cup butter in deep stewpan; when melted, add veal and brown entire surface of meat, watching carefully and turning often, that it may not burn. Add one cup hot water, cover closely, and cook slowly two hours, or until meat is tender, adding more water as needed, using in all about three cups. Remove meat, thicken stock remaining in pan with flour diluted with enough cold water to pour easily. Surround the meat with two cups each boiled turnips and carrots, cut in half-inch cubes, and potatoes cut in balls. Serve gravy in a tureen.

Braised Shoulder of Veal.

Bone, stuff, and sew in shape five pounds shoulder of veal; then cook as Braised Beef, adding with vegetables two sprigs thyme and one of marjoram.

Roast Veal.

The leg, cushion (thickest part of leg), and loin, are suitable pieces for roasting. When leg is to be used, it should be boned at market. Wipe meat, sprinkle with salt and pepper, stuff, and sew in shape. Place on rack in dripping-pan, dredge meat and bottom of pan with flour, and place around meat strips of fat salt pork. Bake three or four hours in moderate oven, basting every fifteen minutes with one-third cup butter, melted in one-half cup boiling water, until used, then baste with fat in pan. Serve with brown gravy.

Fricandeau of Veal.

Lard a cushion of veal and roast or braise.

India Curry.

Wipe a slice of veal one-half inch thick, weighing one and one-half pounds, and cook in frying-pan without butter, quickly searing one side, then the other. Place on a board and cut in one and one-half inch pieces. Fry two sliced onions in one-half cup butter until brown, remove onions, and add to the butter, meat, and one-half tablespoon curry powder, then cover with boiling water. Cook slowly until meat is tender. Thicken with flour diluted with enough cold water to pour easily; then add one teaspoon vinegar. Serve with a border of steamed rice.

Veal Birds.

Wipe slices of veal from leg, cut as thinly as possible, then remove bone, skin, and fat. Pound until one-fourth inch thick and cut in pieces two and one-half inches long by one and one-half inches wide, each piece making a bird. Chop trimmings of meat, adding for every three birds a piece of fat salt pork cut one inch square and one-fourth inch thick; pork also to be chopped. Add to trimmings and pork one-half their measure of fine cracker crumbs, and season highly with salt, pepper, cayenne, poultry seasoning, lemon juice, and onion juice. Moisten with beaten egg and hot water or stock. Spread each piece with thin layer of mixture and avoid having mixture come close to edge. Roll, and fasten with skewers. Sprinkle with salt and pepper, dredge with flour, and fry in hot butter until a golden brown. Put in stewpan, add cream to half cover meat, cook slowly twenty minutes or until tender. Serve on small pieces of toast, straining cream remaining in pan over birds and toast, and garnish with parsley. A Thin White Sauce in place of cream may be served around birds.

Veal Loaf I.

Separate a knuckle of veal in pieces by sawing through bone. Wipe, put in kettle with one pound lean veal and one onion; cover with boiling water and cook slowly until veal is tender. Drain and chop finely meat, season highly with salt and pepper. Garnish bottom of a mould with slices of hard boiled eggs and parsley. Put in layer of meat, layer of thinly sliced hard boiled eggs, sprinkle with finely chopped parsley, and cover with remaining meat. Pour over liquor, which should be reduced to one cupful. Press and chill, turn on a dish, and garnish with parsley.

Veal Loaf II.

Wipe three pounds lean veal, and remove skin and membrane. Chop finely or force through meat chopper, then add two slices fat salt pork cut one-fourth inch thick (also finely chopped), six common crackers (rolled), one-fourth cup melted butter, and one egg slightly beaten. Season highly with salt, pepper, and sage. Pack in a small bread pan, smooth evenly on top, and bake slowly three hours. Cool before turning from pan. Cut in thin slices for serving.

WAYS OF WARMING OVER VEAL.

Minced Veal on Toast.

Prepare as Minced Lamb on Toast, using veal in place of lamb.

Blanquette of Veal.

Reheat two cups cold roast veal, cut in small strips, in one and one-half cups White Sauce I. Serve in a potato border and sprinkle over all finely chopped parsley.

Ragoût of Veal.

Reheat two cups cold roast veal, cut in cubes, in one and one-half cups Brown Sauce seasoned with one teaspoon Worcestershire Sauce, few drops of onion juice, and a few grains of cayenne.

CHAPTER XV.

SWEETBREADS.

A SWEETBREAD is the thymus gland of lamb or calf, but in cookery, veal sweetbreads only are considered. It is prenatally developed, of unknown function, and as soon as calf is taken from liquid food it gradually disappears. Pancreas, stomach sweetbread, is sold in some sections of the country, but in our markets this custom is not practised. Sweetbreads are a reputed table delicacy, and a valuable addition to the menu of the convalescent.

A sweetbread consists of two parts, connected by tubing and membranes. The round, compact part is called the heart sweetbread, as its position is nearer the heart; the other part is called the throat sweetbread. When sweetbread is found in market separated, avoid buying two of the throat sweetbreads, as the heart sweetbread is more desirable.

Sweetbreads spoil very quickly. They should be removed from paper as soon as received from market, plunged into cold water and allowed to stand one hour, drained, and put into acidulated, salted boiling water, then allowed to cook slowly twenty minutes; again drained, and plunged into cold water, that they may be kept white and firm. Sweetbreads are always parboiled in this manner for subsequent cooking.

Broiled Sweetbread.

Parboil a sweetbread, split cross-wise, sprinkle with salt and pepper, and broil five minutes. Serve with Lemon Butter.

Creamed Sweetbread.

Parboil a sweetbread, and cut in one-half inch cubes, or separate in small pieces. Reheat in one cup White Sauce II. Creamed Sweetbread may be served on toast, or used as filling for patty cases or Swedish Timbales.

Creamed Sweetbread and Chicken.

Reheat equal parts of cold cooked chicken, and sweetbread cut in dice, in White Sauce II.

Sweetbread à la Poulette.

Reheat sweetbread, cut in cubes, in one cup Béchamel Sauce.

Larded Sweetbread.

Parboil a sweetbread, lard the upper side, and bake until well browned, basting with Meat Glaze.

Sweetbread Cutlets with Asparagus Tips.

Parboil a sweetbread, split, and cut in pieces shaped like a small cutlet, or cut in circular pieces. Sprinkle with salt and pepper, dip in crumbs, egg, and crumbs, and sauté in butter. Arrange in a circle around Creamed Asparagus Tips.

Sweetbread with Tomato Sauce.

Prepare as Sweetbread Cutlets with Asparagus Tips, sauté in butter or fry in deep fat, and serve with Tomato Sauce.

Sweetbread and Bacon.

Parboil a sweetbread, cut in small pieces, dip in flour, egg, and crumbs, and arrange alternately with pieces of bacon on small skewers, having four pieces sweetbread and three of bacon on each skewer. Fry in deep fat, and drain. Arrange in a circle around mound of green peas.

CHAPTER XVI.

PORK.

PORK is the flesh and fat of pig or hog. Different parts of the creature, when dressed, take different names.

The chine and spareribs, which correspond to the loin in lamb and veal, are used for roasts or steaks. Two ribs are left on the chine. The hind legs furnish *hams*. These are cured, salted, and smoked. Sugar-cured hams are considered the best. Pickle, to which is added light brown sugar, molasses, and saltpetre, is introduced close to bone; hams are allowed to hang one week, then smoked with hickory wood. *Shoulders* are usually corned, or salted and smoked, though sometimes cooked fresh. *Pigs' feet* are boiled until tender, split, and covered with vinegar made from white wine. *Hocks*, the part just above the feet, are corned, and much used by Germans. *Heads* are soused, and cooked by boiling. The flank, which lies just below the ribs, is salted and smoked, and furnishes *bacon*. The best pieces of fat salt pork come from the back, on either side of backbone.

Fat, when separated from flesh and membrane, is tried out and called lard. *Leaf-lard* is the best, and is tried out from the leaf-shaped pieces of solid fat which lie inside the flank. *Sausages* are trimmings of lean and fat meat, minced, highly seasoned, and forced into thin casings made of the prepared entrails. *Little pigs* (four weeks old) are sometimes killed, dressed, and roasted whole.

Pork contains the largest percentage of fat of any meat. When eaten fresh it is the most difficult of digestion, and although found in market through the entire year, it should be but seldom served, and then only during the winter months. By curing, salting, and smoking, pork is rendered more wholesome. *Bacon*, next to butter and cream, is the most easily assimilated of all fatty foods.

Pork Chops.

Wipe chops, sprinkle with salt and pepper, place in a hot frying-pan, and cook slowly until tender, and well browned on each side.

Pork Chops with Fried Apples.

Arrange Pork Chops on a platter, and surround with slices of apples, cut one-half inch thick, fried in the fat remaining in pan.

Roast Pork.

Wipe pork, sprinkle with salt and pepper, place on a rack in a dripping-pan, and dredge meat and bottom of pan with flour. Bake in a moderate oven three or four hours, basting every fifteen minutes with fat in pan. Make a gravy as for other roasts.

Pork Tenderloins with Sweet Potatoes.

Wipe tenderloins, put in a dripping-pan, and brown quickly in a hot oven; then sprinkle with salt, pepper, and powdered sage, and bake forty-five minutes, basting every fifteen minutes.

Sweet Potatoes. Pare six potatoes and parboil ten minutes, drain, put in pan with meat, and cook until soft, basting when basting meat.

Breakfast Bacon.

See Liver and Bacon, page 185.

Fried Salt Pork with Codfish.

Cut fat salt pork in one-fourth inch slices, cut gashes one-third inch apart in slices, nearly to rind. Try out in a hot frying-pan until brown and crisp, occasionally turning off fat from pan. Serve around strips of codfish which have been soaked in pan of lukewarm water and allowed to stand on back of range until soft. Serve with Drawn Butter Sauce, boiled potatoes, and beets.

Broiled Ham.

Soak thin slices of ham one hour in lukewarm water. Drain, wipe, and broil three minutes.

Fried Ham and Eggs.

Wipe ham, remove one-half outside layer of fat, and place in frying-pan. Cover with tepid water and let stand on back of range thirty minutes; drain, and dry on a towel. Heat pan, put in ham, brown quickly on one side, turn and brown other side: or soak ham over night, dry, and cook in hot frying-pan. If cooked too long, ham will become hard and dry. Serve with fried eggs cooked in the tried-out ham fat.

Boiled Ham.

Soak several hours or over night in cold water to cover. Wash thoroughly, trim off ha·d skin near end of bone, put in a kettle, cover with cold water, heat to boiling point, and cook slowly until tender. See Time Table for Cooking, page 32. Remove kettle from range and set aside, that ham may partially cool; then take from water, remove outside skin, sprinkle with sugar and fine cracker crumbs, and stick with cloves one-half inch apart. Bake one hour in a slow oven. Serve cold, thinly sliced.

Roast Ham with Champagne Sauce.

Place a whole baked ham in the oven fifteen minutes before serving time, that outside fat may be heated. Remove to a hot platter, garnish bone end with a paper ruffle, and serve with Champagne Sauce.

Westphalian Ham.

These hams are imported from Germany, and need no additional cooking. Cut in very thin slices for serving.

Broiled Pigs' Feet.

Wipe, sprinkle with salt and pepper, and broil six to eight minutes. Serve with Maître d'Hôtel Butter or Sauce Piquante.

Fried Pigs' Feet.

Wipe, sprinkle with salt and pepper, dip in crumbs, egg, and crumbs, fry in deep fat, and drain.

Sausages.

Cut apart a string of sausages. Pierce each sausage several times with a carving fork. Put in frying-pan, cover with boiling water, and cook fifteen minutes; drain, return to frying-pan, and fry until well browned. Serve with fried apples. Sausages are often broiled.

Boston Baked Beans.

Pick over one quart pea beans, cover with cold water, and soak over night. In morning, drain, cover with fresh water, heat slowly (keeping water below boiling point), and cook until skins will burst, — which is best determined by taking a few beans on the tip of a spoon and blowing on them, when skins will burst if sufficiently cooked. Beans thus tested must, of course, be thrown away. Drain beans, throwing bean-water out of doors, not in sink.

Scald rind of one-half pound fat salt pork, scrape, remove one-fourth inch slice and put in bottom of bean-pot.   Cut through rind of remaining pork every one-half inch, making cuts one inch deep.   Put beans in pot and bury pork in beans, leaving rind exposed.   Mix one tablespoon salt, one tablespoon molasses, and three tablespoons sugar; add one cup boiling water, and pour over beans; then add enough more boiling water to cover beans. Cover bean-pot, put in oven, and bake slowly six or eight hours, uncovering the last hour of cooking, that rind may become brown and crisp.   Add water as needed. Many feel sure that by adding with seasonings one-half tablespoon mustard, the beans are more easily digested. If pork mixed with lean is preferred, use less salt.

The fine reputation which Boston Baked Beans have gained, has been attributed to the earthen bean-pot with small top and bulging sides in which they are supposed to be cooked.   Equally good beans have often been eaten where a five-pound lard pail was substituted for the broken bean-pot.

Yellow-eyed beans are very good when baked.

CHAPTER XVII.

POULTRY AND GAME.

POULTRY includes all domestic birds suitable for food except pigeon and squab. Examples: Chicken, fowl, turkey, duck, goose, etc. Game includes such birds and animals suitable for food as are pursued and taken in field and forest. Examples: Quail, partridge, wild duck, plover, deer, etc.

The flesh of chicken, fowl, and turkey has much shorter fibre than that of ruminating animals, and is not intermingled with fat, — the fat always being found in layers directly under the skin, and surrounding the intestines. Chicken, fowl, and turkey are nutritious, and chicken is specially easy of digestion. The white meat found on breast and wing is more readily digested than the dark meat. The legs, on account of constant motion, are of a coarser fibre and darker color.

Since incubators have been so much used for hatching chickens, small birds suitable for broiling may be always found in market. Chickens which appear in market during January weighing about one and one-half pounds are called *spring chickens*.

Fowl is found in market throughout the year, but is at its best from March until June.

Philadelphia, until recently, furnished our market with Philadelphia chickens and *capons*, but now Massachusetts furnishes equally good ones, which are found in market from December to June. They are very large, plump, and superior eating. At an early age they are deprived of the organs of reproduction, penned, and specially fatted for killing. They are recognized by the presence of head, tail, and wing feathers.

Turkeys are found in market throughout the year, but are best during the winter months. Tame ducks and geese are very indigestible on account of the large quantity of fat they contain. Goose meat is thoroughly infiltrated with fat, containing sometimes from forty to forty-five per cent. Pigeons, being old birds, need long, slow cooking to make them tender. Squabs (young pigeons) make a delicious tidbit for the convalescent, and are often the first meat allowed a patient by the physician.

The flesh of game, with the exception of wild duck and wild geese, is tender, contains less fat than poultry, is of fine though strong flavor, and easy of digestion. Game meat is usually of dark color, partridge and quail being exceptions, and is usually cooked rare. Venison, the flesh of deer, is short fibred, dark colored, highly savored, tender, and easy of digestion; being highly savored, it often disagrees with those of weak digestion.

Geese are in market throughout the year, Massachusetts and Rhode Island furnishing specially good ones. A goose twelve weeks old is known as a *green goose*. They may be found in market from May to September. Young geese which appear in market September first and continue through December are called *goslings*. They have been hatched during May and June, and then fatted for market.

Young ducks, found in market about March first, are called *ducklings*. Canvasback Ducks have gained a fine reputation throughout the country, and are found in market from the last of November until March. Redhead Ducks are in season two weeks earlier, and are about as good eating as Canvasback Ducks, and much less in price. The distinctive flavor of both is due to the wild celery on which they feed. Many other kinds of ducks are found in market during the fall and winter. Examples: Widgeon, Mallard, Lake Erie Teal, Black Ducks, and Butterballs.

Fresh quail are in market from October fifteenth to January first, the law forbidding their being killed at any other time in the year. The same is true of partridge; but both are frozen and kept in cold storage several months. California sends frozen quail in large numbers to Eastern markets. Grouse (*prairie chicken*) are always obtainable, — fresh ones in the fall; later, those kept in cold storage. Plover may be bought from April until December.

To Select Poultry and Game. *A chicken* is known by soft feet, smooth skin, and soft cartilage at end of breastbone. An abundance of pinfeathers always indicates a young bird, while the presence of long hairs denotes age. In a *fowl* the feet have become hard and dry with coarse scales, and cartilage at end of breastbone has ossified. *Cock turkeys* are usually better eating than hen turkeys, unless hen turkey is young, small, and plump. A good turkey should be plump, have smooth dark legs, and cartilage at end of breastbone soft and pliable. Good geese abound in pinfeathers. Small birds should be plump, have soft feet and pliable bills.

To Dress and Clean Poultry. Remove hairs and down by holding the bird over a flame (from gas, alcohol, or burning paper) and constantly changing position until all parts of surface have been exposed to flame; this is known as *singeing.* Cut off the head and draw out pinfeathers, using a small pointed knife. Cut through the skin around the leg one and one-half inches below the leg joint, care being taken not to cut tendons; place leg at this cut over edge of board, press downward to snap the bone, then take foot in right hand, holding bird firmly in left hand, and pull off foot, and with it the tendons. In old birds the tendons must be drawn separately, which is best accomplished by using a steel skewer. Make an incision through skin below breastbone, just large enough to admit the hand. With the hand remove entrails, gizzard, heart, and liver; the last three named constitute what is known as *giblets.* The gall bladder, lying on the under surface of the right lobe of the liver, is removed with liver, and great care must be taken that it is not broken, as a small quantity of the bile which it contains would impart a bitter flavor to the parts with which it came in contact. Enclosed by the ribs, on either side of backbone, may be found the lungs, of spongy consistency and red color. Care must be taken that every part of them is removed. Kidneys, lying in the hollow near end of backbone, must also be removed. By introducing first two fingers under skin close to neck, the windpipe may be easily found and withdrawn; also the crop, which will be found adhering to skin close to breast. Draw down neck skin, and cut off neck close to body, leaving skin long enough to fasten under the back. Remove oil bag, and wash bird by allowing cold water to run through it, not allowing bird to soak in cold water. Wipe inside and outside, looking carefully to see that everything has been withdrawn. If there is disagreeable odor, suggesting that fowl may have been kept too long, clean at once, wash inside and out with soda water, and sprinkle inside with charcoal and place some under wings.

Poultry dressed at market seldom have tendons removed unless so ordered. It is always desirable to have them withdrawn, as they become hard and bony during cooking. It is the practice of market-men to cut a gash through the skin, to easier reach crop and windpipe. This gash must be sewed before stuffing, and causes the bird to look less attractive when cooked.

To Cut up a Fowl. Singe, draw out pinfeathers, cut off head, remove tendons and oil bag. Cut through skin between leg and body close to body, bend back leg (thus breaking ligaments), cut through flesh, and separate at joint. Separate the upper part of leg, *second joint*, from lower part of leg, *drumstick*, as leg is separated from body. Remove wing by cutting through skin and flesh around upper wing joint which lies next to body, then disjoint from body. Cut off tip of wing and separate wing at middle joint. Remove leg and wing from other side.

Separate breast from back by cutting through skin, beginning two inches below breastbone and passing knife between terminus of small ribs on either side and extending cut to collar-bone. Before removing entrails, gizzard, heart, liver, lungs, kidneys, crop, and windpipe, observe their position, that the anatomy of the bird may be understood. The back is sometimes divided by cutting through the middle crosswise. The wishbone, with adjoining meat, is frequently removed, and the breast meat may be separated in two parts by cutting through flesh close to breastbone with cleaver. Wipe pieces, excepting back, with cheese cloth wrung out of cold water. Back piece needs thorough washing.

To Clean Giblets. Remove thin membrane, arteries, veins, and clotted blood around heart. Separate gall bladder from liver, cutting off any of liver that may have a greenish tinge. Cut fat and membranes from gizzard. Make a gash through thickest part of gizzard, and cut as far as inner lining, being careful not to pierce it. Remove the inner sack and discard. Wash giblets and cook until tender, with neck and tips of wings, putting them in cold water and heating water quickly that some of the flavor may be drawn out into stock, which is to be used for making gravy.

To Stuff Poultry. Put stuffing by spoonfuls in neck end, using enough to sufficiently fill the skin, that bird may look plump when served. Where cracker stuffing is used, allowance must be made for the swelling of crackers, otherwise skin may burst during cooking. Put remaining stuffing in body; if body is full, sew skin; if not full, bring skin together with a skewer.

To Truss Fowl. Draw thighs close to body and hold by inserting a steel skewer under middle joint, running it through body, coming out under middle joint on other side. Cut piece three-fourths inch wide from neck skin, and with it fasten legs together at ends; or cross drumsticks, tie securely with a long string, and fasten to tail. Place wings close to body and hold them by inserting a

second skewer through wing, body, and wing on opposite side.   Draw neck skin under back and fasten with a
small wooden skewer.   Turn bird on its breast.   Cross
string attached to tail piece and draw it around each end
of lower skewer, again cross string and draw around each
end of upper skewer; fasten string in a knot and cut off
ends.   In birds that are not stuffed, legs are often passed
through incisions cut in body under bones near tail.

Stuffed and Trussed Chicken.

To Dress Birds for Broiling.   Singe, wipe, and with a
sharp-pointed knife, beginning at back of neck, make a
cut through backbone the entire length of bird.   Lay
open the bird and remove contents from inside.   Cut out
rib bones on either side of backbone, remove breastbone,
then cut through tendons at joints.

To Fillet a Chicken.   Remove skin from breast, and with
a small sharp knife begin at end of collar-bone and cut
through flesh, following close to wish and breastbones
the entire length of meat.   Raise flesh with fingers, and
with knife free the piece of meat from bones which lie
under it.   Cut meat away from wing joint; this solid
piece of breast is meat known as a *fillet*.   This meat is

easily separated in two parts. The upper, larger part is called the *large fillet;* the lower part, the *mignon fillet.* The tough skin on the outside of large fillet should be removed, also the sinew from mignon fillet. To remove tough skin, place large fillet on a board, upper side down, make an incision through flesh at top of fillet, and cut entire length of fillet, holding knife as close to skin as possible. Trim edges, that fillet may look shapely.

Broiled Chicken.

Dress for broiling, following directions on page 218. Sprinkle with salt and pepper, and place in a well-greased broiler. Broil twenty minutes over a clear fire, watching carefully and turning broiler so that all parts may be equally browned. The flesh side must be exposed to the fire the greater part of time, as the skin side will brown quickly. Remove to a hot platter, spread with soft butter, and sprinkle with salt and pepper. Chickens are so apt to burn while broiling that many prefer to partially cook in oven. Place chicken in dripping-pan, skin side down, sprinkle with salt and pepper, dot over with butter, and bake fifteen minutes in hot oven; then broil to finish cooking.

Boiled Fowl.

Dress, clean, and truss a four-pound fowl; tie in a piece of cheese cloth, — otherwise scum will settle on skin and discolor it. Place on trivet in a kettle, half surround with boiling water, cover, and cook slowly until tender, turning occasionally. Add salt the last hour of cooking. Serve with Egg, Oyster, or Celery Sauce. It is not desirable to stuff a boiled fowl.

Boiled Capon with Cauliflower Sauce.

Prepare and cook a capon same as Boiled Fowl, and serve surrounded with Cauliflower Sauce and garnished with parsley.

Chicken à la Providence.

Prepare and boil a chicken, following recipe for Boiled Fowl. The liquor should be reduced to two cups, and used for making sauce, with two tablespoons each butter and flour cooked together. Add to sauce one-half cup each of cooked carrot (cut in fancy shapes) and green peas, one teaspoon lemon juice, yolks two eggs, salt and pepper. Place chicken on hot platter, surround with sauce, and sprinkle chicken and sauce with one-half table-spoon finely chopped parsley.

Roast Chicken.

Dress, clean, stuff, and truss a chicken. Place on its back on rack in a dripping-pan, rub entire surface with salt, and spread breast and legs with three tablespoons butter, rubbed until creamy and mixed with two table-spoons flour. Dredge bottom of pan with flour. Place in a hot oven, and when flour is well browned, reduce the heat, then baste. Continue basting every ten minutes until chicken is cooked. For basting, use one-fourth cup butter, melted in two-thirds cup boiling water, and after this is gone, use fat in pan, and when necessary to prevent flour burning, add one cup boiling water. During cook-ing, turn chicken frequently, that it may brown evenly. If a thick crust is desired, dredge bird with flour two or three times during cooking. If a glazed surface is pre-ferred, spread bird with butter, omitting flour, and do not dredge during baking. When breast meat is tender, bird is sufficiently cooked. A four pound chicken requires about one and one-half hours.

Stuffing I.

1 cup cracker crumbs.	Salt.
⅓ cup butter.	Pepper.
Powdered sage, summer savory, or marjoram.	⅓ cup boiling water.

Melt butter in water, and pour over crackers, to which seasonings have been added.

Stuffing II.

1 cup cracker crumbs.
¼ cup melted butter.
Sage or Poultry Seasoning.

Salt.
Pepper.
⅔ cup scalded milk.

Make as Stuffing I.

Gravy.

Pour off liquid in pan in which chicken has been roasted. From liquid skim off four tablespoons fat; return fat to pan and brown with four tablespoons flour; add two cups stock in which giblets, neck, and tips of wings have been cooked. Cook five minutes, season with salt and pepper, then strain. The remaining fat may be used, in place of butter, for frying potatoes, or for basting when roasting another chicken.

For **Giblet Gravy**, add to the above, giblets (heart, liver, and gizzard) finely chopped.

Braised Chicken.

Dress, clean, and truss a four-pound fowl. Try out two slices fat salt pork, cut one-fourth inch thick; remove scraps and add to fat five slices carrot cut in small cubes, one-half sliced onion, two sprigs thyme, one sprig parsley, and one bay leaf, then cook ten minutes; add two table-spoons butter, and fry fowl, turning often until surface is well browned. Place on trivet in a deep pan, pour over fat, and add two cups boiling water or chicken stock. Cover, and bake in slow oven until tender, basting often, and adding more water if needed. Serve with a sauce made from stock in pan, first straining and removing the fat.

Chicken Fricassee.

Dress, clean, and cut up a fowl. Put in a kettle, cover with boiling water, and cook slowly until tender, adding salt to water when chicken is about half done. Remove from water, sprinkle with salt and pepper, dredge with flour, and sauté in butter or pork fat. Arrange chicken on pieces of dry toast placed on a hot platter, having wings and second joints opposite each other, breast in centre of platter, and drumsticks crossed just below second joints. Pour around White or Brown Sauce. Reduce stock to two cups, strain, and remove the fat. Melt three table-spoons butter, add four tablespoons flour, and pour on gradually one and one-half cups stock. Just before serv-ing, add one-half cup cream, and salt and pepper to taste; or make a sauce by browning butter and flour and adding two cups stock, then seasoning with salt and pepper.

Fowls, which are always made tender by long cooking, are frequently utilized in this way. If chickens are em-ployed, they are sautéd without previous boiling, and al-lowed to simmer fifteen to twenty minutes in the sauce.

Fried Chicken.

Fried chicken is prepared as Chicken Fricassee, with Brown Sauce, chicken always being used, never fowl.

Maryland Chicken.

Dress, clean, and cut up two chickens. Sprinkle with salt and pepper, dip in flour, egg, and crumbs, place in a well-greased dripping-pan, and bake twenty minutes in a hot oven, basting after first five minutes of cooking with one-third cup melted butter. Arrange on platter and pour over two cups Cream Sauce.

Chicken à la Merango.

Dress, clean, and cut up a chicken. Sprinkle with salt and pepper, dredge with flour, and sauté in salt pork fat. Put in a stewpan, cover with sauce, and cook slowly until chicken is tender. Add one-half can mushrooms cut in quarters, and cook five minutes. Arrange chicken on serving dish and pour around sauce; garnish with parsley.

Sauce.

¼ cup butter.
1 tablespoon finely chopped onion.
1 slice carrot, cut in cubes.
1 slice turnip, cut in cubes.
¼ cup flour.

2 cups boiling water.
½ cup stewed and strained tomato.
1 teaspoon salt.
⅛ teaspoon pepper.
Few grains cayenne.

Cook butter five minutes with vegetables. Add flour, with salt, pepper, and cayenne, and cook until flour is well browned. Add gradually water and tomato; cook five minutes, then strain.

Baked Chicken.

Dress, clean, and cut up two chickens. Place in a dripping-pan, sprinkle with salt and pepper, dredge with flour, and dot over with one-fourth cup butter. Bake thirty minutes in a hot oven, basting every five minutes with one-fourth cup butter melted in one-fourth cup boiling water. Serve with gravy made by using fat in pan, one-fourth cup flour, one cup each chicken stock and cream, salt and pepper.

Chicken Gumbo.

Dress, clean, and cut up a chicken. Sprinkle with salt and pepper, dredge with flour, and sauté in pork fat. Fry one-half finely chopped onion in fat remaining in frying-pan. Add four cups sliced okra, sprig of parsley, and one-fourth red pepper finely chopped, and cook slowly fifteen minutes. Add to chicken, with one and one-half cups tomato, three cups boiling water and one and one-half teaspoons salt. Cook slowly until chicken is tender, then add one cup boiled rice.

Chicken Stew.

Dress, clean, and cut up a fowl. Put in a stewpan, cover with boiling water, and cook slowly until tender, adding one-half tablespoon salt and one-eighth teaspoon pepper when fowl is about half cooked. Thicken stock with one-third cup flour diluted with enough cold water to pour easily. Serve with Dumplings. If desired richer, butter may be added.

Chicken Pie.

Dress, clean, and cut up two fowls or chickens. Put in a stewpan with one-half onion, sprig of parsley, and bit of bay leaf; cover with boiling water, and cook slowly until tender. When chicken is half cooked, add one-half tablespoon salt and one-eighth teaspoon pepper. Remove chicken, strain stock, skim off fat, and then cook until reduced to four cups. Thicken stock with one-third cup flour diluted with enough cold water to pour easily. Place a small cup in centre of baking-dish, arrange around it pieces of chicken, removing some of the larger bones; pour over gravy, and cool. Cover with pie crust, in which several incisions have been made that there may be an outlet for escape of steam and gases. Wet edge of crust and put around a rim, having rim come close to edge. Bake in a moderate oven until crust is well risen and browned. Roll remnants of pastry and cut in diamond-shaped pieces, bake, and serve with pie when reheated. If puff paste is used, it is best to bake top separately.

Chicken Curry.

3 lb. chicken.

⅓ cup butter.

2 onions.

1 tablespoon curry powder.

2 teaspoons salt.

1 teaspoon vinegar.

Clean, dress, and cut chicken in pieces for serving. Put butter in a hot frying-pan, add chicken, and cook ten minutes; then add liver and gizzard and cook ten minutes longer. Cut onions in thin slices, and add to chicken with curry powder and salt. Add enough boiling water to cover, and simmer until chicken is tender. Remove chicken; strain and thicken liquor with flour diluted with enough cold water to pour easily. Pour gravy over chicken, and serve with a border of rice or Turkish Pilaf.

Jellied Chicken.

Dress, clean, and cut up a four-pound fowl. Put in a stewpan with two slices onion, cover with boiling water, and cook slowly until meat falls from bones. When half cooked, add one-half tablespoon salt. Remove chicken; reduce stock to three-fourths cup, strain, and skim off fat. Decorate bottom of a mould with parsley and slices of hard boiled eggs. Pack in meat freed from skin and bone and sprinkled with salt and pepper. Pour on stock and place mould under heavy weight. Keep in a cold place until firm. In summer it is necessary to add one teaspoon dissolved granulated gelatine to stock.

Chickens' Livers with Madeira Sauce.

Clean and separate livers, sprinkle with salt and pepper, dredge with flour, and sauté in butter. Brown two tablespoons butter, add two and one-half tablespoons flour, and when well browned add gradually one cup Brown Stock; then add two tablespoons Madeira wine, and reheat livers in sauce.

Chickens' Livers with Bacon.

Clean livers and cut each liver in six pieces. Wrap a thin slice of bacon around each piece and fasten with a small skewer. Put in a broiler, place over a dripping-pan, and bake in a hot oven until bacon is crisp, turning once during cooking.

Sautéd Chickens' Livers.

Cut one slice bacon in small pieces and cook five minutes with two tablespoons butter. Remove bacon, add one finely chopped shallot, and fry two minutes; then add six chickens' livers cleaned and separated, and cook two minutes.   Add two tablespoons flour, one cup Brown Stock, one teaspoon lemon juice, and one-fourth cup sliced mushrooms.   Cook two minutes, turn into a serving dish, and sprinkle with finely chopped parsley.

Chickens' Livers with Curry.

Clean and separate livers.   Dip in seasoned crumbs, egg, and crumbs, and sauté in butter.   Remove livers, and to fat in pan add two tablespoons butter, one-half table-spoon finely chopped onion, and cook five minutes.   Add two tablespoons flour mixed with one-half teaspoon curry powder and one cup stock.   Strain sauce over livers, and serve around livers Rice Timbales.

Boiled Turkey.

Prepare and cook same as Boiled Fowl.   Serve with Oyster or Celery Sauce.

Roast Turkey.

Dress, clean, stuff, and truss a ten-pound turkey, see pages 215–217.   Place on its side on rack in a dripping-pan, rub entire surface with salt, and spread breast, legs, and wings with one-third cup butter, rubbed until creamy and mixed with one-fourth cup flour.   Dredge bottom of pan with flour.   Place in a hot oven, and when flour on turkey begins to brown, reduce heat, baste with fat in pan, and add two cups boiling water.   Continue basting every fifteen minutes until turkey is cooked, which will require about three hours.   For basting, use one-half cup butter melted in one-half cup boiling water, and after this is used baste with fat in pan.   During cooking turn turkey fre-quently, that it may brown evenly.   If turkey is brown-ing too fast, cover with buttered paper to prevent burning. Remove string and skewers before serving.   Garnish with parsley or celery tips.

For stuffing, use double the quantities given in recipes under Roast Chicken. If stuffing is to be served cold, add one beaten egg. Turkey is often roasted with Chestnut Stuffing.

Chestnut Stuffing.

3 cups French chestnuts.	⅛ teaspoon pepper.
½ cup butter.	¼ cup cream.
1 teaspoon salt.	1 cup cracker crumbs.

Shell and blanch chestnuts. Cook in boiling salted water until soft. Drain and mash, using a potato ricer. Add one-half the butter, salt, pepper, and cream. Melt remaining butter, mix with cracker crumbs, then combine mixtures.

Gravy.

Pour off liquid in pan in which turkey has been roasted. From liquid skim off six tablespoons fat; return fat to pan and brown with six tablespoons flour; pour on gradually three cups stock in which giblets, neck, and tips of wings have been cooked, or use liquor left in pan. Cook five minutes, season with salt and pepper; strain. For Giblet Gravy add to the above, giblets (heart, liver, and gizzard) finely chopped.

Chestnut Gravy.

To two cups thin Turkey Gravy add three-fourths cup cooked and mashed chestnuts.

To Carve Turkey.

Bird should be placed on back, with legs at right of platter for carving. Introduce carving fork across breastbone, hold firmly in left hand, and with carving knife in right hand cut through skin between leg and body, close to body. With knife pull back leg and disjoint from body. Then cut off wing. Remove leg and wing from other side. Separate second joints from drum-sticks and divide wings

at joints. Carve breast meat in thin crosswise slices.
Under back on either side of backbone may be found
two small, oyster-shaped pieces of dark meat, which are
dainty tidbits. Chicken and fowl are carved in the same
way. For a small family carve but one side of a turkey,
that remainder may be left in better condition for second
serving.

Roast Goose with Potato Stuffing.

Singe, remove pinfeathers, wash and scrub a goose in
hot soapsuds; then draw (which is removing inside contents). Wash in cold water and wipe. Stuff, truss,
sprinkle with salt and pepper, and lay six thin strips fat
salt pork over breast. Place on rack in dripping-pan,
put in hot oven and bake two hours. Baste every
fifteen minutes with fat in pan. Remove pork last half-
hour of cooking. Place on platter, cut string, and remove
string and skewers. Garnish with watercress and bright
red cranberries, and place Potato Apples between pieces
of watercress. Serve with Apple Sauce.

Potato Stuffing.

2 cups hot mashed potato.	⅓ cup butter.
1¼ cups soft stale bread crumbs.	1 egg.
¼ cup finely chopped fat salt pork.	1½ teaspoons salt.
1 finely chopped onion.	1 teaspoon sage.

Add to potato, bread crumbs, butter, egg, salt, and
sage; then add pork and onion.

To Truss a Goose.

A goose, having short legs, is trussed differently from
chicken, fowl, and turkey. After inserting skewers, wind
string twice around one leg bone, then around other leg
bone, having one inch space of string between legs.
Draw legs with both ends of string, close to back, cross
string under back, then fasten around skewers and tie in
a knot.

Roast Wild Duck.

Dress and clean a wild duck and truss as goose. Place on rack in dripping-pan, sprinkle with salt and pepper, and cover breast with two very thin slices fat salt pork. Bake twenty to thirty minutes in a very hot oven, basting every five minutes with fat in pan; cut string and remove string and skewers. Serve with Orange or Olive Sauce. Currant jelly should accompany a duck course. Domestic ducks should always be well cooked, requiring little more than twice the time allowed for wild ducks.

Ducks are sometimes stuffed with apples, pared, cored, and cut in quarters, or three small onions may be put in body of duck to improve flavor. Neither apples nor onions are to be served. If a stuffing to be eaten is desired, cover pieces of dry bread with boiling water; as soon as bread has absorbed water, press out the water; season bread with salt, pepper, melted butter, and finely-chopped onion.

Braised Duck.

Tough ducks are sometimes steamed one hour, and then braised in same manner as chicken.

Broiled Quail.

Follow recipe for Broiling Chicken, allowing eight minutes for cooking. Serve on pieces of toast, and garnish with parsley and thin slices of lemon. Currant jelly or Rice Croquettes with Jelly should accompany this course.

Roast Quail.

Dress, clean, lard, and truss a quail. Bake same as Larded Grouse, allowing fifteen to twenty minutes for cooking.

Larded Grouse.

Clean, remove pinions, and if it be tough the skin covering breast. Lard breast and insert two lardoons in each leg.

Truss, and place on trivet in small shallow pan; rub with salt, brush over with melted butter, dredge with flour, and surround with trimmings of fat salt pork. Bake twenty to twenty-five minutes in a hot oven, basting three times. Arrange on platter, remove string and skewers, pour around Bread Sauce, and sprinkle bird and sauce with coarse browned bread crumbs. Garnish with parsley.

Broiled or Roasted Plover.

Plover is broiled or roasted same as quail.

Potted Pigeons.

Clean, stuff, and truss six pigeons, place upright in a stewpan, and add one quart boiling water in which celery has been cooked. Cover, and cook slowly three hours or until tender; or cook in oven in a covered earthen dish. Remove from water, cool slightly, sprinkle with salt and pepper, dredge with flour, and brown entire surface in pork fat. Make a sauce with one-fourth cup each butter and flour cooked together and stock remaining in pan; there should be two cups. Place each bird on a slice of dry toast, and pour gravy over all. Garnish with parsley.

Stuffing.

1 cup hot riced potatoes.
¼ teaspoon salt.
⅛ teaspoon pepper.
¼ teaspoon marjoram
    or summer savory.
Few drops onion juice.

1 tablespoon butter.
¼ cup soft stale bread
    crumbs soaked in some
    of the celery water and
    wrung in cheese cloth.
Yolk 1 egg.

Mix ingredients in order given.

Broiled Venison Steak.

Follow recipe for Broiled Beefsteak. Serve with Maître d'Hôtel Butter. Venison should always be cooked rare.

Venison Cutlets.

Clean and trim slices of venison cut from loin. Sprinkle with salt and pepper, brush over with melted butter or olive oil, and roll in soft stale bread crumbs. Place in a broiler and broil five minutes, or sauté in butter. Serve with Port Wine Sauce.

Roast Leg of Venison.

Prepare and cook as Roast Lamb, allowing less time that it may be cooked rare.

Saddle of Venison.

Clean and lard a saddle of venison. Cook same as Saddle of Mutton. Serve with Currant Jelly Sauce.

WAYS OF WARMING OVER POULTRY AND GAME.

Creamed Chicken.

1½ cups cold cooked chicken cut in dice.

1 cup White Sauce II.
⅛ teaspoon celery salt.

Heat chicken dice in sauce, to which celery salt has been added.

Creamed Chicken with Mushrooms.

Add to Creamed Chicken one-fourth cup mushrooms cut in slices.

Chicken with Potato Border.

Serve Creamed Chicken in Potato Border.

Chicken in Baskets.

To three cups hot mashed potatoes add three table-spoons butter, one teaspoon salt, yolks of three eggs slightly beaten, and enough milk to moisten. Shape in form of small baskets, using a pastry-bag and tube. Brush over with white of egg slightly beaten, and brown in oven. Fill with Creamed Chicken. Form handles for baskets of parsley.

Chicken and Oysters à la Métropole.

¼ cup butter.
¼ cup flour.
½ teaspoon salt.
⅛ teaspoon pepper.
2 cups cream.

2 cups cold cooked chicken
    cut in dice.
1 pint oysters cleaned and
    drained.
⅓ cup finely chopped celery.

Make a sauce of first five ingredients, add chicken dice and oysters; cook until oysters are plump. Serve sprinkled with celery.

Luncheon Chicken.

1½ cups cold cooked chicken
    cut in small dice.
2 tablespoons butter.
1 slice carrot cut in small cubes.
1 slice onion.
2 tablespoons flour.

1 cup chicken stock.
Salt.
Pepper.
⅔ cup buttered cracker
    crumbs.
4 eggs.

Cook butter five minutes with vegetables, add flour, and gradually the stock. Strain, add chicken dice, and season with salt and pepper. Turn on a slightly buttered platter and sprinkle with cracker crumbs. Make four nests, and in each nest slip an egg; cover eggs with crumbs, and bake in a moderate oven until whites of eggs are firm.

Blanquette of Chicken.

2 cups cold cooked chicken
    cut in strips.
1 cup White Sauce II.

1 tablespoon finely
    chopped parsley.
Yolks 2 eggs.

2 tablespoons milk.

Add chicken to sauce; when well heated, add yolks of eggs slightly beaten, diluted with milk. Cook two minutes, then add parsley.

Scalloped Chicken.

Butter a baking-dish.   Arrange alternate layers of cold cooked sliced chicken and boiled macaroni or rice.   Pour over White, Brown, or Tomato Sauce, cover with buttered cracker crumbs, and bake in a hot oven until crumbs are brown.

Mock Terrapin.

1½ cups cold cooked chicken or veal cut in dice.
1 cup White Sauce I.
Yolks 2 hard boiled eggs finely chopped.

Whites 2 hard boiled eggs, chopped.
3 tablespoons sherry wine.
¼ teaspoon salt.
Few grains cayenne.

Add to sauce, chicken, yolks and whites of eggs, salt, and cayenne; cook two minutes, and add wine.

Chicken Chartreuse.

Prepare and cook same as Casserole of Rice and Meat, using chicken in place of lamb or veal.   Season chicken with salt, pepper, celery salt, onion juice, and one-half teaspoon finely chopped parsley.

Chicken Soufflé.

2 cups scalded milk.
¼ cup butter.
¼ cup flour.
1 teaspoon salt.
⅛ teaspoon pepper.
½ cup stale soft bread crumbs.

2 cups cold cooked chicken finely chopped.
Yolks 3 eggs well beaten.
1 tablespoon finely-chopped parsley.
Whites 3 eggs beaten stiff.

Make a sauce of first five ingredients, add bread crumbs, and cook two minutes; remove from fire, add chicken, yolks of eggs, and parsley, then fold in whites of eggs. Turn in a buttered pudding-dish, and bake thirty-five minutes in a slow oven.   Serve with White Mushroom Sauce. Veal may be used in place of chicken.

Chicken Hollandaise.

1½tablespoons butter. ⅓ cup finely chopped celery.
1 teaspoon finely chopped onion. ¼ teaspoon salt.
2 tablespoons corn-starch. Few grains paprika.
1 cup chicken stock. 1 cup cold cooked chicken,
1 teaspoon lemon juice. cut in small cubes.

Yolk 1 egg.

Cook butter and onion five minutes, add corn-starch and stock gradually. Add lemon juice, celery, salt, paprika, and chicken; when well heated, add yolk of egg slightly beaten, and cook one minute. Serve with buttered Graham toast.

Scalloped Turkey.

Make one cup of sauce, using two tablespoons butter, two tablespoons flour, one-fourth teaspoon salt, few grains of pepper, and one cup stock (obtained by cooking in water bones and skin of a roast turkey). Cut remnants of cold roast turkey in small pieces; there should be one and one-half cups. Sprinkle bottom of buttered baking-dish with seasoned cracker crumbs, add turkey meat, pour over sauce, and sprinkle with buttered cracker crumbs. Bake in a hot oven until crumbs are brown. Turkey, chicken, or veal may be used separately or in combination.

Minced Turkey.

To one cup cold roast turkey, cut in small dice, add one-third cup soft stale bread crumbs. Make one cup sauce, using two tablespoons butter, two tablespoons flour, and one cup stock (obtained by cooking bones and skin of a roast turkey). Season with salt, pepper, and onion juice. Heat turkey and bread crumbs in sauce. Serve on small pieces of toast, and garnish with poached eggs and toast points.

Salmi of Duck.

Cut cold roast duck in pieces for serving.   Reheat in Spanish Sauce.

Spanish Sauce.   Melt one-fourth cup butter, add one tablespoon finely chopped onion, a stalk of celery, two slices carrot cut in pieces, and two tablespoons finely chopped lean raw ham.   Cook until butter is brown, then add one-fourth cup flour, and when well browned add two cups Consommé, bit of bay leaf, sprig of parsley, blade of mace, two cloves, one-half teaspoon salt, and one-eighth teaspoon pepper; cook five minutes.   Strain, add duck, and when reheated add sherry wine, stoned olives, and mushrooms cut in quarters.   Arrange on dish for serving, and garnish with olives and mushrooms. Grouse may be used in place of duck.

CHAPTER XVIII.

FISH AND MEAT SAUCES.

THE French chef keeps always on hand four sauces, — White, Brown, Béchamel, and Tomato, — and with these as a basis is able to make kinds innumerable. Butter and flour are usually cooked together for thickening sauces. When not browned, it is called *roux;* when browned, *brown roux*. The French mix butter and flour together, put in saucepan, place over fire, stir for five minutes; set aside to cool, again place over fire, and add liquid, stirring constantly until thick and smooth. Butter and flour for brown sauces are cooked together much longer, and watched carefully lest butter should burn. The American cook makes sauce by stirring butter in saucepan until melted and bubbling, adds flour and continues stirring, then adds liquid, gradually stirring or beating until the boiling point is reached. For Brown Sauce, butter should be stirred until well browned; flour should be added and stirred with butter until both are browned before the addition of liquid. The secret in making a Brown Sauce is to have butter and flour well browned before adding liquid.

It is well worth remembering that a sauce of average thickness is made by allowing two tablespoons each of butter and flour to one cup liquid, whether it be milk, stock, or tomato. For Brown Sauce a slightly larger quantity of flour is necessary, as by browning flour its thickening property is lessened, its starch being changed to dextrine. When sauces are set away, put a few bits of butter on top to prevent crust from forming.

Thin White Sauce.

2 tablespoons butter.	1 cup scalded milk.
1½ tablespoons flour.	¼ teaspoon salt.

Few grains pepper.

Put butter in saucepan, stir until melted and bubbling; add flour mixed with seasonings, and stir until thoroughly blended. Pour on gradually the milk, adding about one-third at a time, stirring until well mixed, then beating until smooth and glossy. If a wire whisk is used, all the milk may be added at once; and although more quickly made if milk is scalded, it is not necessary.

Cream Sauce.

Make same as Thin White Sauce, using cream instead of milk.

White Sauce I.

2 tablespoons butter.	1 cup milk.
2 tablespoons flour.	¼ teaspoon salt.

Few grains pepper.

Make same as Thin White Sauce.

White Sauce II.

2 tablespoons butter.	1 cup milk.
3 tablespoons flour.	¼ teaspoon salt.

Few grains pepper.

Make same as Thin White Sauce.

Thick White Sauce (for Cutlets and Croquettes).

2½ tablespoons butter.	1 cup milk.
¼ cup corn-starch or	¼ teaspoon salt.
⅓ cup flour.	Few grains pepper.

Make same as Thin White Sauce.

Sauce Allemande.

To two cups Velouté Sauce add one-half tablespoon lemon juice and yolk one egg.

Velouté Sauce.

2 tablespoons butter.	1 cup White Stock.
2 tablespoons flour.	¼ teaspoon salt.
Few grains pepper.	

Make same as Thin White Sauce.

Soubise Sauce.

2 cups sliced onions.	½ cup cream or milk.
1 cup Velouté Sauce.	Salt and pepper.

Cover onions with boiling water, cook five minutes, drain, again cover with boiling water, and cook until soft; drain, and rub through a sieve. Add to sauce with cream. Season with salt and pepper. Serve with mutton or pork chops.

Drawn Butter Sauce.

⅓ cup butter.	1½ cups hot water.
3 tablespoons flour.	½ teaspoon salt.
⅛ teaspoon pepper.	

Melt one-half the butter, add flour with seasonings, and pour on gradually hot water. Boil five minutes, and add remaining butter in small pieces. To be served with boiled or baked fish.

Shrimp Sauce.

To Drawn Butter Sauce add one egg yolk and one-half can shrimps cleaned and cut in pieces.

Caper Sauce.

To Drawn Butter Sauce add one-half cup capers drained from their liquor. Serve with boiled mutton.

Egg Sauce I.

To Drawn Butter Sauce add two hard boiled eggs cut in one-fourth inch slices.

Egg Sauce II.

To Drawn Butter Sauce add beaten yolks of two eggs and one teaspoon lemon juice.

Brown Sauce I.

2 tablespoons butter.	1 cup Brown Stock.
½ slice onion.	¼ teaspoon salt.
2½ tablespoons flour.	⅛ teaspoon pepper.

Cook onion in butter until slightly browned; remove onion and stir butter constantly until well browned; add flour mixed with seasonings, and brown the butter and flour; then add stock gradually.

Brown Sauce II. (Espagnole).

¼ cup butter.	Sprig of parsley.
1 slice carrot.	6 peppercorns.
1 slice onion.	5 tablespoons flour.
Bit of bay leaf.	2 cups Brown Stock.
Sprig of thyme.	Salt and pepper.

Cook butter with carrot, onion, bay leaf, thyme, parsley, and peppercorns, until brown; add flour, and when well browned, add stock gradually, strain, and season with salt and pepper.

Brown Mushroom Sauce I.

To one cup Brown Sauce add one-fourth can mushrooms, drained, rinsed, and cut in quarters or slices.

Brown Mushroom Sauce II.

1 can mushrooms.	¼ cup flour.
¼ cup butter.	2 cups Consommé or Brown
½ tablespoon lemon juice.	Stock.
Salt and pepper.	

Drain and rinse mushrooms and chop finely one-half of same. Cook five minutes with butter and lemon juice; drain, brown the butter, add flour, and when well browned, add gradually Consommé. Cook fifteen minutes, skim, add remaining mushrooms cut in quarters or slices, and cook two minutes. Season with salt and pepper.

Sauce Piquante.

To one cup Brown Sauce add one tablespoon vinegar, one-half small shallot finely chopped, one tablespoon each chopped capers and pickle, and a few grains of cayenne.

Olive Sauce.

Remove stones from ten olives, leaving meat in one piece. Cover with boiling water and cook five minutes. Drain olives, and add to two cups Brown Sauce I. or II.

Orange Sauce.

¼ cup butter.	Few grains cayenne.
¼ cup flour.	Juice 2 oranges.
1⅓ cups Brown Stock.	2 tablespoons sherry wine.
½ teaspoon salt.	Rind of 1 orange cut in fancy shapes.

Brown the butter, add flour, with salt and cayenne, and stir until well browned. Add stock gradually, and just before serving, orange juice, sherry, and pieces of rind.

Sauce à l'Italienne.

Onion,		Sprig marjoram.
Carrot,	2 tablespoons each, finely chopped.	2 tablespoons butter.
Lean raw ham,		2½ tablespoons flour.
12 peppercorns.		1 cup Brown Stock.
2 cloves.		1¼ cups white wine.

½ tablespoon finely chopped parsley.

Cook first six ingredients with butter five minutes, add flour, and stir until well browned; then add gradually stock and wine. Strain, reheat, and after pouring around fish sprinkle with parsley.

Champagne Sauce.

Simmer two cups Espagnole Sauce until reduced to one and one-half cups. Add two tablespoons mushroom liquor, one-half cup champagne, and one tablespoon powdered sugar.

Tomato Sauce I. (without Stock).

½ can tomatoes or
1¾ cups fresh stewed tomatoes.
1 slice onion.

3 tablespoons butter.
2½ tablespoons flour.
¼ teaspoon salt.

⅛ teaspoon pepper.

Cook onion with tomatoes fifteen minutes, rub through a strainer, and add to butter and flour (to which seasonings have been added) cooked together. If tomatoes are very acid, add a few grains of soda.

Tomato Sauce II.

½ can tomatoes.
2 teaspoons sugar.
8 peppercorns.
Bit of bay leaf.

½ teaspoon salt.
4 tablespoons butter.
4 tablespoons flour.
1 cup Brown Stock.

Cook tomatoes twenty minutes with sugar, peppercorns, bay leaf, and salt; rub through a strainer, and add stock. Brown the butter, add flour, and when well browned, gradually add hot liquid.

Tomato Sauce III.

¼ cup butter.
1 slice carrot.
1 slice onion.
Bit of bay leaf.
Sprig of thyme.

Sprig of parsley.
1 cup stewed and strained
tomatoes.
1 cup Brown Stock.
Salt and pepper.

¼ cup flour.

Brown the butter with carrot, onion, bay leaf, thyme, and parsley; remove seasonings, add flour, stir until well browned, then add tomatoes and stock.

Tomato and Mushroom Sauce.

2 slices chopped bacon or
    small quantity uncooked ham.
1 slice onion.
6 slices carrot.
1 bay leaf.
2 sprigs thyme.
Sprig of parsley.

2 cloves.
½ teaspoon peppercorns.
Few gratings nutmeg.
3 tablespoons flour.
½ can tomatoes.
1½ cups Brown Stock.
Salt and pepper.

½ can mushrooms.

French Chef.

Cook bacon, onion, and carrot five minutes; add bay leaf, thyme, parsley, cloves, peppercorns, nutmeg, and tomatoes, and cook five minutes. Add flour diluted with enough cold water to pour; as it thickens, dilute with stock. Cover, and cook in oven one hour. Strain, add salt and pepper to taste, and one-half can mushrooms, drained from their liquor, rinsed, and cut in quarters; then cook two minutes.

Tomato Cream Sauce.

½ can tomatoes.
Sprig of thyme.
1 stalk celery.
1 slice onion.

Bit of bay leaf.
1 cup White Sauce I.
½ teaspoon salt.
Few grains cayenne.

¼ teaspoon soda.

Cook tomatoes twenty minutes with seasonings; rub through a strainer, add soda, then White Sauce. Serve with Baked Fish or Lobster Cutlets.

Spanish Sauce.

2 tablespoons finely chopped
    lean raw ham.
2 tablespoons chopped celery.
2 tablespoons chopped carrot.
1 tablespoon chopped onion.

¼ cup butter.
¼ cup flour.
1⅓ cups Brown Stock.
⅔ cup stewed and strained
    tomatoes.

Salt and pepper.

Cook ham and vegetables with butter until butter is well browned; add flour, stock, and tomatoes; cook five minutes, then strain. Season with salt and pepper.

Béchamel Sauce.

1½ cups White Stock.
1 slice onion.
1 slice carrot.
Bit of bay leaf.
Sprig of parsley.
6 peppercorns.
¼ cup butter.
¼ cup flour.
1 cup scalded milk.
½ teaspoon salt.
⅛ teaspoon pepper.

Cook stock twenty minutes with onion, carrot, bay leaf, parsley, and peppercorns, then strain; there should be one cupful. Melt the butter, add flour, and gradually hot stock and milk. Season with salt and pepper.

Yellow Béchamel Sauce.

To two cups Béchamel Sauce add yolks of three eggs slightly beaten, first diluting eggs with small quantity of hot sauce.

Oyster Sauce.

1 pint oysters.
¼ cup butter.
¼ cup flour.
1 cup milk or chicken stock.
Salt.
Pepper.
Oyster liquor.

Wash oysters, reserve liquor, heat, strain, add oysters, and cook until plump. Remove oysters, and make a sauce of butter, flour, oyster liquor, and milk. Add oysters, and season with salt and pepper.

Cucumber Sauce.

Grate two cucumbers, drain, and season with salt, pepper, and vinegar. Serve with Broiled Fish.

Celery Sauce.

3 cups celery cut in small pieces. 2 cups Thin White Sauce.

Wash and scrape celery before cutting into pieces. Cook in boiling salted water until soft, drain, rub through a sieve, and add to sauce. Celery sauce is often made from the stock in which a fowl or turkey has been boiled.

Suprême Sauce.

¼ cup butter.	½ cup hot cream.
¼ cup flour.	1 tablespoon mushroom liquor.
1½ cups hot chicken stock.	¾ teaspoon lemon juice.

Salt and pepper.

Make same as Thin White Sauce, and add seasonings.

Anchovy Sauce.

Season Brown, Drawn Butter, or Hollandaise Sauce with Anchovy essence.

Maître d'Hôtel Butter.

¼ cup butter.	⅛ teaspoon pepper.
½ teaspoon salt.	½ tablespoon finely chopped parsley.

¾ tablespoon lemon juice.

Put butter in a bowl, and with small wooden spoon work until creamy. Add salt, pepper, and parsley, then lemon juice very slowly.

Tartar Sauce.

1 tablespoon vinegar.	¼ teaspoon salt.
1 teaspoon lemon juice.	1 tablespoon Worcestershire Sauce.

⅓ cup butter.

The Boston Cook Book.

Mix vinegar, lemon juice, salt, and Worcestershire Sauce in a small bowl, and heat over hot water. Brown the butter in an omelet pan and strain into first mixture.

Lemon Butter.

¼ cup butter.   1 tablespoon lemon juice.

Cream the butter, and add slowly lemon juice.

Anchovy Butter.

¼ cup butter.   Anchovy essence.

Cream the butter, and add Anchovy essence to taste.

Lobster Butter.

¼ cup butter.   Lobster coral.

Clean, wipe, and force coral through a fine sieve. Put in a mortar with butter, and pound until well blended. This butter is used in Lobster Soup and Sauces to give color and richness.

Hollandaise Sauce I.

½ cup butter.   ¼ teaspoon salt.
Yolks 2 eggs.   Few grains cayenne.
1 tablespoon lemon juice.   ⅓ cup boiling water.

Put butter in a bowl, cover with cold water and wash, using a spoon. Divide in three pieces; put one piece in a saucepan with yolks of eggs and lemon juice, place saucepan in a larger one containing boiling water, and stir constantly with a wire whisk until butter is melted; then add second piece of butter, and, as it thickens, third piece. Add water, cook one minute, remove from fire, then add salt and cayenne.

Hollandaise Sauce II.

½ cup butter.   Yolks 2 eggs.
½ tablespoon vinegar.   ¼ teaspoon salt.
Few grains cayenne.

French Chef.

Wash butter, divide in three pieces. Put one piece in a saucepan with vinegar and egg yolks; place saucepan in a larger one containing boiling water, and stir constantly with a wire whisk. Add second piece of butter, and, as it thickens, third piece. Remove from fire, and add salt and cayenne. If left over fire a moment too long it will separate. If a richer sauce is desired, add one-half teaspoon hot water and one-half tablespoon heavy cream.

Lobster Sauce I.

To Hollandaise Sauce I. add one-third cup lobster meat cut in small dice.

Lobster Sauce II.

1¼ lb. lobster. ½ teaspoon salt.
¼ cup butter. Few grains cayenne.
¼ cup flour. ½ tablespoon lemon juice.
3 cups cold water.

Remove meat from lobster, and cut tender claw meat in one-half inch dice. Chop remaining meat, add to body bones, and cover with water; cook until stock is reduced to two cups, strain, and add gradually to butter and flour cooked together, then add salt, cayenne, lemon juice, and lobster dice.

If the lobster contains coral, prepare Lobster Butter, add flour, and thicken sauce therewith.

Sauce Béarnaise.

To Hollandaise Sauce II. add one teaspoon each of finely chopped parsley and fresh tarragon.

Served with mutton chops, steaks, broiled squabs, smelts, or boiled salmon.

Sauce Trianon.

To Hollandaise Sauce II. add gradually, while cooking, one and one-half tablespoons sherry wine.

Sauce Figaro.

To Hollandaise Sauce II. add two tablespoons tomato purée (tomatoes stewed, strained, and cooked until reduced to a thick pulp), one teaspoon finely chopped parsley, and a few grains cayenne.

Horseradish Sauce I.

3 tablespoons grated horse- ¼ teaspoon salt.
radish root. Few grains cayenne.
1 tablespoon vinegar. 4 tablespoons heavy cream.
Mix first four ingredients, and add cream beaten stiff.

Horseradish Sauce II.

3 tablespoons cracker crumbs.
⅓ cup grated horseradish root.
1½ cups milk.

3 tablespoons butter.
½ teaspoon salt.
⅛ teaspoon pepper.

Cook first three ingredients twenty minutes in double boiler. Add butter, salt, and pepper.

Bread Sauce.

2 cups milk.
½ cup fine stale bread crumbs.
1 onion.
6 cloves.

½ teaspoon salt.
Few grains cayenne.
3 tablespoons butter.
½ cup coarse stale bread crumbs.

Cook milk thirty minutes in double boiler, with fine bread crumbs and onion stuck with cloves. Remove onion, add salt, cayenne, and two tablespoons butter. Usually served poured around roast partridge or grouse, and sprinkled with coarse crumbs browned in remaining butter.

Rice Sauce.

3 tablespoons rice.
2 cups milk.
½ onion.

3 cloves.
2 tablespoons butter.
Salt and pepper.

Wash rice, add to milk, and cook in double boiler until soft. Rub through a fine strainer, return to double boiler, add onion stuck with cloves, and cook fifteen minutes. Remove onion, add butter, salt, and pepper.

Cauliflower Sauce.

¼ cup butter.
¼ cup flour.
1 cup hot chicken stock.
1 cup scalded milk.

Cooked flowerets from a small cauliflower.
Salt.
Pepper.

Make same as Thin White Sauce and add flowerets.

Mint Sauce.

¼ cup finely chopped mint leaves.   1 tablespoon powdered
½ cup vinegar.   sugar.

Add sugar to vinegar; when dissolved, pour over mint
and let stand thirty minutes on back of range to infuse.
If vinegar is very strong, dilute with water.

Currant Jelly Sauce.

To one cup Brown Sauce, from which onion has been
omitted, add one-fourth tumbler currant jelly and one
tablespoon sherry wine; or, add currant jelly to one cup
gravy made to serve with roast lamb. Currant Jelly Sauce
is suitable to serve with lamb.

Port Wine Sauce.

To one cup Brown Sauce, from which onion has been
omitted, add one-eighth tumbler currant jelly, two tablespoons port wine, and a few grains cayenne.

Sauce Tartare.

½ teaspoon mustard.   1½ tablespoons vinegar.
1 teaspoon powdered sugar.   Capers,
½ teaspoon salt.   Pickles,   ½ tablespoon each,
Few grains cayenne.   Olives,   finely chopped.
Yolks 2 eggs.   Parsley,
½ cup olive oil.   ½ shallot finely chopped.
                    ¼ teaspoon powdered tarragon.

Mix mustard, sugar, salt, and cayenne; add yolks of
eggs, and stir until thoroughly mixed, setting bowl in pan
of ice water. Add oil, at first drop by drop, stirring
with a wooden spoon or wire whisk. As mixture thickens,
dilute with vinegar, when oil may be added more rapidly.
Keep in cool place until ready to serve, then add remaining ingredients.

Sauce Tyrolienne.

To three-fourths cup Mayonnaise add one-half table-spoon each finely chopped capers and parsley, one finely chopped gherkin, and one-half can tomatoes, stewed, strained, and cooked until reduced to two tablespoons. Serve with any kind of fried fish.

CHAPTER XIX.

VEGETABLES.

Table showing Composition of Vegetables.

Articles.	Proteid.	Fat.	Carbo-hydrates.	Mineral matter.	Water.
Artichokes	2.6	.2	16.7	1.	79.5
Asparagus	1.8	.2	3.3	1.	94.
Beans, Lima, green .	7.1	.7	22.	1.7	68.5
" green string .	2.2	.4	9.4	.7	87.3
Beets	1.6	.1	9.6	1.1	87.6
Brussels sprouts . .	4.7	1.1	4.3	1.7	88.2
Cabbage	2.1	.4	5.8	1.4	90.3
Carrots	1.1	.4	9.2	1.1	88.2
Cauliflower	1.6	.8	6.	.8	90.8
Celery	1.4	.1	3.	1.1	94.4
Corn, green, sweet .	2.8	1.1	14.1	.7	81.3
Cucumbers	.8	.2	2.5	.5	96.
Egg-plant	1.2	.3	5.1	.5	92.9
Kohl-rabi	2.	.1	5.5	1.3	91.1
Lettuce	1.3	.4	3.3	1.	94.
Okra	2.	.4	9.5	.7	87.4
Onions	4.4	.8	.5	1.2	93.5
Parsnips	1.7	.6	16.1	1.7	79.9
Peas, green	4.4	.5	16.1	.9	78.1
Potatoes, sweet . .	1.8	.7	27.1	1.1	69.3
" white . .	2.1	.1	18.	.9	78.9
Spinach	2.1	.5	3.1	1.9	92.4
Squash	1.6	.6	10.4	.9	86.5
Tomatoes	.8	.4	3.9	.5	94.4
Turnips	1.4	.2	8.7	.8	88.9

W. O. Atwater, Ph.D.

Vegetables include, commonly though not botanically speaking, all plants used for food except grains and fruits.

With exception of beans, peas, and lentils, which contain a large amount of proteid, they are chiefly valuable for their potash salts, and should form a part of each day's dietary. Many contain much cellulose, which gives needed bulk to the food. The legumes, peas, beans, and lentils may be used in place of flesh food.

For the various vegetables different parts of the plant are used. Some are eaten in the natural state, others are cooked.

Tubers. White potatoes and Jerusalem artichokes.

Roots. Beets, carrots, parsnips, radishes, sweet potatoes, salsify or oyster plant, and turnips.

Bulbs. Garlic, onions, and shallots.

Stems. Asparagus, celery, and chives.

Leaves. Brussels sprouts, beet greens, cabbages, dandelions, lettuce, sorrel, spinach, and watercress.

Flowers. Cauliflower.

Fruit. Beans, corn, cucumbers, okra, egg-plant, peas, lentils, squash, and tomatoes.

Young, tender vegetables, — as lettuce, radishes, cucumbers, water-cress, and tomatoes, — eaten uncooked, served separately or combined in salads, help to stimulate a flagging appetite, and when dressed with oil furnish considerable nutriment.

Beans, and peas when old, should be employed in making purées and soups; by so doing, the outer covering of cellulose, so irritating to the stomach, is removed.

Care of Vegetables.

Summer vegetables should be cooked as soon after gathering as possible; in case they must be kept, spread on bottom of cool, dry, well-ventilated cellar, or place in ice-box. Lettuce may be best kept by sprinkling with cold water and placing in a tin pail closely covered. Wilted vegetables may be freshened by allowing to stand in cold water. Vegetables which contain sugar lose some of their sweetness by standing; corn and peas are more quickly affected than others. Winter vegetables should be kept in a cold, dry place. Beets, carrots, turnips, potatoes, etc., should be put in barrels or piled in bins, to exclude as much air as possible. Squash should be spread, and needs careful watching; when dark spots appear, cook at once.

In using canned goods, empty contents from can as soon as opened, lest the acid therein act on the tin to produce poisonous compounds, and let stand one hour, that it may become reoxygenated. Beans, peas, asparagus, etc., should be emptied into a strainer, drained, and cold water poured over them and allowed to run through. In using dried vegetables, soak in cold water several hours before cooking. A few years ago native vegetables were alone sold; but now our markets are largely supplied from the Southern States and California, thus allowing us fresh vegetables throughout the year.

Cooking of Vegetables.

A small scrubbing-brush, which may be bought for five cents, and two small pointed knives for preparing vegetables should be found in every kitchen.

Vegetables should be washed in cold water, and cooked until soft in boiling salted water; if cooked in an uncovered vessel, their color is better kept. For peas and beans add salt to water last half hour of cooking. Time for cooking the same vegetable varies according to freshness and age, therefore time-tables for cooking serve only as guides.

Mushrooms and Truffles.

These are classed among vegetables. Mushrooms, which grow about us abundantly, may be easily gathered, and as they contain considerable nutriment, should often be found on the table. While there are hundreds of varieties, one by a little study may acquaint herself with a dozen or more of the most common ones which are valuable as food. Consult W. Hamilton Gibson, "Our Edible Toadstools and Mushrooms." Many might cause illness, but only a few varieties of the *Amanita* family are deadly poison. Mushrooms require heat and moisture, — a severe drought or very wet soil being unfavorable for their growth. Never gather mushrooms in the vicinity of decaying matter. They appear the middle of May, and last until frost comes. *Campestris* is the variety always found in market; French canned are of this family. *Boleti* are dried, canned, and sold as *cepes*.

Truffles.

Truffles belong to the same family as mushrooms, and are grown underground. France is the most famous field for their production, from which country they are exported in tin cans, and are too expensive for ordinary use.

Artichokes.

French artichokes, imported throughout the year, are the ones principally used. They retail from thirty to forty cents each, and are cheapest and best in November, December, and January. Jerusalem artichokes are employed for pickling, and can be bought for fifteen cents per quart.

Boiled Artichokes.

Cut off stem close to leaves, remove outside bottom leaves, trim artichoke, cut off one inch from top of leaves, and with a sharp knife remove choke; then tie artichoke with a string to keep its shape. Soak one-half hour in cold water. Drain, and cook thirty to forty-five minutes in boiling, salted, acidulated water. Remove from water, place upside down to drain, then take off string. Serve with Béchamel or Hollandaise Sauce. Boiled Artichokes often constitute a course at dinner. Leaves are drawn out separately with fingers, dipped in sauce, and fleshy ends only eaten, although the bottom is edible. Artichokes may be cut in quarters, cooked, drained, and served with Sauce Béarnaise. When prepared in this way they are served with mutton.

Fried Artichokes.

Sprinkle Boiled Artichokes cut in quarters with salt, pepper, and finely chopped parsley. Dip in Batter I., fry in deep fat, and drain. In preparing artichokes, trim off tops of leaves closer than when served as Boiled Artichokes.

Artichoke Bottoms.

Remove all leaves and the choke. Trim bottoms in shape, and cook until soft in boiling, salted, acidulated water. Serve with Hollandaise or Béchamel Sauce.

Stuffed Artichokes.

Prepare and cook as Boiled Artichokes, having them slightly underdone. Fill with Chicken Force-meat I. or II., and bake thirty minutes in a moderate oven, basting twice with Thin White Sauce. Remove to serving-dish and pour around them Thin White Sauce.

Asparagus.

Hothouse asparagus is found in market during winter, but is not very satisfactory, and is sold for about one dollar per bunch. Oyster Bay (white asparagus) appears first of May, and commands a very high price. Large and small green stalk asparagus is in season from first of June to middle of July, and cheapest the middle of June.

Boiled Asparagus.

Cut off lower parts of stalks as far down as they will snap, untie bunches, wash, remove scales, and retie. Cook in boiling salted water fifteen minutes or until soft, leaving tips out of water first ten minutes. Drain, remove string, and spread with soft butter, allowing one and one-half tablespoons butter to each bunch asparagus. Asparagus is often broken in inch pieces for boiling, cooking tips a shorter time than stalks.

Asparagus on Toast.

Serve Boiled Asparagus on Buttered or Milk Toast.

Asparagus in White Sauce.

Boil asparagus cut in one-inch pieces, drain, and add to White Sauce I., allowing one cup sauce to each bunch asparagus.

Asparagus à la Hollandaise.

Pour Hollandaise Sauce 1. over Boiled Asparagus.

Asparagus in Crusts.

Remove centres from small rolls, fry shells in deep fat, drain, and fill with Asparagus in White Sauce.

Beans.

String Beans that are obtainable in winter come from California; natives appear in market the last of June and continue until the last of September. There are two varieties, green (pole cranberry being best flavored) and yellow (butter bean).

Shell Beans, including horticultural and sieva, are sold in the pod or shelled, five quarts in pod making one quart shelled. They are found in market during July and August. Common lima and improved lima shell beans are in season in August and September. Dried lima beans are procurable throughout the year.

String Beans.

Remove strings, and snap or cut in one-inch pieces; wash, and cook in boiling water from one to three hours, adding salt last half-hour of cooking. Drain, season with butter and salt.

Shell Beans.

Wash, and cook in boiling water from one to one and a half hours, adding salt last half-hour of cooking. Cook in sufficiently small quantity of water that there may be none left to drain off when beans are cooked. Season with butter and salt.

Cream of Lima Beans.

Soak one cup dried beans over night, drain, and cook in boiling salted water until soft; drain, add three-fourths cup cream, and season with butter and salt. Reheat before serving.

Boiled Beets.

Wash, and cook whole in boiling water until soft; time required being from one to four hours. Old beets will never be tender, no matter how long they may be cooked. Drain and put in cold water, that skins may be easily removed. Serve cut in quarters or slices.

Sugared Beets.

4 hot boiled beets.	1½ tablespoons sugar.
3 tablespoons butter.	½ teaspoon salt.

Cut beets in one-fourth inch slices, add butter, sugar, and salt; reheat for serving.

Pickled Beets.

Slice cold boiled beets and cover with vinegar.

Brussels Sprouts.

Brussels sprouts belong to same family as cabbage, and the small heads grow from one to two inches apart, on the axis of the entire stem, one root yielding about two quarts. They are imported, and also grow in this country, being cheapest and best in December and January.

Brussels Sprouts in White Sauce.

Pick over, remove wilted leaves, and soak in cold water fifteen minutes. Cook in boiling salted water twenty minutes, or until easily pierced with a skewer. Drain, and to each pint add one cup White Sauce I.

Cabbage.

There are four kinds of cabbage in the market, drum-head, sugar-loaf, Savoy, and purple; and some variety may be found throughout the year. The Savoy is best for boiling; drum-head and purple for Cole-Slaw. In buying, select heavy cabbages.

Boiled Cabbage.

Take off outside leaves, cut in quarters, and remove tough stalk. Soak in cold water and cook in an uncovered vessel in boiling salted water, to which is added one-fourth teaspoon soda; this prevents disagreeable odor during cooking. Cook from thirty minutes to one hour, drain and serve; or chop, and season with butter, salt, and pepper.

Escalloped Cabbage.

Cut one-half boiled cabbage in pieces; put in buttered baking-dish, sprinkle with salt and pepper, and add one cup White Sauce I. Lift cabbage with fork that it may be well mixed with sauce, cover with one-half cup buttered crumbs, place on oven grate, and bake until crumbs are brown.

German Cabbage.

Slice red cabbage and soak in cold water. Put one quart in stewpan with two tablespoons butter, one-half teaspoon salt, one tablespoon finely chopped onion, few gratings of nutmeg, and few grains cayenne; cover, and cook until cabbage is tender. Add two tablespoons vinegar and one-half tablespoon sugar, and cook five minutes.

Cole-Slaw.

Select a small, heavy cabbage, take off outside leaves, and cut in quarters; with a sharp knife slice very thinly. Soak in cold water until crisp, drain, dry between towels, and mix with Cream Salad Dressing.

Hot Slaw.

Slice cabbage as for Cole-Slaw, using one-half cabbage. Heat in a dressing made of yolks of two eggs slightly beaten, one-fourth cup cold water, one tablespoon butter, one-fourth cup hot vinegar, and one-half teaspoon salt, stirred over hot water until thickened.

Carrots.

Carrots may always be found in market. New carrots appear last of April, and are sold in bunches; these may be boiled and served, but carrots are chiefly used for flavoring soups, and for garnishing, on account of their bright color. To prepare carrots for cooking, wash and scrape, as best flavor and brightest color are near the skin.

Carrots and Peas.

Wash, scrape, and cut young carrots in small cubes or fancy shapes; cook until soft in boiling salted water or stock. Drain, add an equal quantity of cooked green peas, and season with butter, salt, and pepper.

Cauliflower.

Cauliflowers comprise the stalks and flowerets of a plant which belongs to the same family as Brussels sprouts and cabbage; they may be obtained throughout the year, but are cheapest and best in September and October. In selecting cauliflowers, choose those with white heads and fresh green leaves; if dark spots are on the heads, they are not fresh.

Creamed Cauliflower.

Remove leaves, cut off stalk, and soak thirty minutes (head down) in cold water to cover. Cook (head up) twenty minutes or until soft in boiling salted water; drain, separate flowerets, and reheat in one and one-half cups White Sauce I.

Cauliflower à la Hollandaise.

Prepare as for Creamed Cauliflower, using Hollandaise Sauce I. instead of White Sauce.

Cauliflower au Gratin.

Place a whole cooked cauliflower on dish for serving, cover with buttered crumbs, and place on oven grate to brown crumbs; remove from oven and pour one cup Thin White Sauce around cauliflower.

Cauliflower à la Parmesan.

Prepare as Cauliflower au Gratin. Sprinkle with grated cheese before covering with crumbs.

Celery.

Celery may be obtained from last of July until April. It is best and cheapest in December. Celery stalks are green while growing; but the white celery seen in market has been bleached, with exception of Kalamazoo variety, which grows white. To prepare celery for table, cut off roots and leaves, separate stalks, wash, scrape, and chill in ice water. By adding a slice of lemon to ice water celery is kept white and made crisp. If tops of stalks are gashed several times before putting in water, they will curl back and make celery look more attractive.

Celery in White Sauce.

Wash, scrape, and cut outer celery stalks in one-inch pieces; cook twenty minutes or until soft in boiling salted water; drain, and to two cups celery add one cup White Sauce I.

Chiccory or Endive.

Chiccory or endive may be obtained throughout the year, but during January, February, March, and April, supply is imported. It is used only for salads.

Corn.

Corn may be found in market from first of June to first of October. Until native corn appears it is the most unsatisfactory vegetable. Native corn is obtainable the last of July, but is most abundant and cheapest in August. Among the best varieties are Crosby for early corn and Evergreen for late corn.

Boiled Green Corn.

Remove husks and silky threads. Cook ten to twenty minutes in boiling water. Place on platter covered with napkin; draw corners of napkin over corn; or cut from cob and season with butter and salt.

Succotash.

Cut hot boiled corn from cob, add equal quantity of hot boiled shelled beans; season with butter and salt; reheat before serving.

Corn Oysters.

Grate raw corn from cobs. To one cup pulp add one well beaten egg, one-fourth cup flour, and season highly with salt and pepper. Drop by spoonfuls and fry in deep fat, or cook on a hot, well greased griddle. They should be made about the size of large oysters.

Corn à la Southern.

To one can chopped corn add two eggs slightly beaten, one teaspoon salt, one-eighth teaspoon pepper, one and one-half tablespoons melted butter, and one pint scalded milk; turn into a buttered pudding-dish and bake in slow oven until firm.

Chestnuts.

French and Italian chestnuts are served in place of vegetables.

Chestnut Purée.

Remove shells from chestnuts, cook until soft in boiling salted water; drain, mash, moisten with scalded milk, season with salt and pepper, and beat until light. Chestnuts are often boiled, riced, and piled lightly in centre of dish, then surrounded by meat.

Cucumbers.

Cucumbers may be obtained throughout the year, and are generally served raw. During the latter part of the summer they are gathered and pickled for subsequent use. Small pickled cucumbers are called gherkins.

Sliced Cucumbers.

Remove thick slices from both ends and cut off a thick paring, as the cucumber contains a bitter principle, a large quantity of which lies near the skin and stem end. Cut in thin slices and keep in cold water until ready to serve. Drain, and cover with crushed ice for serving.

Boiled Cucumbers.

Old cucumbers may be pared, cut in pieces, cooked until soft in boiling salted water, drained, mashed, and seasoned with butter, salt, and pepper.

Fried Cucumbers.

Pare cucumbers and cut lengthwise in one-third inch slices. Dry between towels, sprinkle with salt and pepper, dip in crumbs, egg, and crumbs again, fry in deep fat, and drain.

Stuffed Cucumbers.

Pare three cucumbers, cut in halves crosswise, remove seeds, and let stand in cold water thirty minutes. Drain, wipe, and fill with force-meat, using recipe for Chicken Force-meat I. or II., substituting veal for chicken. Place upright on a trivet in a saucepan. Half surround with White Stock, cover, and cook forty minutes. Place on thin slices of dry toast, and pour around one and one-half cups Béchamel Sauce. Serve as a vegetable or entrée.

Fried Egg-plant I.

Pare an egg-plant and cut in very thin slices. Sprinkle slices with salt and pile on a plate. Cover with a weight to express the juice, and let stand one hour. Dredge with flour and sauté slowly in butter until crisp and brown. Egg-plant is in season from September to February.

Fried Egg-plant II.

Pare an egg-plant, cut in one-fourth inch slices, and soak over night in cold salted water. Drain, let stand in cold water one-half hour, drain again, and dry between towels. Sprinkle with salt and pepper, dip in batter, or dip in flour, egg, and crumbs, and fry in deep fat.

Stuffed Egg-plant.

Cook egg-plant fifteen minutes in boiling salted water to cover. Cut a slice from top. and with a spoon remove pulp, taking care not to work too closely to skin. Chop pulp, and add one cup soft stale bread crumbs. Melt two tablespoons butter, add one-half tablespoon finely chopped onion, and cook five minutes; or try out three slices of bacon, using bacon fat in place of butter. Add to chopped pulp and bread, season with salt and pepper, and if necessary moisten with a little stock or water; cook five minutes, cool slightly, and add one beaten egg. Refill egg-plant, cover with buttered bread crumbs, and bake twenty-five minutes in a hot oven.

Greens.

Hothouse beet greens and dandelions appear in market the first of March, when they command a high price. Those grown out of doors are in season from middle of May to first of July.

Boiled Beet Greens.

Wash thoroughly and scrape roots, cutting off ends. Drain, and cook one hour or until tender in a small quantity boiling salted water. Season with butter, salt, and pepper. Serve with vinegar.

Dandelions.

Wash thoroughly, remove roots, drain, and cook one hour or until tender in boiling salted water. Allow two quarts water to one peck dandelions. Season with butter, salt, and pepper. Serve with vinegar.

Lettuce.

Lettuce is obtainable all the year, and is especially valuable during the winter and spring, when other green vegetables in market command a high price. Although containing but little nutriment, it is useful for the large quantity of water and potash salts that it contains, and assists in stimulating the appetite.   Curly lettuce is of less value than Tennis Ball. but makes an effective garnish.

Lettuce should be separated by removing leaves from stalk (discarding wilted outer leaves), washed, kept in cold water until crisp, drained, and so placed on a towel that water may drop from leaves.   A bag made from white mosquito netting is useful for drying lettuce.   Wash lettuce leaves, place in bag, and hang in lower part of ice-box to drain.   Wire baskets are used for the same purpose.   Arrange lettuce for serving in nearly its original shape.

Onions.

The onion belongs to the same family (Lily) as do *shallot*, *garlic*, *leek*, and *chive*.   Onions are cooked and served as a vegetable.   They are wholesome, and contain considerable nutriment, but are objectionable on account of the strong odor they impart to the breath, due to volatile substances absorbed by the blood, and by the blood carried to the lungs, where they are set free.   The common garden onion is obtainable throughout the year, the new ones appearing in market about the first of June.   In large centres Bermuda and Spanish onions are procurable from March 1st to June 1st, and are of delicate flavor.

Shallot, leek, garlic, and chive are principally used to give additional flavor to food.   Shallot, garlic, and chive are used, to some extent, in making salads.

Boiled Onions.

Put onions in cold water and remove skins while under water.   Drain, put in a saucepan, and cover with boiling salted water; boil five minutes, drain, and again cover with boiling salted water.   Cook one hour or until soft, but not broken.   Drain, add a small quantity of milk, cook five minutes, and season with butter, salt, and pepper.

Onions in Cream.

Prepare and cook as Boiled Onions, changing the water twice during boiling; drain, and cover with Cream or Thin White Sauce.

Scalloped Onions.

Cut Boiled Onions in quarters. Put in a buttered baking-dish, cover with White Sauce I., sprinkle with buttered cracker crumbs, and place on centre grate in oven to brown crumbs.

Fried Onions.

Remove skins from four medium-sized onions. Cut in thin slices and put in a hot omelet pan with one and one-half tablespoons butter. Cook until brown, occasionally shaking pan that onions may not burn, or turn onions, using a fork. Sprinkle with salt one minute before taking from fire.

Stuffed Onions.

Remove skins from onions, and parboil ten minutes in boiling salted water to cover. Turn upside down to cool, and remove part of centres. Fill cavities with equal parts of finely chopped cooked chicken, stale soft bread crumbs, and finely chopped onion which was removed, seasoned with salt and pepper, and moistened with cream or melted butter. Place in buttered shallow baking-pan, sprinkle with buttered crumbs, and bake in a moderate oven until onions are soft.

Creamed Oyster Plant (Salsify).

Wash, scrape, and put at once into cold acidulated water to prevent discoloration. Cut in inch slices, cook in boiling salted water until soft, drain, and add to White Sauce I. Oyster plant is in season from October to March.

Salsify Fritters.

Cook oyster plant as for Creamed Oyster Plant. Mash, season with butter, salt, and pepper. Shape in small flat cakes, roll in flour, and sauté in butter.

Parsnips.

Parsnips are not so commonly served as other vegetables; however, they often accompany a boiled dinner. They are raised mostly for feeding cattle. Unless young, they contain a large amount of woody fibre, which extends through centre of roots and makes them undesirable as food.

Parsnips with Drawn Butter Sauce.

Wash and scrape parsnips, and cut in pieces two inches long and one-half inch wide and thick. Cook five minutes in boiling salted water, or until soft. Drain, and to two cups add one cup Drawn Butter Sauce.

Parsnip Fritters.

Wash parsnips and cook forty-five minutes in boiling salted water. Drain, plunge into cold water, when skins will be found to slip off easily. Mash, season with butter, salt, and pepper, shape in small flat round cakes, roll in flour, and sauté in butter.

Peas.

Peas contain, next to beans, the largest percentage of proteid of any of the vegetables, and when young are easy of digestion. They appear in market as early as April, coming from Florida and California, and although high in price are hardly worth buying, they having been picked so long. Native peas may be obtained the middle of June, and last until the first of September. The early June are small peas contained in a small pod. McLean, the best peas, are small peas in large flat pods. Champion peas are large, and the pods are well filled, but they lack sweetness. Marrowfat peas are the largest in the market, and are usually sweet.

Boiled Peas.

Remove peas from pods, cover with cold water, and let stand one-half hour. Skim off undeveloped peas which rise to top of water, and drain remaining peas. Cook until soft in a small quantity of boiling water, adding salt the last fifteen minutes of cooking. (Consult Time Table for Cooking, p. 33.) There should be but little, if any, water to drain from peas when they are cooked. Season with butter, salt, and pepper. If peas have lost much of their natural sweetness, they are improved by the addition of a small amount of sugar.

Creamed Peas.

Drain Boiled Peas, and to two cups peas add three-fourths cup White Sauce II. Canned peas are often drained, rinsed, and reheated in this way.

Stuffed Peppers I.

6 green peppers.
¾ cup hot steamed rice.
½ cup cold cooked meat cut in small dice.

⅓ cup tomatoes stewed and strained.
1 tablespoon melted butter.
Few drops onion juice.

Salt and pepper.

Cut off pieces from stem ends of peppers. Remove seeds and partitions; parboil eight minutes. Fill with rice, meat, tomatoes, and butter, well mixed, and seasoned with onion juice, salt, and pepper. Place in a pan, add one and one-half cups water or stock, and bake forty-five minutes in a moderate oven.

Stuffed Peppers II.

Prepare peppers as for Stuffed Peppers I. Fill with equal parts of finely chopped cold cooked chicken or veal, and softened bread crumbs, seasoned with onion juice, salt, and pepper.

Pumpkins.

Pumpkins are boiled or steamed same as squash, but require longer cooking. They are principally used for making pies.

Radishes.

Radishes may be obtained throughout the year. There are round and long varieties, the small round ones being considered best. They are bought in bunches, six or seven constituting a bunch. Radishes are used merely for a relish, and are served uncooked. To prepare radishes for table, remove leaves, stems, and tip end of root, scrape roots, and serve on crushed ice. Round radishes look very attractive cut to imitate tulips, when they should not be scraped; to accomplish this, begin at root end and make six incisions through skin running three-fourths length of radish. Pass knife under sections of skin, and cut down as far as incisions extend. Place in cold water, and sections of skin will fold back, giving radish a tulip-like appearance.

Spinach.

Spinach is cheapest and best in early summer, but is obtainable throughout the year. It gives variety to winter diet, when most green vegetables are expensive and of inferior quality.

Boiled Spinach.

Remove roots, carefully pick over (discarding wilted leaves), and wash in several waters to be sure that it is free from all sand. When young and tender put in a stewpan, allow to heat gradually, and cook twenty-five minutes, or until tender, in its own juices. Old spinach is better cooked in boiling salted water, allowing two quarts water to one peck spinach. Drain thoroughly, chop finely, reheat, and season with butter, salt, and pepper. Garnish with slices of hard boiled eggs. The green color of spinach is better retained by cooking in a large quantity of water in an uncovered vessel.

Spinach à la Béchamel.

Prepare one-half peck Boiled Spinach. Put three tablespoons butter in hot omelet pan; when melted, add chopped spinach, cook three minutes. Sprinkle with two tablespoons flour, stir thoroughly, and add gradually three-fourths cup milk; cook five minutes.

Squash.

Summer squash, which are in market during the summer months, should be young, tender, and thin skinned. The common varieties are the white round and yellow crookneck. Some of the winter varieties appear in market as early as the middle of August; among the most common are Marrow, Turban, and Hubbard. Turban and Hubbard are usually drier than Marrow. Marrow and Turban have a thin shell, which may be pared off before cooking. Hubbard Squash has a very hard shell, which must be split in order to separate squash in pieces, and squash then cooked in the shell. In selecting winter squash, see that it is heavy in proportion to its size.

Boiled Summer Squash.

Wash squash and cut in thick slices or quarters. Cook twenty minutes in boiling salted water, or until soft. Turn in a cheese cloth placed over a colander, drain, and wring in cheese cloth. Mash, and season with butter, salt, and pepper.

Fried Summer Squash I.

Wash and cut in one-half inch pieces. Sprinkle with salt and pepper, dip in crumbs, egg, and crumbs again, fry in hot fat, and drain.

Fried Summer Squash II.

Follow recipe for Fried Egg-plant I.

Steamed Winter Squash.

Cut in pieces, remove seeds and stringy portion, and pare. Place in a strainer and cook thirty minutes, or until soft, over boiling water. Mash, and season with butter, salt, and pepper. If lacking in sweetness, add a small quantity of sugar.

Boiled Winter Squash.

Prepare as for Steamed Winter Squash. Cook in boiling salted water, drain, mash, and season. Unless squash is very dry, it is much better steamed than boiled.

Baked Winter Squash I.

Cut in pieces two inches square, remove seeds and stringy portion, place in a dripping-pan, sprinkle with salt and pepper, and allow for each square one-half teaspoon molasses and one-half teaspoon melted butter. Bake fifty minutes, or until soft, in a moderate oven, keeping covered the first half-hour of cooking. Serve in the shell.

Baked Winter Squash II.

Cut squash in halves, remove seeds and stringy portion, place in a dripping-pan, cover, and bake two hours, or until soft, in a slow oven. Remove from shell, mash, and season with butter, salt, and pepper.

Tomatoes.

Tomatoes are obtainable throughout the year, but are cheapest and best in September. Hothouse tomatoes are in market during the winter, and command a very high price, sometimes retailing for one and one-half dollars a pound.

Southern tomatoes appear as early as May 1st, and although of good color, lack flavor. Of the many varieties of tomatoes, Acme is among the best.

Sliced Tomatoes.

Wipe, and cover with boiling water; let stand one minute, when they may be easily skinned. Chill thoroughly, and cut in one-third inch slices.

Stewed Tomatoes.

Wipe, pare, cut in pieces, put in stewpan, and cook slowly twenty minutes, stirring occasionally. Season with butter, salt, and pepper.

Scalloped Tomatoes.

Remove contents from one can tomatoes and drain tomatoes from some of their liquor. Season with salt, pepper, a few drops of onion juice, and sugar if preferred sweet. Cover the botton of a buttered baking-dish with buttered cracker crumbs, cover with tomatoes, and sprinkle top thickly with buttered crumbs. Bake in a hot oven until crumbs are brown.

Broiled Tomatoes.

Wipe and cut in halves crosswise, cut off a thin slice from rounding part of each half. Sprinkle with salt and pepper, dip in crumbs, egg, and crumbs again, place in a well-buttered broiler, and broil six to eight minutes.

Tomatoes à la Crême.

Wipe, peel, and slice three tomatoes. Sprinkle with salt and pepper, dredge with flour, and sauté in butter. Place on a hot platter and pour over them one cup White Sauce I.

Devilled Tomatoes.

3 tomatoes.	1 teaspoon mustard.
Salt and pepper.	¼ teaspoon salt.
Flour.	Few grains cayenne.
Butter for sautéing.	Yolk 1 hard boiled egg.
4 tablespoons butter.	1 egg.
2 teaspoons powdered sugar.	2 tablespoons vinegar.

Wipe, peel, and cut tomatoes in slices. Sprinkle with salt and pepper, dredge with flour, and sauté in butter. Place on a hot platter and pour over the dressing made by creaming the butter, adding dry ingredients, yolk of egg rubbed to a paste, egg beaten slightly, and vinegar, then cooking over hot water, stirring constantly until it thickens.

Baked Tomatoes.

Wipe, and remove a thin slice from stem end of six smooth, medium-sized tomatoes. Take out seeds and pulp, and drain off most of the liquid. Add an equal quantity of cracker crumbs, season with salt, pepper, and a few drops onion juice, and refill tomatoes with mixture. Place in a buttered pan, sprinkle with buttered crumbs, and bake twenty minutes in a hot oven.

Stuffed Tomatoes.

Wipe, and remove thin slices from stem end of six medium-sized tomatoes. Take out seeds and pulp, sprinkle inside of tomatoes with salt, invert, and let stand one-half hour. Cook five minutes two tablespoons butter with one-half tablespoon finely chopped onion. Add one-half cup finely chopped cold cooked chicken or veal, one-half cup stale soft bread crumbs, tomato pulp, and salt and pepper to taste. Cook five minutes, then add one egg slightly beaten and cook one minute, and refill tomatoes with mixture. Place in buttered pan, sprinkle with buttered cracker crumbs, and bake twenty minutes in a hot oven.

Turnips.

Turnips are best during the fall and winter; towards spring they become çorky, and are then suitable only for stews and flavoring. The Ruta-baga, a large yellow turnip, is one of the best varieties; the large white French turnip and the small flat Purple Top are also used.

Mashed Turnip.

Wash and pare turnips, cut in slices or quarters, and cook in boiling salted water until soft. Drain, mash, and season with butter, salt, and pepper.

Creamed Turnip.

Wash turnips, and cut in one-half inch cubes. Cook three cups cubes in boiling salted water twenty minutes, or until soft. Drain, and add oné cup White Sauce I.

Turnip Croquettes.

Wash, pare, and cut in quarters new French turnips. Steam until tender, mash, pressing out all water that is possible. This is best accomplished by wringing in cheese cloth. Season one and one-fourth cups with salt and pepper, then add yolks of two eggs slightly beaten. Cool, shape in small croquettes, dip in crumbs, egg, and crumbs again, fry in deep fat, and drain.

Stewed Mushrooms.

Wash one-half pound mushrooms. Remove stems, scrape, and cut in pieces. Peel caps, and break in pieces. Melt three tablespoons of butter, add mushrooms, cook two minutes; sprinkle with salt and pepper, dredge with flour, and add one-half cup hot water or stock. Cook slowly five minutes.

Stewed Mushrooms in Cream.

Prepare mushrooms as for Stewed Mushrooms. Cook with three-fourths cup cream instead of using water or stock. Add a slight grating of nutmeg, pour over small pieces of dry toast, and garnish with toast points.

Broiled Mushrooms.

Wash mushrooms, remove stems, and place caps in a buttered broiler and broil five minutes, having cap side down first half of broiling. Serve on circular pieces of buttered dry toast. Put a small piece of butter in each cap, sprinkle with salt and pepper, and serve as soon as butter has melted. Care must be taken, in removing from broiler, to keep mushrooms cap side up, to prevent loss of juices.

Baked Mushrooms in Cream.

Wash twelve large mushrooms. Remove stems, and peel caps. Put in a shallow buttered pan, cap side up. Sprinkle with salt and pepper, and dot over with butter; add two-thirds cup cream. Bake ten minutes in a hot oven. Place on pieces of dry toast, and pour over them cream remaining in pan.

Sautéd Mushrooms.

Wash, remove stems, peel caps, and break in pieces; there should be one cup of mushrooms. Put two table-spoons butter in a hot omelet pan; when melted, add mushrooms, few drops onion juice, one-fourth teaspoon salt, a few grains pepper, and cook five minutes. Add one teaspoon finely chopped parsley and one-fourth cup boiling water. Cook two minutes, and serve on dry toast.

Mushrooms à la Sabine.

Wash one-half pound mushrooms, remove stems, and peel caps. Sprinkle with salt and pepper, and cook three minutes in a hot frying-pan, with two tablespoons butter. Add one and one-third cups Brown Sauce, and cook slowly five minutes. Sprinkle with three table-spoons grated cheese. As soon as cheese is melted, arrange mushrooms on pieces of toast, and pour over sauce.

Mushrooms à l'Algonquin.

Wash large selected mushrooms. Remove stems, peel caps, and sauté caps in butter. Place in a small buttered shallow pan, cap side being up; place on each a large oyster, sprinkle with salt and pepper, and place on each a bit of butter. Cook in a hot oven until oysters are plump. Serve with Brown or Béchamel Sauce.

Stuffed Mushrooms.

Wash twelve large mushrooms. Remove stems, chop finely, and peel caps. Melt three tablespoons butter, add one-half tablespoon finely chopped shallot and chopped stems, then cook ten minutes. Add one and one-half tablespoons flour, chicken stock to moisten, a slight grating of nutmeg, one-half teaspoon finely chopped parsley, and salt and pepper to taste. Cool, fill caps, well rounding over top, cover with buttered cracker crumbs, and bake fifteen minutes in a hot oven.

CHAPTER XX.

POTATOES.

COMPOSITION.

Water 78.9%.	Proteid 2.1%.
Starch 18%.	Mineral matter .9%.
Fat .1%.	

POTATOES stand pre-eminent among the vegetables used for food. They are tubers belonging to the Nightshade family; their hardy growth renders them easy of cultivation in almost any soil or climate, and, resisting early frosts, they may be raised in a higher latitude than the cereals.

They give needed bulk to food rather than nutriment, and, lacking in proteid, should be used in combination with meat, fish, or eggs.

Potatoes contain an acrid juice, the greater part of which lies near the skin; it passes into the water during boiling of potatoes, and escapes with the steam from a baked potato.

Potatoes are best in the fall, and keep well through the winter. By spring the starch is partially changed to dextrin, giving the potatoes a sweetness, and when cooked a waxiness. The same change takes place when potatoes are frozen. To prevent freezing, keep a pail of cold water standing near them.

Potatoes keep best in a cool dry cellar, in barrels or piled in a bin. When sprouts appear they should be removed; receiving their nourishment from the starch, they deteriorate the potato.

New potatoes may be compared to unripe fruit, the starch grains not having reached maturity; therefore they should not be given to children or invalids.

Sweet Potatoes.

Sweet potatoes, although analogous to white potatoes, are fleshy roots of the plant, belong to a different family (Convolvulus), and contain a much larger percentage of sugar. Our own country produces large quantities of sweet potatoes, which may be grown as far north as New Jersey and Southern Michigan. Kiln-dried sweet potatoes are the best, as they do not so quickly spoil.

Baked Potatoes.

Select smooth, medium-sized potatoes. Wash, using a vegetable brush, and place in dripping-pan. Bake in hot oven forty minutes or until soft, remove from oven and serve at once. If allowed to stand, unless the skin is ruptured for escape of steam, they become soggy. Properly baked potatoes are more easily digested than potatoes cooked in any other way, as some of the starch is changed to dextrin by the intense heat. They are better cooked in boiling water than baked in a slow oven.

Boiled Potatoes.

Select potatoes of uniform size. Wash, pare, and drop at once in cold water to prevent discoloration; soak one half-hour in the fall, and one to two hours in winter and spring. Cook in boiling salted water until soft, which is easily determined by piercing with a skewer. For seven potatoes allow one tablespoon salt, and boiling water to cover. Drain from water, and keep uncovered in warm place until serving time. Avoid sending to table in a covered vegetable dish. In boiling large potatoes, it often happens that outside is soft, while centre is under-done. To finish cooking without potatoes breaking apart, add one pint cold water, which drives heat to centre, thus accomplishing the cooking.

Riced Potatoes.

Force hot boiled potatoes through a potato ricer or coarse strainer. Serve lightly piled in a hot vegetable dish.

Mashed Potatoes.

To five riced potatoes add three tablespoons butter, one teaspoon salt, few grains pepper, and one-third cup hot milk; beat with fork until creamy, reheat, and pile lightly in hot dish.

Potato Omelet.

Prepare Mashed Potatoes, turn in hot omelet pan greased with one tablespoon butter, spread evenly, cook slowly until browned underneath, and fold as an omelet.

Potato Border.

Place a buttered mould on platter, build around it a wall of hot Mashed Potatoes, three and one-half inches high by one inch deep, smooth and crease with case knife. Remove mould, fill with creamed meat or fish, and reheat in oven before serving.

Escalloped Potatoes.

Wash, pare, soak, and cut four potatoes in one-fourth inch slices. Put a layer in buttered baking-dish, sprinkle with salt and pepper, dredge with flour, and dot over with one-half tablespoon butter; repeat. Add hot milk until it may be seen through top layer, bake one and one-fourth hours or until potato is soft.

Potatoes à la Hollandaise.

Wash, pare, soak, and cut potatoes in one-fourth inch slices, shape with French vegetable cutters; or cut in one-half inch cubes. Cover three cups potato with White Stock, cook until soft, and drain. Cream one-third cup butter, add one tablespoon lemon juice, one-half teaspoon salt, and few grains of cayenne. Add to potatoes, cook three minutes, and add one-half tablespoon finely chopped parsley.

Potatoes Baked in Half Shell.

Select six medium-sized potatoes and bake, following recipe for Baked Potatoes. Remove from oven, cut slice from top of each, and scoop out inside. Mash, add two tablespoons butter, salt, pepper, and three tablespoons hot milk; then add whites two eggs well beaten. Refill skins, and bake five to eight minutes in very hot oven. Potatoes may be sprinkled with grated cheese before putting in oven.

Duchess Potatoes.

To two cups hot riced potatoes add two tablespoons butter, one-half teaspoon salt, and yolks of three eggs slightly beaten. Shape, using pastry bag and tube, in form of baskets, pyramids, crowns, leaves, roses, etc. Brush over with beaten egg diluted with one teaspoon water, and brown in a hot oven.

Maître d'Hôtel Potatoes.

Wash, pare, and shape potatoes in balls, using a French vegetable cutter, or cut potatoes in one-half inch cubes. There should be two cups. Soak fifteen minutes in cold water, and cook in boiling salted water to cover until soft. Drain, and add Maître d'Hôtel Butter.

Maître d'Hôtel Butter.

Cream three tablespoons butter, add one teaspoon lemon juice, one-half teaspoon salt, one-eighth teaspoon pepper, and one-half tablespoon finely chopped parsley.

Franconia Potatoes.

Prepare as for Boiled Potatoes, and parboil ten minutes; drain, and place in pan in which meat is roasting; bake until soft, basting with fat in pan when basting meat. Time required for baking about forty minutes.

Brabant Potatoes.

Prepare as for Boiled Potatoes, using small potatoes, and trim egg-shaped; parboil ten minutes, drain, and place in baking-pan and bake until soft, basting three times with melted butter.

Potato Balls.

Select large potatoes, wash, pare, and soak. Shape in balls with a French vegetable cutter. Cook in boiling salted water until soft; drain, and to one pint potatoes add one cup Thin White Sauce. Turn into hot dish, and sprinkle with finely chopped parsley.

FRIED POTATOES.

Shadow Potatoes (Saratoga Chips).

Wash and pare potatoes. Slice thinly (using vegetable slicer) into a bowl of cold water. Let stand two hours, changing water twice. Drain, plunge in a kettle of boiling water and boil one minute. Drain again, and cover with cold water. Take from water and dry between towels. Fry in deep fat until light brown, keeping in motion with a skimmer. Drain on brown paper and sprinkle with salt.

Shredded Potatoes.

Wash, pare, and cut potatoes in one-eighth inch slices. Cut slices in one-eighth inch strips. Soak one hour in cold water. Take from water, dry between towels, and fry in deep fat. Drain on brown paper and sprinkle with salt. Serve around fried or baked fish.

French Fried Potatoes.

Wash and pare small potatoes, cut in eighths lengthwise, and soak one hour in cold water. Take from water, dry between towels, and fry in deep fat. Drain on brown paper and sprinkle with salt.

Care must be taken that fat is not too hot, as potatoes must be cooked as well as browned.

Potato Marbles.

Wash and pare potatoes. Shape in balls, using a French vegetable cutter. Soak fifteen minutes in cold water, take from water and dry between towels. Fry in deep fat, drain, and sprinkle with salt.

Fried Potato Balls.

To one cup hot riced potatoes add one tablespoon butter, one-fourth teaspoon salt, one-eighth teaspoon celery salt, and few grains cayenne. Cool slightly, and add one-half beaten egg and one-half teaspoon finely chopped parsley. Shape in small balls, roll in flour, fry in deep fat, and drain.

Potato Fritters.

2 cups hot riced potatoes.	Few gratings nutmeg.
2 tablespoons cream.	Few grains cayenne.
2 tablespoons wine.	3 eggs.
1 teaspoon salt.	Yolks 2 eggs.

½ cup flour.

Add cream, wine, and seasonings to potatoes; then add eggs well beaten, having bowl containing mixture in pan of ice water, and beat until cold. Add flour, and when well mixed, drop by spoonfuls in deep fat, fry until delicately browned, and drain on brown paper.

Potato Curls.

Wash and pare large long potatoes. Shape with a potato curler, soak one hour in cold water, drain, dry between towels, fry in deep fat, drain, and sprinkle with salt.

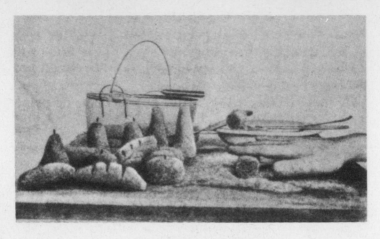

Potato Croquettes.

Potato Croquettes.

2 cups hot riced potatoes.	¼ teaspoon celery salt.
2 tablespoons butter.	Few drops onion juice.
½ teaspoon salt.	Yolk 1 egg.
⅛ teaspoon pepper.	1 teaspoon finely chopped parsley.

Mix ingredients in order given, and beat thoroughly. Shape, dip in crumbs, egg, and crumbs again, fry one minute in deep fat, and drain on brown paper. Croquettes are shaped in a variety of forms. The most common way is to first form a smooth ball by rolling one rounding tablespoon mixture between hands. Then roll on a board until of desired length, and flatten ends.

French Potato Croquettes.

2 cups hot riced potatoes.	Yolks 3 eggs.
2 tablespoons butter.	/ ½ teaspoon salt.
Few grains cayenne.	

Mix ingredients in order given, and beat thoroughly. Shape in balls, then in rolls, pointed at ends. Roll in flour, mark in three places on top of each with knife blade to represent a small French loaf. Fry in deep fat, and drain on brown paper. *Makes 10 small rolls.*

Potato Apples.

2 cups hot riced potatoes.	Few grains cayenne.
2 tablespoons butter.	Slight grating nutmeg.
⅓ cup grated cheese.	2 tablespoons thick cream.
½ teaspoon salt.	Yolks 2 eggs.

Mix ingredients in order given, and beat thoroughly. Shape in form of small apples, roll in flour, egg, and crumbs, fry in deep fat, and drain on brown paper. Insert a clove at both stem and blossom end of each apple.

Potatoes en Surprise.

Make Potato Croquette mixture, omitting parsley. Shape in small nests and fill with Creamed Chicken, shrimp, or peas. Cover nests with Croquette mixture, then roll in form of croquettes. Dip in crumbs, egg, and crumbs again; fry in deep fat, and drain on brown paper.

SWEET POTATOES.

Baked Sweet Potatoes.

Prepare and bake as white potatoes.

Boiled Sweet Potatoes.

Select potatoes of uniform size. Wash, pare, and cook twenty minutes in boiling salted water to cover. Many boil sweet potatoes with the skins on.

Mashed Sweet Potatoes.

To ~~two~~ 4 cups riced sweet potatoes, add three tablespoons butter, one-~~half~~ teaspoon salt, and hot milk to moisten. Beat until light, and pile on a vegetable dish.

Butter custard cups or muffin pans, fill, and bake until brown.

Glazed Sweet Potatoes.

Wash and pare six medium-sized potatoes. Cook ten minutes in boiling salted water. Drain, cut in halves lengthwise, and put in a buttered pan.. Make a syrup by boiling three minutes one-half cup sugar and four table-spoons water; add one tablespoon butter. Brush pota-toes with syrup and bake ~~fifteen minutes~~, *until brown* basting ~~twice~~ with remaining syrup.

Sweet Potato Balls.

To two cups hot riced sweet potatoes add three table-spoons butter, one-half teaspoon salt, few grains pepper, and one beaten egg. Shape in small balls, roll in flour, fry in deep fat, and drain. If potatoes are very dry, it will be necessary to add hot milk to moisten.

Sweet Potato Croquettes.

Prepare mixture for Sweet Potato Balls. Shape in croquettes, dip in crumbs, egg, and crumbs again, fry in deep fat, and drain.

WARMED–OVER POTATOES.

Potato Cakes.

Shape cold mashed potato in small cakes, and roll in flour. Butter hot omelet pan, put in cakes, brown one side, turn and brown other side, adding butter as needed to prevent burning; or pack potato in small buttered pan as soon as it comes from table, and set aside until ready for use. Turn from pan, cut in pieces, roll in flour, and cook same as Potato Cakes.

Creamed Potatoes.

Reheat two cups cold boiled potatoes, cut in dice, in one and one-fourth cups White Sauce I.

Potatoes au Gratin.

Put Creamed Potatoes in buttered baking-dish, cover with buttered crumbs, and bake on centre grate until crumbs are brown.

Delmonico Potatoes.

To Potatoes au Gratin add one-third cup grated mild cheese, arranging potatoes and cheese in alternate layers before covering with crumbs.

Hashed Brown Potatoes.

Try out fat salt pork cut in small cubes, remove scraps; there should be about one-third cup of fat. Add ~~two~~ *4* cups cold boiled potatoes finely chopped, one-eighth teaspoon pepper, and salt if needed. Mix potatoes thoroughly with fat; cook three minutes, stirring constantly; let stand to brown underneath. Fold as an omelet and turn on hot platter. *parsley + onion juice.*

Sautéd Potatoes.

Cut cold boiled potatoes in one-fourth inch slices, season with salt and pepper, put in a hot, well-greased frying-pan, brown on one side, turn and brown on other side

Chartreuse Potatoes.

Cut cold boiled potatoes in one-fourth inch slices, sprinkle with salt, pepper, and a few drops onion juice, put together in pairs, dip in Batter I., fry in deep fat, and drain on brown paper.

Lyonnaise Potatoes I.

Cook five minutes three tablespoons butter with one small onion, cut in thin slices; add three cold boiled potatoes cut in one-fourth inch slices and sprinkled with salt and pepper; stir until well mixed with onion and butter; let stand until potato is brown underneath, fold, and turn on a hot platter. This dish is much improved and potatoes brown better by addition of two tablespoons Brown Stock. Sprinkle with finely chopped parsley if desired.

Lyonnaise Potatoes II.

Slice cold boiled potatoes to make two cups. Cook five minutes one and one-half tablespoons butter with one tablespoon finely chopped onion. Melt three tablespoons butter, season with salt and pepper, add potatoes, and cook until potatoes have absorbed butter, occasionally shaking pan. Add butter and onion, and when well mixed, add one-half tablespoon finely chopped parsley.

French Chef.

Oak Hill Potatoes.

Cut four cold boiled potatoes and four hard boiled eggs in one-fourth inch slices. Put layer of potatoes in buttered baking-dish, sprinkle with salt and pepper, cover with layer of eggs; repeat, and pour over two cups Thin White Sauce. Cover with buttered ~~cracker~~ crumbs and bake until crumbs are brown.

CHAPTER XXI.

SALADS AND SALAD DRESSINGS.

SALADS, which constitute a course in almost every dinner, but a few years since seldom appeared on the
table.   They are now made in an endless variety of ways,
and are composed of meat, fish, vegetables (alone or in
combination) or fruits, with the addition of a dressing.
The salad plants, lettuce, watercress, chiccory, cucumbers, etc., contain but little nutriment, but are cooling,
refreshing, and assist in stimulating the appetite.   They
are valuable for the water and potash salts they contain.
The olive oil, which usually forms the largest part of the
dressing, furnishes nutriment, and is of much value to the
system.

Salads made of greens should always be served crisp
and cold.   The vegetables should be thoroughly washed,
allowed to stand in cold or ice water until crisp, then
drained and spread on a towel and set aside in a cold
place until serving time.   See Lettuce, page 263.   Dressing may be added at table or just before sending to
table.   If greens are allowed to stand in dressing they
will soon wilt.   It should be remembered that winter
greens are raised under glass and should be treated as
any other hothouse plant.   Lettuce will be affected by a
change of temperature and wilt just as quickly as delicate
flowers.

Canned or cold cooked left-over vegetables are well
utilized in salads, but are best mixed with French Dressing and allowed to stand in a cold place one hour before
serving.   Where several vegetables are used in the same

salad they should be marinated separately, and arranged for serving just before sending to table.

Meat for salads should be freed from skin and gristle, cut in small cubes, and allowed to stand mixed with French Dressing before combining with vegetables. Fish should be flaked or cut in cubes.

Where salads are dressed at table, first sprinkle with salt and pepper, add oil, and lastly vinegar. If vinegar is added before oil, the greens will become wet, and oil will not cling, but settle to bottom of bowl.

A Chapon. Remove a small piece from end of French loaf and rub over with a clove of garlic, first dipped in salt. Place in bottom of salad bowl before arranging salad. A chapon is often used in vegetable salads, and gives an agreeable additional flavor.

To Marinate. The word marinate, used in cookery, means to add salt, pepper, oil, and vinegar to a salad ingredient or mixture and let stand until well seasoned.

SALAD DRESSINGS.

French Dressing.

½ teaspoon salt.   2 tablespoons vinegar.
¼ teaspoon pepper.   4 tablespoons olive oil.

Mix ingredients and stir until well blended. French Dressing is more easily prepared and largely used than any other dressing.

Cream Dressing I.

½ tablespoon salt.   1 egg slightly beaten.
½ tablespoon mustard.   2½ tablespoons melted butter.
1¼ tablespoons sugar.   ¾ cup cream.
                   ¼ cup vinegar.

Mix ingredients in order given, adding vinegar very slowly. Cook over boiling water, stirring constantly until mixture thickens, strain and cool.

Cream Dressing II.

1 teaspoon mustard.	Few grains cayenne.
1 teaspoon salt.	1 teaspoon melted butter.
2 teaspoons flour.	Yolk 1 egg.
2 teaspoons powdered sugar.	⅓ cup hot vinegar.

½ cup thick cream.

Mix dry ingredients, add butter, egg, and vinegar slowly. Cook over boiling water, stirring constantly until mixture thickens; cool, and add to heavy cream, beaten until stiff.

Boiled Dressing.

½ tablespoon salt.	½ tablespoon flour.
1 teaspoon mustard.	Yolks 2 eggs.
1½ tablespoons sugar.	1½ tablespoons melted butter.
Few grains cayenne.	¾ cup milk.

¼ cup vinegar.

Mix dry ingredients, add yolks of eggs slightly beaten, butter, milk, and vinegar very slowly. Cook over boiling water until mixture thickens; strain, and cool.

German Dressing.

½ cup thick cream.	¼ teaspoon salt.
3 tablespoons vinegar.	Few grains pepper.

Beat cream until stiff, using Dover Egg-beater. Add salt, pepper, and vinegar very slowly, continuing the beating.

Chicken Salad Dressing.

½ cup rich chicken stock.	1 teaspoon salt.
½ cup vinegar.	¼ teaspoon pepper.
Yolks 5 eggs.	Few grains cayenne.
2 tablespoons mixed mustard.	½ cup thick cream.

⅓ cup melted butter.

Reduce stock in which a fowl has been cooked to one-half cupful. Add vinegar, yolks of eggs slightly beaten, mustard, salt, pepper, and cayenne. Cook over boiling water, stirring constantly until mixture thickens. Strain, add cream and melted butter, then cool.

Oil Dressing I.

4 hard boiled eggs.	½ teaspoon mustard.
4 tablespoons oil.	½ teaspoon salt.
4 tablespoons vinegar.	Few grains cayenne.
½ tablespoon sugar.	White 1 egg.

Rub yolks of eggs until smooth, add dry ingredients, then gradually oil and vinegar. Stir in lightly white of egg beaten until stiff.

Oil Dressing II.

1½ teaspoons mustard.	2 tablespoons oil.
1 teaspoon salt.	⅓ cup vinegar diluted with
2 teaspoons powdered sugar.	cold water to make one-
Few grains cayenne.	half cup.
2 eggs slightly beaten.	

Mix dry ingredients, add egg and oil gradually, stirring constantly until thoroughly mixed ; then add diluted vinegar. Cook over boiling water until mixture thickens ; strain and cool.

Mayonnaise Dressing I.

1 teaspoon mustard.	Yolks 2 eggs.
1 teaspoon salt.	2 tablespoons lemon juice.
1 teaspoon powdered sugar.	2 tablespoons vinegar.
Few grains cayenne.	1½ cups olive oil.

Mix dry ingredients, add egg yolks, and when well mixed, add one-half teaspoon of vinegar. Add oil gradually, at first drop by drop, and stir constantly. As mixture thickens, thin with vinegar or lemon juice. Add oil, and vinegar or lemon juice alternately, until all is used, stirring or beating constantly. If oil is added too rapidly, dressing will have a curdled appearance. A smooth consistency may be restored by taking yolk of another egg and adding curdled mixture slowly to it. It is desirable to have bowl containing mixture placed in a larger bowl of crushed ice, to which a small quantity of water has been added. Olive oil for making Mayonnaise should always be thoroughly chilled. A silver fork, wire whisk, small wooden spoon, or Dover Egg-beater may be used as preferred. If one has a Keystone Egg-beater, dressing may be made very quickly by its use. Mayonnaise should be stiff enough to hold its shape. It soon liquefies when added to meat or vegetables; therefore it should be added just before serving time.

Mayonnaise Dressing II.

Use same ingredients as for Mayonnaise Dressing I., adding mashed yolk of a hard boiled egg to dry ingredients.

French Chef.

Cream Mayonnaise Dressing.

To Mayonnaise Dressing I. or II. add one-third cup thick cream, beaten until stiff. This recipe should be used only when dressing is to be eaten the day it is made.

Colored Mayonnaise Dressing.

Lobster coral, rubbed through a fine sieve, added to Mayonnaise, makes *Red Mayonnaise*.

Finely chopped parsley leaves pounded with a small quantity of lemon juice, strained through cheese cloth and added to Mayonnaise makes *Green Mayonnaise ;* or Spinach Green may be used if desired.

Potato Mayonnaise.

Very small baked potato.	1 teaspoon powdered sugar.
1 teaspoon mustard.	2 tablespoons vinegar.
1 teaspoon salt.	¾ cup olive oil.

Remove and mash the inside of potato. Add mustard, salt, and powdered sugar; add one tablespoon vinegar, and rub mixture through a fine sieve.   Add slowly oil and remaining vinegar.   By the taste one would hardly realize eggs were not used in the making.

SALADS.

Dressed Lettuce.

Prepare lettuce as directed on page 263.   Serve with French Dressing.

Lettuce and Cucumber Salad.

Place a chapon in bottom of salad bowl.   Wash, drain, and dry one head lettuce, arrange in bowl, and place between leaves one cucumber cut in thin slices.   Serve with French Dressing.

Lettuce and Radish Salad.

Prepare and arrange as for Dressed Lettuce.   Place between leaves six radishes which have been washed, scraped, and cut in thin slices.   Garnish with round radishes cut to represent tulips.   See page 268.   Serve with French Dressing.

Lettuce and Tomato Salad.

Peel and chill three tomatoes.   Cut in halves crosswise, arrange each half on a lettuce leaf.   Garnish with Mayonnaise Dressing forced through a pastry bag and tube. If tomatoes are small, cut in quarters, and allow one tomato to each lettuce leaf.

Dressed Watercress.

Wash, remove roots, drain, and chill watercress.   Arrange in salad dish, and serve with French Dressing.

Watercress and Cucumber Salad.

Prepare watercress and add one cucumber, pared, chilled, and cut in one-half inch dice.   Serve with French Dressing.

Cucumber and Tomato Salad.

Arrange on a bed of lettuce leaves, sliced tomatoes. Pile on each slice, cucumber cubes cut one-half inch square. Serve with French or Mayonnaise Dressing.

Dressed Celery.

Wash, scrape, and cut stalks of celery in thin slices. Mix with Cream Dressing I.

Celery and Cabbage Salad.

Remove outside leaves from a small solid white cabbage, and cut off stalk close to leaves. Cut out centre and with a sharp knife shred finely. Let stand one hour in cold or ice water. Drain, wring in double cheese cloth, to make as dry as possible. Mix with equal parts celery cut in small pieces. Moisten with Cream Dressing and refill cabbage. Arrange on a folded napkin and garnish with celery tips and parsley between folds of napkin and around top of cabbage.

String Bean Salad.

String Bean Salad.

Marinate two cups cold string beans with French Dressing. Add one teaspoon finely cut chives. Pile in centre of salad dish and arrange around base thin slices of radishes, overlapping one another.   Garnish top with radish cut to represent a tulip.

Potato Salad.

Potato Salad.

Cut cold boiled potatoes in one-half inch cubes. Sprinkle four cupfuls with one-half tablespoon salt and one-fourth teaspoon pepper. Add four tablespoons oil and mix thoroughly; then add two tablespoons vinegar. A few drops of onion juice may be added, or one-half tablespoon chives finely cut. Arrange in a mound and garnish with whites and yolks of two hard boiled eggs, cold boiled red beets, and parsley. Chop whites and arrange on one-fourth of the mound; chop beets finely, mix with one tablespoon vinegar, and let stand fifteen minutes; then arrange on fourths of mound next to whites. Arrange on remaining fourth of mound, yolks chopped or forced through a potato ricer. Put small sprigs of parsley in lines dividing beets from eggs; also garnish with parsley at base.

Potato and Celery Salad.

To two cups boiled potatoes cut in one-half inch cubes add one-half cup finely cut celery and a medium-sized apple, pared, cut in eighths, then eighths cut in thin slices. Marinate with French Dressing. Arrange in a mound and garnish with celery tips and sections of bright red apple.

Macédoine Salad.

Marinate separately cold cooked cauliflower, peas, and carrots, cut in small cubes, and outer stalks of celery finely cut. Arrange peas and carrots in alternate piles in centre of a salad dish. Pile cauliflower on top. Arrange celery in four piles at equal distances. At top of each pile place a small gherkin cut lengthwise in very thin slices, beginning at blossom end and cutting nearly to stem end. Open slices to represent a fan. Place between piles of celery a slice of tomato.

Almost any cold cooked vegetables on hand may be used for a Macédoine Salad, and if care is taken in arrangement, they make a very attractive dish.

Individual Salads.
1. Stuffed Tomato.   2. Sweetbread and Cucumber.

Stuffed Tomato Salad.

Peel medium-sized tomatoes. Remove thin slice from top of each and take out seeds and some of pulp. Sprinkle inside with salt, invert, and let stand one-half hour. Fill tomatoes with cucumbers cut in small cubes and mixed with Mayonnaise Dressing. Arrange on lettuce leaves and garnish top of each with Mayonnaise Dressing forced through a pastry-bag and tube.

Tomato Jelly Salad.

To one can stewed and strained tomatoes add one tea-spoon each of salt and powdered sugar, and one box gelatine which has soaked fifteen minutes in one-half cup cold water. Pour into small cups and chill. Run a knife around inside of moulds, so that when taken out shapes may have a rough surface suggesting a fresh tomato. Place on lettuce leaves and garnish top of each with Mayonnaise Dressing.

Salad à la Russe.

Peel six tomatoes, remove thin slices from top of each, and take out seeds and pulp. Sprinkle inside with salt, invert, and let stand one-half hour. Place seeds and pulp removed from tomatoes in a strainer to drain. Mix one-third cup cucumbers cut in dice, one-third cup cold cooked peas, one-fourth cup pickles finely chopped, one-third cup tomato pulp, and two tablespoons capers. Season with salt, pepper, and vinegar. Put in a cheese cloth and squeeze; then add one-half cup cold cooked chicken cut in very small dice. Mix with Mayonnaise Dressing, re-fill tomatoes, sprinkle with finely chopped parsley, and place each on a lettuce leaf.

Spinach Salad.

Pick over, wash, and cook one-half peck spinach. Drain, and chop finely. Season with salt, pepper, and lemon juice, and add one tablespoon melted butter. Butter slightly small tin moulds and pack solidly with mixture. Chill, remove from moulds, and arrange on thin slices of cold boiled tongue cut in circular pieces. Garnish base of each with a wreath of parsley, and serve on top of each Sauce Tartare.

Egg Salad I.

Cut six hard boiled eggs in halves crosswise, keeping whites in pairs. Remove yolks, and mash or put through a potato ricer. Add slowly enough Oil Dressing II. to moisten. Make into balls the size of original yolks and refill whites. Arrange on a bed of lettuce and pour Oil Dressing II. around eggs.

Egg Salad II.

Cut four hard boiled eggs in halves crosswise in such a way that tops of halves may be cut in small points. Remove yolks, mash, and add an equal amount of finely chopped cooked chicken. Moisten with Oil Dressing I., shape in balls size of original yolks, and refill whites. Arrange on lettuce leaves and serve with Oil Dressing I.

Lenten Salad.

Separate yolks and whites of four hard boiled eggs. Chop whites finely, marinate with French Dressing, and arrange on lettuce leaves. Force yolks through a potato ricer and pile on the centre of whites. Serve with French Dressing.

Cheese Salad.

Arrange one head of lettuce on a salad dish, sprinkle with one-fourth pound Edam cheese broken in very small pieces, and pour over it French Dressing.

Nut Salad.

Mix one cup chopped English walnut meat and two cups shredded lettuce. Arrange on lettuce leaves and garnish with Mayonnaise Dressing.

Nut and Celery Salad.

Mix equal parts of English walnut or pecan nut meat cut in pieces, and celery cut in small pieces. Marinate with French Dressing. Serve with a border of shredded lettuce.

Banana Salad.

Remove one section of skin from each of four bananas. Take out fruit, scrape, and cut fruit from one banana in thin slices, fruit from other three bananas in one-half inch cubes.   Marinate cubes with French Dressing.   Refill skins and garnish each with slices of banana.   Stack around a mound of lettuce leaves.

Salmon Salad.

Flake remnants of cold boiled salmon.   Mix with French, Mayonnaise, or Cream Dressing.   Arrange on nests of lettuce leaves.   Garnish with the yolk of a hard boiled egg forced through a potato ricer, and white of egg cut in strips.

Shrimp Salad.

Remove shrimps from can, cover with cold or ice water, and let stand twenty minutes.   Drain, dry between towels, remove intestinal veins, and break in pieces, reserving six of the finest.   Moisten with Cream Dressing II., and arrange on nests of lettuce leaves.   Put a spoonful of dressing on each, and garnish with a whole shrimp, capers, and an olive cut in quarters.

Sardine Salad.

Remove skin and bones from sardines, and mix with an equal quantity of the mashed yolks of hard boiled eggs. Arrange in nests of lettuce leaves and serve with Mayonnaise Dressing.

Lobster Salad I.

Remove lobster meat from shell, cut in one-half inch cubes, and marinate with a French Dressing.   Mix with a small quantity of Mayonnaise Dressing and arrange in nests of lettuce leaves.   Put a spoonful of Mayonnaise on each, and sprinkle with lobster coral rubbed through a fine sieve. Garnish with small lobster claws around outside of dish. Cream Dressing I. or II. may be used in place of Mayonnaise Dressing.

Lobster Salad II.

Lobster Salad II.

Prepare lobster as for Lobster Salad I. Add an equal quantity of celery cut in small pieces, kept one hour in cold or ice water, then drained and dried in a towel. Moisten with any cream or oil dressing. Arrange on a salad dish, pile slightly in centre, cover with dressing, sprinkle with lobster coral forced through a fine sieve, and garnish with a border of curled celery.

To Curl Celery. Cut thick stalks of celery in two-inch pieces. With a sharp knife, beginning at outside of stalks, make five cuts parallel with each other, extending one-third the length of pieces. Make six cuts at right-angles to cuts already made. Put pieces in cold or ice water and let stand over night or for several hours, when they will curl back and celery will be found very crisp. Both ends of celery may be curled if one cares to take the trouble.

Lobster Salad III.

Remove large claws and split a lobster in two lengthwise by beginning the cut on inside of tail end and cutting through entire length of tail and body. Open lobster, remove tail meat, liver, and coral, and set aside. Discard intestinal vein, stomach, and fat, and wipe inside thoroughly with cloth wrung out of cold water. Body meat and small claws are left on shell. Remove meat from upper parts of large claws and cut off (using scissors or can opener) one-half the shell from lower parts, taking

Lobster Salad III.

out meat and leaving the parts in suitable condition to refill. Cut lobster meat in one-half inch cubes and mix with an equal quantity of finely cut celery. Season with salt, pepper, and vinegar, and moisten with Mayonnaise Dressing. Refill tail, body, and under half of large claw shells. Mix liver and coral, rub through a sieve, add one tablespoon Mayonnaise Dressing and a few drops anchovy essence, with enough more Mayonnaise Dressing to cover lobster already in shell. Arrange on a bed of lettuce leaves, and sprinkle top with finely chopped parsley.

Chicken Salad I.

Cut cold boiled fowl or remnants of roast chicken in one-half inch cubes, and marinate with French Dressing. Add an equal quantity of celery, washed, scraped, cut in small pieces, chilled in cold or ice water, drained, and dried in a towel. Just before serving moisten with Cream, Oil, or Mayonnaise Dressing. Mound on a salad dish, and garnish with yolks of hard boiled eggs forced through a potato ricer, capers, and celery tips.

Chicken Salad II.

Cut cold boiled fowl or remnants of roast chicken in one-half inch dice. To two cups add one and one-half cups celery cut in small pieces, and moisten with Cream Dressing II. Mound on a salad dish, cover with dressing, and garnish with capers, thin slices cut from small pickles, and curled celery.

Chicken and Oyster Salad.

Clean, parboil, and drain one pint oysters. Remove tough muscles, and mix soft parts with an equal quantity of cold boiled fowl cut in one-half inch dice. Moisten with any salad dressing, and serve on a bed of lettuce leaves.

Sweetbread and Cucumber Salad.

Parboil a pair of sweetbreads twenty minutes; drain, cool, and cut in one-half inch cubes. Mix with an equal quantity of cucumber cut in one-half inch dice. Season with salt and pepper, and moisten with German Dressing. Arrange in nests of lettuce leaves or in cucumber cups, and garnish with watercress. To prepare cucumber cups, pare cucumbers, remove thick slices from each end, and cut in halves crosswise. Take out centres, put cups in cold water, and let stand until crisp; drain, and dry for refilling. Small cucumbers may be pared, cut in halves lengthwise, centres removed, and cut pointed at ends to represent a boat.

CHAPTER XXII.

ENTRÉES.

Batters and Fritters.

Batter I.

1 cup bread flour.   Few grains pepper.
½ teaspoon salt.   ⅔ cup milk.
              2 Eggs.

Mix flour, salt, and pepper.   Add milk gradually, and eggs well beaten.

Batter II.

1 cup bread flour.   ⅔ cup water.
1 tablespoon sugar.   ½ tablespoon olive oil.
¼ teaspoon salt.   White 1 egg.

Mix flour, sugar, and salt.   Add water gradually, then olive oil and white of egg beaten until stiff.

Batter III.

1⅓ cups flour.   ¼ teaspoon salt.
2 teaspoons baking powder. ⅔ cup milk.
              1 egg.

Mix and sift dry ingredients, add milk gradually, and egg well beaten.

Batter IV.

1 cup flour.   ¼ teaspoon salt.
1½ teaspoons baking powder. ⅓ cup milk.
3 tablespoons powdered sugar. 1 egg.

Mix and sift dry ingredients. add milk gradually, and egg well beaten.

Batter V.

1 cup flour
¼ teaspoon salt.
⅔ cup milk or water.

Yolks 2 eggs.
Whites 2 eggs.
1 tablespoon melted butter
or olive oil.

Mix salt and flour, add milk gradually, yolks of eggs beaten until thick, butter and whites of eggs beaten until stiff.

Apple Fritters I.

2 medium-sized sour apples. Batter III.
Powdered sugar.

Pare, core, and cut apples in eighths, then cut eighths in slices and stir into batter. Drop by spoonfuls and fry in deep fat. (See Rules for Testing Fat, page 23.) Drain on brown paper, and sprinkle with powdered sugar. Serve hot on a folded napkin.

Apple Fritters II.

2 medium-sized sour apples. Batter IV.
Prepare and cook as Apple Fritters I.

Apple Fritters III.

Sour apples.
Powdered sugar.

Lemon juice.
Batter II.

Core, pare, and cut apples in one-third inch slices. Sprinkle with powdered sugar and few drops lemon juice; cover, and let stand one-half hour. Drain, dip pieces in batter, fry in deep fat, and drain. Arrange on a folded napkin in form of a circle, and serve with Sabyon or Hard Sauce.

Banana Fritters I.

4 bananas.
Powdered sugar.
Batter V.

½ tablespoon lemon juice.
3 tablespoons sherry wine.

Remove skins from bananas. Scrape bananas, cut in halves lengthwise, and cut halves in two pieces crosswise.

Sprinkle with powdered sugar, lemon-juice, and wine; cover, and let stand thirty minutes; drain, dip in batter, fry in deep fat, and drain on brown paper. Sprinkle with powdered sugar, and serve on a folded napkin.

Banana Fritters II.

3 bananas.	¼ teaspoon salt.
1 cup bread flour.	¼ cup milk.
2 teaspoons baking powder.	1 egg.
1 tablespoon powdered sugar.	1 tablespoon lemon juice.

Mix and sift dry ingredients. Beat egg until light, add milk, and combine mixtures; then add lemon juice and banana fruit forced through a sieve. Drop by spoonfuls and fry in deep fat. Drain on brown paper. Serve with Lemon Sauce.

Orange Fritters.

Peel two oranges and separate into sections. Make an opening in each section just large enough to admit of passage for seeds, which should be removed. Dip sections in Batter II., III., IV., or V., and fry and serve same as other fritters.

Fruit Fritters.

Fresh peaches, apricots, or pears may be cut in pieces, dipped in batter, and fried same as other fritters. Canned fruits may be used, after draining from their syrup.

Cauliflower Fritters.

Cold cooked cauliflower.   Batter V.
Salt and pepper.

Sprinkle pieces of cauliflower with salt and pepper and dip in Batter I. or V. Fry in deep fat, and drain on brown paper.

Fried Celery.

Celery cut in three-inch
 pieces.

Salt and pepper.
Batter I., III., or V.

Parboil celery until soft, drain, sprinkle with salt and pepper, dip in batter, fry in deep fat, and drain on brown paper.   Serve with Tomato Sauce.

Tomato Fritters.

1 can tomatoes.
6 cloves.
¼ cup sugar.
3 slices onion.
   1 egg. ¾ c. flour

1 teaspoon salt.
Few grains cayenne.
¼ cup butter.
~~⅓ cup corn-starch~~.

Cook first four ingredients twenty minutes, rub all through a sieve except seeds, and season with salt and pepper.   Melt butter, and when bubbling, add corn-starch and tomato gradually; cook two minutes, then add egg slightly beaten.   Pour into a buttered shallow tin and cool.   Turn on a board, cut in squares, diamonds, or strips.   Roll in crumbs, eggs, and crumbs again, fry in deep fat, and drain.

Cherry Fritters.

2 cups scalded milk.
¼ cup corn-starch.
¼ cup flour.
½ cup sugar.

¼ teaspoon salt.
¼ cup cold milk.
Yolks 3 eggs.
½ cup Maraschino cherries
 cut in halves.

Mix corn-starch, flour, sugar, and salt.   Dilute with cold milk and add beaten yolks; then add gradually to scalded milk and cook fifteen minutes in double boiler, stirring constantly until thickened.   Add cherries, pour into a buttered shallow tin, and cool.   Turn on a board, cut in squares, diamonds, or strips, dip in flour, egg, and crumbs, fry in deep fat, and drain.   Serve with Maraschino Sauce.

Maraschino Sauce.

⅔ cup boiling water.
⅓ cup sugar.
2 tablespoons corn-starch.
½ tablespoon butter.

¼ cup Maraschino cherries
cut in halves.
½ cup Maraschino syrup.

Mix sugar and corn-starch, add gradually to boiling water, stirring constantly. Boil five minutes, and add cherries, syrup, and butter.

Farina Cakes with Jelly.

3 2 cups scalded milk.
½ cup farina (scant).
1 egg.

¼ cup sugar.
½ teaspoon salt.

Add farina, sugar, and salt to milk, and cook in double boiler twenty minutes, stirring constantly until mixture has thickened. Add egg slightly beaten, pour into a buttered shallow pan, and brush over with one egg slightly beaten and diluted with one tablespoon milk. Brown in oven. Cut in squares, and serve with a cube of jelly on each square.

Gnocchi à la Romaine.

¼ cup butter.
¼ cup flour.
¼ cup corn-starch.
¾ cup grated cheese.

½ teaspoon salt.
2 cups scalded milk.
Yolks 2 eggs.

Melt butter, and when bubbling, add flour, corn-starch, salt, and milk, gradually. Cook three minutes, stirring constantly. Add yolks of eggs slightly beaten, and one-half cup cheese. Pour into a buttered shallow pan, and cool. Turn on a board, cut in squares, diamonds, or strips. Place on a platter, sprinkle with remaining cheese, and brown in oven.

Chocolate Fritters with Vanilla Sauce.

Make Queen Fritters, fill with Chocolate Cream Filling, and serve with Vanilla Sauce; filling to be cold and sauce warm.

Queen Fritters.

¼ cup butter (scant).   ½ cup flour.
½ cup boiling water.   2 eggs.
Fruit preserve or marmalade.

Put butter in small saucepan and pour on water. As soon as water again reaches boiling point, add flour all at once, and stir until mixture leaves sides of saucepan, cleaving to spoon. Remove from fire and add eggs unbeaten, one at a time, beating mixture thoroughly between addition of eggs. Drop by spoonfuls and fry in deep fat until well puffed and browned. Drain, make an opening, and fill with preserve or marmalade. Sprinkle with powdered sugar and serve on a folded napkin.

Sponge Fritters.

2⅔ cups flour.   ⅓ cup melted butter.
⅓ cup sugar.   ¼ teaspoon salt.
⅞ cup scalded milk.   2 eggs.
⅓ yeast cake dissolved in 2   Grated rind ½ lemon.
   tablespoons lukewarm water.   Quince marmalade.
Currant jelly.

Make a sponge of one-half the flour, sugar, milk, and dissolved yeast cake; let rise to double its bulk. Add remaining ingredients and let rise again. Toss on a floured board, roll to one-fourth inch thickness, shape with a small biscuit cutter (first dipped in flour), cover, and let rise on board. Take each piece and hollow in centre to form a nest. In one-half the pieces put one-half teaspoon of currant jelly and quince marmalade mixed in the proportion of one part jelly to two parts marmalade. Brush with milk, edges of filled pieces. Cover with unfilled pieces and press edges closely together with fingers first dipped in flour. If this is not carefully done fritters will separate during frying. Fry in deep fat, drain on brown paper, and sprinkle with powdered sugar.

Croquettes.

Before making Croquettes, consult Rules for Testing Fat for Frying, page 23; Egging and Crumbing, page 25; Uses for Stale Bread, page 69; and Potato Croquettes, page 282.

Cheese Croquettes.

3 tablespoons butter.	1 cup mild cheese cut in
¼ cup flour.	very small cubes.
⅔ cup milk.	½ grated Gruyère cheese.
Yolks 2 eggs.	Salt and pepper.
Few grains cayenne.	

Make a thick white sauce, using butter, flour, and milk, add yolks of eggs without first beating, and stir until well mixed; then add cheese. As soon as grated cheese melts, remove from fire and season with salt, pepper, and cayenne. Spread in a shallow pan and cool. Turn on a board, cut in small squares or strips, dip in crumbs, egg, and crumbs again, fry in deep fat, and drain on brown paper. Serve for a cheese course.

Chestnut Croquettes.

1 cup mashed French chestnuts.	Yolks 2 eggs.
2 tablespoons thick cream.	1 teaspoon sugar.
¼ teaspoon vanilla.	

Mix ingredients in order given. Shape in balls, dip in crumbs, egg, and crumbs again, fry in deep fat, and drain.

Rice Croquettes with Jelly.

½ cup rice.	½ teaspoon salt.
½ cup boiling water.	Yolks 2 eggs.
1 cup scalded milk.	1 tablespoon butter.

Wash rice, add to water with salt, cover, and steam until rice has absorbed water. Then add milk, stir lightly with a fork, cover, and steam until rice is soft. Remove from fire, add egg yolks and butter; spread on a shallow plate to cool. Shape in balls, roll in crumbs, then shape in form of nests. Dip in egg, again in crumbs, fry in deep fat, and drain. Put a cube of jelly in each croquette. Arrange on a folded napkin and garnish with parsley, or serve around game.

Sweet Rice Croquettes.

To rice croquette mixture add two tablespoons powdered sugar and grated rind one-half lemon. Shape in cylinder forms, dip in crumbs, egg, and crumbs again, fry in deep fat, and drain.

Rice and Tomato Croquettes.

½ cup rice.	2 cloves.
¾ cup stock.	¼ teaspoon peppercorns.
½ can tomatoes.	1 teaspoon sugar.
1 slice onion.	1 egg.
1 slice carrot.	¼ cup grated cheese.
1 sprig parsley.	1 tablespoon butter.
1 sprig thyme.	½ teaspoon salt.

Few grains cayenne.

Wash rice, and steam in stock until rice has absorbed stock; then add tomatoes which have been cooked twenty minutes with onion, carrot, parsley, thyme, cloves, peppercorns, and sugar, and then rubbed through a strainer. Remove from fire, add egg slightly beaten, cheese, butter, salt, and cayenne. Spread on a plate to cool. Shape in form of cylinders, dip in crumbs, egg, and crumbs again, fry in deep fat, and drain.

Oyster and Macaroni Croquettes.

⅓ cup macaroni broken in ½ inch pieces.	Few grains cayenne. Few grains mace.
1 pint oysters.	½ teaspoon lemon juice.
1 cup Thick White Sauce.	¼ cup grated cheese.

Cook macaroni in boiling salted water until soft, drain in a colander, and pour over macaroni two cups cold water. Clean and parboil oysters, remove tough muscles, and cut soft parts in pieces. Reserve one-half cup oyster liquor and use in making Thick White Sauce in place of all milk. Mix macaroni and oysters, add Thick White Sauce and seasonings. Spread on a plate to cool. Shape, dip in crumbs, egg, and crumbs again, fry in deep fat, and drain.

Salmon Croquettes.

1¾ cups cold flaked salmon.	Few grains cayenne.
1 cup Thick White Sauce.	1 teaspoon lemon juice.
Salt.	

Add sauce to salmon, then add seasonings. Spread on a plate to cool. Shape, dip in crumbs, egg, and crumbs again, fry in deep fat, and drain.

Salmon Cutlets.

Mix equal parts of cold flaked salmon and hot mashed potatoes. Season with salt and pepper. Shape in form of cutlets, dip in crumbs, egg, and crumbs again, fry in deep fat, and drain. Arrange in a circle, having cutlets overlap one another, on a folded napkin. Garnish with parsley.

Lobster Croquettes.

2 cups chopped lobster meat.	Few grains cayenne.
½ teaspoon salt.	1 teaspoon lemon.
¼ teaspoon mustard.	1 cup Thick White Sauce.

Add seasonings to lobster, then add Thick White Sauce. Cool, shape, dip in crumbs, egg, and crumbs again, fry in deep fat, and drain. Serve with Tomato Cream Sauce.

Lobster Cutlets.

2 cups chopped lobster meat.	1 teaspoon lemon juice.
½ teaspoon salt.	Yolk 1 egg.
Few grains cayenne.	1 teaspoon finely chopped
Few gratings nutmeg.	parsley.
1 cup Thick White Sauce.	

Mix ingredients in order given, and cool. Shape in form of cutlets, crumb, and fry same as croquettes. Make

Lobster Cutlets.

a cut at small end of each cutlet, and insert in each the tip end of a small claw. Stack around a mound of parsley. Serve with Sauce Tartare.

Lamb Croquettes.

1 tablespoon finely chopped onion.
2 tablespoons butter.
¼ cup flour.
1 cup stock.

1 cup cold cooked lamb cut in small cubes.
⅔ cup boiled potato cubes.
Salt and pepper.
1 teaspoon finely chopped parsley.

Fry onion in butter five minutes, then remove onion. To butter add flour and stock, and cook two minutes. Add meat, potato, salt, and pepper. Simmer until meat and potato have absorbed sauce. Add parsley, and spread on a shallow dish to cool. Shape, dip in crumbs, egg, and crumbs again, fry in deep fat, and drain. Serve with Tomato Sauce.

Veal Croquettes.

2 cups chopped cold cooked veal.
½ teaspoon salt.
⅛ teaspoon pepper.

Few grains cayenne.
Few drops onion juice.
Yolk 1 egg.

1 cup thick sauce.

Mix ingredients in order given. In making the thick sauce, use rich white stock in place of milk. Cool, shape, crumb, and fry same as other croquettes.

Chicken Croquettes I.

1¾ cups chopped cold cooked
    fowl.
½ teaspoon salt.
¼ teaspoon celery salt.
Few grains cayenne.

1 teaspoon lemon juice.
Few drops onion juice.
1 teaspoon finely chopped
    parsley.
1 cup Thick White Sauce.

Mix ingredients in order given.   Cool, shape, crumb, and fry same as other croquettes.

White meat of fowl absorbs more sauce than dark meat. This must be remembered if dark meat alone is used. Croquette mixtures should always be as soft as can be conveniently handled, when croquettes will be soft and creamy inside.

Chicken Croquettes II.

Clean and dress a four-pound fowl.   Put into a kettle with six cups boiling water, seven slices carrot, two slices turnip, one small onion, one stalk celery, one bay leaf, and three sprigs thyme.   Cook slowly until fowl is tender. Remove fowl; strain liquor, cool, and skim off fat.   Make a thick sauce, using one-fourth cup butter, one-half cup flour, one and one-third cups chicken stock, and one-half cup cream.   Remove meat from chicken, chop, and moisten with sauce.   Season with salt, cayenne, and slight grating of nutmeg; then add one beaten egg, cool, shape, crumb, and fry same as other croquettes.   Arrange around a mound of green peas, and serve with Cream Sauce or Wine Jelly.

Chicken and Mushroom Croquettes.

Make as Chicken Croquettes I., using one and one-third cups chicken meat and two-thirds cup chopped mushrooms.

Cutlets of Sweetbreads à la Victoria.

2 pairs parboiled sweetbreads.	Slight grating nutmeg.
2 teaspoons lemon juice.	1 teaspoon finely chopped
½ teaspoon salt.	parsley.
⅛ teaspoon pepper.	1 egg.

1 cup Thick White Sauce.

Chop the sweetbreads, of which there should be two cups; if not enough, add chopped mushrooms to make two cups, then season. Add egg slightly beaten to sauce, and combine mixtures. Cool, shape, crumb, and fry. Make a cut in small end of each cutlet, and insert in each a piece of cold boiled macaroni, one and one-half inches long. Serve with Allemande Sauce.

Cutlets of Sweetbreads à la Victoria.

Swedish Timbales.

¾ cup flour.	½ cup milk.
½ teaspoon salt.	1 egg.
1 teaspoon sugar.	1 tablespoon olive oil.

Mix dry ingredients, add milk gradually, and beaten egg; then add olive oil. Shape, using a hot timbale iron, fry in deep fat until crisp and brown; take from iron and invert on brown paper to drain.

To Heat Timbale Iron.   Heat fat until nearly hot enough to fry uncooked mixtures.   Put iron into hot fat, having fat deep enough to more than cover it, and let stand until heated.   The only way of knowing when iron is of right temperature is to take it from fat, shake what fat may drip from it, lower in batter to three-fourths its depth, raise from batter, then immerse in hot fat.   If batter does not cling to iron, or drops from iron as soon as immersed in fat, it is either too hot or not sufficiently heated.

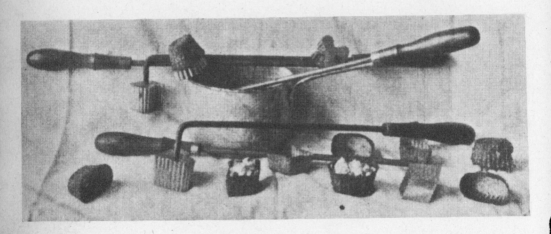

Timbale irons and cases.

To Form Timbales.   Turn timbale batter into a cup. Lower hot iron into cup, taking care that batter covers iron to only three-fourths its depth.   When immersed in fat, mixture will rise to top of iron, and when crisp and brown may be easily slipped off.   If too much batter is used, in cooking it will rise over top of iron, and in order to remove timbale it must be cut around with a sharp knife close to top of iron.   If the cases are soft rather than crisp, batter is too thick and must be diluted with milk.

Fill cases with Creamed Oysters, Chicken, Sweetbreads, or Chicken and Sweetbreads in combination with Mushrooms.

Strawberry Baskets.

Fry Swedish Timbales, making cases one inch deep. Fill with selected strawberries, sprinkled with powdered sugar. Serve as a first course at a ladies' luncheon.

Rice Timbales.

Pack hot boiled rice in slightly buttered small tin moulds. Let stand in hot water ten minutes. Use as a garnish for curried meat, fricassee, or boiled fowl.

Macaroni Timbales.

Line slightly buttered Dario moulds with boiled macaroni. Cut strips the length of height of mould, and place closely together around inside of mould. Fill with Chicken, or Salmon Force-meat. Put in a pan, half surround with hot water, cover with buttered paper, and bake thirty minutes in a moderate oven. Serve with Lobster, Béchamel, or Hollandaise Sauce I.

Spaghetti Timbales.

Line bottom and sides of slightly buttered Dario moulds with long strips of boiled spaghetti coiled around the inside. Fill and bake as Macaroni Timbales.

Halibut Timbales.

1 lb halibut.	Few grains cayenne.
⅓ cup thick cream.	1½ teaspoons lemon juice.
¾ teaspoon salt.	Whites 3 eggs.

Cook halibut in boiling salted water, drain, and rub through a sieve. Season with salt, cayenne, and lemon juice; add cream beaten until stiff, then beaten whites of eggs. Turn into small, slightly buttered moulds, put in a pan, half surround with hot water, cover with buttered paper, and bake twenty minutes in a moderate oven. Remove from moulds, arrange on a serving-dish, pour around Béchamel Sauce or Lobster Sauce II., and garnish with parsley.

Lobster Timbales.

Sprinkle slightly buttered Dario or timbale moulds with lobster coral rubbed through a strainer. Line moulds with Fish Force-meat I., fill centres with Creamed Lobster, and cover with force-meat. Put in a pan, half surround with hot water, place over moulds buttered paper, and bake twenty minutes in a moderate oven. Serve with Lobster or Béchamel Sauce.

Lobster Cream.

Lobster Cream.

2 lb. lobster.	2 teaspoons Anchovy essence.
½ cup soft stale bread crumbs.	½ teaspoon salt.
½ cup milk.	Few grains cayenne.
¼ cup cream.	Whites 3 eggs.

Remove lobster meat from shell and chop finely. Cook bread and milk ten minutes. Add cream, seasonings, and whites of eggs beaten until stiff. Turn into one slightly buttered timbale mould and two slightly buttered Dario moulds. Bake as Lobster Timbales. Remove to serving-dish, having larger mould in centre, smaller moulds one at either end. Pour around Lobster Sauce II., sprinkle with coral rubbed through a sieve, and garnish with pieces of lobster shell from tail, and parsley

Chicken Timbales.

Garnish slightly buttered Dario moulds with chopped truffles or slices of truffles cut in fancy shapes. Line with Chicken Force-meat I., fill centres with Creamed Chicken and Mushrooms, to which has been added a few chopped truffles. Cover with force-meat, and bake as Lobster Timbales. Serve with Béchamel or Yellow Béchamel Sauce.

Suprême of Chicken.

Breast and second joints of un-cooked chicken weighing 4 lbs.	4 eggs. ⅔ cup thick cream. Salt and pepper.

Force chicken through a meat chopper, or chop very finely. Beat eggs separately, add one at a time, stirring until mixture is smooth. Add cream, and season with salt and pepper. Turn into slightly buttered Dario moulds, and bake as Lobster Timbales, allowing thirty minutes for baking. Serve with Suprême or Béchamel Sauce.

Devilled Oysters.

1 pint oysters. ¼ cup butter. ¼ cup flour. ⅔ cup milk. Yolk 1 egg.	½ tablespoon finely chopped parsley. ½ teaspoon salt. Few grains cayenne. 1 teaspoon lemon juice.

Buttered cracker crumbs.

Clean, drain, and slightly chop oysters. Make a sauce of butter, flour, and milk; add egg yolk, seasonings, and oysters. Arrange buttered scallop shells in a dripping-pan, half fill with mixture, cover with buttered crumbs, and bake twelve to fifteen minutes in a hot oven. Deep oyster shells may be used in place of scallop shells.

Devilled Crabs.

1 cup chopped crab meat.	Yolks 2 eggs.
¼ cup mushrooms finely chopped.	2 tablespoons sherry wine.
2 tablespoons butter.	1 teaspoon finely chopped
2 tablespoons flour.	parsley.
⅔ cup White Stock.	Salt and pepper.

Make a sauce of butter, flour, and stock; add yolks of eggs, seasonings (except parsley), crab meat, and mushrooms. Cook three minutes, add parsley, and cool mixture. Wash and trim crab shells, fill rounding with mixture, sprinkle with stale bread crumbs mixed with a small quantity of melted butter. Crease on top with a case knife, having three lines parallel with each other across shell and three short lines branching from outside parallel lines.

Devilled Scallops.

1 quart scallops.	1 teaspoon salt.
⅓ cup butter.	Few grains cayenne.
⅓ teaspoon made mustard.	⅔ cup buttered cracker
	crumbs.

Clean scallops, drain, and heat to the boiling point; drain again, and reserve liquor. Cream the butter, add mustard, salt, cayenne, two-thirds cup reserved liquor, and scallops chopped. Let stand one-half hour. Put in a baking-dish, cover with crumbs, and bake twenty minutes.

Fried Oyster Crabs.

Wash and drain crabs. Roll in flour and shake in a sieve to remove superfluous flour. Fry in a basket in deep fat, having fat same temperature as for cooked mixtures. Drain and place on a napkin, and garnish with parsley and slices of lemon. Serve with Sauce Tyrolienne.

Cutlets of Chicken.

Remove fillets from two chickens; for directions, see page 218. Make six parallel slanting incisions in each mignon fillet and insert in each a slice of truffle, having the part of truffle exposed cut in points on edge. Arrange small fillets on large fillets. Garnish with truffles cut in small shapes, and Chicken Force-meat forced through a pastry bag and tube. Place in a greased pan, add one-third cup White Stock, cover with buttered paper, and bake fifteen minutes in a hot oven. Serve with Suprême or Béchamel Sauce.

Fillets of Game.

Remove skin from breasts of three partridges. Cut off breasts, leaving wing joints attached. Separate large from mignon fillets. Make five parallel slanting incisions in each mignon fillet, and insert in each a slice of truffle, having part of truffle exposed cut in points on edge. Beginning at outer edge of large fillets make deep cuts, nearly separating fillets in two parts, and stuff with Chicken Force-meat I. or II. Arrange small fillets on large fillets. Place in a greased baking-pan, brush over with butter, add one tablespoon Madeira wine and two tablespoons mushroom liquor. Cover with buttered paper, and bake twelve minutes in a hot oven. Serve with Suprême Sauce.

Chickens' Livers en Brochette.

Cut each liver in four pieces. Alternate pieces of liver and pieces of thinly sliced bacon on skewers, allowing one liver and five pieces of bacon for each skewer. Balance skewers in upright positions on rack in dripping-pan. Bake in a hot oven until bacon is crisp. Serve garnished with watercress.

Cheese Fondue.

1 cup scalded milk.

1 cup soft stale bread crumbs.

¼ lb. mild cheese cut in small pieces.

1 tablespoon butter.

½ teaspoon salt.

Yolks 3 eggs.

Whites 3 eggs.

Mix first five ingredients, add yolks of eggs beaten until lemon-colored. Cut and fold in whites of eggs beaten until stiff. Pour in a buttered baking-dish, and bake twenty minutes in a moderate oven.

Cheese Soufflé.

2 tablespoons butter.

3 tablespoons flour.

½ cup scalded milk.

½ teaspoon salt.

Few grains cayenne.

¼ cup grated Old English or Young America cheese.

Yolks 3 eggs.

Whites 3 eggs.

Melt butter, add flour, and when well mixed add gradually scalded milk. Then add salt, cayenne, and cheese. Remove from fire, add yolks of eggs beaten until lemon-colored. Cool mixture, and cut and fold in whites of eggs beaten until stiff and dry. Pour into a buttered baking-dish, and bake twenty minutes in a slow oven. Serve at once.

Ramequins Soufflés.

Bake Cheese Soufflé mixture in ramequin dishes. Serve for a course in a dinner.

Watrouskis.

½ cup grated mild cheese.

¼ teaspoon salt.

Few grains cayenne.

Few grains mace.

1 egg.

Yolk 1 egg.

1 tablespoon melted butter.

Mix cheese with seasonings. Beat egg and yolk of egg slightly, add butter, and mix with cheese. Fill buttered ramequin dishes with mixture, and bake fifteen minutes in a moderate oven.

Compote of Rice with Peaches.

Wash two-thirds cup rice, add one cup boiling water, and steam until rice has absorbed water; then add one and one-third cups hot milk, one teaspoon salt, and one-fourth cup sugar. Cook until rice is soft. Turn into a slightly buttered round shallow mould. When shaped, remove from mould to serving-dish, and arrange on top sections of cooked peaches drained from their syrup and dipped in macaroon dust. Garnish between sections with candied cherries and angelica cut in leaf-shapes. Angelica may be softened by dipping in hot water. Color peach syrup with fruit red, and pour around mould.

Compote of Rice and Pears.

Cook and mould rice as for Compote of Rice with Peaches. Arrange on top, quarters of cooked pears, and pour around pear syrup.

Croustades of Bread.

Cut stale bread in diamonds, squares, or circles. Remove centres, leaving cases. Fry in deep fat or brush over with melted butter, and brown in oven. Fill with creamed vegetables, fish, or meat.

Rice Croustades.

Wash one cup rice, and steam in White Stock. Cool, and mix with three-fourths cup Thick White Sauce, to which has been added beaten yolk of one egg, slight grating of nutmeg, one-half teaspoon salt, and one-eighth teaspoon pepper. Spread mixture in buttered pan two inches thick, cover with buttered paper, and place weight on top. Let stand until cold. Turn f m pan, cut in rounds, remove centres, leaving cases; dip in crumbs, egg, and crumbs, and fry in deep fat. Fill with creamed fish.

Soufflé au Rhum.

Yolks 2 eggs.   1 tablespoon rum.
¼ cup powdered sugar.   Whites 4 eggs.
                    Few grains salt.

Beat yolks of eggs until lemon-colored. Add sugar, salt, and rum. Cut and fold in whites of eggs beaten until stiff and dry.   Butter a hot omelet pan, pour in one-half mixture, brown underneath, fold gradually, turn on a hot serving-dish, and sprinkle with powdered sugar. Cook remaining mixture in same way. Soufflé au Rhum should be slightly underdone inside. At gentlemen's dinners rum is sometimes poured around soufflé and lighted when sent to table.

Omelet Soufflé.

Yolks 2 eggs.   ½ teaspoon vanilla.
¼ cup powdered sugar.   Whites 4 eggs.
                    Few grains salt.

Prepare as Soufflé au Rhum. Mound three-fourths of mixture on a slightly buttered platter. Decorate mound with remaining mixture forced through a pastry bag and tube. Sprinkle with powdered sugar, and bake ten minutes in a moderate oven.

Patties.

Patty shells are filled with Creamed Oysters, Oysters in Brown Sauce, Creamed Chicken, Creamed Chicken and Mushrooms, or Creamed Sweetbreads. They are arranged on a folded napkin, and are served for a course at dinner or luncheon.

Bouchées.

Small pastry shells filled with creamed meat are called bouchées.

Vol-au-vents.

Vol-au-vents are filled as patty shells.

Rissoles.

Roll puff paste to one-eighth inch thickness, and cut in rounds. Place one teaspoon finely chopped seasoned meat moistened with Thick White Sauce on each round. Brush each piece with cold water half-way round close to edge. Fold like a turnover, and press edges together. Dip in egg slightly beaten and diluted with one tablespoon water. Roll in gelatine, fry in deep fat, and drain. Granulated gelatine cannot be used.

Filling for Rissoles. Mix one-half cup finely chopped cold cooked chicken with one-fourth cup finely chopped cooked ham. Moisten with Thick White Sauce, and season with salt and cayenne:

Cheese Soufflé with Pastry.

2 eggs.
⅔ cup thick cream.
½ cup Swiss cheese cut
    in small dice.
½ cup grated American cheese.

⅓ cup grated Parmesan
    cheese.
Salt and pepper.
Few grains cayenne.
Few gratings nutmeg.

Add eggs to cream and beat slightly, then add cheese and seasonings. Line the sides of ramequin dishes with strips of puff paste. Fill dishes with mixture until two-thirds full. Bake fifteen minutes in a hot oven.

Aspic Jelly.

Carrot, ⎫
Onion, ⎬ 2 tablespoons each,
Celery, ⎭   cut in cubes.
2 sprigs parsley.
2 sprigs thyme.
1 sprig savory.
2 cloves.
½ teaspoon peppercorns.
1 bay leaf.

⅞ cup white wine.
1 box gelatine.
1 quart White Stock for
    vegetables and white
    meat, or
1 quart Brown Stock for
    dark meat.
Juice 1 lemon.
Whites 3 eggs.

Aspic jelly is always made with meat stock, and is principally used in elaborate entrées where fish, chicken, game, or vegetables are to be served moulded in jelly. In making Aspic Jelly, use as much liquid as the pan which is to contain moulded dish will hold.

Put vegetables, seasonings, and wine (except two tablespoons) in a saucepan; cook eight minutes, and strain, reserving liquid. Add gelatine to stock, then add lemon juice. Heat to boiling point and add strained liquid. Season with salt and cayenne. Beat whites of eggs slightly, add two tablespoons wine, and dilute with one cup hot mixture. Add slowly to remaining mixture, stirring constantly until boiling point is reached. Place on back of range and let stand thirty minutes. Strain through a double cheese cloth placed over a fine wire strainer, or through a jelly bag.

Tomatoes in Aspic.

Peel six small firm tomatoes, and remove pulp, having opening in tops as small as possible. Sprinkle insides with salt, invert, and let stand thirty minutes. Fill with vegetable or chicken salad. Cover tops with Mayonnaise to which has been added a small quantity of dissolved gelatine, and garnish with capers and sliced pickles. Place a pan in ice water, cover bottom with aspic jelly mixture, and let stand until jelly is firm. Arrange tomatoes on jelly garnished side down. Add more aspic jelly mixture, let stand until firm, and so continue until all is used. Chill thoroughly, turn on a serving-dish, and garnish around base with parsley.

Tongue in Aspic.

Cook a tongue according to directions on page 184. After removing skin and roots, run a skewer through tip of tongue and fleshy part, thus keeping tongue in shape. When cool, remove skewer. Put a round pan in ice water, cover bottom with brown aspic, and when firm decorate with cooked carrot, turnip, beet cut in fancy shapes, and parsley. Cover with aspic jelly mixture, adding it by spoonfuls so as not to disarrange vegetables. When this layer of mixture is firm, put in tongue, adding gradually remaining mixture as in Tomatoes in Aspic.

Birds in Aspic.

Clean, bone, stuff, and truss a bird, then steam over body bones or roast. If roasted, do not dredge with flour. Put a pan in ice water, cover bottom with aspic jelly mixture, and when firm garnish with truffles and egg custard thinly sliced and cut in fancy shapes. The smaller the shapes the more elaborate may be the designs. When garnishing with small shapes, pieces are so difficult to handle that they should be taken on the pointed end of a larding-needle, and placed as desired on jelly. Add aspic mixture by spoonfuls, that designs may not be disturbed. When mixture is added, and firm to the depth of three-fourths inch, place in the bird, breast down. If sides of mould are to be decorated, dip pieces in jelly and they will cling to pan. Add remaining mixture gradually as in Tomatoes in Aspic. Small birds, chicken, or turkey, may be put in aspic.

Egg Custard for Decorating.

Separate yolks from whites of two eggs. Beat yolks slightly, add two tablespoons milk and few grains salt. Strain into a buttered cup, put in a saucepan, surround with boiling water to one-half depth of cup, cover, put on back of range, and steam until custard is firm. Beat whites slightly, add few grains salt, and cook as yolks. Cool, turn from cups, cut in thin slices, then in desired shapes.

Stuffing for Chicken in Aspic.

Chop finely breast and meat from second joints of an uncooked chicken, or one pound of uncooked lean veal. Add one-half cup cracker crumbs, hot stock to moisten, salt, pepper, celery salt, cayenne, lemon juice, and one egg slightly beaten. In stuffing boned chicken, stuff body, legs, and wings, being careful that too much stuffing is not used, as an allowance must be made for the swelling of cracker crumbs.

Chaud-froid of Chicken.

2 tablespoons butter.	¾ teaspoon granulated gelatine dissolved in one tablespoon hot water.
3 tablespoons flour.	
1 cup White Stock.	
Yolk 1 egg.	Aspic jelly.
2 tablespoons cream.	Truffles.
1 tablespoon lemon juice.	6 pieces cooked chicken shaped in form of cutlets.
Salt and pepper.	

Make a sauce of butter, flour, and stock; add egg yolk diluted with cream, lemon juice, salt, and pepper; then add dissolved gelatine. Dip chicken in sauce which has been allowed to cool. When chicken has cooled, garnish upper side with truffles cut in shapes. Brush over with aspic jelly mixture, and chill. Arrange a bed of lettuce; in centre pile cold cooked asparagus tips or celery cut in small pieces, marinated with French Dressing, and place chicken at base of salad.

Rum Cakes.

Shape Brioche dough in the form of large biscuits and put into buttered individual tin moulds, having moulds two-thirds full; cover, and let rise to fill moulds. Bake twenty-five minutes in a moderate oven. Remove from moulds and dip in Rum Sauce. Arrange on a dish and pour remaining sauce around cakes.

Rum Sauce.

½ cup sugar.	1 cup boiling water.
¼ cup rum or wine.	

Make a syrup by boiling sugar and water five minutes; then add rum or wine.

Flûtes.

Shape Brioche dough in sticks similar to Bread Sticks. Place on a buttered sheet, cover, and let rise fifteen minutes. Brush over with white of one egg slightly beaten and diluted with one-half tablespoon cold water. Sprinkle with powdered sugar and bake ten minutes. These are delicious served with coffee or chocolate.

CHAPTER XXIII.

HOT PUDDINGS.

Rice Pudding.

5 4 cups milk.   ½ teaspoon salt.
⅓ cup rice.   ⅓ cup sugar.
              Grated rind ½ lemon.

Wash rice, mix ingredients, and pour into buttered
pudding-dish; bake three hours in very slow oven, stirring three times during first hour of baking to prevent rice
from settling.

Poor Man's Pudding.

4 cups milk.   ½ teaspoon salt.
½ cup rice.   ½ teaspoon cinnamon.
⅓ cup molasses.   1 tablespoon butter.

Wash rice, mix and bake same as Rice Pudding.   At
last stirring, add butter.

Indian Pudding.

5 cups scalded milk.   ½ cup molasses.
⅓ cup Indian meal.   1 teaspoon salt.
              1 teaspoon ginger.

Pour milk slowly on meal, cook in double boiler twenty
minutes, add molasses, salt, and ginger; pour into buttered pudding-dish and bake two hours in slow oven;
serve with cream. If baked too rapidly it will not whey.
Ginger may be omitted.

Cerealine Pudding (Mock Indian).

4 cups scalded milk.	½ cup molasses.
2 cups cerealine.	1½ teaspoons salt.

1½ tablespoons butter.

Pour milk on cerealine, add remaining-ingredients, pour into buttered pudding-dish, and bake one hour in slow oven. Serve with cream.

Apple Tapioca.

¾ cup pearl tapioca.	½ teaspoon salt.
Cold water.	7 sour apples.
2½ cups boiling water.	½ cup sugar.

Soak tapioca one hour in cold water to cover, drain, add boiling water and salt; cook in double boiler until transparent. Core and pare apples, arrange in buttered pudding-dish, fill cavities with sugar, pour over tapioca, and bake in moderate oven until apples are soft. Serve with sugar and cream or Cream Sauce I.

Tapioca Custard Pudding.

4 cups scalded milk.	½ cup sugar.
⅔ cup pearl tapioca.	1 teaspoon salt.
3 eggs.	1 tablespoon butter.

Soak tapioca one hour in cold water to cover, drain, add to milk, and cook in double boiler thirty minutes; beat eggs slightly, add sugar and salt, pour on gradually hot mixture, turn into buttered pudding-dish, add butter, bake thirty minutes in slow oven.

Peach Tapioca.

1 can peaches.	Boiling water.
¼ cup powdered sugar.	½ cup sugar.
1 cup tapioca.	½ teaspoon salt.

Drain peaches, sprinkle with powdered sugar, and let stand one hour; soak tapioca one hour in cold water to cover; to peach syrup add enough boiling water to make three cups; heat to boiling point, add tapioca drained from cold water, sugar, and salt; then cook in double boiler until transparent. Line a mould or pudding-dish with peaches cut in quarters, fill with tapioca, and bake in moderate oven thirty minutes; cool slightly, turn on a dish, and serve with Cream Sauce I.

Scalloped Apples.

1 small stale baker's loaf.	¼ cup sugar.
¼ cup butter.	¼ teaspoon grated nutmeg.
1 quart sliced apples.	Grated rind and juice of ½ lemon.

Cut loaf in halves, remove soft part, and crumb by rubbing through a colander; melt butter and stir in lightly with fork; cover bottom of buttered pudding-dish with crumbs and spread over one-half the apples, sprinkle with one-half sugar, nutmeg, lemon juice and rind mixed together; repeat, cover with remaining crumbs, and bake forty minutes in moderate oven. Cover at first to prevent crumbs browning too rapidly. Serve with sugar and cream.

Bread Pudding.

2 cups stale bread crumbs.	2 eggs.
1 quart scalded milk.	½ teaspoon salt.
⅓ cup sugar.	1 teaspoon vanilla or
¼ cup melted butter.	¼ teaspoon spice.

2 tbsp. [handwritten note]

Soak bread crumbs in milk, set aside until cool; add sugar, butter, eggs slightly beaten, salt, and flavoring; bake one hour in buttered pudding-dish in slow oven; serve with Vanilla Sauce. In preparing bread crumbs for puddings avoid using outside crusts. With a coarse grater there need be but little waste.

Cracker Custard Pudding.

Make same as Bread Pudding, using two-thirds cup cracker crumbs in place of bread crumbs; after baking, cover with meringue made of whites two eggs, one-fourth cup powdered sugar, and one tablespoon lemon juice; return to oven to cook meringue.

Bread and Butter Pudding.

1 small stale baker's loaf.	½ cup sugar.
Butter.	¼ teaspoon salt.
3 eggs.	1 quart milk.

Remove end crusts from bread, cut loaf in one-half inch slices, spread each slice generously with butter; arrange in buttered pudding-dish, buttered side down. Beat eggs slightly, add sugar, salt, and milk; strain, and pour over bread; let stand thirty minutes. Bake one hour in slow oven, covering the first half-hour of baking. The top of pudding should be well browned. Serve with Hard or Creamy Sauce. Three-fourths cup raisins, parboiled in boiling water to cover, and seeded, may be sprinkled between layers of bread.

Chocolate Bread Pudding.

2 cups stale bread crumbs.	⅔ cup sugar.
4 cups scalded milk.	3 2 eggs. *use whites for mereing*
2 squares Baker's chocolate.	¼ teaspoon salt.
1 teaspoon vanilla.	

Soak bread in milk thirty minutes; melt chocolate in saucepan placed over hot water, add one-half sugar and enough milk taken from bread and milk to make of consistency to pour; add to mixture with remaining sugar, salt, vanilla, and eggs slightly beaten; turn into buttered pudding-dish and bake one hour in a moderate oven. Serve with Hard or Cream Sauce I.

Cottage Pudding.

¼ cup butter.	1 cup milk.
½ cup sugar.	2 cups flour.
1 egg.	3 teaspoons baking powder.
½ teaspoon salt.	

Cream the butter, add sugar gradually, and egg well beaten; mix and sift flour, baking powder, and salt; add alternately with milk to first mixture; turn into buttered cake-pan; bake thirty-five minutes. Serve with Vanilla or Hard Sauce.

Strawberry Cottage Pudding.

⅓ cup butter.   ½ cup milk.
1 cup sugar.   1¾ cups flour.
1 egg.   3 teaspoons baking powder.

Mix same as Cottage Pudding, and bake twenty-five minutes in shallow pan; cut in squares and serve with strawberries (sprinkled with sugar and slightly mashed) and Cream Sauce I. *Sliced peaches* may be used in place of strawberries.

Orange Puffs.

⅓ cup butter.   ½ cup milk.
1 cup sugar.   1¾ cups flour.
2 eggs.   3 teaspoons baking powder.

Mix same as Cottage Pudding, and bake in buttered individual tins. Serve with Orange Sauce.

Custard Soufflé.

3 tablespoons butter.   1 cup scalded milk.
¼ cup flour.   4 eggs.
                    ¼ cup sugar.

Melt butter, add flour, and gradually hot milk; when well thickened, pour on to yolks of eggs beaten until thick and lemon colored, and mixed with sugar; cool, and cut and fold in whites of eggs beaten stiff and dry. Turn into buttered pudding-dish, and bake from thirty to thirty-five minutes in slow oven; take from oven and serve at once, — if not served immediately it is sure to fall; serve with Creamy or Foamy Sauce.

Lemon Soufflé.

Yolks 4 eggs.	1 cup sugar.
Grated rind and juice 1 lemon.	Whites 4 eggs.

Beat yolks until thick and lemon colored, add sugar gradually and continue beating, then add lemon rind and juice. Cut and fold in whites of eggs beaten until dry; turn into buttered pudding-dish, set in pan of hot water, and bake thirty-five to forty minutes. Serve with or without sauce.

Fruit Soufflé.

¾ cup fruit pulp, peach, apricot, or quince.	Whites 3 eggs. Sugar.

Rub fruit through sieve; if canned fruit is used, first drain from syrup. Heat and sweeten if needed; beat whites of eggs until stiff, add gradually hot fruit pulp, and continue beating; turn into buttered and sugared individual moulds, having them three-fourths full; set moulds in pan of hot water and bake in slow oven until firm, which may be determined by pressing with finger; serve with Sabyon Sauce.

Spanish Soufflé.

¼ cup butter.	2 tablespoons sugar.
½ cup stale bread crumbs.	3 eggs.
1 cup milk.	½ teaspoon vanilla.

Melt butter, add crumbs, cook until slightly browned, stirring often; add milk and sugar, cook twenty minutes in double boiler; remove from fire, add unbeaten yolks of eggs, then cut and fold in whites of eggs beaten until stiff, and flavor. Bake as Fruit Soufflé.

Chestnut Soufflé.

¼ cup sugar.	1 cup chestnut purée.
2 tablespoons flour.	½ cup milk.
Whites 3 eggs.	

Mix sugar and flour, add chestnuts and milk gradually; cook five minutes, stirring constantly; beat whites of eggs until stiff, and cut and fold into mixture.   Bake as Fruit Soufflé; serve with Cream Sauce.

Steamed Apple Pudding.

2 cups flour.	2 tablespoons butter.
4 teaspoons baking powder.	¾ cup milk.
½ teaspoon salt.	4 apples cut in eighths.

Mix and sift dry ingredients; work in butter with tips of fingers, add milk gradually, mixing with a knife; toss on floured board, pat and roll out, place apples on middle of dough, and sprinkle with one tablespoon sugar mixed with one-fourth teaspoon each of salt and nutmeg; bring dough around apples and carefully lift into buttered mould or five-pound lard pail; or apples may be sprinkled over dough, and dough rolled like a jelly roll; cover closely and steam one hour and twenty minutes; serve with Vanilla or Cold Sauce.   Twice the number of apples may be sprinkled with sugar and cooked until soft in granite kettle placed on top of range, covered with dough, rolled size to fit in kettle, then kettle covered tightly and dough steamed fifteen minutes.   When turned on dish for serving, apples will be on top.

Steamed Blueberry Pudding.

Mix and sift dry ingredients and work in butter same as for Steamed Apple Pudding.   Add one cup each of milk, and blueberries rolled in flour; turn into buttered mould and steam one and one-half hours.   Serve with Creamy Sauce.

Steamed Cranberry Pudding.

½ cup butter.	3½ cups flour.
1 cup sugar.	1¼ tablespoons baking powder.
3 eggs.	½ cup milk.
1½ cups cranberries.	

Cream the butter, add sugar gradually, and eggs well beaten.   Mix and sift flour and baking powder and add alternately with milk to first mixture, stir in berries previously washed, turn into buttered mould, cover, and steam three hours. Serve with thin cream, sweetened and flavored with nutmeg.

Ginger Pudding.

⅓ cup butter.	3½ teaspoons baking powder.
½ cup sugar.	¼ teaspoon salt.
1 egg.	2 teaspoons ginger.
2¼ cups flour.	1 cup milk.

Cream the butter, add sugar gradually, and egg well beaten; mix and sift dry ingredients; add alternately with milk to first mixture. Turn into buttered mould, cover, and steam two hours; serve with Vanilla Sauce.

Harvard Pudding.

⅓ cup butter.	3½ teaspoons baking powder.
½ cup sugar.	¼ teaspoon salt.
2½ cups flour.	1 egg.
1 cup milk.	

Mix and sift dry ingredients and work in butter with tips of fingers; beat egg, add milk, and combine mixtures; turn into buttered mould, cover, and steam two hours; serve with warm apple sauce and Hard Sauce.

Apple Sauce. Pick over and wash dried apples, soak over night in cold water to cover; cook until soft; sweeten, and flavor with lemon juice.

Swiss Pudding.

½ cup butter.	Grated rind one lemon.
⅞ cup flour.	5 eggs.
2 cups milk.	⅓ cup powdered sugar.

Cream the butter, add flour gradually; scald milk with lemon rind, add to first mixture, and cook five minutes in double boiler. Beat yolks of eggs until thick and lemon colored, add sugar gradually, then add to cooked mixture; cool, and cut and fold in whites of eggs beaten stiff.   Turn into buttered mould, cover, and steam one and one-fourth hours; while steaming, be sure water surrounds mould to half its depth.

Snow Balls.

½ cup butter.	2¼ cups flour.
1 cup sugar.	3½ teaspoons baking powder.
½ cup milk.	Whites 4 eggs.

Cream the butter, add sugar gradually, milk, and flour mixed and sifted with baking powder; then add the whites of eggs beaten stiff.   Steam thirty-five minutes in buttered cups; serve with preserved fruit, quince marmalade, or strawberry sauce.

Graham Pudding.

¼ cup butter.	1½ cups Graham flour.
½ cup molasses.	½ teaspoon soda.
½ cup milk.	1 teaspoon salt.
1 egg.	1 cup raisins seeded and cut in pieces.

Melt butter, add molasses, milk, egg well beaten, dry ingredients mixed and sifted, and raisins; turn into buttered mould, cover, and steam two and one-half hours. Serve with Wine Sauce.   Dates or figs cut in small pieces may be used in place of raisins.

St. James Pudding.

3 tablespoons butter.	Salt,
½ cup molasses.	Clove,
½ cup milk.	Allspice, } ¼ teaspoon each.
1½ cups flour.	Nutmeg,
½ teaspoon soda.	½ lb. dates stoned and cut in pieces.

Mix and steam same as Graham Pudding.   A simple, delicious pudding without egg.   Puddings may be nicely steamed in buttered one-pound baking-powder boxes, and are attractive in shape and easy to serve.

Suet Pudding.

1 cup finely chopped suet.
1 cup molasses.
1 cup milk.
3 cups flour.
1 teaspoon soda.

1½ teaspoons salt.
Ginger,
Clove, } ½ teaspoon each.
Nutmeg,
1 teaspoon cinnamon.

Mix and sift dry ingredients. Add molasses and milk to suet; combine mixtures. Turn into buttered mould, cover, and steam three hours; serve with Egg Sauce. Raisins and currants may be added.

Thanksgiving Pudding.

4 cups scalded milk.
1¼ cups rolled crackers.
1 cup sugar.
4 eggs.

⅓ cup melted butter.
½ grated nutmeg.
1 teaspoon salt.
1½ cups raisins.

Pour milk over crackers and let stand until cool; add sugar, eggs slightly beaten, nutmeg, salt, and butter; parboil raisins until soft, by cooking in boiling water to cover; seed, and add to mixture; turn into buttered pudding-dish and bake slowly two and one-half hours, stirring after first half-hour to prevent raisins from settling; serve with Brandy Sauce.

Hunters' Pudding.

1 cup finely chopped suet.
1 cup molasses.
1 cup milk.
3 cups flour.
1 teaspoon soda.
1½ teaspoons salt.

Clove,
Mace, } ½ teaspoon each.
Allspice,
1 teaspoon cinnamon.
1½ cups raisins.
2 tablespoons flour.

Mix same as Suet Pudding. Stone, cut, and flour raisins, then add to mixture. Turn into buttered mould, cover, and steam three hours.

French Fruit Pudding.

1 cup finely chopped suet.	½ teaspoon clove.
1 cup molasses.	½ teaspoon salt.
1 cup sour milk.	1¼ cups raisins seeded
1½ teaspoons soda.	and chopped.
1 teaspoon cinnamon.	¾ cup currants.

2½ cups flour.

Add molasses and sour milk to suet; add two cups
flour mixed and sifted with soda, salt, and spices; add
fruit mixed with remaining flour. Turn into buttered
mould, cover, and steam four hours. Serve with Sterling
Sauce.

English Plum Pudding.

½ lb. stale bread crumbs.	¼ lb. finely chopped figs.
1 cup scalded milk.	2 oz. finely cut citron.
¼ lb. sugar.	½ lb. suet.
4 eggs.	¼ cup wine and brandy mixed.
½ lb. raisins, seeded, cut	½ grated nutmeg.
in pieces, and floured.	¾ teaspoon cinnamon.
¼ lb. currants.	⅓ teaspoon clove.

⅓ teaspoon mace.

Soak bread crumbs in milk, let stand until cool, add
sugar, beaten yolks of eggs, raisins, currants, figs, and
citron; chop suet, and cream by using the hand; combine mixtures, then add wine, brandy, nutmeg, cinnamon,
clove, mace, and whites of eggs beaten stiff. Turn into
buttered mould, cover, and steam six hours.

CHAPTER XXIV.

PUDDING SAUCES.

Lemon Sauce I.

¾ cup sugar.   2 teaspoons butter.
¼ cup water.   1 tablespoon lemon juice.

Make a syrup by boiling sugar and water eight minutes; remove from fire; add butter and lemon juice.

Lemon Sauce II.

½ cup sugar.   2 tablespoons butter
1 cup boiling water.   1½ tablespoons lemon juice.
2 tablespoons corn-starch.   Few gratings nutmeg.

Mix sugar and corn-starch, add water gradually, stirring constantly; boil five minutes, remove from fire, add butter, lemon juice, and nutmeg.

Vanilla Sauce.

Make as Lemon Sauce II., using one teaspoon vanilla in place of lemon juice and nutmeg.

Molasses Sauce.

1 cup molasses.   2 tablespoons lemon juice or
1½ tablespoons butter.   1 tablespoon vinegar.

Boil molasses and butter five minutes; remove from fire and add lemon juice.

Cream Sauce I.

¾ cup thick cream.　　　⅓ cup powdered sugar.
¼ cup milk.　　　　　　　½ teaspoon vanilla.

Mix cream and milk, beat until stiff, using egg beater; add sugar and vanilla.

Cream Sauce II.

1 egg.　　　　　　　　　½ cup thick cream.
1 cup powdered sugar.　　¼ cup milk.
　　　　½ teaspoon vanilla.

Beat white of egg until stiff; add yolk of egg well beaten, and sugar gradually; dilute cream with milk, beat until stiff, combine mixtures, and flavor.

Yellow Sauce I.

2 eggs.　　　　　　　　1 teaspoon vanilla or
1 cup sugar.　　　　　　½ teaspoon vanilla and
　　　　　　　　　　　1 tablespoon brandy.

Beat eggs until very light, add sugar gradually and continue beating; then flavor.

Yellow Sauce II.

2 eggs.　　　　　　　　　1 cup powdered sugar.
　　　　3 tablespoons wine.

Beat yolks of eggs until thick, add one-half sugar gradually; beat whites of eggs until stiff, add gradually remaining sugar; combine mixtures, and add wine.

Orange Sauce.

Whites 3 eggs.　　　　　Juice and rind 2 oranges.
1 cup powdered sugar.　　Juice 1 lemon.

Beat whites until stiff, add sugar gradually and continue beating; add rind and fruit juices; use blood oranges when possible.

Strawberry Sauce.

⅓ cup butter. 1 cup powdered sugar.
⅔ cup strawberries.

Make as Hard Sauce, add strawberries, and beat until berries are well mashed.

Creamy Sauce I.

¼ cup butter. 2 tablespoons milk.
½ cup powdered sugar. 2 tablespoons wine.

Cream the butter, add sugar gradually, and milk and wine drop by drop. If liquids are added too fast the sauce will have a curdled appearance; it should be of soft, smooth consistency.

Creamy Sauce II.

Use same proportions as given in Recipe I. If not careful in adding liquids, it will curdle; but this will make no difference, as the sauce is to be warmed over hot water. By careful watching and constant stirring, the ingredients will be perfectly blended; it should be creamy in consistency.

Foamy Sauce I.

½ cup butter. 1 egg.
1 cup powdered sugar. 2 tablespoons wine.

Cream the butter, add gradually sugar, egg well beaten, and wine; beat while heating over hot water.

Foamy Sauce II.

Whites 2 eggs. ½ cup hot milk.
1 cup powdered sugar. 1 teaspoon vanilla.

Beat eggs until stiff, add sugar gradually and continue beating; add milk and vanilla.

Chocolate Sauce.

2 cups milk.
1½ tablespoons corn-starch.
2 squares Baker's chocolate.
4 tablespoons powdered sugar.

2 tablespoons hot water.
2 eggs.
⅔ cup powdered sugar.
1 teaspoon vanilla.

Scald one and three-fourths cup milk, add corn-starch diluted with remaining milk, and cook eight minutes in double boiler; melt chocolate over hot water, add four tablespoons sugar and hot water, stir until smooth, then add to cooked mixture; beat whites of eggs until stiff, add gradually powdered sugar and continue beating, then add unbeaten yolks, and stir into cooked mixture; cook one minute, add vanilla, and cool before serving.

Sabyon Sauce.

Grated rind and juice ½ lemon.
½ cup white wine or
¼ cup sherry.

⅓ cup sugar.
2 eggs.

Mix lemon, wine, sugar, and yolks of eggs; stir vigorously over fire until it thickens, using a wire whisk; pour on to whites of eggs beaten stiff.

Hard Sauce.

⅓ cup butter.
1 cup powdered sugar.

⅓ teaspoon lemon extract.
⅔ teaspoon vanilla.

Cream the butter, add sugar gradually, and flavoring.

Sterling Sauce.

½ cup butter.
1 cup brown sugar.

1 teaspoon vanilla or
2 tablespoons wine.
4 tablespoons cream or milk.

Cream the butter, add sugar gradually, and milk and flavoring drop by drop to prevent separation.

Wine Sauce.

½ cup butter.   3 tablespoons sherry or
1 cup powdered sugar.   Madeira wine.
Slight grating nutmeg.

Cream the butter, add sugar gradually, and wine slowly; pile on glass dish, and sprinkle with grated nutmeg.

Brandy Sauce.

¼ cup butter.   Yolks 2 eggs.
1 cup sugar.   Whites 2 eggs.
2 tablespoons brandy.   ½ cup milk or cream.

Cream the butter, add sugar gradually, then brandy very slowly, well beaten yolks, and milk or cream. Cook over hot water until it thickens as a custard, pour on to beaten whites.

CHAPTER XXV.

COLD DESSERTS.

Irish Moss Blanc-Mange.

⅓ cup Irish moss.   ¼ teaspoon salt.
4 cups milk.   1½ teaspoons vanilla.

Soak moss fifteen minutes in cold water to cover, drain, pick over, and add to milk; cook in double boiler thirty minutes; the milk will seem but little thicker than when put on to cook, but if cooked longer blanc-mange will be too stiff. Add salt, strain, flavor, re-strain, and fill individual moulds previously dipped in cold water; chill, turn on glass dish, surround with thin slices of banana, and place a slice on each mould. Serve with sugar and cream.

Chocolate Blanc-Mange.

Irish Moss Blanc-Mange flavored with chocolate. Melt one and one-half squares Baker's chocolate, add one-fourth cup sugar and one-third cup boiling water, stir until perfectly smooth, adding to milk just before taking from fire. Serve with sugar and cream.

Rebecca Pudding.

4 cups scalded milk.   ¼ teaspoon salt.
½ cup corn-starch.   ½ cup cold milk.
¼ cup sugar.   1 teaspoon vanilla.
           Whites 3 eggs.

Mix corn-starch, sugar, and salt, dilute with cold milk, add to scalded milk, stirring constantly until mixture thickens, afterwards occasionally; cook fifteen minutes. Add flavoring and whites of eggs beaten stiff, mix thoroughly, mould, chill, and serve with Yellow Sauce I. or II.

Moulded Snow.

Make as Rebecca Pudding, and serve with Chocolate Sauce.

Chocolate Cream.

2 cups scalded milk.	⅓ cup cold milk.
5 tablespoons corn-starch.	1½ squares Baker's chocolate.
½ cup sugar.	3 tablespoons hot water.
¼ teaspoon salt.	Whites 3 eggs.

1 teaspoon vanilla.

Mix corn-starch, sugar, and salt, dilute with cold milk, add to scalded milk, and cook over hot water ten minutes, stirring constantly until thickened; melt chocolate, add hot water, stir until smooth, and add to cooked mixture; add whites of eggs beaten stiff, and vanilla. Mould, chill, and serve with cream.

Pineapple Pudding.

2¾ cups scalded milk.	¼ cup sugar.
¼ cup cold milk.	¼ teaspoon salt.
⅓ cup corn-starch.	½ can grated pineapple.

Whites 3 eggs.

Follow directions for Rebecca Pudding, and add pineapple just before moulding. Fill individual moulds, previously dipped in cold water. Serve with cream.

Boiled Custard.

2 cups scalded milk.	¼ cup sugar.
Yolks 3 eggs.	⅛ teaspoon salt.

½ teaspoon vanilla.

Beat eggs slightly, add sugar and salt; stir constantly while adding gradually hot milk. Cook in double boiler, continue stirring until mixture thickens and a coating is formed on the spoon, strain immediately; chill and flavor. If cooked too long the custard will curdle; should this happen, by using a Dover egg-beater it may be restored to a smooth consistency, but custard will not be as thick. Eggs should be beaten slightly for custard, that it may be of smooth, thick consistency. To prevent scum from forming, cover with a perforated tin. When eggs are scarce, use yolks two eggs and one-half tablespoon corn-starch.

Tipsy Pudding.

Flavor Boiled Custard with sherry wine, and pour over slices of stale sponge cake; cover with Cream Sauce I. or II.

Peach Custard.

Arrange alternate layers of stale cake and sections of canned peaches in glass dish and pour over Boiled Custard. Bananas may be used instead of peaches; it is then called *Banana Custard*.

Orange Custard.

Arrange slices of sweet oranges in glass dish, pour over them Boiled Custard; chill, and cover with Meringue I.

Apple Meringue.

Use Meringue I. and pile lightly on baked apples, brown in oven, cool, and serve with Boiled Custard. Canned peaches, drained from their liquor, may be prepared in the same way; it is then called *Peach Meringue*.

Apple Snow.

Whites 3 eggs. ¾ cup apple pulp.
Powdered sugar.

Pare, quarter, and core four sour apples, steam until soft, and rub through sieve; there should be three-fourths cup apple pulp. Beat on a platter whites of eggs until stiff (using wire whisk), add gradually apple sweetened to taste, and continue beating. Pile lightly on glass dish, chill, and serve with Boiled Custard.

Prune Whip.

⅓ lb. prunes.   ½ cup sugar.
Whites 5 eggs.   ½ tablespoon lemon juice.

Pick over and wash prunes, then soak several hours in cold water to cover; cook in same water until soft; remove stones and rub prunes through a strainer, add sugar, and cook five minutes; the mixture should be of the consistency of marmalade. Beat whites of eggs until stiff, add prune mixture gradually when cold, and lemon juice. Pile lightly on buttered pudding-dish, bake twenty minutes in slow oven. Serve cold with Boiled Custard.

Raspberry Whip.

1¼ cups raspberries.   1 cup powdered sugar.
White 1 egg.

Put ingredients in bowl and beat with wire whisk until stiff enough to hold in shape; about thirty minutes will be required for beating. Pile lightly on dish, chill, surround with lady fingers, and serve with Boiled Custard.

Strawberry Whip may be prepared in same way.

Baked Custard.

4 cups scalded milk.   ½ cup sugar.
4 to 6 eggs.   ¼ teaspoon salt.
Few gratings nutmeg.

Beat eggs slightly, add sugar and salt, pour on slowly scalded milk; strain in buttered mould, set in pan of hot water. Sprinkle with nutmeg, and bake in slow oven until firm, which may be readily determined by running a silver knife through custard; if knife comes out clean, custard is done. During baking, care must be taken that water surrounding mould does not reach boiling point, or custard will whey. Always bear in mind that eggs and milk in combination must be cooked at a low temperature. For *cup custards* allow four eggs to four cups milk; for large moulded custard, six eggs; if less eggs are used custard is liable to crack when turned on a serving-dish.

Caramel Custard.

4 cups scalded milk.	½ teaspoon salt.
5 eggs.	1 teaspoon vanilla.
½ cup sugar.	

Put sugar in omelet pan, stir constantly over hot part of range until melted to a syrup of light brown color. Add gradually to milk, being careful that milk does not bubble up and go over, as is liable on account of high temperature of sugar. As soon as sugar is melted in milk, add mixture gradually to eggs slightly beaten; add salt and flavoring, then strain in buttered mould. Bake as custard. Chill, and serve with Caramel Sauce.

Caramel Sauce.

½ cup sugar.	½ cup boiling water.

Miss Parloa.

Melt sugar as for Caramel Custard, add water, simmer ten minutes; cool before serving.

Tapioca Cream.

¼ cup pearl tapioca.	⅓ cup sugar.
2 cups scalded milk.	¼ teaspoon salt.
2 eggs.	1 teaspoon vanilla.

Pick over tapioca and soak one hour in cold water to cover, drain, add to milk, and cook in double boiler until tapioca is transparent. Add half the sugar to milk and remainder to egg yolks slightly beaten, and salt. Combine by pouring hot mixture slowly on egg mixture, return to double boiler, and cook until it thickens. Remove from range and add whites of eggs beaten stiff. Chill and flavor.

Norwegian Prune Pudding.

½ lb. prunes.
2 cups cold water.
1 cup sugar.

1 inch piece stick cinnamon.
1 cup boiling water.
⅓ cup corn-starch.

Pick over and wash prunes, then soak one hour in cold water, and boil until soft; remove stones, obtain meat from stones and add to prunes; then add sugar, cinnamon, boiling water, and simmer ten minutes. Dilute corn-starch with enough cold water to pour easily, add to prune mixture, and cook eight minutes in double boiler. Remove cinnamon, mould, then chill, and serve with Cream Sauce I. or II.

Apples in Bloom.

Select eight red apples, cook in boiling water until soft, turning them often. Have water half surround apples. Remove skins carefully, that the red color may remain, and arrange on serving-dish. To the water add one cup sugar, grated rind one-half lemon, and juice one orange; simmer until reduced to one cup. Cool, and pour over apples. Serve with Cream Sauce I. or II.

Neapolitan Baskets.

Bake sponge cake in gem pans, cool, and remove centres. Fill with Cream Sauce II., flavoring half the sauce with chocolate. Melt chocolate, dilute with hot water, cool, and add cream sauce slowly to chocolate. Garnish with candied cherries and angelica.

Wine Cream.

Arrange lady fingers or slices of sponge cake in a dish, pour over cream made as follows: Mix one-third cup sugar, grated rind and juice one-half lemon, one-fourth cup sherry wine, and yolks of two eggs; place over fire and stir vigorously with wire whisk until it thickens and is frothy, then pour over beaten whites of two eggs and continue beating

Orange Salad.

Arrange layers of sliced oranges, sprinkling each layer with powdered sugar and shredded cocoanut. Sliced oranges when served alone should not stand long after slicing, as they are apt to become bitter.

Fruit Salad I.

Arrange alternate layers of shredded pineapple, sliced bananas, and sliced oranges, sprinkling each layer with powdered sugar. Chill before serving.

To Shred Pineapple. Pare and cut out eyes, pick off small pieces with a silver fork, continuing until all soft part is removed. *To Slice Oranges*. Remove skin and white covering, slice lengthwise that the tough centre may not be served; seeds should be removed.

Fruit Salad II.

Pare a pineapple and cut in one-quarter inch slices, remove hard centres, sprinkle with powdered sugar, set aside one hour in a cool place; drain, spread on serving-dish, arrange a circle of thin slices of banana on each piece, nearly to the edge, pile strawberries in centre, pour over syrup drained from pineapple, sprinkle with powdered sugar, and serve with or without Cream Sauce.

Fruit Salad with Wine Dressing

Arrange alternate layers of sliced fruit, using pineapples, bananas, oranges, and grapes; pour over all Wine Dressing, and let stand one hour in a cold place.

Wine Dressing.

Mix one-half cup sugar, one-third cup sherry wine, and two tablespoons Madeira.

Cream Whips.

Sweeten thin cream, flavor with vanilla, brandy, or wine, then whip; half fill frappé glasses with any preserve, pile on lightly the whip.

Lemon Jelly.

½ box gelatine or
2½ tablespoons granulated
    gelatine.

½ cup cold water.
2½ cups boiling water.
1 cup sugar.

½ cup lemon juice.

Soak gelatine twenty minutes in cold water, dissolve in boiling water, strain, and add to sugar and lemon juice. Turn into mould, and chill.

Orange Jelly.

½ box gelatine or
2½ tablespoons granulated
    gelatine.
½ cup cold water.

1½ cups boiling water.
1 cup sugar.
1½ cups orange juice.
3 tablespoons lemon juice.

Make same as Lemon Jelly.

To Remove Juice from Oranges. Cut fruit in halves crosswise, remove with spoon pulp and juice from sections, and strain through double cheese cloth; or use a glass lemon squeezer.

Coffee Jelly.

½ box gelatine or
2½ tablespoons granulated
    gelatine.

½ cup cold water.
1 cup boiling water.
⅓ cup sugar.

2 cups boiled coffee.

Make same as Lemon Jelly. Serve with sugar and cream.

Cider Jelly.

½ box gelatine or
2½ tablespoons granulated
    gelatine.

½ cup cold water.
1 cup boiling water.
2 cups cider.

Make same as Lemon Jelly.

Wine Jelly I.

½ box gelatine or
2½ tablespoons granulated
    gelatine.
½ cup cold water.
1⅔ cups boiling water.

1 cup sugar.
1 cup sherry or Madeira
    wine.
⅓ cup orange juice.
3 tablespoons lemon juice.

Soak gelatine twenty minutes in cold water, dissolve in boiling water; add sugar, wine, orange juice, and lemon juice; strain, mould, and chill. If a stronger jelly is desired, use additional wine in place of orange juice.

Wine Jelly II.

½ box gelatine or
2½ tablespoons granulated
    gelatine.
½ cup cold water.
1⅔ cups boiling water.
1 cup sugar.

½ cup sherry wine.
2 tablespoons brandy.
Kirsch.
⅓ cup orange juice.
3 tablespoons lemon juice.
Fruit red.

Soak gelatine twenty minutes in cold water, dissolve in hot water, add sugar, fruit juices, sherry, brandy, and enough Kirsch to make one cup of strong liquor, then color with fruit red. Strain, mould, and chill.

Russian Jelly.

¼ box gelatine or
1¼ tablespoons granulated
    gelatine.
¼ cup cold water.

1 cup boiling water.
⅔ cup sugar.
½ cup Sauterne.
¼ cup orange juice.

1½ tablespoons lemon juice.

Make same as other jellies, cool, and beat until frothy and firm enough to mould.

Jelly in Glasses.

Use recipe for Wine or Russian Jelly. Fill Apollinaris glasses three-fourths full, reserving one-fourth of the mixture, which, after cooling, is to be beaten until frothy and placed on top of jelly in glasses. This is a most attractive way of serving jelly to one who is ill.

Jellied Prunes.

⅓ lb. prunes.
2 cups cold water.
Boiling water.
½ cup cold water.
½ box gelatine or
2½ tablespoons granulated
    gelatine.
1 cup sugar.
¼ cup lemon juice.

Pick over, wash, and soak prunes for several hours in two cups cold water, and cook in same water until soft; remove prunes; stone, and cut in quarters. To prune water add enough boiling water to make two cups. Soak gelatine in half-cup cold water, dissolve in hot liquid, add sugar, lemon juice, then strain, add prunes, mould, and chill. Stir twice while cooling to prevent prunes from settling. Serve with sugar and cream.

Jellied Walnuts.

¼ box gelatine or
1¼ tablespoons granulated
    gelatine.
¼ cup cold water.
⅓ cup boiling water.
¾ cup sugar.
½ cup sherry wine.
½ cup orange juice.
3 tablespoons lemon juice.

Make same as other jellies and cover bottom of shallow pan with mixture. When firm, place over it, one inch apart, halves of English walnuts. Cover with remaining mixture. Chill, and cut in squares for serving.

Apricot and Wine Jelly.

½ box gelatine or
2½ tablespoons granulated
    gelatine.
½ cup cold water.
1 cup boiling water.
1 cup apricot juice.
1 cup wine.
1 cup sugar.
1 tablespoon lemon juice.

Garnish individual moulds with halves of apricots, fill with mixture made same as for other jellies, and chill. Serve with Cream Sauce I.

Snow Pudding I.

¼ box gelatine or   1 cup boiling water.
1¼ tablespoons granulated gelatine.   1 cup sugar.
¼ cup cold water.   ¼ cup lemon juice.
Whites 3 eggs.

Soak gelatine in cold water, dissolve in boiling water, add sugar and lemon juice, strain, and set aside in cool place; occasionally stir mixture, and when quite thick, beat with wire spoon or whisk until frothy; add whites of eggs beaten stiff, and continue beating until stiff enough to hold its shape. Mould, or pile by spoonfuls on glass dish; serve cold with Boiled Custard. A very attractive dish may be prepared by coloring half the mixture with fruit red.

Amber Pudding.

Make as Snow Pudding I., using cider instead of boiling water, and one-fourth cup boiling water to dissolve gelatine, omitting lemon juice.

Snow Pudding II.

Beat whites of four eggs until stiff, add one-half tablespoon granulated gelatine dissolved in three tablespoons boiling water, beat until thoroughly mixed, add one-fourth cup powdered sugar, and flavor with one-half teaspoon lemon extract. Pile lightly on dish, serve with Boiled Custard.

Pudding à la Macédoine.

Make fruit or wine jelly mixture. Place a mould in pan of ice water, pour in mixture one-half inch deep; when firm, decorate with slices of banana from which radiate thin strips of figs (seed side down), cover fruit, adding mixture by spoonfuls lest the fruit be disarranged. When firm, add more fruit and mixture; repeat until all is used, each time allowing mixture to stiffen before fruit

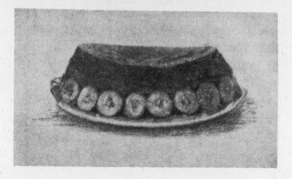

Pudding à la Macédoine.

is added. In preparing this dish various fruits may be used: oranges, bananas, dates, figs, and English walnuts. Serve with Cream Sauce I.

Fruit Chartreuse.

Make fruit or wine jelly mixture. Place a mould in pan of ice water, pour in mixture one-half inch deep; when firm, decorate with candied cherries and angelica; add by spoonfuls more mixture to cover fruit; when this is firm, place a smaller mould in the centre on jelly, and fill with ice water. Pour gradually remaining jelly mixture between moulds; when firm, invert to empty smaller mould of ice water; then pour in some tepid water; let stand a few seconds, when small mould may easily be removed. Fill space thus made with fresh sweetened fruit, using shredded pineapple, sliced bananas, and strawberries.

Spanish Cream.

¼ box gelatine or 1¼ tablespoons granulated gelatine.
3 cups milk.
Whites 3 eggs.

Yolks 3 eggs.
½ cup sugar (scant).
¼ teaspoon salt.
1 teaspoon vanilla or 3 tablespoons wine

Scald milk with gelatine, add sugar, pour slowly on yolks of eggs slightly beaten. Return to double boiler and cook until thickened, stirring constantly; remove from range, add salt, flavoring, and whites of eggs beaten stiff. Turn into individual moulds, first dipped in cold water, and chill; serve with cream. More gelatine will be required if large moulds are used.

Columbian Pudding.

Cover the bottom of a fancy mould with Wine Jelly. Line the upper part of mould with figs, cut in halves cross-wise, which have been soaked in jelly, having seed side next to mould. Fill centre with Spanish Cream; chill, and turn on a serving dish. Garnish with cubes of Wine Jelly.

Macaroon Cream.

¼ box gelatine or	Yolks 3 eggs.
1¼ tablespoons granulated	⅓ cup sugar.
gelatine.	⅛ teaspoon salt.
¼ cup cold water.	⅔ cup pounded macaroons.
2 cups scalded milk.	1 teaspoon vanilla.

Whites 3 eggs.

Soak gelatine in cold water. Make custard of milk, yolks of eggs, sugar, and salt; add soaked gelatine; when dissolved, strain into pan set in ice water. Add macaroons and flavoring, stirring until it begins to thicken; then add whites of eggs beaten stiff, mould, chill, and serve garnished with macaroons.

Cold Cabinet Pudding.

¼ box gelatine or	⅓ cup sugar.
1¼ tablespoons granulated gelatine.	⅛ teaspoon salt.
¼ cup cold water.	1 teaspoon vanilla.
2 cups scalded milk.	1 tablespoon brandy,
Yolks 3 eggs.	5 lady fingers.

6 macaroons.

Soak gelatine in cold water and add to custard made of milk, eggs, sugar, and salt; strain, cool slightly, and flavor. Place a mould in pan of ice water, decorate with candied cherries and angelica, cover with mixture, added carefully by spoonfuls; when firm, add layer of lady fingers (first soaked in custard), then layer of macaroons (also soaked in custard); repeat, care being taken that each layer is firm before another is added. Garnish, and serve with Cream Sauce I. and candied cherries.

Mont Blanc.

Remove shells from three cups French chestnuts, cook in small quantity of boiling water until soft, when there will be no water remaining. Mash, sweeten to taste with powdered sugar, and moisten with hot milk; cook two minutes. Rub through strainer, cool, flavor with vanilla, Kirsch or Maraschino. Pile in form of pyramid, cover with Cream Sauce I., garnish base with Cream Sauce I. forced through pastry bag and tube.

French Chef.

Crême aux Fruits.

¼ box gelatine or
1¼ tablespoons granulated gelatine.
¼ cup cold water.
¼ cup scalded milk.
½ cup sugar.

Whites 2 eggs.
½ pint thick cream.
⅓ cup milk.
⅓ cup cooked prunes
   cut in pieces.

⅓ cup chopped figs.

Soak gelatine in cold water, dissolve in scalded milk, and add sugar. Strain in pan set in ice water, stir constantly, and when it begins to thicken add whites of eggs beaten stiff, cream (diluted with milk and beaten), prunes, and figs. Mould and chill.

To Whip Cream.

Thin and heavy cream are both used in making and garnishing desserts.

Heavy cream is bought in half-pint, pint, and quart glass jars, and usually retails at sixty cents per quart; *thin* or *strawberry cream* comes in glass jars or may be bought in bulk, and usually retails for thirty cents per quart.   Heavy cream is very rich; for which reason, when whipped without being diluted, it is employed as a garnish; even when so used, it is generally diluted with one-fourth to one-third its bulk in milk; when used in

Whipping of cream.

combination with other ingredients for making desserts, it is diluted from one-half to two-thirds its bulk in milk. Thin cream is whipped without being diluted.   Cream should be thoroughly chilled for whipping.   Turn cream to be whipped in a bowl (care being taken not to select too large a bowl), and set in pan of crushed ice, to which water is added that cream may be quickly chilled; without addition of water, cream will not be so thoroughly chilled.

For whipping heavy cream undiluted, or diluted with one-third or less its bulk in milk, use Dover egg-beater: undiluted heavy cream if beaten a moment too long will come to butter.   Heavy cream diluted, whipped, sweetened, and flavored, is often served with puddings, and called Cream Sauce.

Thin cream is whipped by using a whip churn, as is heavy cream when diluted with one-half to two-thirds its bulk in milk. Place churn in bowl containing cream, hold down cover with left hand, with right hand work dasher with quick downward and slow upward motions; avoid raising dasher too high in cylinder, thus escaping spattering of cream. The first whip which appears should be stirred into cream, as air bubbles are too large and will break; second whip should be removed by spoonfuls to a strainer, strainer to be placed in a pan, as some cream will drain through. The first which drains through may be turned into bowl to be re-whipped, and continue whipping as long as possible.

There will be some cream left in bowl, which does not come above perforations in whip churn, and cannot be whipped. Cream which remains may be scalded and used to dissolve gelatine when making desserts which require gelatine. Cream should treble its bulk in whipping. By following these directions one need have no difficulty, if cream is of right consistency; always bearing in mind heavy cream calls for Dover egg-beater, thin cream for whip churn.

Charlotte Russe.

¼ box gelatine or
1¼ tablespoons granulated
   gelatine.
¼ cup cold water.
⅓ cup scalded cream.

⅓ cup powdered sugar.
Whip from 3½ cups thin
   cream.
1½ teaspoons vanilla.
6 lady fingers.

Soak gelatine in cold water, dissolve in scalded cream, strain into a bowl, and add sugar and vanilla. Set bowl in pan of ice water and stir constantly until it begins to thicken, then fold in whip from cream, adding one-third at a time. Should gelatine mixture become too thick, melt over hot water, and again cool before adding whip. Trim ends and sides of lady fingers, place around inside of a mould, crust side out, one-half inch apart. Turn in mixture, spread evenly, and chill. Serve on glass dish and garnish with cubes of Wine Jelly. Charlotte Russe is sometimes made in individual moulds; these are often garnished on top with some of mixture forced through a pastry bag and tube. Individual moulds are frequently lined with thin slices of sponge cake cut to fit moulds.

Charlotte Russe garnished with cubes of Wine Jelly.

Orange Trifle.

½ box gelatine or	1 cup sugar.
2½ tablespoons granulated gelatine.	1 cup orange juice.
	Grated rind 1 orange.
⅓ cup cold water.	1 tablespoon lemon juice.
½ cup boiling sugar.	Whip from 3½ cups cream.

Make same as Charlotte Russe, and mould; or make orange jelly, color with fruit red, and cover bottom of mould one-half inch deep; chill, and when firm fill with Orange Trifle mixture. Cool remaining jelly in shallow pan, cut in cubes, and garnish base of mould.

Banana Cantaloupe.

½ box gelatine or	⅔ cup sugar.
2½ tablespoons granulated gelatine.	4 bananas, mashed pulp.
½ cup cold water.	1 tablespoon lemon juice.
Whites 2 eggs.	Whip from 3½ cups cream.
¼ cup powdered sugar.	
¾ cup scalded cream.	12 lady fingers.

Soak gelatine in cold water, beat whites of eggs slightly, add powdered sugar, and gradually hot cream, cook over hot water until it thickens; add soaked gelatine and remaining sugar, strain into a pan set in ice water, add bananas and lemon juice, stir until it begins to thicken, then fold in whip from cream. Line a melon mould with lady fingers trimmed to just fit sections of mould, turn in the mixture, spread evenly, and chill.

Chocolate Charlotte.

¼ box gelatine or
1¼ tablespoons granulated gelatine.
¼ cup cold water.
⅓ cup scalded cream.

1½ squares Baker's chocolate.
3 tablespoons hot water.
⅔ cup powdered sugar.
Whip from 3 cups cream.
1 teaspoon vanilla.

6 lady fingers.

Melt chocolate, add half the sugar, dilute with boiling water, and add to gelatine mixture while hot. Proceed same as in recipe for Charlotte Russe.

Caramel Charlotte Russe.

¼ box gelatine or
1¼ tablespoons granulated gelatine.
¼ cup cold water.
½ cup scalded cream.

⅓ cup sugar caramelized.
¼ cup powdered sugar.
1½ teaspoons vanilla.
Whip from 3½ cups cream.
6 lady fingers.

Make same as Charlotte Russe, adding caramelized sugar to scalded cream before putting into gelatine mixture.

Burnt Almond Charlotte.

½ box gelatine or
2½ tablespoons granulated gelatine.
½ cup cold water.
¾ cup scalded milk.
½ cup sugar.

⅓ cup sugar caramelized.
¾ cup blanched and finely chopped almonds.
1 teaspoon vanilla.
Whip from 3½ cups cream.
6 lady fingers.

Make same as Caramel Charlotte Russe, adding nuts before folding in cream.

Ginger Cream.

¼ box gelatine or
1¼ tablespoons granulated
    gelatine.
¼ cup cold water.
1 cup milk.
Yolks 2 eggs.
¼ cup sugar.

Few grains salt.
1 tablespoon wine.
½ tablespoon brandy.
2 tablespoons ginger syrup.
¼ cup Canton ginger cut in
    pieces.
Whip from 2½ cups cream.

Soak gelatine, and add to custard made of milk, eggs, sugar, and salt.   Strain, chill in pan of ice water, add flavorings, and when it begins to thicken fold in whip from cream.

Orange Charlotte.

⅓ box gelatine or
1⅔ tablespoons granulated
    gelatine.
⅓ cup cold water.
⅓ cup boiling water.

1 cup sugar.
3 tablespoons lemon juice.
1 cup orange juice and pulp.
Whites 3 egg.
Whip from 2 cups cream.

Soak gelatine in cold water, dissolve in boiling water, strain, and add sugar, lemon juice, orange juice, and pulp. Chill in pan of ice water; when quite thick, beat with wire spoon or whisk until frothy, then add whites of eggs beaten stiff, and fold in cream.   Line a mould with sections of oranges, turn in mixture, smooth evenly, and chill.

Strawberry Sponge.

⅓ box gelatine or
1⅔ tablespoons granulated
    gelatine.
⅓ cup cold water.
⅓ cup boiling water.

1 cup sugar.
1 tablespoon lemon juice.
1 cup strawberry juice.
Whites 3 eggs.
Whip from 2 cups cream.

Make same as Orange Charlotte.

Orange Baskets.

Cut two pieces from each orange, leaving what remains in shape of basket with handle, remove pulp from baskets and pieces, and keep baskets in ice water until ready to fill. From orange juice make orange jelly with which to fill baskets. Serve garnished with Cream Sauce.

Orange Jelly in Ambush.

Cut oranges in halves lengthwise, remove pulp and juice. With juice make Orange Jelly to fill half the pieces. Fill remaining pieces with Charlotte Russe mixture. When both are firm, put together in pairs and tie together with narrow white ribbon.

Bavarian Cream (Quick).

½ lemon, grated rind and juice.	2 eggs.
½ cup white wine.	1 teaspoon granulated gelatine.
⅓ cup sugar.	1 tablespoon cold water.

Mix lemon, wine, sugar, and yolks of eggs; stir vigorously over fire until mixture thickens, add gelatine soaked in water, then pour over whites of eggs beaten stiff. Set in pan of ice water and beat until thick enough to hold its shape. Turn into a mould lined with lady fingers, and chill. Orange juice may be used in place of wine, and the cream served in orange baskets.

2 oranges ½ C. sugar ⅛ lb lady fingers + serve with orange Sauce.

Strawberry Bavarian Cream.

Line a mould with large, fresh strawberries cut in halves, fill with Charlotte Russe mixture.

Pineapple Bavarian Cream.

½ box gelatine or 2½ tablespoons granulated gelatine.	1 can grated pineapple.
	½ cup sugar.
½ cup cold water.	1 tablespoon lemon juice.
	Whip from 3 cups cream.

Soak gelatine in cold water. Heat pineapple, add sugar, lemon juice, and soaked gelatine; chill in pan of ice water, stirring constantly; when it begins to thicken, fold in whip from cream, mould, and chill.

Royal Diplomatic Pudding.

Place mould in pan of ice water and pour in Wine Jelly II. one-half inch deep. When firm, decorate with candied cherries and angelica, proceed as for Fruit Chartreuse, filling the centre with Charlotte Russe mixture or Fruit Cream.

Fruit Cream.

Peel four bananas, mash, and rub through a sieve; add pulp and juice of two oranges, one tablespoon lemon juice, one tablespoon sherry wine, two-thirds cup powdered sugar, and one and one-fourth tablespoons granulated gelatine dissolved in one-fourth cup boiling water. Cool in ice water, stirring constantly, and fold in whip from two cups cream.

CHAPTER XXVI.

ICES, ICE CREAMS, AND OTHER FROZEN DESSERTS.

ICES and other frozen dishes comprise the most popular desserts. Hygienically speaking, they cannot be recommended for the final course of a dinner, as cold mixtures reduce the temperature of the stomach, thus retarding digestion until the normal temperature is again reached. But how cooling, refreshing, and nourishing, when properly taken, and of what inestimable value in the sick room!

Frozen dishes include: —

Water Ice, — fruit juice sweetened, diluted with water, and frozen.

Sherbet, — water ice to which is added a small quantity of dissolved gelatine or beaten whites of eggs.

Frappé, — water ice frozen to consistency of mush; in freezing, equal parts of salt and ice being used to make it granular.

Punch, — water ice to which is added spirit and spice.

Sorbet, — strictly speaking, frozen punch; the name is often given to a water ice where several kinds of fruit are used.

Philadelphia Ice Cream, — thin cream, sweetened, flavored, and frozen.

Plain Ice Cream, — custard foundation, thin cream, and flavoring.

Mousse, — heavy cream, beaten until stiff, sweetened, flavored, placed in a mould, packed in equal parts salt and ice, and allowed to stand three hours; or whip from thin cream may be used folded into mixture containing small quantity of gelatine.

How to Freeze Desserts.

The prejudice of thinking a frozen dessert difficult to prepare has long since been overcome. With ice cream freezer, burlap bag, wooden mallet or axe, small saucepan, sufficient ice and coarse rock salt, the process neither takes much time nor patience. Snow may be used instead of ice; if not readily acted on by salt, pour in one cup cold water. Crush ice finely by placing in bag and giving a few blows with mallet or broad side of axe; if there are any coarse pieces, remove them. Place can containing mixture to be frozen in wooden tub, cover, and adjust top. Turn crank to make sure can fits in socket. Allow three level measures ice to one of salt, and repeat until ice and salt come to top of can, packing solidly, using handle of mallet to force it down. If only small quantity is to be frozen, the ice and salt need come only little higher in the tub than mixture to be frozen. These are found the best proportions of ice and salt to insure smooth, fine-grained cream, sherbet, or water ice, while equal parts of salt and ice are used for freezing frappé. If a larger proportion of salt is used, mixture will freeze in shorter time and be of granular consistency, which is desirable only for frappé·

The mixture increases in bulk during freezing, so the can should never be more than three-fourths filled; by overcrowding can, cream will be made coarse grained. Turn the crank slowly and steadily to expose as large surface of mixture as possible to ice and salt. After frozen to a mush, the crank may be turned more rapidly, adding more ice and salt if needed; never draw off salt water until mixture is frozen, unless there is possibility of its getting into the can, for salt water is what effects freezing; until ice melts, no change will take place. After freezing is accomplished, draw off water, remove dasher, and with spoon pack solidly. Put cork in opening of cover, then put on cover. Re-pack freezer, using four measures ice to one of salt. Place over top newspapers or piece of carpet; when serving time comes, remove can, wipe carefully, and place in vessel of cool water; let stand one minute, remove cover, and run a knife around edge of cream, invert can on serving-dish, and frozen mixture will slip out. Should there be any difficulty, a cloth wrung out of hot water, passed over can, will aid in removing mixture.

To Line a Mould.

Allow mould to stand in salt and ice until well chilled. Remove cover, put in mixture by spoonfuls, and spread with back of spoon or a case knife evenly three-quarters inch thick.

To Mould Frozen Mixtures.

When frozen mixtures are to be bricked or moulded, avoid freezing too hard. Pack mixture solidly in moulds and cover with buttered paper, buttered side up. Have moulds so well filled that mixture is forced down sides of mould when cover is pressed down. Repack in salt and ice, using four parts ice to one part salt. If these directions are carefully followed, one may feel no fear that salt water will enter cream, even though moulds be immersed in salt water.

Lemon Ice.

4 cups water.   2 cups sugar.
¾ cup lemon juice.

Make a syrup by boiling water and sugar twenty minutes; add lemon juice; cool, strain, and freeze. See directions for freezing, page 366.

Orange Ice.

4 cups water.   ¼ cup lemon juice.
2 cups sugar.   Grated rind and juice of
2 cups orange juice.   two oranges.

Make syrup as for Lemon Ice; add fruit juice and grated rind; cool, strain, and freeze.

Pomegranate Ice.

Same as Orange Ice, made from blood oranges.

Raspberry Ice.

4 cups water.	2 cups raspberry juice.
1⅔ cups sugar.	2 tablespoons lemon juice.

Make a syrup as for Lemon Ice, cool, add raspberries mashed, and squeezed through double cheese cloth, and lemon juice; strain and freeze.

Strawberry Ice.

4 cups water.	2 cups strawberry juice.
1½ cups sugar.	1 tablespoon lemon juice.

Prepare and freeze same as Raspberry Ice.

Currant Ice.

4 cups water.	1½ cups sugar.
	2 cups currant juice.

Prepare and freeze same as Raspberry Ice.

Raspberry and Currant Ice.

4 cups water.	⅔ cup raspberry juice.
1⅓ cups sugar.	1⅓ cups currant juice.

Prepare and freeze same as Raspberry Ice.

Crême de Menthe Ice.

4 cups water.	⅓ cup Crême de Menthe cordial.
1 cup sugar.	Burnett's Leaf Green.

Make a syrup as for Lemon Ice, add cordial and coloring; strain and freeze.

Canton Sherbet.

4 cups water.	¼ lb. Canton ginger.
1 cup sugar.	½ cup orange juice.

⅓ cup lemon juice.

Cut ginger in small pieces, add water and sugar, boil fifteen minutes; add fruit juice, cool, strain, and freeze. To be used in place of punch at a course dinner. This quantity is enough to serve twelve persons.

Milk Sherbet.

4 cups milk.	1½ cups sugar.

Juice 3 lemons.

Mix juice and sugar, stirring constantly while slowly adding milk; if added too rapidly mixture will have a curdled appearance, which is unsightly, but will not affect the quality of sherbet; freeze and serve.

Pineapple Frappé.

2 cups water.	4 cups ice water.
1 cup sugar.	1 can grated pineapple or
Juice 3 lemons.	1 pineapple shredded.

Make a syrup by boiling water and sugar fifteen minutes; add pineapple and lemon juice; cool, strain, add ice water, and freeze to a mush, using equal parts ice and salt. Serve in frappé glasses. If fresh fruit is used, more sugar will be required.

Sorbet.

2 cups water.	1⅓ cups orange juice.
2 cups sugar.	½ cup lemon juice.
1 can grated pineapple or	1 quart Apollinaris.
1 pineapple shredded.	

Prepare and freeze same as Pineapple Frappé.

Café Frappé.

White 1 egg.   ½ cup ground coffee.
½ cup cold water.   4 cups boiling water.
                1 cup sugar.

Beat white of egg slightly, add cold water, and mix
with coffee; turn into scalded coffee-pot, add boiling
water, and boil one minute; place on back of range ten
minutes; strain, add sugar, cool, and freeze as Pineapple
Frappé. Serve in frappé glasses, with whipped cream,
sweetened and flavored.

Clam Frappé.

20 clams.   ½ cup cold water.

Wash clams thoroughly, changing water several times;
put in stewpan with cold water, cover closely, and steam
until shells open. Strain the liquor, cool, and freeze to
a mush.

Frozen Apricots.

1 can apricots.   1½ cups sugar.
                Water.

Drain apricots, and cut in small pieces. To the syrup
add enough water to make four cups, and cook with sugar
five minutes; strain, add apricots, cool, and freeze.
Peaches may be used instead of apricots. To make a
richer dessert, add the whip from two cups cream when
frozen to a mush, and continue freezing.

Pineapple Cream.

2 cups water.   1 can grated pineapple.
1 cup sugar.   2 cups cream.

Make syrup by boiling sugar and water fifteen minutes;
strain, cool, add pineapple, and freeze to a mush. Fold
in whip from cream; let stand thirty minutes before
serving.

Cardinal Punch.

4 cups water.	⅓ cup lemon juice.
2 cups sugar.	¼ cup brandy.
⅔ cup orange juice.	¼ cup Curaçoa.

¼ cup tea infusion.

Make syrup as for Lemon Ice, add fruit juice and tea, freeze to a mush; add strong liquors and continue freezing. Serve in frappé glasses.

Punch Hollandaise.

4 cups water.	Rind one lemon.
1⅓ cups sugar.	1 can grated pineapple.
⅓ cup lemon juice.	¼ cup brandy.

2 tablespoons gin.

Cook sugar, water, and lemon rind fifteen minutes, add lemon juice and pineapple, cool, strain, freeze to a mush, add strong liquors, and continue freezing.

Victoria Punch.

3½ cups water.	Grated rind two oranges.
2 cups sugar.	1 cup angelica wine.
½ cup lemon juice.	1 cup cider.
½ cup orange juice.	1½ tablespoons gin.

Prepare same as Cardinal Punch; strain before freezing, to remove orange rind.

London Sherbet.

2 cups sugar.	3 tablespoons lemon juice.
2 cups water.	1 cup fruit syrup.
⅓ cup seeded and finely cut raisins.	¼ grated nutmeg.
	¼ cup port wine.
¾ cup orange juice.	Whites 3 eggs.

Make syrup by boiling water and sugar ten minutes; pour over raisins, cool, and add fruit syrup and nutmeg; freeze to a mush, then add wine and whites of eggs beaten stiff, and continue freezing. Serve in glasses. Fruit syrup may be used which has been left from canned peaches, pears, or strawberries.

Roman Punch.

4 cups water.	½ cup orange juice.
2 cups sugar.	½ cup tea infusion.
½ cup lemon juice.	½ cup rum.

Prepare and freeze same as Cardinal Punch.

Vanilla Ice Cream I. (Philadelphia).

1 quart thin cream.	¾ cup sugar.

1½ tablespoons vanilla.

Mix ingredients, and freeze.

Vanilla Ice Cream II.

2 cups scalded milk.	1 egg.
1 tablespoon flour.	⅛ teaspoon salt.
1 cup sugar.	1 quart thin cream.

2 tablespoons vanilla.

Mix flour, sugar, and salt, add egg slightly beaten, and milk gradually; cook over hot water twenty minutes, stirring constantly at first; should custard have curdled appearance, it will disappear in freezing. When cool, add cream and flavoring; strain and freeze.

Vanilla Ice Cream Croquettes.

Shape Vanilla Ice Cream in individual moulds, roll in macaroon dust made by pounding and sifting dry macaroons.

Chocolate Ice Cream I.

1 quart thin cream.	1½ squares Baker's chocolate or
1 cup sugar.	¼ cup prepared cocoa.
Few grains salt.	1 tablespoon vanilla.

Melt chocolate and dilute with hot water to pour easily, add to cream; then add sugar, salt, and flavoring, and freeze.

Chocolate Ice Cream II.

Use recipe for Vanilla Ice Cream II. Melt two squares Baker's chocolate, and pour hot custard slowly on chocolate; then cool before adding cream.

Strawberry Ice Cream.

3 pints thin cream.	1¾ cups sugar.
2 boxes strawberries.	2 cups milk.

1½ tablespoons arrowroot.

Wash and hull berries, sprinkle with sugar, let stand one hour, mash, and rub through strainer. Scald one and one-half cups milk; dilute arrowroot with remaining milk, add to hot milk, and cook ten minutes in double boiler; cool, add cream, freeze to a mush, add fruit, and finish freezing.

Pineapple Ice Cream

3 pints cream.	½ cup sugar.

1 can grated pineapple.

Add pineapple to cream, let stand thirty minutes; strain, add sugar, and freeze.

Coffee Ice Cream.

1 quart cream.	1¼ cups sugar.
1½ cups milk.	¼ teaspoon salt.
⅓ cup Mocha coffee.	Yolks 4 eggs.

Scald milk with coffee, add one cup sugar; mix egg yolks slightly beaten with one-fourth cup sugar, and salt; combine mixtures, cook over hot water until thickened, add one cup cream, and let stand on back of range twenty-five minutes; cool, add remaining cream, and strain through double cheese cloth; freeze. Coffee Ice Cream may be served with Maraschino cherries.

Caramel Ice Cream.

1 quart cream.	1 egg.
2 cups milk.	1 tablespoon flour.
1⅓ cups sugar.	⅛ teaspoon salt.

1½ tablespoons vanilla.

Prepare same as Vanilla Ice Cream II., using one-half sugar in custard; remaining half caramelize, and add slowly to hot custard. See Caramelization of Sugar, page 505.

Burnt Almond Ice Cream.

It is made same as Caramel Ice Cream, with the addition of one cup finely chopped blanched almonds.

Brown Bread Ice Cream.

3 pints cream.	⅞ cup sugar.
1¼ cups dried brown bread crumbs.	¼ teaspoon salt.

Soak crumbs in one quart cream, let stand fifteen minutes, rub through sieve, add sugar, salt, and remaining cream; then freeze.

Bisque Ice Cream.

Make custard as for Vanilla Ice Cream II., add one quart cream, one tablespoon vanilla, and one cup hickory nut or English walnut meat finely chopped.

Macaroon Ice Cream.

1 quart cream.	¾ cup sugar.
1 cup macaroons.	1 tablespoon vanilla.

Dry, pound, and measure macaroons; add to cream, sugar, and vanilla, then freeze.

Banana Ice Cream.

1 quart cream.	1½ tablespoons lemon juice.
4 bananas.	1 cup sugar.

Remove skins, and rub bananas through a sieve; add remaining ingredients; then freeze.

Ginger Ice Cream.

To recipe for Vanilla Ice Cream II., using one-half quantity vanilla, add one-half cup Canton ginger cut in small pieces, three tablespoons ginger syrup, and two tablespoons wine; then freeze.

Pistachio Ice Cream.

Prepare as Vanilla Ice Cream II., using for flavoring one tablespoon vanilla and one teaspoon almond extract; color with Burnett's Leaf Green.

Pistachio Bisque.

To Pistachio Ice Cream add one-half cup each of pounded macaroons, chopped almonds and peanuts. Mould, and serve with or without Claret Sauce.

Neapolitan or Harlequin Ice Cream.

Two kinds of ice cream and an ice moulded in a brick.

Baked Alaska.

Whites 6 eggs.	2 quart brick of ice cream.
6 tablespoons powdered sugar.	Thin sheet sponge cake.

Make meringue of eggs and sugar as in Meringue I., cover a board with white paper, lay on sponge cake, turn ice cream on cake (which should extend one-half inch beyond cream), cover with meringue, and spread smoothly. Place on oven grate and brown quickly in hot oven.

The board, paper, cake, and méringue are poor conductors of heat, and prevent the cream from melting. Slip from paper on ice cream platter.

Pudding Glacé.

2 cups milk.	¼ teaspoon salt.
⅔ cup raisins.	1 quart thin cream.
1 cup sugar.	½ cup almonds.
1 egg.	½ cup candied pineapple.
1 tablespoon flour.	⅓ cup Canton ginger.
3 tablespoons wine.	

Scald raisins in milk fifteen minutes, strain, make custard of milk, egg, sugar, flour, and salt; strain, cool, add pineapple, ginger cut in small pieces, nuts finely chopped, wine, and cream; then freeze. The raisins should be rinsed and saved for a pudding.

Frozen Pudding I.

2½ cups milk.	2 eggs.
1 cup sugar.	1 cup heavy cream.
⅛ teaspoonful salt.	¼ cup rum.
1 cup candied fruit, cherries, pineapples, pears, and apricots.	

Cut fruit in pieces, and soak several hours in brandy to cover, which prevents fruit freezing; make custard of first four ingredients; strain, cool, add cream and rum, then freeze. Fill a brick mould with alternate layers of the cream and fruit; pack in salt and ice and let stand two hours.

Frozen Pudding II.

1 quart cream.	¼ cup rum.
¾ cup sugar.	1 cup candied fruit.
8 lady fingers.	

Cut fruit in pieces, and soak several hours in brandy to cover. Mix cream, sugar, and rum, then freeze. Line a two quart melon mould with lady fingers, crust side down; fill with alternate layers of the cream and fruit, cover, pack in salt and ice, and let stand two hours. Brandied peaches cut in pieces, with some of their syrup added, greatly improve the pudding.

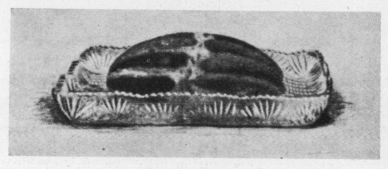

Frozen Pudding.

Delmonico Ice Cream with Angel Food.

2 cups milk.	⅛ teaspoon salt.
¾ cup sugar.	2½ cups thin cream.
Yolks 7 eggs.	1 tablespoon vanilla.
1 teaspoon lemon.	

Make custard of milk, sugar, eggs, and salt; cool, strain, and flavor; whip cream, remove whip; there should be two quarts; add to custard, and freeze. Serve plain or with Angel Food.

Angel Food.

Whites 3 eggs.	1 quart cream whip.
½ cup powdered sugar.	1½ teaspoons vanilla.

Beat eggs until stiff, fold in sugar, cream whip, and flavoring; line a mould with Delmonico Ice Cream, fill with the mixture, cover, pack in salt and ice, and let stand two hours.

Sultana Roll with Claret Sauce.

Line one-pound baking-powder boxes with Pistachio Ice Cream; sprinkle with sultana raisins which have been soaked one hour in brandy; fill centres with Vanilla Ice Cream or whipped cream, sweetened, and flavored with vanilla; cover with Pistachio Ice Cream; pack in salt and ice, and let stand one and one-half hours.

Claret Sauce.

1 cup sugar.   ¼ cup water.
                ⅓ cup claret.

Boil sugar and water eight minutes; cool slightly, and add claret.

Café Parfait.

1 cup milk.   ⅛ teaspoon salt.
¼ cup Mocha coffee.   1 cup sugar.
Yolks 3 eggs.   3 cups thin cream.

Scald milk with coffee, and add one-half the sugar; without straining, use this mixture for making custard, with eggs, salt, and remaining sugar; add one cup cream and let stand thirty minutes; cool, strain through double cheese cloth, add remaining cream, and freeze. Line a mould, fill with Italian Meringue, cover, pack in salt and ice, and let stand three hours.

Italian Meringue.

½ cup sugar.   Whites 3 eggs.
¼ cup water.   1 cup thin cream.
1 tablespoon gelatine or   ½ tablespoon vanilla.
¼ teaspoon granulated gelatine.

Make syrup by boiling sugar and water; pour slowly on beaten whites of eggs, and continue beating. Place in pan of ice water, and beat until cold; dissolve gelatine in small quantity boiling water; strain into mixture; whip cream, fold in whip, and flavor.

Bombe Glacée.

Line a mould with sherbet or water ice; fill with ice cream or thin Charlotte Russe mixture; cover, pack in salt and ice, and let stand two hours. The mould may be lined with ice cream. Pomegranate Ice and Vanilla or Macaroon Ice Cream make a good combination.

Nesselrode Pudding.

3 cups milk. ½ teaspoon salt.
1½ cups sugar. 1 pint thin cream.
Yolks 5 eggs. ¼ cup pineapple syrup.
1½ cups prepared French chestnuts.

Make custard of first four ingredients, strain, cool; add cream, pineapple syrup, and chestnuts; then freeze. To prepare chestnuts, shell, cook in boiling water until soft, and force through a strainer. Line a two-quart melon mould with part of mixture; to remainder add one-half cup candied fruit cut in small pieces, one-quarter cup sultana raisins, and eight chestnuts broken in pieces, first soaked several hours in Maraschino syrup. Fill mould, cover, pack in salt and ice, and let stand two hours. Serve with whipped cream, sweetened and flavored with Maraschino syrup.

Strawberry Mousse.

1 quart thin cream. ¼ box gelatine (scant) or
1 box strawberries. 1¼ tablespoons granulated gelatine.
1 cup sugar 2 tablespoons cold water.
3 tablespoons hot water.

Wash and hull berries, sprinkle with sugar, and let stand one hour; mash, and rub through a fine sieve; add gelatine soaked in cold and dissolved in boiling water. Set in pan of ice water and stir until it begins to thicken; then fold in whip from cream, put in mould, cover, pack in salt and ice, and let stand four hours. Raspberries may be used in place of strawberries.

Coffee Mousse.

Make same as Strawberry Mousse, using one cup boiled coffee in place of fruit juice.

Mousse Marron.

1 quart vanilla ice cream.	1 teaspoon granulated gelatine.
½ cup sugar.	1½ cups prepared French chestnuts.
¼ cup water.	1 pint cream.
Whites two eggs.	½ tablespoon vanilla.

Cook sugar and water five minutes, pour on to beaten whites of eggs; dissolve gelatine in one and one-half tablespoons boiling water, and add to first mixture. Set in a pan of ice water, and stir until cold; add chestnuts, and fold in whip from cream and vanilla. Line a mould with ice cream, and fill with mixture; cover, pack in salt and ice, and let stand three hours.

Cardinal Mousse, with Iced Madeira Sauce.

Line a mould with Pomegranate Ice; fill with Italian Meringue made of three-fourths cup sugar, one-third cup hot water, whites two eggs, and one and one-half teaspoons granulated gelatine dissolved in two tablespoons boiling water. Beat until cold, and fold in whip from two cups cream; flavor with one teaspoon vanilla, cover, pack in salt and ice, and let stand three hours.

Iced Madeira Sauce.

¼ cup orange juice.	½ cup sugar.
2 tablespoons lemon juice.	1 cup boiling water.
½ cup Madeira wine.	Whites 2 eggs.

Freeze fruit juice and wine; boil sugar and water, pour on slowly to beaten whites of eggs, set in a pan of salted ice water, and stir until cold   Add to frozen mixture.

Demi-glacé aux Fraises.

Line a brick mould with Vanilla Ice Cream, put in layer of Lady Fingers, and fill the centre with preserved strawberries or large fresh fruit cut in halves; cover with ice cream, pack in salt and ice, and let stand one hour. For ice cream, make custard of two and one-half cups milk, yolks four eggs, one cup sugar, and one-fourth teaspoon salt; strain, cool, add one cup heavy cream and one tablespoon vanilla; then freeze.

CHAPTER XXVII.

PASTRY.

PASTRY cannot be easily excluded from the menu of the New Englander. Who can dream of a Thanksgiving dinner without a pie! The last decade has done much to remove pies from the *daily* bill of fare, and in their place are found delicate puddings and seasonable fruits.

If pastry is to be served, have it of the best, — light, flaky, and tender.

To pastry belongs, 1st, Puff Paste; 2d, Plain Paste.

Puff paste, which to many seems so difficult of preparation, is rarely attempted by any except professionals. As a matter of fact, one who has never handled a rolling pin is less liable to fail, under the guidance of a good teacher, than an old cook, who finds it difficult to overcome the bad habit of using too much force in rolling. It is necessary to work rapidly and with a light touch. A cold room is of great advantage.

For making pastry, pastry flour and the best shortenings, thoroughly chilled, are essential. Its lightness depends on the amount of air enclosed and expansion of that air in baking. The flakiness depends upon kind and amount of shortening used. Lard makes more tender crust than butter, but lacks flavor which butter gives. Puff paste is usually shortened with butter, though some chefs prefer beef suet. Eggs and ice were formerly used, but are not essentials.

Butter should be washed if pastry is to be of the best, so as to remove salt and buttermilk, thus making it of a waxy consistency, easy to handle.

Rules for Washing Butter. Scald and chill an earthen bowl. Heat palms of hands in hot water, and chill in cold water. By following these directions, butter will not adhere to bowl nor hands. Wash butter in bowl by squeezing with hands until soft and waxy, placing bowl under a cold-water faucet and allowing water to run. A small amount of butter may be washed by using a wooden spoon in place of the hands.

For rolling paste, use a smooth wooden board, and wooden rolling-pin with handles.

Puff paste should be used for vol-au-vents, patties, rissoles, bouchées, cheese straws, tarts, etc. It may be used for rims and upper crusts of pies, but never for lower crusts. Plain paste may be used where pastry is needed, except for vol-au-vents and patties.

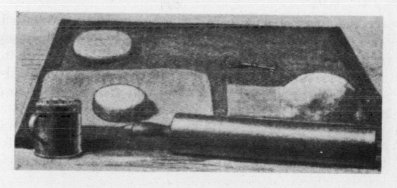

Puff paste before and after folding in butter.

Puff Paste.

1 pound butter.   1 pound pastry flour.
Cold water.

Wash the butter, pat and fold until no water flies. Reserve two tablespoons of butter, and shape remainder into a circular piece one-half inch thick, and put on floured board. Work two tablespoons of butter into flour with the tips of fingers of the right hand. Moisten to a dough with cold water, turn on slightly floured board, and knead one minute. Cover with towel, and let stand five minutes.

Pat and roll one-fourth inch thick, keeping paste a little wider than long, and corners square. If this cannot be accomplished with rolling-pin, draw into shape with fingers. Place butter on centre of lower half of paste. Cover butter by folding upper half of paste over it. Press edges firmly to enclose as much air as possible.

Fold right side of paste over enclosed butter, the left side under enclosed butter. Turn paste half-way round, cover, and let stand five minutes. Pat and roll one-fourth inch thick, having paste longer than wide, lifting often to prevent paste from sticking, and dredging board slightly with flour when necessary. Fold from ends towards centre, making three layers. Cover, and let stand five minutes. Repeat twice, turning paste half-way round each time before rolling. After fourth rolling, fold from ends to centre, and double, making four layers. Put in cold place to chill; if outside temperature is not sufficiently cold, fold paste in a towel, put in a dripping-pan, and place between dripping pans of crushed ice. If paste is to be kept for several days, wrap in a napkin, put in tin pail and cover tightly, then put in cold place; if in ice box, do not allow pail to come in direct contact with ice.

To Bake Puff Paste.

Baking of puff paste requires as much care and judgment as making. After shaping, chill thoroughly before baking. Puff paste requires hot oven, greatest heat coming from the bottom, that the paste may properly rise. While rising it is often necessary to decrease the heat by lifting covers or opening the check to stove. Turn frequently that it may rise evenly. When it has risen its full height, slip a pan under the sheet on which paste is baking to prevent burning on the bottom. Puff paste should be baked on a tin sheet covered with a double thickness of brown paper, or dripping-pan may be used, lined with brown paper. The temperature for baking of patties should be about the same as for raised biscuit; vol-au-vents require less heat, and are covered for first half-hour to prevent scorching on top.

Patty Shells.

Roll puff paste one-quarter inch thick, shape with a patty cutter, first dipped in flour; remove centres from one-half the rounds with smaller cutter. Brush over with cold water the larger pieces near the edge, and fit on rings, pressing lightly. Place in towel between pans of crushed ice, and chill until paste is stiff; if cold weather, chill out of doors. Place on iron or tin sheet covered with brown paper, and bake twenty-five minutes in hot oven. The shells should rise their full height and begin to brown in twelve to fifteen minutes; continue browning, and finish baking in twenty-five minutes. Pieces cut from centre of rings of patties may be baked and used for patty covers, or put together, rolled, and cut for unders. Trimmings from puff paste should be carefully laid on top of each other, patted, and rolled out.

Vol-au-vents.

Roll puff paste one-third inch thick, mark an oval on paste with cutter or mould, and cut out with sharp knife, first dipped in flour. Brush over near the edge with cold water, put on a rim three-fourths inch wide, press lightly, chill, and bake. Vol-au-vents require for baking forty-five minutes to one hour. During the first half-hour they should be covered, watched carefully, and frequently turned. The paste cut from centre of rim should be rolled one-quarter inch thick, shaped same size as before rolling, chilled, baked, and used for cover to the Vol-au-vent.

Plain Paste.

1½ cups flour.   ¼ cup butter.
¼ cup lard.   ½ teaspoon salt.
                 Cold water.

Wash butter, pat, and form in circular piece.   Add salt to flour, and work in lard with tips of fingers or case knife. Moisten to dough with cold water; ice water is not an essential, but is desirable in summer.   Toss on board dredged sparingly with flour, pat, and roll out; fold in butter as for puff paste, pat, and roll out.   Fold so as to make three layers, turn half-way round, pat, and roll out; repeat.   The pastry may be used at once; if not, fold in cheese cloth, put in covered tin, and keep in cold place, but never in direct contact with ice.   Plain paste requires a moderate oven.   This is superior paste and quickly made.

Quick Paste.

1½ cups flour.   ¼ cup cottolene or cocoanut
¾ teaspoon salt.   butter.
                 Cold water.

Mix salt with flour, cut in shortening with knife.   Moisten to dough with cold water.   Toss on floured board, pat, roll out, and roll up like a jelly roll.   Use one-third cup of shortening if a richer paste is desired.

Paste with Lard.

1½ cups flour.   ⅓ cup lard.
½ teaspoon salt.   Cold water.

Mix salt with flour.   Reserve one and one-fourth table-spoons lard, work in remainder to flour, using tips of fin-gers or a case knife.   Moisten to a dough with water. Toss on a floured board, pat, and roll out.   Spread with one tablespoon reserved lard, dredge with flour, roll up like a jelly roll, pat, and roll out; again roll up.   Cut from the end of roll a piece large enough to line a pie plate. Pat and roll out, keeping the paste as circular in form as possible. With care and experience there need be no trimmings. Worked-over pastry is never as satisfactory. The remaining one-fourth tablespoon lard is used to dot over upper crust of pie just before sending to oven; this gives the pie a flaky appearance. Ice water has a similar effect. If milk is brushed over the pie it has a glazed appearance. This quantity of paste will make one pie with two crusts and a few puffs, or two pies with one crust where the rim is built up and fluted.

CHAPTER XXVIII.

PIES.

PASTE for pies should be one-fourth inch thick and rolled a little larger than the plate to allow for shrinking. In dividing paste for pies, allow more for upper than under crusts. Always perforate upper crusts that steam may escape. Some make a design, others pierce with a large fork.

Flat rims for pies should be cut in strips three-fourths inch wide. Under crusts should be brushed with cold water before putting on rims, and rims slightly fulled, otherwise they will shrink from edge of plate. The pastry-jagger, a simple device for cutting paste, makes rims with fluted edges.

Pies requiring two crusts sometimes have a rim between the crusts. This is mostly confined to mince pies, where there is little danger of juice escaping. Sometimes a rim is placed over upper crust. Where two pieces of paste are put together, the under piece should always be brushed with cold water, the upper piece placed over, and the two pressed lightly together; otherwise they will separate during baking.

When juicy fruit is used for filling pies, some of the juices are apt to escape during baking. As a precaution, bind with a strip of cotton cloth wrung out of cold water and cut one inch wide and long enough to encircle the plate. Squash, pumpkin, and custard pies are much less care during baking when bound. Where cooked fruits are used for filling, it is desirable to bake crusts separately. This is best accomplished by covering an inverted deep pie plate with paste and baking for under crust. Prick with a fork before baking. Slip from plate and fill. For upper crusts, roll a piece of paste a little larger than the pie plate, prick, and bake on a tin sheet.

For baking pies, perforated tin plates are used. They may be bought shallow or deep. By the use of such plates the under crust is well cooked. Pastry should be thoroughly baked and well browned. Pies require from thirty-five to forty-five minutes for baking. Never grease a pie plate; good pastry greases its own tin. Slip pies, when slightly cooled, to earthen plates.

Apple Pie I.

4 or 5 sour apples.	⅛ teaspoon salt.
⅓ cup sugar.	1 teaspoon butter.
¼ teaspoon grated nutmeg.	1 teaspoon lemon juice.
Few gratings lemon rind.	

Line pie plate with paste. Pare, core, and cut the apples into eighths, put row around plate one-half inch from edge, and work towards centre until plate is covered; then pile on remainder. Mix sugar, nutmeg, salt, lemon juice, and grated rind, and sprinkle over apples. Dot over with butter. Wet edges of under crust, cover with upper crust, and press edges together.

Bake forty to forty-five minutes in moderate oven. A very good pie may be made without butter, lemon juice and grated rind. Cinnamon may be substituted for nutmeg. Evaporated apples may be used in place of fresh fruit. If used, they should be soaked over night in cold water.

Apple Pie II.

Use same ingredients as for Apple Pie I. Place in small earthen baking-dish and add hot water to prevent apples from burning. Cover closely and bake three hours in very slow oven, when apples will be a dark red color. Brown sugar may be used instead of white sugar, a little more being required. Cool, and bake between two crusts.

Blackberry Pie.

Pick over and wash one and one-half cups berries. Stew until soft with enough water to prevent burning. Add sugar to taste and one-eighth teaspoon salt. Line plate with paste, put on a rim, fill with berries (which have been cooled); arrange six strips pastry across the top, cut same width as rim; put on an upper rim. Bake thirty minutes in moderate oven.

Blueberry Pie.

2½ cups berries.   ½ cup supar.
Flour.   ⅛ teaspoon salt.

Line a deep plate with Plain Paste, fill with berries slightly dredged with flour; sprinkle with sugar and salt, cover, and bake forty-five to fifty minutes in a moderate oven. For sweetening, some prefer to use one-third molasses, the remaining two-thirds to be sugar. Six green grapes (from which seeds have been removed) cut in small pieces much improve the flavor, particularly where huckleberries are used in place of blueberries.

Cranberry Pie.

1½ cups cranberries.   ½ cup water.
                 ¾ cup sugar.

Put ingredients in saucepan in order given, and cook ten minutes; cool, and bake in one crust, with a rim, and strips across the top.

Currant Pie.

1 cup currants.   ¼ cup flour.
1 cup sugar.   2 egg yolks.
                 2 tablespoons water.

Mix flour and sugar, add yolks of eggs slightly beaten and diluted with water. Wash currants, drain, remove stems, then measure; add to first mixture and bake in one crust; cool, and cover with Meringue I. Cook in slow oven until delicately browned.

Cream Pie.

Bake three crusts on separate pie plates. Put together with Cream Filling and dust over with powdered sugar. If allowed to stand after filling for any length of time, the pastry will soften.

Custard Pie.

2 eggs.	⅛ teaspoon salt.
3 tablespoons sugar.	1½ cups milk.

Few gratings nutmeg.

Beat eggs slightly, add sugar, salt, and milk. Line plate with paste, and build up a fluted rim. Strain in the mixture and sprinkle with few gratings nutmeg. Bake in quick oven at first to set rim, decrease the heat afterwards, as egg and milk in combination need to be cooked at low temperature.

Date Pie.

2 cups milk.	2 eggs.
⅓ pound sugar dates.	¼ teaspoon salt.

Few gratings nutmeg.

Cook dates with milk twenty minutes in top of double boiler. Strain and rub through sieve, then add eggs and salt. Bake same as Custard Pie.

Lemon Pie I.

½ cup chopped apple.	¼ cup rolled common crackers.
1 cup sugar.	2 tablespoons lemon juice.
1 beaten egg.	Grated rind 1 lemon.

1 teaspoon melted butter.

Mix ingredients in order given and bake with two crusts.

Lemon Pie II.

¾ cup sugar.	2 egg yolks.
¾ cup boiling water.	3 tablespoons lemon juice.
3 tablespoons corn-starch.	Grated rind 1 lemon.

1 teaspoon butter.

Mix corn-starch and sugar, add boiling water, stirring constantly. Cook two minutes, add butter, egg yolks, and rind and juice of lemon. Line plate with paste same as for Custard Pie. Turn in mixture which has been cooled, and bake until pastry is well browned. Cool slightly and cover with Meringue I.; then return to oven and bake meringue.

Lemon Pie III.

4 eggs.	1 lemon.
6 tablespoons sugar.	1¼ cups milk.
Few grains salt.	1 cup powdered sugar.

Beat yolks of eggs slightly, add sugar, salt, grated rind of lemon, and milk. Line plate with paste as for Custard Pie. Pour in mixture. Bake in moderate oven until set. Remove, cool slightly, and cover with Meringue III.

Lemon Pie IV.

Lemon Pie IV.

3 eggs.	¼ cup lemon juice.
⅔ cup sugar.	Grated rind ½ lemon.
2 tablespoons water.	

Beat eggs slightly, add sugar, lemon juice, grated rind, and water. Bake in one crust. Cool slightly, cover with Meringue II., then return to oven and bake meringue.

Mince Pies.

Mince pies should be always baked with two crusts. For Thanksgiving and Christmas pies, Puff Paste is often used for rims and upper crusts.

Mince Pie Meat.

4 lbs. lean beef.	3 lbs. currants.
2 lbs. beef suet.	½ lb. finely cut citron.
Baldwin apples.	1 quart cooking brandy.
3 quinces.	1 tablespoon cinnamon and mace.
3 lbs. sugar.	1 tablespoon powdered clove.
2 cups molasses.	2 grated nutmegs.
2 quarts cider.	1 teaspoon pepper.
4 lbs. raisins seeded	Salt to taste.
and cut in pieces.	

Cover meat and suet with boiling water and cook until tender, cool in water in which they were cooked; the suet will rise to top, forming a cake of fat, which may be easily removed. Finely chop meat, and add it to twice the amount of finely chopped apples. The apples should be quartered, cored, and pared, previous to chopping, or skins may be left on, which is not an objection if apples are finely chopped. Add quinces finely chopped, sugar, molasses, cider, raisins, currants, and citron; also suet, and stock in which meat and suet were cooked, reduced to one and one-half cups. Heat gradually, stir occasionally, and cook slowly two hours; then add brandy and spices.

English Mince Meat.

5 lbs. raisins seeded.	5 lbs. currants.
5 lbs. suet,	5 lbs. light brown sugar.
5 lbs. apples,	½ teaspoon mace.
4 lbs. citron, — finely chopped.	½ teaspoon cinnamon.
1½ lbs. blanched almonds,	2½ cups brandy.

Cook raisins, suet, apples, citron, currants, and sugar slowly for one and one-half hours; then add almonds, spices, and brandy.

Mince Meat (without Liquor).

Mix together one cup chopped apple, one-half cup raisins seeded and chopped, one-half cup currants, one-fourth cup butter, one tablespoon molasses, one table-spoon boiled cider, one cup sugar, one teaspoon cinnamon, one-half teaspoon cloves, one-half nutmeg grated, one salt-spoon of mace, and one teaspoon salt. Add enough stock in which meat was cooked to moisten; heat gradually to boiling point and simmer one hour; then add one cup chopped meat and two tablespoons Barberry Jelly. Cook fifteen minutes.

Mock Mince Pie.

4 common crackers rolled.	1 cup raisins seeded and
1½ cups sugar.	chopped.
1 cup molasses.	½ cup butter.
⅓ cup lemon juice or vinegar.	2 eggs well beaten.
	Spices.

Mix ingredients in order given, adding spices to taste. Bake between crusts. This quantity will make two pies.

Peach Pie.

Remove skins from peaches. This may be done easily after allowing peaches to stand in boiling water one minute. Cut in eighths, cook until soft with enough water to prevent burning; sweeten to taste. Cool, and fill crust previously baked. Cover with whipped cream, sweetened and flavored.

Prune Pie.

½ lb. prunes.	1 tablespoon lemon juice.
½ cup sugar (scant).	1½ teaspoons butter.
	1 tablespoon flour.

Wash prunes and soak in enough cold water to cover. Cook in same water until soft. Remove stones, cut prunes in quarters, and mix with sugar and lemon juice. Reduce liquor to one and one-half tablespoons. Line plate with paste, cover with prunes, pour over liquor, dot over with butter, and dredge with flour. Bake with an upper crust.

Rhubarb Pie.

1½ cups rhubarb.	1 egg.
⅞ cup sugar.	2 tablespoons flour.

Skin and cut stalks of rhubarb in half-inch pieces before measuring. Mix sugar, flour, and egg; add to rhubarb and bake between crusts. Many prefer to scald rhubarb before using; if so prepared, losing some of its acidity, less sugar is required.

Squash Pie.

1¼ cups steamed and strained squash.	¼ teaspoon cinnamon, ginger, nutmeg, or
¼ cup sugar.	½ teaspoon lemon extract.
½ teaspoon salt.	1 egg.
	⅞ cup milk.

Mix sugar, salt, and spice or extract, add squash, egg slightly beaten, and milk gradually. Bake in one crust, following directions for Custard Pie. If a richer pie is desired, use one cup squash, one-half cup each of milk and cream, and an additional egg yolk.

Pumpkin Pie.

Pumpkin Pie is made same as Squash Pie, using pumpkin in place of squash.

2 c. pumpkin
⅓ c. sugar
½ tsp. Salt
2 tsp. lemon juice
1 tbsp. Butter

1 tsp. cinn.
1 tsp. ginger
½ tsp. nutmeg
2 eggs
⅞ c. milk

CHAPTER XXIX.

PASTRY DESSERTS.

Banbury Tarts.

1 cup raisins.	1 egg.
1 cup sugar.	1 cracker.

Juice and grated rind 1 lemon.

Stone and chop raisins, add sugar, egg slightly beaten, cracker finely rolled, and lemon juice and rind. Roll pastry one-eighth inch thick, and cut pieces three and one-half inches long by three inches wide. Put two teaspoons of mixture on each piece. Moisten edge with cold water half-way round, fold over, press edges together with three-tined fork, first dipped in flour. Bake twenty minutes in slow oven.

Cheese Cakes.

1 cup sweet milk.	Juice and grated rind 1 lemon.
1 cup sour milk.	¼ cup almonds blanched and
1 cup sugar.	chopped.
Yolks 4 eggs.	¼ teaspoon salt.

Scald sweet and sour milk, strain through cheese cloth. To curd add sugar, yolks of eggs slightly beaten, lemon, and salt. Line patty pans with paste, fill with mixture, and sprinkle with chopped almonds. Bake until mixture is firm to the touch.

Cheese Straws.

Roll puff or plain paste one-fourth inch thick, sprinkle one-half with grated cheese to which has been added few grains of salt and cayenne. Fold, press edges firmly

together, fold again, pat and roll out one-fourth inch
thick. Sprinkle with cheese and proceed as before; repeat twice. Cut in strips five inches long and one-fourth
inch wide. Bake eight minutes in hot oven. Parmesan
cheese or equal parts of Parmesan and Edam cheese may
be used. Cheese straws are piled log cabin fashion and
served with cheese or salad course.

Condés.

Whites 2 eggs.   ¾ cup powdered sugar.
2 oz. almonds, blanched and finely chopped.

Beat whites of eggs until stiff, add sugar gradually,
then almonds. Roll paste and cut in strips three and
one-half inches long by one and one-half inches wide.
Spread with mixture; avoid having it come close to edge.
Dust with powdered sugar and bake fifteen minutes in
moderate oven.

Cream Horns.

Roll puff paste in a long rectangular piece, one-eighth
inch thick. Cut in strips three-fourths inch wide. Roll
paste over wooden forms bought for the purpose, having
edges overlap. Bake in hot oven until well puffed and
slightly browned. Brush over with white of egg slightly
beaten, diluted with one teaspoon water, then sprinkle
with sugar. Return to oven and finish cooking, and remove from forms. When cold, fill with Cream Filling or
whipped cream sweetened and flavored.

Florentine Meringue.

Roll puff or plain paste one-eighth inch thick; cut a
piece ten inches long by seven inches wide; place on a
sheet, wet edges, and put on a half-inch rim. Prick with
fork six times, and bake in hot oven. Cool and spread
with jam, cover with Meringue II., and almonds blanched
and shredded, sprinkle with powdered sugar, and bake.

Napoleons.

Bake three sheets of pastry, pricking before baking. Put between the sheets Cream Filling; spread top with Confectioners' Frosting, crease in pieces about two and one-half by four inches, and cut with sharp knife.

Orange Sticks.

Cut puff or plain paste rolled one-eighth inch thick in strips five inches long by one inch wide, and bake in hot oven. Put together in pairs, with Orange Filling between.

Lemon Sticks.

Lemon Sticks may be made in same manner as Orange Sticks, using Lemon Filling.

Palm Leaves.

Roll remnants of puff paste one-eighth inch thick; sprinkle one-half surface with powdered sugar, fold, press edges together, pat and roll out, using sugar for dredging board; repeat three times. After the last rolling fold four times. The pastry should be in long strip one and one-half inches wide. From the end, cut pieces one-inch wide; place on baking-sheet, broad side down, one-inch apart, and separate layers of pastry at one end to suggest a leaf. Bake eight minutes in hot oven; these will spread while baking.

Raspberry Puffs.

Roll plain paste one-eighth inch thick, and cut in pieces four by three and one-half inches. Put one-half tablespoon raspberry jam on centre of lower half of each piece, wet edges half-way around, fold, press edges firmly together, prick tops, place on sheet, and bake twenty minutes in hot oven. Mince meat or apple sauce may be used for filling.

Tarts.

Roll puff paste one-eighth inch thick. Shape with a fluted round cutter, first dipped in flour; with a smaller cutter remove centres from half the pieces, leaving rings one-half inch wide. Brush with cold water the larger pieces near the edge; fit on rings, pressing lightly. Chill thoroughly, and bake fifteen minutes in hot oven. By brushing tops of rings with beaten yolk of egg diluted with one teaspoonful water, they will have a glazed appearance. Cool, and fill with jam or jelly.

Polish Tartlets.

Roll puff or plain paste one-eighth inch thick, and cut in two and one-half inch squares; wet the corners, fold toward the centre, and press lightly; bake on a sheet; when cool, press down the centres and fill, using two-thirds quince marmalade and one-third currant jelly.

MERINGUES.

For Pies, Puddings, and Desserts.

Eggs for meringues should be thoroughly chilled, and beaten with silver fork, wire spoon or whisk. Where several eggs are needed, much time is saved by using a whisk. Meringues on pies, puddings, or desserts, may be spread evenly, spread and piled in the centre, put on lightly by spoonfuls, or spread evenly with part of the mixture, the remainder being forced through a pastry bag and tube.

Meringues I. and III. should be baked fifteen minutes in slow oven. Meringue II. should be cooked eight minutes in moderate oven; if removed from oven before cooked, the eggs will liquefy and meringue settle; if cooked too long, meringue is tough.

Meringue I.

Whites 2 eggs.   ½ tablespoon lemon juice or
2 tablespoons powdered sugar.   ¼ teaspoon vanilla.

Beat whites until stiff, add sugar gradually and continue beating, then add flavoring.

Meringue II.

Whites 3 eggs.   ½ teaspoon lemon extract or
7½ tablespoons powdered sugar.   ⅓ teaspoon vanilla.

Beat whites until stiff, add four tablespoons sugar gradually, and beat vigorously; fold in remaining sugar, and add flavoring.

Meringue III.

Whites 4 eggs.   ⅞ cup powdered sugar.
          2 tablespoons lemon juice.

Put whites of eggs and sugar in bowl, beat mixture until stiff enough to hold its shape, add lemon juice drop by drop, continuing the beating. It will take thirty minutes to beat mixture sufficiently stiff to hold its shape, but when baked it makes a most delicious meringue.

Meringues Glacées, or Kisses.

Whites 4 eggs.   1¼ cups powdered sugar or
½ teaspoon vanilla.   1 cup fine granulated.

Beat whites until stiff, add gradually two-thirds of sugar, and continue beating until mixture will hold its shape; fold in remaining sugar, and add flavoring. Shape with a spoon or pastry bag and tube on wet board covered with letter paper. Bake thirty minutes in very slow oven, remove from paper and put together in pairs, or if intending to fill with whipped cream or ice cream remove soft part with spoon and place meringues in oven to dry.

Nut Meringues.

To Meringue Glacée mixture add chopped nut meat; almonds, English walnuts, or hickory nuts are preferred. Shape by dropping mixture from tip of spoon in small piles one-half inch apart, or by using pastry bag and tube. Sprinkle with nut meat and bake.

Meringues (Mushrooms).

Shape Meringue Glacée mixture in rounds the size of mushroom caps, using pastry bag and tube; sprinkle with grated chocolate. Shape stems like mushroom stems. Bake, remove from paper, and place caps on stems.

Meringues Panachées.

Fill Meringues Glacées with ice cream, or ice cream and water ice. Garnish with whipped cream forced through pastry bag and tube, and candied cherries.

CHAPTER XXX.

GINGERBREADS, COOKIES, AND WAFERS.

Hot Water Gingerbread.

1 cup molasses.	1 teaspoon soda.
½ cup boiling water.	1½ teaspoons ginger.
2¼ cups floor.	½ teaspoon salt.

3 tablespoons melted butter.

Add water to molasses. Mix and sift dry ingredients, combine mixtures, add butter, and beat vigorously. Pour into a buttered shallow pan, and bake twenty-five minutes in a moderate oven. Chicken fat tried out and clarified furnishes an excellent shortening, and may be used in place of butter.

Sour Milk Gingerbread.

1 cup molasses.	1¾ teaspoons soda.
1 cup sour milk.	2 teaspoons ginger.
2⅓ cups flour.	½ teaspoon salt.

¼ cup melted butter.

Add milk to molasses. Mix and sift dry ingredients, combine mixtures, add butter, and beat vigorously. Pour into a buttered shallow pan, and bake twenty-five minutes in a moderate oven.

Soft Molasses Gingerbread.

1 cup molasses.	1 egg.
⅓ cup butter.	2 cups flour.
1¾ teaspoons soda.	2 teaspoons ginger
½ cup sour milk.	½ teaspoon salt.

Put butter and molasses in saucepan and cook until boiling point is reached. Remove from fire, add soda.

and beat vigorously.   Then add milk, egg well beaten,
and remaining ingredients mixed and sifted.   Bake fifteen
minutes in buttered small tin pans, having pans two-thirds
filled with mixture.

Cambridge Gingerbread.

⅓ cup butter.	1½ teaspoons soda.
⅔ cup boiling water.	½ teaspoon salt.
1 cup molasses.	1 teaspoon cinnamon.
1 egg.	1 teaspoon ginger.
3 cups flour.	¼ teaspoon clove.

Melt butter in water, add molasses, egg well beaten,
and dry ingredients mixed and sifted.   Bake in a buttered
shallow pan.

Soft Sugar Gingerbread.

2 eggs.	3 teaspoons baking powder.
1 cup sugar.	½ teaspoon salt.
1¾ cups flour.	1½ teaspoons ginger.
⅔ cup thin cream.	

Beat eggs until light, and add sugar gradually.   Mix
and sift dry ingredients, and add alternately with cream to
first mixture.   Turn into a buttered cake pan, and bake
thirty minutes in a moderate oven.

Gossamer Gingerbread.

⅓ cup butter.	½ cup milk.
1 cup sugar.	1⅞ cups flour.
1 egg.	3 teaspoons baking powder.
1 teaspoon yellow ginger.	

Cream the butter, add sugar gradually, then egg well
beaten.   Add milk, and dry ingredients mixed and sifted.
Spread in a buttered dripping-pan as thinly as possible,
using the back of mixing-spoon.   Bake fifteen minutes.
Sprinkle with sugar, and cut in small squares or diamonds
before removing from pan.

Fairy Gingerbread.

½ cup butter.   ½ cup milk.
1 cup light brown sugar.   1⅞ cups bread flour.
                2 teaspoons ginger.

Cream the butter, add sugar gradually, and milk very slowly. Mix and sift flour and ginger, and combine mixtures. Spread very thinly with a broad, long-bladed knife on a buttered, inverted dripping pan. Bake in a moderate oven. Cut in squares before removing from pan. Watch carefully and turn pan frequently during baking, that all may be evenly cooked. If mixture around edge of pan is cooked before that in the centre, pan should be removed from oven, cooked part cut off, and remainder returned to oven to finish cooking.

Hard Sugar Gingerbread.

¾ cup butter.   5 cups flour.
1½ cups sugar.   ¾ tablespoon baking powder.
¾ cup milk.   1½ teaspoons salt.
                ¾ tablespoon ginger.

Cream the butter, add sugar gradually, milk, and dry ingredients mixed and sifted. Put some of mixture on an inverted dripping-pan and roll as thinly as possible to cover pan. Mark dough with a coarse grater. Sprinkle with sugar and bake in a moderate oven. Before removing from pan, cut in strips four and one-half inches long by one and one-half inches wide.

Molasses Drop Cakes.

1 cup molasses.   1 cup hot water.
½ cup melted butter.   1 egg.
1 cup sugar.   2 teaspoons ginger.
2 teaspoons soda.   ½ teaspoon salt.
                4 cups flour.

Mix molasses, butter, and sugar. Add soda and beat thoroughly, then add water, egg well beaten, and flour mixed and sifted with ginger and salt.   Drop by spoonfuls on a buttered sheet.   Bake twelve to fifteen minutes in a hot oven.

Ginger Snaps.

Good.

1 cup molasses.	½ teaspoon soda.
⅓ cup shortening.	1 tablespoon ginger.
3¼ cups flour. *More*	1½ teaspoons salt.

2 c. brown sugar   of the spice

Heat molasses to boiling point and pour over shortening. Add dry ingredients mixed and sifted.   Chill thoroughly. Toss one-fourth of mixture on a floured board and roll as thinly as possible; shape with a small round cutter, first dipped in flour.   Place near together on a buttered sheet and bake in a moderate oven.   Gather up the trimmings and roll with another portion of dough.   During rolling, the bowl containing mixture should be kept in a cool place, or it will be necessary to add more flour to dough, which makes cookies hard rather than crisp and short.

Molasses Cookies.

Good.

1 cup molasses.	1 tablespoon ginger.
½ cup shortening, butter	1 tablespoon soda.
and lard mixed.	2 tablespoons warm milk.
2 cups bread flour.	

Heat molasses to boiling point, add shortening, ginger, soda dissolved in warm milk, and flour.   Proceed as for Ginger Snaps.

Soft Molasses Cookies.

not good.

1 cup molasses.	½ cup shortening melted.
1¾ teaspoons soda.	2 teaspoons ginger.
1 cup sour milk.	1 teaspoon salt.
Flour.	

Add soda to molasses and beat thoroughly; add milk, shortening, ginger, salt, and flour.   Enough flour must be used to make mixture of right consistency to drop easily from spoon.   Let stand several hours in a cold place to thoroughly chill.   Toss one-half mixture at a time on slightly floured board and roll lightly to one-fourth inch thickness. Shape with a round cutter, first dipped in flour. Bake on a buttered sheet.

Spice Cookies.

½ cup molasses.
¼ cup sugar.
1½ tablespoons butter.
1½ tablespoons lard.
1 tablespoon milk.
3 cups flour.
½ teaspoon soda.
½ teaspoon salt.
½ teaspoon clove.
½ teaspoon cinnamon.
½ teaspoon nutmeg.

Heat molasses to boiling point. Add sugar, shortening, and milk. Mix and sift dry ingredients, and add to first mixture. Chill, and proceed as with Ginger Snaps.

Scotch Wafers.

1 cup fine oatmeal.
1 cup Quaker Rolled Oats
2 cups flour.
¼ cup sugar.
1 teaspoon salt.
⅛ teaspoon soda.
¼ cup butter or lard.
½ cup hot water.

Mix first six ingredients. Melt shortening in water and add to first mixture. Toss on a floured board, pat and roll as thinly as possible. Shape with a cutter, or with a sharp knife cut in strips. Bake on a buttered sheet in a slow oven. These are well adapted for children's luncheons, and are much enjoyed by the convalescent, taken with a glass of milk.

Oatmeal Cookies.

1 egg.
¼ cup sugar.
¼ cup thin cream.
¼ cup milk.
½ cup fine oatmeal.
2 cups flour.
2 teaspoons baking powder.
1 teaspoon salt.

Beat egg until light, add sugar, cream, and milk; then add oatmeal, flour, baking powder, and salt, mixed and sifted. Toss on a floured board, roll, cut in shape, and bake in a moderate oven.

Vanilla Wafers.

⅓ cup butter and lard in
    equal proportions.
1 cup sugar.
1 egg.

¼ cup milk.
2½ cups flour.
2 teaspoons baking powder.
½ teaspoon salt.

2 teaspoons vanilla.

Cream the butter, add sugar, egg well beaten, milk, and
vanilla.   Mix and sift dry ingredients and add to first
mixture.   Proceed as with Ginger Snaps.

Cream Cookies.

⅓ cup butter.
1 cup sugar.
2 eggs.
½ cup thin cream.

2 teaspoons baking powder.
1 teaspoon salt.
2 teaspoons yellow ginger.
Flour to roll.

Mix and bake same as Vanilla Wafers.

Imperial Cookies.

½ cup butter.
1 cup sugar.
2 eggs.
1 tablespoon milk.

3 cups flour.
2 teaspoons baking powder.
½ teaspoon lemon extract.
½ teaspoon grated nutmeg.

Mix and bake same as Vanilla Wafers.

Hermits.

⅓ cup butter.
⅔ cup sugar.
1 egg.
2 tablespoons milk.
2 cups flour.
2 teaspoons baking powder.

⅓ cup raisins stoned and cut
    in small pieces.
½ teaspoon cinnamon.
¼ teaspoon clove.
¼ teaspoon mace.
¼ teaspoon nutmeg.

Cream the butter, add sugar gradually, then raisins, egg
well beaten, and milk.   Mix and sift dry ingredients and
add to first mixture.   Roll mixture a little thicker than
for Vanilla Wafers.

Boston Cookies.

1 cup butter.	½ teaspoon salt.
1½ cups sugar.	1 teaspoon cinnamon.
3 eggs.	1 cup chopped nut meat,
1 teaspoon soda.	hickory or English walnut.
1½ tablespoons hot water.	½ cup currants.
3¼ cups flour.	½ cup raisins seeded and chopped.

Cream the butter, add sugar gradually, and eggs well beaten. Add soda dissolved in water, one-half flour mixed and sifted with salt and cinnamon; then add nut meat, fruit, and remaining flour. Drop by spoonfuls one inch apart on a buttered sheet, and bake in a moderate oven.

Cocoanut Cream Cookies.

2 eggs.	½ cup shredded cocoanut.
1 cup sugar.	3½ cups flour.
1 cup thick cream.	3 teaspoons baking powder.
	1 teaspoon salt.

Beat eggs until light, add sugar gradually, cocoanut, cream, and flour mixed and sifted with baking powder. Chill, toss on a floured board, pat and roll one-half inch thick. Sprinkle with cocoanut, roll one-fourth inch thick, and shape with a small round cutter, first dipped in flour. Bake on a buttered sheet.

Peanut Cookies.

2 tablespoons butter.	¼ teaspoon salt.
¼ cup sugar.	½ cup flour.
1 egg.	2 tablespoons milk.
1 teaspoon baking powder.	½ cup finely chopped peanuts.
	½ teaspoon lemon juice.

Cream the butter, add sugar, and egg well beaten. Mix and sift baking powder, salt, and flour; add to first mixture; then add milk, peanuts, and lemon juice. Drop from a teaspoon on an unbuttered sheet one-inch apart, and place one-half peanut on top of each. Bake twelve to fifteen minutes in a slow oven. This recipe will make twenty-four cookies.

Seed Cakes.

Follow recipe for Cocoanut Cream Cookies, using one and one-half tablespoons caraway seeds in place of cocoanut.

Chocolate Cookies.

½ cup butter.
1 cup sugar.
1 egg.
¼ teaspoon salt.

2 oz. Baker's chocolate.
2½ cups flour (scant).
2 teaspoons baking powder.
¼ cup milk.

Cream the butter, add sugar gradually, egg well beaten, salt, and chocolate melted. Beat well, and add flour mixed and sifted with baking powder alternately with milk. Chill, roll very thin, then shape with a small cutter, first dipped in flour, and bake in a hot oven.

Sand Tarts.

½ cup butter.
1 cup sugar.
1 egg.
1¾ cups flour.

2 teaspoons baking powder.
White 1 egg.
Blanched almonds.
1 tablespoon sugar.

¼ teaspoon cinnamon.

Cream the butter, add sugar gradually, and egg well beaten; then add flour mixed and sifted with baking powder. Chill, toss one-half mixture on a floured board, and roll one-eighth inch thick. Shape with a doughnut cutter. Brush over with white of egg, and sprinkle with sugar mixed with cinnamon. Split almonds, and arrange three halves on each at equal distances. Place on a buttered sheet, and bake eight minutes in a slow oven.

Rolled Wafers tied in bundles of three with baby ribbon.

Rolled Wafers.

¼ cup butter.   ¼ cup milk.
½ cup powdered sugar.   ⅞ cup bread flour.
½ teaspoon vanilla.

Cream the butter, add sugar gradually, and milk drop by drop; then add flour and flavoring. Spread very thinly with a broad, long-bladed knife on a buttered inverted dripping pan. Crease in three-inch squares, and bake in a slow oven until delicately browned. Place pan on back of range, cut squares apart with a sharp knife, and roll while warm in tubular or cornucopia shape. If squares become too brittle to roll, place in oven to soften. If rolled tubular shape, tie in bunches with narrow ribbon. These are very attractive, and may be served with sherbet, ice cream, or chocolate. If rolled cornucopia shape, they may be filled with whipped cream just before sending to table. Colored wafers may be made from this mixture by adding leaf green or fruit red. If colored green, flavor with one-fourth teaspoon almond and three-fourths teaspoon vanilla. If colored pink, flavor with rose. Colored wafers must be baked in a very slow oven to prevent browning.

Almond Wafers tied together with ribbon.

Almond Wafers.

Before baking Rolled Wafers, sprinkle with almonds blanched and chopped.

CHAPTER XXXI.

CAKE.

THE mixing and baking of cake requires more care and judgment than any other branch of cookery; notwithstanding, it seems the one most frequently attempted by the inexperienced.

Two kinds of cake mixtures are considered : —

I. Without butter.   Example : Sponge Cakes.

II. With butter.   Examples : Cup and Pound Cakes.

In cake making (1) the best ingredients are essential; (2) great care must be taken in measuring and combining ingredients; (3) pans must be properly prepared; (4) oven heat must be regulated, and cake watched during baking.

Best tub butter, fine granulated sugar, fresh eggs, and pastry flour are essentials for good cake.   Coarse granulated sugar, bought by so many, if used in cake making, gives a coarse texture and hard crust.   Pastry flour contains more starch and less gluten than bread flour, therefore makes a lighter, more tender cake.   If bread flour must be used, allow two tablespoons less for each cup than the recipe calls for.   Flours differ greatly in thickening properties; for this reason it is always well when using from a new bag to try a small cake, as the amount of flour given may not make the perfect loaf.   In winter, cake may be made of less flour than in summer.

Before attempting to mix cake, study How to Measure (p. 27) and How to Combine Ingredients (p. 29).

Look at the fire, and replenish by sprinkling on a small quantity of coal if there is not sufficient heat to effect the baking.

To Mix Sponge Cake. Separate yolks from whites of eggs. Beat yolks until thick and lemon colored, using an egg beater; add sugar gradually, and continue beating; then add flavoring. Beat whites until stiff and dry, — when they will fly from the beater, — and add to the first mixture. Mix and sift flour with salt, and cut and fold in at the last. If mixture is beaten after the addition of flour, much of the work already done of enclosing a large amount of air will be undone by breaking air bubbles. These rules apply to a mixture where baking powder is not employed.

To Mix Butter Cakes. An earthen bowl should always be used for mixing cake, and a wooden cake-spoon with slits lightens the labor. Measure dry ingredients, and mix and sift baking powder and spices, if used, with flour. Count out number of eggs required, breaking each separately that there may be no loss should a stale egg chance to be found in the number, separating yolks from whites if rule so specifies. Measure butter, then liquid. Having everything in readiness, the mixing may be quickly accomplished. If butter is very hard, by allowing it to stand a short time in a warm room it is measured and creamed much easier. If time cannot be allowed for this to be done, warm bowl by pouring in some hot water, letting stand one minute, then emptying and wiping dry. Avoid overheating bowl, as butter will become oily rather than creamy. Put butter in bowl, and cream by working with a wooden spoon until soft and of a creamy consistency; then add sugar gradually, and continue beating. Add yolks of eggs or whole eggs beaten until light, liquid, and flour mixed and sifted with baking powder; or liquid and flour may be added alternately. When yolks and whites of eggs are beaten separately, whites are usually added at the last, as is the case when whites of eggs alone are used. A cake can be made fine grained only by long beating, although light and delicate with a small amount of beating. Never stir cake after the final beating, remembering that beating motion should always be the last used. Fruit, when added to cake, is usually floured to prevent its settling to the bottom. This is not necessary if it is added directly after the sugar, which is desirable in all dark cakes. If a light fruit cake is made, fruit added in this way discolors the loaf. Citron is first cut in thin slices, then in strips, floured, and put in between layers of cake mixtures. Raisins are seeded and cut, rather than chopped. *To seed raisins*, wet tips of fingers in a cup of warm water. Then break skins with fingers, or cut with a vegetable knife; remove seeds, and put in cup of water. This is better than covering raisins with warm water; if this be done, water clings to fruit, and when dredged with flour a pasty mass is formed on the outside. Washed currants, put up in packages, are quite free from stems and foreign substances, and need only picking over and rolling in flour. Currants bought in bulk need thorough cleaning. First roll in flour, which helps to start dirt; wash in cold water, drain, and spread to dry; then roll again in flour before using.

To Butter and Fill Pans. Grease pans with melted fat, applying the same with a butter brush. If butter is used, put in a small saucepan and place on back of range; when melted, salt will settle to the bottom; butter is then called *clarified*. Just before putting in mixture, dredge pans thoroughly with flour, invert, and shake pan to remove all superflous flour, leaving only a thin coating which adheres to butter. This gives to cake a smooth under surface, which is especially desirable if cake is to be frosted. Pans may be lined with paper. If this is done, paper should just cover bottom of pan and project over sides. Then ends of pan and paper are buttered.

In filling pans, have the mixture come well to the corners and sides of pans, leaving a slight depression in the centre, and when baked the cake will be perfectly flat on top. Cake pans should be filled nearly two-thirds full if cake is expected to rise to top of pan.

To Bake Cake. The baking of cake is more critical than the mixing. Many a well-mixed cake has been spoiled in the baking. No oven thermometer has yet proved practical, and although many teachers of cookery have given oven tests, experience alone has proved the most reliable teacher. In baking cake, divide the time required into quarters. During the first quarter the mixture should begin to rise; second quarter, continue rising and begin to brown; third quarter, continue browning; fourth quarter, finish baking and shrink from pan. If oven is too hot, open check and raise back covers, or leave oven door ajar. It is sometimes necessary to cover cake with brown paper; there is, however, danger of cake adhering to paper. Cake should be often looked at during baking, and providing oven door is opened and closed carefully, there is no danger of this causing cake to fall. Cake should not be moved in oven until it has risen its full height; after this time it is usually desirable to move it that it may be evenly browned. Cake when done shrinks from the pan, and in most cases this is a sufficient test; however, in pound cakes this rule does not apply. Pound and rich fruit cakes are tested by pressing surface with tip of finger. If cake feels firm to touch and follows finger back into place, it is safe to remove it from the oven. When baking cake arrange to have nothing else in the oven, and place loaf or loaves as near the centre of oven as possible. If placed close to fire box, one side of loaf is apt to become burned before sufficiently risen to turn. If cake is put in too slow an oven, it often rises over sides of pan and is of very coarse texture; if put in too hot an oven, it browns on top before sufficiently risen, and in its attempt to rise breaks through the crust, thus making an unsightly loaf. Cake will also crack on top if too much flour has been used. The oven should be kept at as nearly uniform temperature as possible. Small and layer cakes require a hotter oven than loaf cakes.

To Remove Cake from Pans.   Remove cake from pans as soon as it comes from the oven, by inverting pan on a wire cake cooler, or on a board covered with a piece of old linen.   If cake is inclined to stick, do not hurry it from pan, but loosen with knife around edges, and rest pan on its four sides successively, thus by its own weight cake may be helped out.

To Frost Cake.   Where cooked frostings are used, it makes but little difference whether they are spread on hot or cold cake.   Where uncooked frostings are used, it is best to have the cake slightly warm, with the exception of Confectioners' Frosting, where boiling water is employed.

Hot Water Sponge Cake.

Yolks 2 eggs.
1 cup sugar.
⅜ cup hot water.
¼ teaspoon lemon extract.

Whites 2 eggs.
1 cup flour.
1½ teaspoons baking powder.
¼ teaspoon salt.

Beat yolks of eggs until thick and lemon-colored, add one-half the sugar gradually, and continue beating; then add water, remaining sugar, lemon extract, whites of eggs beaten until stiff, and flour mixed and sifted with baking powder and salt.   Bake twenty-five minutes in a moderate oven in a buttered and floured shallow pan.

Cheap Sponge Cake.

Yolks 3 eggs.
1 cup sugar.
1 tablespoon hot water.
1 cup flour.

1½ teaspoons baking powder.
¼ teaspoon salt.
Whites 3 eggs.
2 teaspoons vinegar.

Beat yolks of eggs until thick and lemon-colored, add sugar gradually, and continue beating; then add water, flour mixed and sifted with baking powder and salt, whites of eggs beaten until stiff, and vinegar.   Bake thirty-five minutes in a moderate oven, in a buttered and floured cake pan.

Cream Sponge Cake.

Yolks 4 eggs.
1 cup sugar.
3 tablespoons cold water.
1½ tablespoons corn-starch.

Flour.
1½ teaspoons baking powder.
¼ teaspoon salt.
Whites 4 eggs.

1 teaspoon lemon extract.

Beat yolks of eggs until thick and lemon-colored, add sugar gradually, and beat two minutes; then add water. Put corn-starch in a cup and fill cup with flour. Mix and sift corn-starch and flour with baking powder and salt, and add to first mixture. When thoroughly mixed add whites of eggs beaten until stiff, and flavoring. Bake thirty minutes in a moderate oven.

Sponge Cake.

Yolks 6 eggs.
1 cup sugar.
1 tablespoon lemon juice.

Grated rind one-half lemon.
Whites 6 eggs.
1 cup flour.

¼ teaspoon salt.

Beat yolks until thick and lemon-colored, add sugar gradually, and continue beating, using Dover egg-beater. Add lemon-juice, rind, and whites of eggs beaten until stiff and dry. When whites are partially mixed with yolks, remove beater, and carefully cut and fold in flour mixed and sifted with salt. Bake one hour in a slow oven, in an angel cake pan or deep narrow pan.

Genuine sponge cake contains no rising properties, but is made light by the quantity of air beaten into both yolks and whites of eggs, and the expansion of that air in baking. It requires a slow oven. All so-called sponge cakes which have the addition of soda and cream of tartar or baking powder require same oven temperature as butter cakes. When failures are made in Sunshine and Angel Cake, they are usually traced to baking in too slow an oven, and removing from oven before thoroughly cooked.

Sunshine Cake.

Whites 10 eggs   1 teaspoon lemon extract.
1½ cups powdered sugar.   1 cup flour.
Yolks 6 eggs.   1 teaspoon cream of tartar.

Beat whites of eggs until stiff and dry, add sugar gradually, and continue beating; then add yolks of eggs beaten until thick and lemon colored, and extract. Cut and fold in flour mixed and sifted with cream of tartar. Bake fifty minutes in a moderate oven in an angel cake pan.

Angel Cake.

1 cup white of eggs.   ⅓ cup flour.
¾ cup sugar.   ½ teaspoon salt.
¼ cup corn-starch.   1 teaspoon cream of tartar.
                1 teaspoon vanilla.

Beat whites of eggs until stiff and dry, add sugar gradually and continue beating, then add flavoring. Cut and fold in corn-starch, flour, salt, and cream of tartar, mixed and sifted. Bake forty-five to fifty minutes in an unbuttered angel cake pan in a moderate oven.

Lady Fingers.

Whites 3 eggs.   ⅓ cup of flour.
⅓ cup powdered sugar.   ⅛ teaspoon salt.
Yolks 2 eggs.   ¼ teaspoon vanilla.

Beat whites of eggs until stiff and dry, add sugar gradually, and continue beating. Then add yolks of eggs beaten until thick and lemon colored, and flavoring. Cut and fold in flour mixed and sifted with salt. Shape four and one-half inches long and one inch wide on a tin sheet covered with unbuttered paper, using a pastry bag and tube. Sprinkle with powdered sugar, and bake eight minutes in a moderate oven. Remove from paper with a knife. Lady Fingers are much used for lining moulds that are to be filled with whipped cream mixtures. They are often served with frozen desserts, and sometimes put together in pairs with a thin coating of whipped cream between, when they are attractive for children's parties.

Sponge Drop.

Drop Lady Finger mixture from tip of spoon on unbuttered paper. Sprinkle with powdered sugar, and bake eight minutes in a moderate oven.

Jelly Roll.

3 eggs.	1½ teaspoons baking powder.
1 cup sugar.	¼ teaspoon salt.
½ tablespoon milk.	1 cup flour.

1 tablespoon melted butter.

Beat egg until light, add sugar gradually, milk, flour mixed and sifted with baking powder and salt, then butter. Line the bottom of a dripping-pan with paper; butter paper and sides of pan. Cover bottom of pan with mixture, and spread evenly. Bake twelve minutes in a moderate oven. Take from oven and turn on a ~~damp~~ *damp* ~~paper sprinkled with powdered sugar.~~ *towel* Quickly remove paper, and cut off a thin strip from sides and ends of cake. Spread with jelly or jam which has been beaten to consistency to spread easily, and roll. After cake has been rolled, roll paper around cake that it may better keep in shape. The work must be done quickly, or cake will crack in rolling.

Aunt Caddie's Cake.

¼ cup butter.	1 teaspoon salt.
½ cup sugar.	1 teaspoon cinnamon.
1 cup molasses.	⅓ teaspoon clove.
1 cup sour milk.	2½ cups flour.
1½ teaspoons soda.	¾ cup raisins seeded and cut in pieces.

Cream the butter, add sugar gradually, molasses, sour milk, and raisins. Mix and sift remaining ingredients, and combine mixtures. Bake fifty minutes in a deep pan.

Election Cake.

½ cup butter.
1 cup bread dough.
1 egg.
1 cup brown sugar.
½ cup sour milk.
⅔ cup raisins seeded and
cut in pieces.

8 finely chopped figs.
1⅓ cups flour.
½ teaspoon soda.
1 teaspoon cinnamon.
¼ teaspoon clove.
¼ teaspoon mace.
¼ teaspoon nutmeg.

1 teaspoon salt.

Work butter into dough, using the hand. Add egg well beaten, sugar, milk, fruit dredged with two table-spoons flour, and flour mixed and sifted with remaining ingredients. Put into a well-buttered bread pan, cover, and let rise one and one-fourth hours. Bake one hour in a slow oven. Cover with Boiled Milk Frosting.

One Egg Cake.

¼ cup of butter.
½ cup sugar.
1 egg.

½ cup of milk.
1½ cups flour.
2½ teaspoons baking powder.

Cream the butter, add sugar gradually, and egg well beaten. Mix and sift flour and baking powder, add alternately with milk to first mixture. Bake thirty minutes in a shallow pan. Spread with Chocolate Frosting.

Chocolate Cake.

3 tablespoons butter.
½ cup sugar.
1 egg.
½ cup milk.

1⅓ cups flour.
2 teaspoons baking powder.
1 square chocolate melted.
½ teaspoon vanilla.

Cream the butter, add one-half sugar, egg well beaten, and remaining sugar. Mix and sift flour and baking powder, add alternately with milk to first mixture. Then add chocolate and vanilla. Bake thirty minutes in a shallow pan.

Chocolate Nougat Cake.

¼ cup butter.	3 teaspoons baking powder.
1½ cups powdered sugar.	½ teaspoon vanilla.
1 egg.	2 squares chocolate melted.
1 cup milk.	⅓ cup powdered sugar.
2 cups bread flour.	⅔ cup almonds blanched and shredded.

Cream the butter, add gradually one and one-half cups sugar, and egg unbeaten; when well mixed, add two-thirds milk, flour mixed and sifted with baking powder, and vanilla. To melted chocolate add one-third cup powdered sugar; place on range, add gradually remaining milk, and cook until smooth. Cool slightly, and add to cake mixture. Bake fifteen to twenty minutes in round layer cake pans. Put between layers and on top of cake White Mountain Cream sprinkled with almonds.

Cream Pie I.

⅓ cup butter.	½ cup milk.
1 cup sugar.	1¾ cups flour.
2 eggs.	2½ teaspoons baking powder.

Mix as One Egg Cake. Bake in round layer cake pans. Put Cream Filling between layers and sprinkle top with powdered sugar.

Cream Pie II.

Make as Cream Pie I., using French Cream Filling in place of Cream Filling.

Cocoanut Pie.

Mix and bake as Cream Pie. Put Cocoanut Filling between layers and on top.

Washington Pie.

Mix and bake as Cream Pie. Put raspberry jam or jelly between layers and sprinkle top with powdered sugar.

Chocolate Pie.

2 tablespoons butter.	½ cup milk.
¾ cup sugar.	1⅓ cups flour.
1 egg.	2 teaspoons baking powder.

Mix and bake as Cream Pie. Split layers, and spread between and on top of each a thin layer of Chocolate Frosting.

Orange Cake.

¼ cup butter.	½ cup milk.
1 cup sugar.	1⅔ cups flour.
2 eggs.	2½ teaspoons baking powder.

Cream the butter, add sugar gradually, eggs well beaten, and milk. Then add flour mixed and sifted with baking powder. Bake in a thin sheet in a dripping-pan. Cut in halves, spread one-half with Orange Filling. Put over other half, and cover with Orange Frosting.

Quick Cake.

⅓ cup soft butter.	1¾ cups flour.
1⅓ cups brown sugar.	3 teaspoons baking powder.
2 eggs.	½ teaspoon cinnamon.
½ cup milk.	½ teaspoon grated nutmeg.
½ lb. dates stoned and cut in pieces.	

Put ingredients in a bowl and beat all together for three minutes. Bake in a cake pan thirty-five to forty minutes. If directions are followed this makes a most satisfactory cake; but if ingredients are added separately it will not prove a success.

Boston Favorite Cake.

⅔ cup butter.	1 cup milk.
2 cups sugar.	3½ cups flour.
4 eggs.	5 teaspoons baking powder.

Cream the butter, add sugar gradually, eggs beaten until light, then milk and flour mixed and sifted with baking powder. This recipe makes two loaves.

Cream Cake

2 eggs.	2½ teaspoons baking powder.
1 cup sugar.	½ teaspoon salt.
⅔ cup thin cream.	½ teaspoon cinnamon.
1⅔ cups flour.	¼ teaspoon mace.

¼ teaspoon ginger.

Put unbeaten eggs in a bowl, add sugar and cream, and beat vigorously. Mix and sift remaining ingredients, then add to first mixture. Bake thirty minutes in a shallow cake pan.

Currant Cake.

½ cup butter.	½ cup milk.
1 cup sugar.	2 cups flour.
2 eggs.	3 teaspoons baking powder.
Yolk 1 egg.	1 cup currants mixed with
	1 tablespoon flour.

Cream the butter, add sugar gradually, and eggs and egg yolk well beaten. Then add milk, flour mixed and sifted with baking powder, and currants. Bake forty minutes in a buttered and floured cake pan.

Velvet Cake.

½ cup butter.	1½ cups flour.
1½ cups sugar.	½ cup corn-starch.
Yolks 4 eggs.	4 teaspoons baking powder.
½ cup cold water	Whites 4 eggs.

⅓ cup almonds blanched and shredded.

Cream the butter, add sugar gradually, yolks of eggs well beaten, and water. Mix and sift flour, corn-starch, and baking powder, and add to first mixture; then add whites of eggs beaten until stiff. After putting in pan, cover with almonds and sprinkle with powdered sugar. Bake forty minutes in a moderate oven.

Walnut Cake.

½ cup butter.   1¾ cups flour.
1 cup sugar.   2½ teaspoons baking powder.
Yolks 3 eggs.   Whites 2 eggs.
½ cup milk.   ¾ cup walnut meat broken in
                              pieces.

Mix ingredients in order given. Bake forty-five minutes in a moderate oven. Cover with White Mountain Cream, crease in squares, and put one-half walnut on each square.

Spanish Cake.

½ cup butter.   1¾ cups flour.
1 cup sugar.   3 teaspoons baking powder.
Yolks 2 eggs.   1 teaspoon cinnamon.
½ cup milk.   Whites 2 eggs.

Mix ingredients in order given. Bake in shallow tins and spread between and on top Caramel Frosting.

Cup Cake.

⅔ cup butter.   1 cup milk.
2 cups sugar.   3¼ cups flour.
4 eggs.   4 teaspoons baking powder.
            ¼ teaspoon mace.

Put butter and sugar in a bowl, and stir until well mixed; add eggs well beaten, then milk, and flour mixed and sifted with baking powder and mace. Bake in individual tins. Cover with Chocolate Frosting.

Brownies.

⅓ cup butter.   1 egg well beaten.
⅓ cup powdered sugar.   ⅞ cup bread flour.
⅓ cup Porto Rico molasses. 1 cup pecan meat cut in pieces.

Mix ingredients in order given. Bake in small, shallow fancy cake tins, garnishing top of each cake with one-half pecan.

Ribbon Cake.

½ cup butter.
2 cups sugar.
Yolks 4 eggs.
1 cup milk.
3½ cups flour.
5 teaspoons baking powder.
Whites 4 eggs.

½ teaspoon cinnamon.
¼ teaspoon mace.
¼ teaspoon nutmeg.
⅓ cup raisins seeded and
    cut in pieces.
⅓ cup figs finely chopped.
1 tablespoon molasses.

Mix first seven ingredients in order given. Bake two-thirds of the mixture in two layer cake pans. To the remainder add spices, fruit, and molasses, and bake in a layer cake pan. Put layers together with jelly (apple usually being preferred as it has less flavor), having the dark layer in the centre.

Coffee Cake.

¼ cup butter.
½ cup sugar.
½ cup raisins seeded and
    cut in pieces.
½ cup molasses.
¼ cup boiled coffee.

2 eggs.
2½ cups flour.
3 teaspoons baking powder.
½ teaspoon salt.
½ teaspoon cinnamon.
½ teaspoon allspice.

½ nutmeg grated.

Follow directions for mixing butter cake mixtures.

Rich Coffee Cake.

1 cup butter.
2 cups sugar.
4 eggs.
2 tablespoons molasses.
1 cup cold boiled coffee.
3¾ cups flour.
5 teaspoons baking powder.
1 teaspoon cinnamon.

½ teaspoon clove.
½ teaspoon mace.
½ teaspoon allspice.
¾ cup raisins seeded and
    cut in pieces.
¾ cup currants.
¼ cup citron thinly sliced
    and cut in strips.

2 tablespoons brandy.

Follow directions for mixing butter cake mixtures. Bake in deep cake pans.

Dark Fruit Cake.

½ cup butter.
¾ cup brown sugar.
¾ cup raisins seeded and
    cut in pieces.
¾ cup currants.
½ cup citron thinly sliced
    and cut in strips.
½ cup molasses.

2 eggs.
½ cup milk.
2 cups flour.
½ teaspoon soda.
1 teaspoon cinnamon.
½ teaspoon allspice.
¼ teaspoon mace.
¼ teaspoon clove.

½ teaspoon lemon extract.

Follow directions for mixing butter cake mixtures. Bake in deep cake pans one and one-quarter hours.

Nut Cakes.

Meat from 1 lb. pecans.
1 lb. powdered sugar.

¼ cup flour.
Whites 6 eggs.

1 teaspoon vanilla.

Pound nut meat and mix with sugar and flour. Beat whites of eggs until stiff, add first mixture and vanilla. Drop from tip of tablespoon (allowing one spoonful for each drop) on a tin sheet covered with buttered paper. Bake twenty minutes in a moderate oven.

Snow Cake.

¼ cup butter.
1 cup sugar.
½ cup milk.
1⅔ cups flour.

2½ teaspoons baking powder.
Whites 2 eggs.
½ teaspoon vanilla or
¼ teaspoon almond extract.

Follow recipe for mixing butter cakes. Bake forty-five minutes in a deep narrow pan.

Lily Cake.

⅓ cup butter.
1 cup sugar.
½ cup milk.
1¾ cups flour.

2½ teaspoons baking powder.
Whites 3 eggs.
⅓ teaspoon lemon extract.
⅔ teaspoon vanilla.

Follow recipe for mixing butter cakes.

Corn-starch Cake.

1 cup butter.	4½ teaspoons baking powder.
2 cups sugar.	Whites 5 eggs.
1 cup milk.	¾ teaspoon vanilla or
1 cup corn-starch.	½ teaspoon almond extract.
2 cups flour.	

Follow recipe for mixing butter cakes. This mixture makes two loaves.

Prune Almond Cake.

Bake one-half Corn-starch Cake mixture in a dripping-pan. Cut in two crosswise, spread between layers Prune Almond Filling, and cover top with White Mountain Cream.

Prune Almond Filling. To one-half the recipe for White Mountain Cream add eight soft prunes stoned and cut in pieces, and one-fourth cup almonds blanched and cut in pieces.

Marshmallow Cake.

½ cup butter.	3 teaspoons baking powder.
1½ cups sugar.	¼ teaspoon cream of tartar.
½ cup milk.	Whites 5 eggs.
2 cups flour.	1 teaspoon vanilla.

Follow recipe for mixing butter cakes. Bake in shallow pans, and put Marshmallow Cream between the layers and on the top.

Fig Éclair.

½ cup butter (scant).	1⅞ cups flour.
1 cup sugar.	3 teaspoons baking powder.
½ cup milk.	Whites 4 eggs.
½ teaspoon vanilla.	

Follow recipe for mixing butter cakes. Bake in shallow pans, put between layers Fig Filling, and sprinkle top with powdered sugar.

Banana Cake.

Mix and bake Fig Éclair mixture; put between layers White Mountain Cream covered with thin slices of banana, and frost the top. This should be eaten the day it is made.

Bride's Cake.

½ cup butter.
1½ cups sugar.
½ cup milk.
2½ cups flour.

3 teaspoons baking powder.
¼ teaspoon cream of tartar.
Whites six eggs.
½ teaspoon almond extract.

Follow recipe for mixing butter cakes. Bake forty-five to fifty minutes in deep, narrow pans. Cover with white frosting.

Light Fruit Cake.

To Fig Éclair mixture add one-half cup raisins seeded and cut in pieces, two ounces citron thinly sliced and cut in strips, and one-third cup walnut meat cut in pieces. In making mixture, reserve one tablespoon flour to use for dredging fruit.

White Nut Cake.

¾ cup butter.
1½ cups sugar.
½ cup milk.
2½ cups flour.

½ teaspoon cream of tartar.
3 teaspoons baking powder.
Whites 8 eggs.
1 cup walnut meat cut in pieces.

Follow recipe for mixing butter cakes. This mixture makes two loaves.

Golden Cake.

¼ cup butter.
½ cup sugar.
Yolks 5 eggs.

½ cup milk.
⅞ cup flour.
1½ teaspoons baking powder.

1 teaspoon orange extract.

Cream the butter, add sugar gradually, and yolks of eggs beaten until thick and lemon colored, and extract.

Mix and sift flour and baking powder, and add alternately with milk to first mixture. Omit orange extract, add one-half cup nut meat cut in small pieces, and bake in individual tins.

Mocha Cake.

Bake a sponge cake mixture in sheets. Shape in small rounds, and cut in three layers. Put layers together with a thin coating of frosting. Spread frosting around sides and roll in shredded cocoanut. Ornament top with frosting forced through a pastry bag and tube, using the rose tube. Begin at centre of top and coil frosting around until surface is covered. Garnish centre of top with a candied cherry.

Frosting. Wash one-third cup butter, add one cup powdered sugar gradually, and beat until creamy. Then add one cup Cream Filling which has been cooled. Flavor with one-half teaspoon vanilla and one and one-half squares melted chocolate.

This frosting is sometimes colored pink, yellow, green, or lavender, and flavored with rose, vanilla, or a combination of almond and vanilla. Large Mocha Cakes are baked in two round layer cake tins, each cake being cut in two layers. Layers are put together as small cakes. The top is spread smoothly with frosting, then ornamented with large pieces of candied fruits arranged in a design, and frosting forced through pastry bag and tube.

Cream Cakes.

½ cup butter.   4 eggs.
1 cup boiling water.   1 cup flour.

Put butter and water in saucepan and place on front of range. As soon as boiling point is reached, add flour all at once, and stir vigorously. Remove from fire as soon as mixed, and add unbeaten eggs one at a time, beating, until thoroughly mixed, between the addition of eggs. Drop by spoonfuls on a buttered sheet, one and one-half inches apart, shaping with handle of spoon as nearly circular as possible, having mixture slightly piled in centre. Bake thirty minutes in a moderate oven. With a sharp knife make a cut in each large enough to admit of Cream Filling. This recipe makes eighteen small cream cakes. For flavoring cream filling use lemon extract. If cream cakes are removed from oven before being thoroughly cooked, they will fall. If in doubt, take one from oven, and if it does not fall, this is sufficient proof that others are cooked.

French Cream Cakes.

Fill Cream Cakes with Cream Sauce I.

French Strawberry Cream Cakes.

Shape cream cake mixture oblong, making twelve cakes. Split and fill with Strawberry Cream Filling.

Éclairs.

Shape cream cake mixture four and one-half inches long by one inch wide, by forcing through a pastry bag and tube. Bake twenty-five minutes in a moderate oven. Split and fill with vanilla, coffee, or chocolate cream filling. Frost with Confectioners' Frosting to which is added one-third cup melted Fondant, dipping top of éclairs in frosting while it is hot.

Lemon Queens.

¼ lb. butter.
½ lb. sugar.
Grated rind 1 lemon.
¾ tablespoon lemon juice.
Whites 4 eggs.

Yolks 4 eggs.
5 oz. flour.
¼ teaspoon salt.
¼ teaspoon soda.

Cream the butter, add sugar gradually, and continue beating. Then add grated rind, lemon juice, and yolks of eggs beaten until thick and lemon colored. Mix and sift soda, salt, and baking powder ; add to first mixture and beat thoroughly. Add whites of eggs beaten stiff. Bake from twenty to twenty-five minutes in small tins.

Queen Cake.

⅔ cup butter.   Whites 6 eggs.
2 cups flour (scant).   1¼ cups powdered sugar.
¼ teaspoon soda.   1½ teaspoons lemon juice.

Cream the butter, add flour gradually, mixed and sifted with soda, then add lemon juice. Beat whites of eggs until stiff; add sugar gradually, and combine the mixtures. Bake fifty minutes in a long shallow pan. Cover with Opera Caramel Frosting.

Pound Cake.

1 lb. butter.   Whites 10 eggs.
1 lb. sugar.   1 lb. flour.
Yolks 10 eggs.   ½ teaspoon mace.
2 tablespoons brandy. *1 tsp. bak. powd* [handwritten]

Cream the butter, add sugar gradually, and continue beating; then add yolks of eggs beaten until thick and lemon colored, whites of eggs beaten until stiff and dry, flour, mace, and brandy. Beat vigorously five minutes. Bake in a deep pan one and one fourth hours in a slow oven; or if to be used for fancy ornamented cakes, bake thirty to thirty-five minutes in a dripping-pan.

English Fruit Cake.

1 lb. butter.   2 tablespoons milk.
1 lb. light brown sugar.   3 lbs. currants.
9 eggs.   2 lbs. raisins seeded and
1 lb. flour.   finely chopped.
2 teaspoons mace.   ½ lb. almonds blanched and
2 teaspoons cinnamon,   shredded.
1 teaspoon soda.   1 lb. citron thinly sliced and
                 cut in strips.

Cream the butter, add sugar gradually, and beat thoroughly. Separate yolks from whites of eggs; beat yolks until thick and lemon colored, whites until stiff and dry, and add to first mixture. Then add milk, fruit, and flour mixed and sifted with mace, cinnamon, and soda.

Put in deep pans, cover with buttered paper, steam three hours, and bake one and one-half hours in a slow oven, or bake four hours in a very slow oven.

Imperial Cake.

½ lb. butter.
½ lb. sugar.
Yolks 5 eggs.
Whites 5 eggs.
Grated rind ½ lemon.
2 teaspoons lemon juice.

½ lb. raisins seeded and
  cut in pieces.
½ cup walnut meat broken
  in pieces.
½ lb. flour.
¼ teaspoon soda.

Mix same as Pound Cake, adding raisins dredged with flour, and nuts at the last.

Wedding Cake.

1 lb. butter.
1 lb. sugar. *brown*
12 eggs.
1 lb. flour.
2 teaspoons cinnamon.
Nutmeg, ⎫
Allspice, ⎬ ¾ teaspoon
Mace, ⎭ each.

½ teaspoon clove.
or 2 3 lbs. raisins seeded and
  cut in pieces.
+
or 2 1 lb. currants.
1 lb. citron thinly sliced
  and cut in strips.
(1 lb. figs finely chopped.)
¼ cup brandy.

2 tablespoons lemon juice.

(1 lb. almonds + nig. walnuts.)

Cream the butter, add sugar gradually, and beat thoroughly. Separate yolks from whites of eggs; beat yolks until thick and lemon colored, whites until stiff and dry, and add to first mixture. Add flour (excepting one-third cup, which should be reserved to dredge fruit) mixed and sifted, with spices, brandy, and lemon juice. Then add fruit, except citron, dredged with reserved flour. Dredge citron with flour and put in layers between cake mixture when putting in the pan. Bake same as English Fruit Cake.

CHAPTER XXXII.

CAKE FILLINGS AND FROSTINGS.

Cream Filling.

⅞ cup sugar.
⅓ cup flour.
⅛ teaspoon salt.

2 eggs.
2 cups scalded milk.
1 teaspoon vanilla or
½ teaspoon lemon extract.

Mix dry ingredients, add eggs slightly beaten, and pour on gradually scalded milk. Cook fifteen minutes in double boiler, stirring constantly until thickened, afterwards occasionally. Cool slightly and flavor.

Chocolate Cream Filling.

Put one and one-fourth squares Baker's chocolate in a saucepan and melt over hot water. Add to Cream Filling, using in making one cup sugar in place of seven-eighths cup.

Coffee Cream Filling.

Flavor Cream Filling with one and one-half tablespoons coffee extract.

French Cream Filling.

¾ cup thick cream
¼ cup milk.

¼ cup powdered sugar.
White one egg.
½ teaspoon vanilla.

Dilute cream with milk and beat until stiff, using Dover egg-beater. Add sugar, white of egg beaten until stiff, and vanilla.

Strawberry Filling.

1 cup thick cream.	White 1 egg.
⅓ cup sugar.	½ cup strawberries.

¼ teaspoon vanilla.

Beat cream until stiff, using Dover egg-beater, add sugar, white of egg beaten until stiff, strawberries mashed, and vanilla.

Lemon Filling.

1 cup sugar.	¼ cup lemon juice.
2½ tablespoons flour.	1 egg.
Grated rind 2 lemons.	1 teaspoon butter.

Mix sugar and flour, add grated rind, lemon juice, and egg slightly beaten.   Put butter in saucepan; when melted, add mixture, and stir constantly until boiling point is reached.   Care must be taken that mixture does not adhere to bottom of saucepan.   Cool before spreading.

Orange Filling.

½ cup sugar.	¼ cup orange juice.
2½ tablespoons flour.	½ tablespoon lemon juice.
Grated rind ½ orange.	1 egg slightly beaten.

1 teaspoon butter.

Mix ingredients in order given.   Cook ten minutes in double boiler, stirring constantly.   Cool before spreading.

Chocolate Filling.

2½ squares chocolate.	3 tablespoons milk.
1 cup powdered sugar.	Yolk 1 egg.

½ teaspoon vanilla.

Melt chocolate over hot water, add one-half the sugar, and milk; add remaining sugar, and yolk of egg; then cook in double boiler until it thickens, stirring constantly at first, that mixture may be perfectly smooth.   Cool slightly, flavor, and spread.

Nut or Fruit Filling.

To White Mountain Cream add chopped walnuts, almonds, figs, dates, or raisins, separately or in combination.

Cocoanut Filling.

Whites 2 eggs.   Fresh grated cocoanut.
                 Powdered sugar.

Beat whites of eggs on a platter with a fork until stiff.
Add enough powdered sugar to spread. Spread over
cake, sprinkle thickly with cocoanut. Use for layer cake,
having filling between and on top.

Lemon Cocoanut Cream.

Juice and grated rind 1 lemon.   Yolks 2 eggs.
1 cup sugar.   1 cup shredded cocoanut.

Mix lemon juice and rind with sugar and yolks of eggs
slightly beaten; cook ten minutes in double boiler, stirring constantly; then add cocoanut. Cool and use as a
filling for Corn-starch Cake.

Fig Filling.

½ lb. figs finely chopped.   ⅓ cup boiling water.
⅓ cup sugar.   1 tablespoon lemon juice.

Mix ingredients in the order given and cook in double
boiler until thick enough to spread.

Marshmallow Paste.

¾ cup sugar.   ¼ lb. marshmallows.
¼ cup milk.   2 tablespoons hot water.
                 ½ teaspoon vanilla.

Put sugar and milk in a saucepan, heat slowly to boiling point without stirring, and boil six minutes. Break
marshmallows in pieces and melt in double boiler, add hot
water and cook until mixture is smooth, then add hot
syrup gradually, stirring constantly. Beat until cool
enough to spread, then add vanilla. This may be used
for both filling and frosting.

Pistachio Paste.

To Marshmallow Paste add a few drops extract of almond, one-third cup pistachio nuts blanched and chopped,
and leaf green to color. Use same as Marshmallow Paste.

Prune Almond Filling.

To White Mountain Cream add one-half cup selected prunes, stoned and cut in pieces, and one-third cup almonds blanched and chopped.

Confectioners' Frosting.

2 tablespoons boiling water.   Confectioners' sugar.
Flavoring.

To water add enough sifted sugar to make of right consistency to spread; then add flavoring.   Fresh fruit juice may be used in place of boiling water.   This is a most satisfactory frosting, and is both easily and quickly made.

Orange Frosting.

Grated rind 1 orange.   1 tablespoon orange juice.
1 teaspoon brandy.   Yolk 1 egg.
½ teaspoon lemon juice.   Confectioners' sugar.

Add rind to brandy and fruit juices; let stand fifteen minutes.   Strain, and add gradually to yolk of egg slightly beaten.   Stir in confectioners' sugar until of right consistency to spread.

Gelatine Frosting.

2½ tablespoons boiling water.   ¾ cup confectioners'
½ teaspoon granulated gelatine.   sugar.
½ teaspoon vanilla.

Dissolve gelatine in boiling water.   Add sugar and flavoring and beat until of right consistency to spread. Crease in squares when slightly hardened.

Plain Frosting.

White 1 egg.   ½ teaspoon vanilla or
2 teaspoons cold water.   ½ tablespoon lemon juice.
¾ cup confectioners' sugar.

Beat white of egg until stiff; add water and sugar. Beat thoroughly, then add flavoring.   Use more sugar if needed.   Spread with a broad-bladed knife.

Chocolate Frosting.

1½ squares chocolate.
⅓ cup scalded cream.
Few grains salt.

Yolk 1 egg.
½ teaspoon melted butter.
Confectioners' sugar. *1 C.*

½ teaspoon vanilla.

Melt chocolate over hot water, add cream gradually, salt, yolk of egg, and butter. Stir in confectioners' sugar until of right consistency to spread; then add flavoring.

White Mountain Cream.

cup sugar.
⅓ cup boiling water.
White 1 egg.

1 teaspoon vanilla or
½ tablespoon lemon juice.

Put sugar and water in saucepan, and stir to prevent sugar from adhering to saucepan; heat gradually to boiling point, and boil without stirring until syrup will thread when dropped from tip of spoon or tines of silver folk. Pour syrup gradually on beaten white of egg, beating mixture constantly, and continue beating until of right consistency to spread; then add flavoring and pour over cake, spreading evenly with back of spoon. Crease as soon as firm. If not beaten long enough, frosting will run; if beaten too long, it will not be smooth. Frosting beaten too long may be improved by adding a few drops of lemon juice or boiling water. This frosting is soft inside, and has a glossy surface. If frosting is to be ornamented with nuts or candied cherries, place them on frosting as soon as spread.

Boiled Frosting.

1 cup sugar.
½ cup water.
Whites 2 eggs.

1 teaspoon vanilla or
½ tablespoon lemon juice.

Make same as White Mountain Cream. This frosting, on account of the larger quantity of egg, does not stiffen so quickly as White Mountain Cream, therefore is more successfully made by the inexperienced.

Boiled Chocolate Frosting.

To White Mountain Cream or Boiled Frosting add one and one-half squares melted chocolate as soon as syrup is added to whites of eggs.

Brown Frosting.

Make same as Boiled Frosting, using brown sugar in place of white sugar.

Maple Sugar Frosting.

1 lb. soft maple sugar.   ½ cup boiling water.
Whites 2 eggs.

Break sugar in small pieces, put in saucepan with boiling water, and stir occasionally until sugar is dissolved. Boil without stirring until syrup will thread when dropped from tip of spoon. Pour syrup gradually on beaten whites, beating mixture constantly, and continue beating until of right consistency to spread.

Cream Maple Sugar Frosting.

1 lb. soft maple sugar.   1 cup cream.

Break sugar in small pieces, put in saucepan with cream, and stir occasionally until sugar is dissolved. Boil without stirring until a ball can be formed when mixture is tried in cold water. Beat until of right consistency to spread.

Milk Frosting.

1½ cups sugar.   1 teaspoon butter.
½ cup milk.   ½ teaspoon vanilla.

Put butter in saucepan; when melted, add sugar and milk. Stir to be sure that sugar does not adhere to saucepan, heat to boiling point, and boil without stirring thirteen minutes. Remove from fire, and beat until of right consistency to spread; then add flavoring and pour over cake, spreading evenly with back of spoon. Crease as soon as firm.

Caramel Frosting.

Make as Milk Frosting, adding one and one-half squares melted chocolate as soon as boiling point is reached.

Opera Caramel Frosting.

1½ cups brown sugar.   ¾ cup thin cream.
½ tablespoon butter.

Boil ingredients together until a ball can be formed when mixture is tried in cold water. It takes about forty minutes for boiling. Beat until of right consistency to spread.

Fondant Icing.

The mixture in which small cakes are dipped for icing is fondant, the recipe for which may be found in chapter on Confections. Cakes for dipping must first be glazed.

To Glaze Cakes. Beat white of one egg slightly, and add one tablespoon powdered sugar. Apply with a brush to top and sides of cakes. After glazing, cakes should stand over night before dipping.

To Dip Cakes. Melt fondant over hot water, and color and flavor as desired. Stir to prevent crust from forming on top. Take cake to be dipped on a three-tined fork and lower in fondant three-fourths the depth of cake. Remove from fondant, invert, and slip from fork to a board. Decorate with ornamental frosting and nut meat, candied cherries, angelica, or candied violets. For small ornamented cakes, pound cake mixture is baked a little more than one inch thick in shallow pans, and when cool cut in squares, diamonds, triangles, circles, crescents, etc.

Ornamental Frosting I.

2 cups sugar.   Whites 3 eggs.
1 cup water.   ¼ teaspoon tartaric acid.

Boil sugar and water until syrup when dropped from tip of spoon forms a long thread. Pour syrup gradually on beaten whites of eggs, beating constantly; then add acid and continue beating. When stiff enough to spread, put a thin coating over cake. Beat remaining frosting until cold and stiff enough to keep in shape after being forced through a pastry tube. After first coating on cake has hardened, cover with a thicker layer, and crease for cutting. If frosting is too stiff to spread smoothly, thin with a few drops of water. With a pastry bag and variety of tubes, cake may be ornamented as desired.

Cake being ornamented with Ornamental Frosting.

Ornamental Frosting II.

Whites 3 eggs.   1 tablespoon lemon juice.
Confectioners' sugar, sifted.

Put eggs in a large bowl, add two tablespoons sugar, and beat three minutes, using a perforated wooden spoon. Repeat until one and one-half cups sugar are used. Add lemon juice gradually, as mixture thickens. Continue adding sugar by spoonfuls, and beating until frosting is stiff enough to spread. This may be determined by taking up some of mixture on back of spoon, and with a case knife making a cut through mixture; if knife makes a clean cut and frosting remains parted, it is of right consistency. Spread cake thinly with frosting; when this has hardened, put on a thicker layer, having mixture somewhat stiffer than first coating, and then crease for cutting.   To remaining frosting add enough more sugar, that frosting may keep in shape after being forced through a pastry bag and tube.

With a pastry bag and variety of tubes, cake may be ornamented as desired.

CHAPTER XXXIII.

FANCY CAKES AND CONFECTIONS.

A LMOND paste for making macaroons and small fancy cakes may be bought of dealers who keep confectioners' supplies, although sometimes a resident baker or confectioner will sell a small quantity. Almond paste is put up in five-pound tin pails, and retails for one and one-half dollars per pail. During the cold weather it will keep after being opened for a long time.

Macaroons.

½ lb. almond paste.   Whites 3 eggs.
⅜ lb. powdered sugar.

Work together almond paste and sugar on a smooth board or marble slab. Then add whites of eggs gradually, and work until mixture is perfectly smooth. Confectioners at first use the hand, afterward a palette knife, which is not only of use for mixing but for keeping board clean. Shape, using a pastry bag and tube, on a tin sheet covered with buttered paper, one-half inch apart; or drop mixture from tip of spoon in small piles. Macaroon mixture is stiff enough to hold its shape, but in baking spreads. Bake fifteen to twenty minutes in a slow oven. If liked soft, they should be slightly baked. After removing from oven, invert paper, and wet with a cloth wrung out of cold water, when macaroons will easily slip off.

Almond Macaroons.

Sprinkle Macaroons, before baking, with almonds blanched and shredded, or chopped.

Crescents.

¼ lb. almond paste.
2 oz. confectioners' sugar.
White 1 small egg.

Almonds blanched and finely chopped.

Mix same as Macaroons. Shape mixture, which is quite soft, in a long roll. Cut pieces from roll three-fourths inch long. Roll each separately in chopped nuts, at the same time shaping to form a crescent. Bake twenty minutes on a buttered tin sheet in a slow oven. Cool and frost with Confectioners' Frosting, made thin enough to apply with a brush, and flavored with lemon juice until quite acid. Other nuts may be used in place of almonds.

Cinnamon Bars.

10 oz. almond paste.
5 oz. confectioners' sugar.

White 1 egg.
½ teaspoon cinnamon.

Mix same as Macaroons. Dredge a board with sugar, knead mixture slightly, and shape in a long roll. Pat and roll one-fourth inch thick, using a rolling-pin. After rolling, the piece should be four inches wide. Spread with frosting made of white of one egg and two-thirds cup confectioners' sugar beaten together until stiff enough to spread. Cut in strips four inches long by three-fourths inch wide. This must be quickly done, as a crust soon forms over frosting. To accomplish this, use two knives, one placed through mixture where dividing line is to be made, and the other used to make a clean sharp cut on both sides of first knife. Knives should be kept clean by wiping on a damp cloth. Remove strips, as soon as cut, to a tin sheet, greased with lard and then floured. Bake twenty minutes on centre grate in a slow oven.

Horseshoes.

Use Cinnamon Bar mixture. Cover with frosting colored with fruit red. Cut in strips six inches long by one-half inch wide. As soon as cut, shape quickly, at the same time carefully, in form of horseshoes. Bake same as Cinnamon Bars. When cool, make eight dots with chocolate frosting to represent nails.

Cocoanut Cakes I.

½ lb. fresh grated cocoanut.   6 oz. sugar and glucose,
Whites 1½ eggs.   using one mixing-spoon
                                              glucose.

                                              German Confectioner.

Cook cocoanut, sugar and glucose, in double boiler until mixture clings to spoon, add whites of eggs, stir vigorously, and cook until mixture feels sticky when tried between the fingers. Spread in a wet pan, cover with wet paper, and chill on ice. Shape in small balls, first dipping hands in cold water. Bake twenty minutes in a slow oven on a tin sheet greased with white wax.

Cocoanut Cakes II.

1 lb. fresh grated cocoanut.   ¾ lb. sugar.
                 Whites 2 eggs.

Cook, shape, and bake same as Cocoanut Cakes I.

Stuffed Dates I.

Make a cut the entire length of dates and remove stones. Fill cavities with castanea nuts, English walnuts, or blanched almonds, and shape in original form. Roll in granulated sugar. Pile in rows on a small plate covered with a doily. If castanea nuts are used, with a sharp knife cut off the brown skin which lies next to shell.

Stuffed Dates II.

Remove stones from dates and fill cavities with Neufchatel cheese.

Salted Almonds I.

Blanch one-fourth pound Jordan almonds and dry on a towel. Put one-third cup olive oil in a very small saucepan. When hot, put in one-fourth of the almonds and fry until delicately browned, stirring to keep almonds constantly in motion. Remove with a spoon or small skimmer, taking up as little oil as possible. Drain on brown paper and sprinkle with salt; repeat until all are fried. It may be necessary to remove some of the salt by wiping nuts with a napkin.

Salted Almonds II.

Prepare almonds as for Salted Almonds I. Fry in one-third cup fat, using half lard and half clarified butter or all cocoanut butter. Drain and sprinkle with salt.

Salted Peanuts.

In buying peanuts for salting, get those which have not been roasted. Remove skins and fry same as Salted Almonds I. or II.

Salted Pecans.

Shelled pecans may be bought by the pound, which is much the best way when used for salting, as it is difficult to remove the nut meat without breaking. Fry same as Salted Almonds I. or II. Care must be taken that they do not remain in fat too long; having a dark skin, color does not determine when they are sufficiently cooked.

Parisian Sweets.

1 lb. figs.	1 lb. English walnut meat.
1 lb. dates.	Confectioners' sugar.

Pick over and remove stems from figs and stones from dates. Mix fruit with walnut meat, and force through a meat-chopper. Work, using the hands, on a board dredged with confectioners' sugar, until well blended. Roll to one-fourth inch thickness, using confectioners' sugar for dredging board and pin. Shape with a small round cutter, first dipped in sugar, or cut with a sharp knife in three-fourth inch squares. Roll each piece in confectioners' sugar, and shake to remove superfluous sugar. Pack in layers in a tin box, putting paper between each layer. These confections may be used at dinner in place of bonbons or ginger chips. A combination of nut meat (walnut, almond, and filbert) may be used in equal proportions.

Molasses Candy.

2 cups Porto Rico molasses.	3 tablespoons butter.
⅔ cup sugar.	1 tablespoon vinegar.

An iron kettle with a rounding bottom (Scotch kettle), or copper kettle is best for candy making. If one has no copper kettle, a granite kettle is best for sugar candies.

Put butter in kettle, place over fire, and when melted, add molasses and sugar. Stir until sugar is dissolved. During the first of the boiling, stirring is unnecessary; but when nearly cooked, it should be constantly stirred. Boil until, when tried in cold water, mixture will become brittle. Add vinegar just before taking from fire. Pour into a well buttered pan. When cool enough to handle, pull until porous and light colored, allowing candy to come in contact with tips of fingers and thumbs, not to be squeezed in the hand. Cut in small pieces, using large shears or a sharp knife, and then arrange on slightly buttered plates to cool.

Velvet Molasses Candy.

1 cup molasses.	3 tablespoons vinegar.
3 cups sugar.	½ teaspoon cream of tartar.
1 cup boiling water.	½ cup melted butter.
¼ teaspoon soda.	

Put first four ingredients in kettle placed over front of range. As soon as boiling point is reached, add cream of tartar. Boil until, when tried in cold water, mixture will become brittle. Stir constantly during last part of cooking. When nearly done, add butter and soda. Pour into a buttered pan and pull same as Molasses Candy. While pulling, add one teaspoon vanilla, one-half teaspoon lemon extract, few drops oil of peppermint, or few drops oil of wintergreen.

Buttercups.

2 cups molasses.	2 tablespoons butter.
1 cup sugar.	⅓ teaspoon cream of tartar.
½ cup boiling water.	Fondant flavored with vanilla.

Boil ingredients (except fondant) until, when tried in cold water, a firm ball may be formed in the fingers, not stirring until the last few minutes of cooking. Pour on a buttered platter, and when cool enough to handle, pull until light colored. Shape on a floured board, having strip wide enough to enclose a roll of fondant one inch in diameter. Place fondant on candy, bring edges of candy together, and press firmly over fondant. With both hands pull candy into a long strip. Cut in small pieces; each piece will consist of fondant encircled with molasses candy. Care must be taken that candy is not cooked too long, as it should be soft rather than brittle.

Vinegar Candy.

2 cups sugar.	½ cup vinegar.
2 tablespoons butter.	

Put butter into kettle; when melted, add sugar and vinegar. Stir until sugar is dissolved, afterwards occasionally. Boil until, when tried in cold water, mixture will become brittle. Turn on a buttered platter to cool. Pull and cut same as Molasses Candy.

Ice Cream Candy.

3 cups sugar.	½ cup boiling water.
¼ teaspoon cream of tartar.	½ tablespoon vinegar.

Boil ingredients together without stirring, until, when tried in cold water, mixture will become brittle. Turn on a well buttered platter to cool. As edges cool, fold towards centre. As soon as it can be handled, pull until white and glossy. While pulling, flavor as desired, using vanilla, orange extract, coffee extract, oil of sassafras, or melted chocolate. Cut in sticks or small pieces.

Butter Scotch.

1 cup sugar.	2 tablespoons vinegar.
¼ cup molasses.	2 tablespoons boiling water.
½ cup butter.	

Boil ingredients together until, when tried in cold water, mixture will become brittle. Turn into a well buttered pan; when slightly cool, mark with a sharp-pointed knife in squares. This candy is much improved by cooking a small piece of vanilla bean with other ingredients.

Butter Taffy.

2 cups light brown sugar.	2 tablespoons water.
¼ cup molasses.	⅞ teaspoon salt.
2 tablespoons vinegar.	¼ cup butter.
2 teaspoons vanilla.	

Boil first five ingredients until, when tried in cold water, mixture will become brittle. When nearly done, add butter, and just before turning into pan, vanilla. Cool, and mark in squares.

Horehound Candy.

¾ square inch pressed horehound.	2 cups boiling water.
	3 cups sugar.
½ teaspoon cream of tartar.	

Pour boiling water over horehound which has been separated in pieces; let stand one minute, then strain through double cheese cloth. Put into a granite kettle with remaining ingredients, and boil until, when tried in cold water, mixture will become brittle. Turn into a buttered pan, cool slightly, then mark in small squares. Small square packages of horehound may be bought for five cents.

Chocolate Caramels.

2½ tablespoons butter. ½ cup milk.
2 cups molasses. 3 squares chocolate.
1 cup brown sugar. 1 teaspoon vanilla.

Put butter into kettle; when melted, add molasses, sugar, and milk. Stir until sugar is dissolved, and when boiling point is reached, add chocolate, stirring constantly until chocolate is melted. Boil until, when tried in cold water, a firm ball may be formed in the fingers. Add vanilla just after taking from fire. Turn into a buttered pan, cool, and mark in small squares.

Nut Chocolate Caramels.

To Chocolate Caramels add the meat from one pound English walnuts broken in pieces, or one-half pound almonds blanched and chopped.

Peanut Nougat.

1 lb. sugar. 1 quart peanuts.

Shell, remove skins, and finely chop peanuts. Sprinkle with one-fourth teaspoon salt. Put sugar in a perfectly smooth granite saucepan, place on range, and stir constantly until melted to a syrup, taking care to keep sugar from sides of pan. Add nut meat, pour at once into a warm buttered tin, and mark in small squares. If sugar is not removed from range as soon as melted, it will quickly caramelize.

Nut Bar.

Cover the bottom of a buttered shallow pan with one and one-third cups nut meat (castaneas, English walnuts, or almonds) cut in quarters. Pour over one pound sugar, melted as for Peanut Nougat. Mark in bars.

French Nougat.

½ lb. confectioners' sugar.   ½ lb. almonds blanched
                                     and finely chopped.
              Confectioners' chocolate.

Put sugar in a saucepan, place on range, and stir constantly until melted; add almonds, and pour on an oiled marble. Fold mixture as it spreads with a broad-bladed knife, keeping it constantly in motion. Divide in four parts, and as soon as cool enough to handle shape in long rolls about one-third inch in diameter, keeping rolls in motion until almost cold. When cold, snap in pieces one and one-half inches long. This is done by holding roll at point to be snapped over the sharp edge of a broad-bladed knife and snapping. Melt confectioners' chocolate over hot water, beat with a fork until light and smooth, and when slightly cooled dip pieces in chocolate and with a two-tined fork or bonbon dipper remove from chocolate to oiled paper, drawing dipper through top of each the entire length, thus leaving a ridge. Chocolate best adapted for dipping bonbons and confections must be bought where confectioners' supplies are kept.

Nougatine Drops.

Drop French Nougat mixture from the tip of a spoon on an oiled marble very soon after taking from fire. These drops have a rough surface. When cold, dip in melted confectioners' chocolate.

Wintergreen Wafers.

1 oz. gum tragacanth.   Confectioners' sugar.
1 cup cold water.   Oil of wintergreen.

Soak gum tragacanth in water twenty-four hours, and rub through a fine wire sieve; add enough confectioners' sugar to knead. Flavor with a few drops oil of wintergreen. If liked pink, color with fruit red. Roll until very thin on a board or marble dredged with sugar. Shape with a small round cutter or cut in three-fourths inch squares. Spread wafers, cover, and let stand until dry and brittle. This mixture may be flavored with oil of lemon, clove, sassafras, etc., and colored as desired.

Cocoanut Cream Candy.

1½ cups sugar.	2 teaspoons butter.
½ cup milk.	⅓ cup shredded cocoanut.

½ teaspoon vanilla.

Put butter into granite saucepan; when melted, add sugar and milk, and stir until sugar is dissolved. Heat to boiling point, and boil twelve minutes; remove from fire, add cocoanut and vanilla, and beat until creamy and mixture begins to sugar slightly around edge of saucepan. Pour at once into a buttered pan, cool slightly, and mark in squares. One-half cup nut meat, broken in pieces, may be used in place of cocoanut.

Chocolate Cream Candy.

2 cups sugar.	1 tablespoon butter.
⅔ cup milk.	2 squares chocolate.

1 teaspoon vanilla.

Put butter into granite saucepan; when melted, add sugar and milk. Heat to boiling point; then add chocolate, and stir constantly until chocolate is melted. Boil thirteen minutes, remove from fire, add vanilla, and beat until creamy and mixture begins to sugar slightly around edge of saucepan. Pour at once into a buttered pan, cool slightly, and mark in squares. Omit vanilla, and add, while cooking, one-fourth teaspoon cinnamon.

Maple Sugar Candy.

1 lb. soft maple sugar.	¼ cup boiling water.
¾ cup thin cream.	⅔ cup English walnut or pecan meat cut in pieces.

Break sugar in pieces; put into a saucepan with cream and water. Bring to boiling point, and boil until a soft ball is formed when tried in cold water. Remove from fire, beat until creamy, add nut meat, and pour into a buttered tin. Cool slightly, and mark in squares.

Sultana Caramels.

2 cups sugar.
½ cup milk.
¼ cup molasses.
¼ cup butter.

2 squares chocolate.
1 teaspoon vanilla.
½ cup English walnut or hickory nut meat cut in pieces.

2 tablespoons Sultana raisins.

Put butter into a saucepan; when melted, add sugar, milk, and molasses. Heat to boiling point, and boil seven minutes. Add chocolate, and stir until chocolate is melted; then boil seven minutes longer. Remove from fire, beat until creamy, add nuts, raisins, and vanilla, and pour at once into a buttered tin. Cool slightly, and mark in squares.

Pralines.

1⅞ cups powdered sugar.
1 cup maple syrup.
½ cup cream.

2 cups hickory nut or pecan meat cut in pieces.

Boil first three ingredients until, when tried in cold water, a soft ball may be formed. Remove from fire, and beat until of a creamy consistency; add nuts, and drop from tip of spoon in small piles on buttered paper.

Creamed Walnuts.

White 1 egg.
½ tablespoon cold water.

¾ teaspoon vanilla.
1 lb. confectioners' sugar.

English walnuts.

Put egg, water, and vanilla in a bowl, and beat until well blended. Add sugar gradually until stiff enough to knead. Shape in balls, flatten, and place halves of walnuts opposite each other on each piece. Sometimes all the sugar will not be required.

Peppermints.

1½ cups sugar.   ½ cup boiling water.
6 drops oil of peppermint.

Put sugar and water into a granite saucepan and stir until sugar is dissolved. Boil ten minutes; remove from fire, add peppermint, and beat until of right consistency. Drop from tip of spoon on slightly buttered paper.

BOILED SUGAR FOR CONFECTIONS.

Eleven tests are considered for boiling sugar: —

Small thread,	215° F.	The feather,	232°.
Large thread,	217°.	Soft ball,	238°.
Pearl,	220°.	Hard ball,	248°.
Large pearl,	222°.	Small crack,	290°.
The blow,	230°.	Crack,	310°.

Caramel, 350°.

Fondant, the basis of all French candy, is made of sugar and water boiled together (with a small quantity of cream of tartar to prevent sugar from granulating) to soft ball, 238° F. The professional confectioner is able to decide when syrup has boiled to the right temperature by sound while boiling, and by testing in cold water; these tests at first seem somewhat difficult to the amateur, but only a little experience is necessary to make fondant successfully. A sugar thermometer is often employed, and proves valuable, as by its use one need not exercise his judgment.

White Fondant.

2½ lbs. sugar.   1½ cups hot water.
¼ teaspoon cream of tartar.

Put ingredients into a smooth granite stewpan. Stir, place on range, and heat gradually to boiling point. Boil without stirring until, when tried in cold water, a soft ball may be formed that will just keep in shape, which is 238° F After a few minutes' boiling, sugar will adhere to sides of kettle; this should be washed off with the hand first dipped in cold water.   Have a pan of cold water near at hand, dip hand in cold water, then quickly wash off a small part of the sugar with tips of fingers, and repeat until all sugar adhering to side of saucepan is removed.   If this is quickly done, there is no danger of burning the fingers.   Pour slowly on a slightly oiled marble slab. Let stand a few minutes to cool, but not long enough to become hard around the edge.   Scrape fondant with chopping knife to one end of marble, and work with a wooden spatula until white and creamy.   It will quickly change from this consistency, and begin to lump, when it should be kneaded with the hands until perfectly smooth.

Put into a bowl, cover with oiled paper to exclude air, that a crust may not form on top, and let stand twenty-four hours.   A large oiled platter and wooden spoon may be used in place of marble slab and spatula.   Always make fondant on a clear day, as a damp, heavy atmosphere has an unfavorable effect on the boiling of sugar.

Coffee Fondant.

2½ lbs. sugar.	¼ cup ground coffee.
1½ cups cold water.	¼ teaspoon cream of tartar.

Put water and coffee in saucepan, and heat to boiling point.   Strain through double cheese cloth; then add sugar and cream of tartar.   Boil and work same as White Fondant.

Maple Fondant.

1¼ lbs. maple sugar.	1 cup hot water.
1¼ lbs. sugar.	¼ teaspoon cream of tartar.

Break maple sugar in pieces, and add to remaining ingredients.   Boil and work same as White Fondant.

Bonbons.

The centres of bonbons are made of fondant shaped in small balls.   If White Fondant is used, flavor as desired, — vanilla being usually preferred.   For cocoanut centres, work as much shredded cocoanut as possible into a small quantity of fondant; for nut centres, surround pieces of nut meat with fondant, using just enough to cover. French candied cherries are often used in this way. Allow balls to stand over night, and dip the following day.

To Dip Bonbons. Put fondant in saucepan, and melt over hot water; color and flavor as desired. In coloring fondant, dip a small wooden skewer in coloring paste, take up a small quantity, and dip skewer in fondant. If care is not taken, the color is apt to be too intense. During dipping, keep fondant over hot water that it may be kept of right consistency. For dipping, use a two-tined fork or confectioners' bonbon dipper. Drop centres in fondant one at a time, stir until covered, remove from fondant, put on oiled paper, and bring end of dipper over the top of bonbon, thus leaving a tail-piece which shows that bonbons have been hand dipped. Stir fondant between dippings to prevent a crust from forming.

Cream Mints.

Melt fondant over hot water, flavor with a few drops of oil of peppermint, wintergreen, clove, cinnamon, or orange, and color if desired. Drop from tip of spoon on oiled paper. Confectioners use rubber moulds for shaping cream mints; but these are expensive for home use, unless one is to make mints in large quantities.

Cream Nut Bars.

Melt fondant and flavor, stir in any kind of nut meat, cut in pieces. Turn in an oiled pan, cool, and cut in bars with a sharp knife. Maple Fondant is delicious with nuts.

Dipped Walnuts.

Melt fondant and flavor. Dip halves of walnuts as bonbon centres are dipped. Halves of pecan or whole blanched almonds may be similarly dipped.

Tutti-Frutti Candy.

Fill an oiled border-mould with three layers of melted fondant. Have bottom layer maple, well mixed with English walnut meat; the second layer colored pink, flavored with rose, and mixed with candied cherries cut in quarters and figs finely chopped; the third layer white, flavored with vanilla, mixed with nuts, candied cherries cut in quarters, and candied pineapple cut in small pieces. Cover mould with oiled paper, and let stand over night. Remove from mould, and place on a plate covered with a lace paper napkin. Fill centre with Bonbons and Glacé Nuts.

Glacé Nuts.

2 cups sugar.   1 cup boiling water.
⅛ teaspoon cream of tartar.

Put ingredients in a smooth saucepan, stir, place on range, and heat to boiling point. Boil without stirring until syrup begins to discolor, which is 310° F. Wash off sugar which adheres to sides of saucepan as in making fondant. Remove saucepan from fire, and place in larger pan of cold water to instantly stop boiling. Remove from cold water and place in a saucepan of hot water during dipping. Take nuts separately on a long pin, dip in syrup to cover, remove from syrup, and place on oiled paper.

Glacé Fruits.

For Glacé Fruits, grapes, strawberries, sections of mandarins and oranges, and candied cherries are most commonly used. Take grapes separately from clusters, leaving a short stem on each grape. Dip in syrup made as for Glacé Nuts, holding by stem with pincers. Remove to oiled paper. Glacé fruits keep but a day, and should only be attempted in cold and clear weather.

Spun Sugar.

2 lbs. sugar.   2 cups boiling water.
1/4 teaspoon cream of tartar.

Put ingredients in a smooth saucepan. Boil without stirring until syrup begins to discolor, which is 310° F. Wash off sugar which adheres to sides of saucepan as in making fondant. Remove saucepan from fire, and place in a larger pan of cold water to instantly stop boiling. Remove from cold water, and place in saucepan of hot water. Place two broomstick-handles over backs of chairs, and spread paper on the floor under them. When syrup is slightly cooled, put dipper in syrup, remove from syrup, and shake quickly back and forth over broom-handles. Carefully take off spun sugar as soon as formed, and shape in nests or pile lightly on a cold dish. Syrup may be colored if desired. Spun Sugar is served around bricks or moulds of frozen creams and ices.

Dippers for spinning sugar are made of coarse wires; about twenty wires, ten inches long, are put in a bundle, and fastened with wire coiled round and round to form a handle.

CHAPTER XXXIV.

SANDWICHES AND CANAPÉS.

IN preparing bread for sandwiches, cut slices as thinly as possible, and remove crusts. If butter is used, cream the butter, and spread bread before cutting from loaf. Spread half the slices with mixture to be used for filling, cover with remaining pieces, and cut in squares, oblongs, or triangles. If sandwiches are shaped with round or fancy cutters, bread should be shaped before spreading, that there may be no waste of butter. Sandwiches which are prepared several hours before serving-time may be kept fresh and moist by wrapping in a napkin wrung as dry as possible out of hot water, and keeping in a cool place. Paraffine paper is often used for the same purpose. Bread for sandwiches cuts better when a day old. Serve sandwiches piled on a plate covered with a doily.

Rolled Bread.

Cut fresh bread, while still warm, in as thin slices as possible, using a very sharp knife. Spread evenly with butter which has been creamed. Roll slices separately, and tie each with baby ribbon.

Bread and Butter Folds.

Remove end slice from bread. Spread end of loaf sparingly and evenly with butter which has been creamed. Cut off as thin a slice as possible. Repeat until the number of slices required are prepared. Remove crusts, put together in pairs, and cut in squares, oblongs, or triangles. Use white, entire wheat, Graham, or brown bread.

Lettuce Sandwiches.

Put fresh, crisp lettuce leaves, washed and thoroughly dried, between thin slices of buttered bread prepared as for Bread and Butter Folds, having a teaspoon of Mayonnaise on each leaf.

Egg Sandwiches.

Chop finely the whites of hard boiled eggs; force the yolks through a strainer or potato ricer. Mix yolks and whites, season with salt and pepper, and moisten with Mayonnaise or Cream Salad Dressing. Spread mixture between thin slices of buttered bread prepared as for Bread and Butter Folds.

Sardine Sandwiches.

Remove skin and bones from sardines, and mash to a paste. Add to an equal quantity of yolks of hard boiled eggs rubbed through a sieve. Season with salt, cayenne, and a few drops of lemon juice; moisten with olive oil or melted butter. Spread mixture between thin slices of buttered bread prepared as for Bread and Butter Folds.

Sliced Ham Sandwiches.

Slice cold boiled ham as thinly as possible. Put between thin slices of buttered bread prepared as for Bread and Butter Folds.

Chopped Ham Sandwiches.

Finely chop cold boiled ham, and moisten with Sauce Tartare. Spread between thin slices of buttered bread prepared as for Bread and Butter Folds.

Anchovy Sandwiches.

Rub the yolks of hard boiled eggs to a paste. Moisten with soft butter and season with Anchovy essence. Spread mixture between thin slices of buttered bread prepared as for Bread and Butter Folds.

Chicken Sandwiches.

Chop cold boiled chicken, and moisten with Mayonnaise or Cream Salad Dressing; or season with salt and pepper, and moisten with rich chicken stock. Prepare as other sandwiches.

Lobster Sandwiches.

Remove lobster meat from shell, and chop. Season with salt, cayenne, made mustard, and lemon juice; or moisten with any salad dressing. Spread mixture on a crisp lettuce leaf, and prepare as other sandwiches.

Oyster Sandwiches.

Arrange fried oysters on crisp lettuce leaves, allowing two oysters for each leaf, and one leaf for each sandwich. Prepare as other sandwiches.

Nut and Cheese Sandwiches.

Mix equal parts of grated Gruyère cheese and chopped English walnut meat; then season with salt and cayenne. Prepare as other sandwiches.

Ginger Sandwiches.

Cut preserved Canton ginger in very thin slices. Prepare as other sandwiches.

Fruit Sandwiches.

Remove stems and finely chop figs; add a small quantity of water, cook in double boiler until a paste is formed, then add a few drops of lemon juice. Cool mixture and spread on thin slices of buttered bread; sprinkle with finely chopped peanuts and cover with pieces of buttered bread.

Brown Bread Sandwiches.

Brown Bread to be used for sandwiches is best steamed in one-pound baking-powder boxes. Spread and cut bread as for other sandwiches.   Put between layers finely chopped peanuts seasoned with salt; or grated cheese mixed with chopped English walnut meat and seasoned with salt.

Russian Sandwiches.

Spread zephyrettes with thin slices of Neufchatel cheese, cover with finely chopped olives moistened with Mayonnaise Dressing.   Place a zephyrette over each and press together.

Jelly Sandwiches.

Spread zephyrettes with quince jelly and sprinkle with chopped English walnut meat.   Place a zephyrette over each and press together.

Cheese Wafers.

Sprinkle zephyrettes with grated cheese mixed with a few grains of cayenne.   Put on a sheet and bake until the cheese melts.

Canapés.

Canapés are made by cutting bread in slices one-fourth inch thick, and cutting slices in strips four inches long by one and one-half inches wide, or in circular pieces. Then bread is toasted, fried in deep fat, or buttered and browned in the oven, and covered with a seasoned mixture of eggs, cheese, fish, or meat, separately or in combination.   Canapés are served hot or cold, and used in place of oysters at a dinner or luncheon.   At a gentlemen's dinner they are served with a glass of sherry before entering the dining-room.

Cheese Canapés I.

Toast circular pieces of bread, sprinkle with a thick layer of grated cheese, seasoned with salt and cayenne. Place on a tin sheet and bake until cheese is melted. Serve at once.

Cheese Canapés II.

Spread circular pieces of toasted bread with French Mustard, then proceed as for Cheese Canapés I.

Sardine Canapés.

Spread circular pieces of toasted bread with sardines (from which bones have been removed) rubbed to a paste, with a small quantity of creamed butter and seasoned with Worcestershire Sauce and a few grains cayenne. Place in the centre of each a stuffed olive, made by removing stone and filling cavity with sardine mixture. Around each arrange a border of the finely chopped whites of hard boiled eggs.

Anchovy Canapés.

Spread circular pieces of toasted bread with Anchovy Butter. Chop separately yolks and whites of hard boiled eggs. Cover canapés by quarters with egg, alternating yolks and whites. Divide yolks from whites with anchovies split in two lengthwise, and pipe around a border of Anchovy Butter, using a pastry bag and tube.

Canapés Lorenzo.

Toast slices of bread cut in shape of horseshoes, cream two tablespoons butter, and add one teaspoon white of egg. Spread rounding with Crab Mixture, cover with creamed butter, sprinkle with cheese, and brown in the oven. Serve on a napkin, ends toward centre of dish, and garnish with parsley.

Crab Mixture. Finely chop crab meat, season with salt, cayenne, and a few drops of lemon juice, then moisten with Thick White Sauce. Lobster meat may be used in place of crab meat.

CHAPTER XXXV.

RECIPES FOR THE CHAFING-DISH.

THE chafing-dish, which, within the last few years, has gained so much favor, is by no means a utensil of modern invention, as its history may be traced to the time of Louis XIV. It finds its place on the breakfast table, when the eggs may be cooked to suit the most fastidious; on the luncheon table, when a dainty hot dish may be prepared to serve in place of the so-oft-seen cold meat; but it is made of greatest use for the cooking of late suppers, and always seems to accompany hospitality and good cheer.

It is appreciated and enjoyed by the housekeeper who does her own work, or has but one maid, as well as by the society girl who, by its use, first gains a taste for the art of cooking. The simple tin chafing-dishes may be bought for as small a sum as ninety cents, while the elaborate silver ones command as high a price as one hundred dollars. Very attractive dishes are made of granite ware, nickel, or copper. The latest patterns have the lamp with a screw adjustment to regulate the flame, and a metal tray on which to set dish, that it may be moved if necessary while hot, without danger of burnt fingers, and that it may not injure the polished table.

A chafing-dish has two pans, the under one for holding hot water, the upper one with long handle for holding food to be cooked. A blazer differs from a chafing-dish, inasmuch as it has no hot-water pan.

Wood alcohol, which is much lower in price than high-proof spirits, is generally used in chafing-dishes.

The Davy Toaster may be used over the chafing-dish for toasting bread and broiling.

List of dishes previously given that may be prepared on the Chafing-Dish : —

German Toast.
Dropped Eggs.
Eggs à la Finnoise.
Eggs à la Suisse.
Scrambled Eggs.
Scrambled Eggs with Tomato Sauce.
Scrambled Eggs with Anchovy Toast.
Buttered Eggs.
Buttered Eggs with Tomatoes.
Curried Eggs.
French Omelet.
Spanish Omelet.
Creamed Fish.
Halibut à la Rarebit.
Creamed Oysters.

Buttered Lobster.
Creamed Lobster.
Broiled Meat Cakes.
Salmi of Lamb.
Creamed Sweetbreads.
Sautéd Sweetbreads.
Chickens' Livers with Madeira Sauce.
Chickens' Livers with Curry.
Sautéd Chickens' Livers.
Creamed Chicken.
Chicken and Oysters à la Métropole.
Stewed Mushrooms.
Sautéd Mushrooms.
Mushrooms à la Sabine.
Soufflé au Rhum.

Scrambled Eggs with Sweetbreads.

4 eggs.
½ teaspoon salt.
⅛ teaspoon pepper.
½ cup milk.
1 sweetbread parboiled and cut in dice.
2 tablespoons butter.

Beat eggs slightly with silver folk, add salt, pepper, milk, and sweetbread. Put butter in hot chafing-dish; when melted, pour in the mixture. Cook until of creamy consistency, stirring and scraping from bottom of pan.

Scrambled Eggs with Calf's Brains.

Follow recipe for Scrambled Eggs with Sweetbreads, using calf's brains in place of sweetbreads.

To Prepare Calf's Brains. Soak one hour in cold water to cover. Remove membrane, and parboil twenty minutes in boiling, salted, acidulated water. Drain, put in cold water; as soon as cold, drain again, and separate in small pieces.

Cheese Omelet.

2 eggs.	⅛ tablespoon salt.
1 tablespoon melted butter.	Few grains cayenne.
1 tablespoon grated cheese.	

Beat eggs slightly, add one-half teaspoon melted butter, salt, cayenne, and cheese. Melt remaining butter, add mixture, and cook until firm, without stirring. Roll, and sprinkle with grated cheese.

Eggs au Beurre Noir.

Butter.	Pepper.
Salt.	4 eggs.
1 teaspoon vinegar.	

Put one tablespoon butter in a hot chafing-dish; when melted, slip in carefully four eggs, one at a time. Sprinkle with salt and pepper, and cook until whites are firm. Remove to a hot platter, care being taken not to break yolks. In same dish brown two tablespoons butter, add vinegar, and pour over eggs.

Eggs à la Caracas.

2 oz. smoked dried beef.	Few grains cinnamon.
1 cup tomatoes.	Few grains cayenne.
¼ cup grated cheese.	2 tablespoons butter.
Few drops onion juice.	3 eggs.

Pick over beef and chop finely, add tomatoes, cheese, onion juice, cinnamon, and cayenne. Melt butter, add mixture, and when heated, add eggs well beaten. Cook until eggs are of creamy consistency, stirring and scraping from bottom of pan.

Union Grill.

Clean one pint of oysters and drain off all the liquor possible. Put oysters in chafing-dish, and as liquor flows from oysters, remove with a spoon, and so continue until oysters are plump. Sprinkle with salt and pepper, and add two tablespoons butter. Serve on zephyrettes

Oysters à la D'Uxelles.

1 pint oysters.	½ teaspoon salt.
2 tablespoons chopped mushrooms.	½ teaspoon lemon juice.
2 tablespoons butter.	Few grains cayenne.
2 tablespoons flour.	1 egg yolk.

1 tablespoon sherry wine.

Clean oysters, heat to boiling point, and drain. Reserve liquor and strain through cheese cloth; there should be three-fourths cup. Cook butter and mushrooms five minutes, add flour, and oyster liquor gradually; then cook three minutes. Add seasonings, oysters, egg, and sherry. Serve on pieces of toasted bread or zephyrettes.

Oysters à la Thorndike.

1 pint oysters.	Few grains cayenne.
2 tablespoons butter.	Slight grating nutmeg.
½ teaspoon salt.	¼ cup thin cream.

Yolks 2 eggs.

Clean and drain oysters. Melt butter, add oysters, and cook until plump. Then add seasonings, cream, and egg yolks. Cook until sauce is slightly thickened. Serve on zephyrettes.

Lobster à la Delmonico.

2 lb. lobster.	Few grains cayenne.
¼ cup butter.	Slight grating nutmeg.
¾ tablespoons flour.	1 cup thin cream.
½ teaspoon salt.	Yolks 2 eggs.

2 tablespoons sherry wine.

Remove lobster meat from shell and cut in small cubes. Melt butter, add flour, seasonings, and cream, gradually. Add lobster, and when heated, add egg yolks and wine.

Lobster à la Newburg.

2 lb. lobster.	Slight grating nutmeg.
¼ cup butter.	1 tablespoon sherry.
½ teaspoon salt.	1 tablespoon brandy.
Few grains cayenne.	⅓ cup thin cream.

Yolks 2 eggs.

Remove lobster meat from shell and cut in slices.   Melt butter, add lobster, and cook three minutes.   Add seasonings and wine, cook one minute, then add cream and yolks of eggs slightly beaten.   Stir until thickened.   Serve with toast or Puff Paste Points.

Clams à la Newburg.

1 pint clams.	3 tablespoons sherry or
tablespoons butter.	Madeira wine.
½ teaspoon salt.	½ cup thin cream.
Few grains cayenne.	Yolks 3 eggs.

Clean clams, remove soft parts, and finely chop hard parts.   Melt butter, add chopped clams, seasonings, and wine.   Cook eight minutes, add soft part of clams, and cream.   Cook two minutes, then add egg yolks slightly beaten, diluted with some of the hot sauce.

Shrimps à la Newburg.

1 pint shrimps.	1 teaspoon lemon juice.
3 tablespoons butter.	1 teaspoon flour.
½ teaspoon salt.	½ cup cream.
Few grains cayenne.	Yolks 2 eggs.

2 tablespoons sherry wine.

Clean shrimps and cook three minutes in two tablespoons butter.   Add salt, cayenne, and lemon juice, and cook one minute.   Remove shrimps, and put remaining butter in chafing-dish, add flour and cream; when thickened, add yolks of eggs slightly beaten, shrimps, and wine.   Serve with toast or Puff Paste Points.

Fish à la Provençale.

¼ cup butter.	Yolks 4 hard boiled eggs.
2½ tablespoons flour.	1 teaspoon Anchovy essence.
2 cups milk.	2 cups cold boiled flaked fish.

Make a sauce of butter, flour, and milk. Mash yolks of eggs and mix with Anchovy essence, add to sauce, then add fish. Serve as soon as heated.

Grilled Sardines.

Drain twelve sardines and cook in a chafing-dish until heated, turning frequently. Place on small oblong pieces of dry toast, and serve with Maître d' Hôtel or Lemon Butter.

Sardines with Anchovy Sauce.

Drain twelve sardines and cook in a chafing-dish until heated, turning frequently. Remove from chafing-dish. Make one cup Brown Sauce with one and one-half tablespoons sardine oil, two tablespoons flour, and one cup Brown Stock. Season with Anchovy essence. Reheat sardines in sauce. Serve with Brown Bread Sandwiches, having a slice of cucumber marinated with French Dressing between slices of bread.

Welsh Rarebit I.

1 tablespoon butter.	¼ teaspoon salt.
1 teaspoon corn-starch.	¼ teaspoon mustard.
½ cup thin cream.	Few grains cayenne.
½ lb. mild soft cheese cut in small pieces.	Toast or zephyrettes.

Melt butter, add corn-starch, stir until well mixed, then add cream gradually and cook two minutes. Add cheese, and stir until cheese is melted. Season, and serve on zephyrettes or bread toasted on one side, rarebit being poured over untoasted side.

Welsh Rarebit II.

1 tablespoon butter.
½ lb. mild soft cheese.
   cut in small pieces.
¼ teaspoon salt.

¼ teaspoon mustard.
Few grains cayenne.
⅓ to ½ cup ale or
   lager beer.

1 egg.

Put butter in chafing-dish, and when melted, add cheese and seasonings; as cheese melts, add ale gradually; then egg slightly beaten. Serve as Welsh Rarebit I.

Oyster Rarebit.

1 cup oysters.
2 tablespoons butter.
½ lb. soft mild cheese.
   cut in small pieces.

¼ teaspoon salt.
Few grains cayenne.
2 eggs.

Clean, parboil, and drain oysters, reserving liquor; then remove and discard tough muscle. Melt butter, add cheese and seasonings; as cheese melts, add gradually oyster liquor, and eggs slightly beaten. As soon as mixture is smooth, add soft part of oysters.

English Monkey.

1 cup stale bread crumbs.
1 cup milk.
1 tablespoon butter.

½ cup soft mild cheese
   cut in small pieces.
1 egg.
½ teaspoon salt.

Few grains cayenne.

Soak bread crumbs fifteen minutes in milk. Melt butter, add cheese, and when cheese has melted, add soaked crumbs, egg slightly beaten, and seasonings. Cook three minutes, and pour over toasted crackers.

Breaded Tongue with Tomato Sauce.

Cut cold boiled corned tongue in slices one-third inch thick. Sprinkle with salt and pepper, dip in egg and crumbs, and sauté in butter. Serve with Tomato Sauce I.

Scotch Woodcock.

4 hard boiled eggs.	1 cup milk.
3 tablespoons butter.	¼ teaspoon salt.
1½ tablespoons flour.	Few grains cayenne.

Anchovy essence.

Make a thin white sauce of butter, flour, milk, and seasonings; add eggs finely chopped, and season with Anchovy essence.   Serve as Welsh Rarebit I.

Shredded Ham with Currant Jelly Sauce.

½ tablespoon butter.	Few grains cayenne.
⅓ cup currant jelly.	¼ cup sherry wine.

1 cup cold cooked ham cut in small strips.

Put butter and currant jelly into the chafing-dish.   As soon as melted, add cayenne, wine, and ham; simmer five minutes.

Venison Cutlets with Apples.

Wipe, core, and cut four apples in one-fourth inch slices. Sprinkle with powdered sugar, and add one-third cup port wine; cover, and let stand thirty minutes.   Drain, and sauté in butter.   Cut a slice of venison one-half inch thick in cutlets.   Sprinkle with salt and pepper, and cook three or four minutes in a hot chafing-dish, using just enough butter to prevent sticking.   Remove from dish; then melt three tablespoons butter, add wine drained from apples, and twelve candied cherries cut in halves. Reheat cutlets in sauce, and serve with apples.

Mutton with Currant Jelly Sauce.

2 tablespoons butter.	1 cup Brown Stock.
tablespoons flour.	⅓ cup currant jelly.
¼ teaspoon salt.	1½ tablespoons sherry wine.
Few grains pepper.	6 slices cold cooked mutton.

Brown the butter, add flour, seasonings, and stock, gradually; then add jelly, and when melted, add mutton. When meat is heated, add wine.   If mutton gravy is at hand, use instead of making a Brown Sauce.

Minced Mutton.

2 cups chopped cooked mutton.　　Salt.
Yolks 6 hard boiled eggs.　　　　Cayenne.
¾ teaspoon mixed mustard.　　　1 cup of cream.
　　　　　　¼ cup wine.

Mash the yolks, and season with mustard, salt, and cayenne. Add cream and mutton. When thoroughly heated, add wine. Serve on toast.

Devilled Bones.

2 tablespoons butter.　　　　　Drumsticks, second joints, and
1 tablespoon Chili sauce.　　　　　wings of a cooked chicken.
1 tablespoon Worcestershire　　Salt.
　　sauce.　　　　　　　　　　Pepper.
1 tablespoon Walnut Catsup.　　Flour.
1 teaspoon made mustard.　　　½ cup hot stock.
Few grains cayenne.　　　　　Finely chopped parsley.

Melt butter, and add Chili Sauce, Worcestershire sauce, Walnut Catsup, mustard, and cayenne. Cut four small gashes in each piece of chicken. Sprinkle with salt and pepper, dredge with flour, and cook in the seasoned butter until well browned. Pour on stock, simmer five minutes, and sprinkle with chopped parsley.

Devilled Almonds.

2 oz. blanched and shredded　　2 tablespoons chopped pickles.
　　almonds.　　　　　　　　1 tablespoon Worcestershire
Butter.　　　　　　　　　　　　sauce.
1 tablespoon Chutney.　　　　¼ teaspoon salt.
　　　　　　Few grains cayenne.

Fry almonds until well browned, using enough butter to prevent almonds from burning. Mix remaining ingredients, pour over nuts, and serve as soon as thoroughly heated. Serve with oysters.

Devilled Chestnuts.

Shell one cup chestnuts, cut in thin slices, and fry until well browned, using enough butter to prevent chestnuts from burning.   Season with Tabasco Sauce or few grains paprika.

Fruit Canapés.

Make German Toast in circular pieces, cover with stewed prunes, figs, or jam.   Serve with Cream Sauce I.

Peach Canapés.

Sauté circular pieces of sponge cake in butter until delicately browned.   Drain canned peaches, sprinkle with powdered sugar, few drops lemon juice, and slight grating nutmeg.   Melt one tablespoon butter, add peaches, and when heated, serve on cake.

Fig Cups.

½ lb. washed figs.	2 tablespoons sugar.
Chopped salted almonds.	1 teaspoon lemon juice.

½ cup wine.

Stuff figs with almonds.   Put sugar, lemon juice, and wine in chafing-dish; when heated add figs, cover, and cook until figs are tender, turning and basting often. Serve with Lady Fingers.

CHAPTER XXXVI.

COOKING, PRESERVING, AND CANNING FRUITS.

FRUITS are usually at their best when served ripe and in season; however, a few cannot be taken in their raw state, and still others are rendered more easy of digestion by cooking. The methods employed are stewing and baking. Fruit should be cooked in earthen or granite ware utensils, and silver or wooden spoons should be employed for stirring. It must be remembered that all fruits contain one or more acids, and when exposed to air and brought in contact with an iron or tin surface, a poisonous compound may be formed.

Baked Apples.

Wipe and core sour apples. Put in a baking-dish, and fill cavities with sugar and spice. Allow one-half cup sugar and one-fourth teaspoon cinnamon or nutmeg to eight apples. If nutmeg is used, a few drops lemon juice and few gratings from rind of lemon to each apple is an improvement. Cover bottom of dish with boiling water, and bake in a hot oven until soft, basting often with syrup in dish. Serve hot or cold with cream. Many prefer to pare apples before baking. When this is done, core before paring, that fruit may keep in shape. In the fall, when apples are at their best, do not add spices to apples, as their flavor cannot be improved; but towards spring they become somewhat tasteless, and spice is an improvement.

Baked Sweet Apples.

Wipe and core eight sweet apples. Put in a baking-dish, and fill cavities with sugar, allowing one-third cup, or sweeten with molasses. Add two-thirds cup boiling water. Cover, and bake three hours in a slow oven, adding more water if necessary.

Apple Sauce.

Wipe, quarter, core, and pare eight sour apples. Make a syrup by boiling seven minutes one cup sugar and one cup water with thin shaving from rind of a lemon. Remove lemon, add enough apples to cover bottom of saucepan, watch carefully during cooking, and remove as soon as soft. Continue until all are cooked. Strain remaining syrup over apples.

Spiced Apple Sauce.

Wipe, quarter, core, and pare eight sour apples. Put in a saucepan, sprinkle with one cup sugar, add eight cloves, and enough water to prevent apples from burning. Cook to a mush, stirring occasionally.

Apple Ginger.

Wipe, quarter, core, pare, and chop two and one-half pounds sour apples. Put in a stewpan and add one and one-half pounds light brown sugar, juice and rind of one and one-half lemons, one-half ounce ginger root, and enough water to prevent apples from burning. Cover, and cook slowly four hours, adding water as necessary. Apple Ginger may be kept for several weeks.

Apple Porcupine.

Make a syrup by boiling eight minutes one and one-half cups sugar and one and one-half cups water. Wipe, core, and pare eight apples. Put apples in syrup as soon as pared, that they may not discolor. Cook until soft, occasionally skimming syrup during cooking. Apples cook better covered with the syrup; therefore it is better to use a deep saucepan, and have two cookings. Drain apples from syrup, cool, fill cavities with jelly, marmalade, or preserved fruit, and stick apples with almonds blanched and split in halves lengthwise. Serve with Cream Sauce I.

Baked Bananas.

Remove skins from six bananas and cut in halves lengthwise. Put in a shallow granite pan or on an old platter. Mix two tablespoons melted butter, one-third cup sugar, and two tablespoons lemon juice. Baste bananas with one-half the mixture. Bake twenty minutes in a slow oven, basting during baking with remaining mixture.

Sautéd Bananas.

Remove skins from bananas, cut in halves lengthwise, and again cut in halves crosswise. Dredge with flour, and sauté in clarified butter. Drain, and sprinkle with powdered sugar.

Baked Peaches.

Peel, cut in halves, and remove stones from six peaches. Place in a shallow granite pan. Fill each cavity with one teaspoon sugar, one-half teaspoon butter, few drops lemon juice, and a slight grating nutmeg. Cook twenty minutes, and serve on circular pieces of buttered dry toast.

Baked Pears.

Wipe, quarter, and core pears. Put in a deep pudding-dish, sprinkle with sugar or add a small quantity of molasses, then add water to prevent pears from burning. Cover, and cook two or three hours in a very slow oven. Small pears may be baked whole. Seckel pears are delicious when baked.

Baked Quinces.

Wipe, quarter, core, and pare eight quinces. Put in a baking-dish, sprinkle with three-fourths cup sugar, add one and one-half cups water, cover, and cook until soft in a slow oven. Quinces require a long time for cooking.

Cranberry Sauce.

Pick over and wash three cups cranberries. Put in a stewpan, add one and one-fourth cups sugar and one cup boiling water. Cover, and boil ten minutes. Care must be taken that they do not boil over. Skim and cool.

Cranberry Jelly.

Pick over and wash four cups cranberries. Put in a stewpan with one cup boiling water, and boil twenty minutes. Rub through a sieve, add two cups sugar, and cook five minutes. Turn into a mould or glasses.

Stewed Prunes.

Wash and pick over prunes. Put in a saucepan, cover with cold water, and soak two hours; then cook until soft in same water. When nearly cooked, add sugar or molasses to sweeten. Many prefer the addition of a small quantity of lemon juice.

Rhubarb Sauce.

Peel and cut rhubarb in one-inch pieces. Put in a saucepan, sprinkle generously with sugar, and add enough water to prevent rhubarb from burning. Rhubarb contains such a large percentage of water that but little additional water is needed. Cook until soft. If rhubarb is covered with boiling water, allowed to stand five minutes, then drained and cooked, less sugar will be required. Rhubarb is sometimes baked in an earthen pudding-dish. If baked slowly for a long time it has a rich red color.

JELLIES.

Jellies are made of cooked fruit juice and sugar, in nearly all cases the proportions being equal. Where failures occur, they may usually be traced to the use of too ripe fruit.

To Prepare Glasses for Jelly. Wash glasses, and put in a kettle of cold water; place on range, and heat water gradually to boiling point. Remove glasses, and drain. Place glasses while filling on a cloth wrung out of hot water.

To Cover Jelly Glasses. Cut letter paper in circular pieces to just fit in top of glasses. Dip in brandy, and cover jelly. Put on tin covers or circular pieces of paper cut larger than the glasses, and fastened securely over the edge with mucilage.

To Make a Jelly Bag. Fold two opposite corners of a piece of cotton and wool flannel three-fourths yard long. Sew up in the form of a cornucopia, rounding at the end. Fell the seam to make more secure. Bind the top with tape, and furnish with two or three heavy loops by which it may be hung.

Apple Jelly.

Wipe apples, remove stem and blossom ends, and cut in quarters. Put in a granite or porcelain-lined preserving kettle, and add cold water to come nearly to top of apples. Cover, and cook slowly until apples are soft; mash, and drain through a coarse sieve. Avoid squeezing apples, which makes jelly cloudy. Then allow juice to drip through a double thickness of cheese cloth or a jelly bag. Boil twenty minutes, and add an equal quantity of heated sugar; boil five minutes, skim, and turn in glasses. Put in a sunny window, and let stand twenty-four hours. Cover, and keep in a cool, dry place. Porter apples make a delicious flavored jelly. If apples are pared, a much lighter jelly may be made. Gravenstein apples make a very spicy jelly.

To Heat Sugar. Put in a granite dish, place in oven, leaving oven door ajar, and stir occasionally.

Quince Jelly.

Follow recipe for Apple Jelly, using quinces in place of apples, and removing seeds from fruit. Quince parings are often used for jelly, the better part of the fruit being used for canning.

Crab Apple Jelly.

Follow recipe for Apple Jelly, leaving apples whole instead of cutting in quarters.

Currant Jelly.

Currants are in the best condition for making jelly between June twenty-eighth and July third, and should not be picked directly after a rain. Cherry currants make the best jelly. Equal proportions of red and white currants are considered desirable, and make a lighter colored jelly.

Pick over currants, but do not remove stems; wash and drain. Mash a few in the bottom of a preserving kettle, using a wooden potato masher; so continue until berries are used. Cook slowly until currants look white. Strain through a coarse strainer, then allow juice to drop through a double thickness of cheese cloth or a jelly bag. Measure, bring to boiling point, and boil five minutes; add an equal measure of heated sugar, boil three minutes, skim, and pour into glasses. Place in a sunny window, and let stand twenty-four hours. Cover, and keep in a cool, dry place.

Currant and Raspberry Jelly.

Follow recipe for Currant Jelly, using equal parts of currants and raspberries.

Blackberry Jelly.

Follow recipe for Currant Jelly, using blackberries in place of currants.

Raspberry Jelly.

Follow recipe for Currant Jelly, using raspberries in place of currants. Raspberry Jelly is the most critical to make, and should not be attempted if fruit is thoroughly ripe, or if it has been long picked.

Barberry Jelly.

Barberry Jelly is firmer and of better color if made from fruit picked before the frost comes, while some of the berries are still green. Make same as Currant Jelly, allowing one cup water to one peck barberries.

Grape Jelly.

Grapes should be picked over, washed, and stems removed before putting into a preserving kettle. Heat to boiling point, mash, and boil thirty minutes; then proceed as for Currant Jelly. Wild grapes make the best jelly.

Green Grape Jelly.

Grapes should be picked when just beginning to turn. Make same as Grape Jelly.

Venison Jelly.

1 peck wild grapes.   Whole cloves, } ¼ cup
1 quart vinegar.   Stick cinnamon, } each.
6 pounds sugar.

Put first four ingredients into a preserving kettle, heat slowly to the boiling point, and cook until grapes are soft. Strain through a double thickness of cheese cloth or a jelly bag, and boil liquid twenty minutes; then add sugar heated, and boil five minutes. Turn into glasses.

Damson Jelly.

Wipe and pick over damsons; then prick several times with a large pin. Make same as Currant Jelly, using three-fourths as much sugar as fruit juice.

JAMS.

Raspberries and blackberries are the fruits most often employed for making jams, and require equal weight of sugar and fruit.

Raspberry Jam.

Pick over raspberries. Mash a few in the bottom of a preserving kettle, using a wooden potato masher, and so continue until the fruit is used. Heat slowly to boiling point, and add gradually an equal quantity of heated sugar. Cook slowly forty-five minutes. Put in a stone jar or tumblers.

Blackberry Jam.

Follow recipe for Raspberry Jam, using blackberries in place of raspberries.

MARMALADES.

Marmalades are made of the pulp and juice of fruits with sugar.

Grape Marmalade.

Pick over, wash, drain, and remove stems from grapes. Separate pulp from skins. Put pulp in preserving kettle. Heat to boiling point, and cook slowly until seeds separate from pulp; then rub through a hair sieve. Return to kettle with skins, add an equal measure of sugar, and cook slowly thirty minutes, occasionally stirring to prevent burning. Put in a stone jar or tumblers.

Quince Marmalade.

Wipe quinces, remove blossom ends, cut in quarters, remove seeds; then cut in small pieces. Put into a preserving kettle, and add enough water to nearly cover.

Cook slowly until soft. Rub through a hair sieve, and add three-fourths its measure of heated sugar. Cook slowly twenty minutes, stirring occasionally to prevent burning. Put in tumblers.

Orange Marmalade.

Select sour, smooth-skinned oranges. Weigh oranges, and allow three-fourths their weight in cut sugar. Remove peel from oranges in quarters. Cook peel until soft in enough boiling water to cover; drain, remove white part from peel by scraping it with a spoon. Cut thin yellow rind in strips, using a pair of scissors. This is more quickly accomplished by cutting through two or three pieces at a time. Divide oranges in sections, remove seeds and tough part of skin. Put into a preserving kettle and heat to boiling point, add sugar gradually, and cook slowly one hour; add rind, and cook one hour longer. Turn into glasses.

Orange and Rhubarb Marmalade.

Remove peel in quarters from eight oranges and prepare as for Orange Marmalade. Divide oranges in sections, remove seeds and tough part of skin. Put into a preserving kettle, add five pounds rhubarb, skinned and cut in one-half inch pieces. Heat to boiling point, and boil one-half hour; then add four pounds cut sugar and cut rind. Cook slowly two hours. Turn into glasses.

CANNING AND PRESERVING.

Preserving fruit is cooking it with from three-fourths to its whole weight of sugar. By so doing, much of the natural flavor of the fruit is destroyed; therefore canning is usually preferred to preserving.

Canning fruit is preserving sterilized fruit in sterilized air-tight jars, the sugar being added to give sweetness. Fruits may be canned without sugar if perfectly sterilized, that is, freed from all germ life.

Directions for Canning.

Fruit for canning should be fresh, firm, of good quality, and not over-ripe. If over-ripe, some of the spores may survive the boiling, then fermentation will take place in a short time.

For canning fruit, allow one third its weight in sugar, and two and one-half to three cups water to each pound of sugar, Boil sugar and water ten minutes to make a thin syrup; then cook a small quantity of the fruit at a time in the syrup; by so doing, fruit may be kept in perfect shape. Hard fruits like pineapple and quince are cooked in boiling water until nearly soft, then put in syrup to finish cooking. Sterilized jars are then filled with fruit, and enough syrup added to overflow jars. If there is not sufficient syrup, add boiling water, as jars must be filled to overflow. Introduce a spoon between fruit and jar, that air bubbles may rise to the top and break; then quickly put on rubbers and screw on steril- ized covers. Let stand until cold, again screw covers, being sure this time that jars are air tight. While filling jars place them on a cloth wrung out of hot water.

To Sterilize Jars.

Wash jars and fill with cold water. Set in a kettle on a trivet, and surround with cold water. Heat gradually to boiling point, remove from water, empty, and fill while hot. Put covers in hot water and let stand five minutes. Dip rubber bands in hot water, but do not allow them to stand. New rubbers should be used each season, and care must be taken that rims of covers are not bent, as jars cannot then be hermetically sealed.

Canned Porter Apples.

Wipe, quarter, core, and pare Porter apples, then weigh. Make a syrup by boiling for ten minutes one- third their weight in sugar with water, allowing two and one-half cups to each pound of sugar. Cook apples in syrup until soft, doing a few at a time. Fill jars, following Directions for Canning.

Canned Peaches.

Wipe peaches and put in boiling water, allowing them to stand just long enough to easily loosen skins. Remove skins and cook fruit at once, that it may not discolor, following Directions for Canning. Some prefer to pare peaches, sprinkle with sugar, and let stand over night. In morning drain, add water to fruit syrup, bring to boiling point, and then cook fruit. Peaches may be cut in halves, or smaller pieces if desired.

Canned Pears.

Wipe and pare fruit. Cook whole with stems left on, or remove stems, cut in quarters, and core. Follow Directions for Canning. A small piece of ginger root or a few slicings of lemon rind may be cooked with syrup. Bartlett pears are the best for canning.

Canned Pineapples.

Remove skin and eyes from pineapples; then cut in half-inch slices, and slices in cubes, at the same time discarding the core. Follow Directions for Canning. Pineapples may be shredded and cooked in one-half their weight of sugar without water, and then put in jars. When put up in this way they are useful for the making of sherbets and fancy desserts.

Canned Quinces.

Wipe, quarter, core, and pare quinces. Follow Directions for Canning. Quinces may be cooked with an equal weight of sweet apples; in this case use no extra sugar for apples.

Canned Cherries.

Use large white or red cherries. Wash, remove stems, then follow Directions for Canning.

Canned Huckleberries.

Pick over and wash berries, then put in a preserving kettle with a small quantity of water to prevent berries from burning. Cook until soft and put in jars. No sugar is required, but a sprinkling of salt is an agreeable addition.

Canned Rhubarb.

Pare rhubarb and cut in one-inch pieces. Pack in a jar, put under cold water faucet, and let water run twenty minutes, then screw on cover. Rhubarb canned in this way has often been known to keep a year.

Canned Tomatoes.

Wipe tomatoes, cover with boiling water, and let stand until skins may be easily removed. Cut in pieces and cook until thoroughly scalded; skim often during cooking. Fill jars, following directions given.

Damson Preserves.

Wipe damsons, and prick each fruit five or six times, using a large needle; then weigh. Make a syrup by boiling three-fourths their weight in sugar with water, allowing one cup to each pound of sugar. As soon as syrup reaches boiling point, skim, and add plums, a few at a time, that fruit may better keep in shape during cooking. Cook until soft. It is well to use two kettles, that work may be more quickly done, and syrup need not cook too long a time. Put into glass or stone jars.

Strawberry Preserves.

Pick over, wash, drain, and hull strawberries; then weigh. Fill jars with berries. Make a syrup same as for Damson Preserve, cooking syrup fifteen minutes. Add syrup to fruit to overflow jars; let stand fifteen minutes, when fruit will have shrunk, and more fruit must be added to fill jars. Screw on covers, put in a kettle of cold water, heat water to boiling point, and keep just below boiling point one hour.

Raspberries may be preserved in the same way.

Pear Chips.

8 lbs. pears.   ¼ lb. Canton ginger.
4 lbs. sugar.   4 lemons.

Wipe pears, remove stems, quarter, and core; then cut in small pieces. Add sugar and ginger, and let stand over night. In the morning add lemons cut in small pieces, rejecting seeds, and cook slowly three hours. Put into a stone jar.

Raspberry and Currant Preserve.

6 lbs. currants.   6 lbs. sugar.
8 quarts raspberries.

Pick over, wash, and drain currants. Put into a preserving kettle, adding a few at a time, and mash. Cook one hour, strain through double thickness of cheese cloth. Return to kettle, add sugar, heat to boiling point, and cook slowly twenty minutes. Add one quart raspberries when syrup again reaches boiling point, skim out raspberries, put in jar, and repeat until raspberries are used. Fill jars to overflowing with syrup, and screw on tops.

Brandied Peaches.

1 peck peaches.   Half their weight in sugar.
1 quart high-proof alcohol or brandy.

Remove skins from peaches, and put alternate layers of peaches and sugar in a stone jar; then add alcohol. Cover closely, having a heavy piece of cloth under cover of jar.

Tutti-Frutti.

Put one pint brandy into a stone jar, add the various fruits as they come into market; to each quart of fruit add the same quantity of sugar, and stir the mixture each morning until all the fruit has been added. Raspberries, strawberries, apricots, peaches, cherries, and pineapples are the best to use.

Preserved Melon Rind.

Pare and cut in strips the rind of ripe melons. Soak in alum water to cover, allowing two teaspoons powdered alum to each quart of water. Heat gradually to boiling point and cook slowly ten minutes. Drain, cover with ice water, and let stand two hours; again drain, and dry between towels. Weigh, allow one pound sugar to each pound of fruit. and one cup water to each pound of sugar. Boil sugar and water ten minutes. Add melon rind, and cook until tender. Remove rind to a stone jar, and cover with syrup. Two lemons cut in slices may be cooked ten minutes in the syrup.

Tomato Preserve.

1 lb. yellow pear tomatoes.	2 oz. preserved Canton ginger.
1 lb. sugar.	2 lemons.

Peel tomatoes, cover with sugar, and let stand over night. In the morning pour off syrup and boil until quite thick; skim, then add tomatoes, ginger, and lemons which have been sliced and the seeds removed. Cook until tomatoes have a clarified appearance.

PICKLING.

Pickling is preserving in any salt or acid liquor.

Spiced Currants.

7 lbs. currants.	3 tablespoons cinnamon.
5 lbs. brown sugar.	3 tablespoons clove.
1 pint vinegar.	

Pick over currants, wash, drain, and remove stems. Put in a preserving kettle, add sugar, vinegar, and spices tied in a piece of muslin. Heat to boiling point, and cook slowly one and one-half hours.

Sweet Pickled Pears.

Follow recipe for Sweet Pickled Peaches, using pears in place of peaches.

Sweet Pickled Peaches.

½ peck peaches.
2 lbs. brown sugar.

1 pint vinegar.
1 oz. stick cinnamon.

Cloves.

Boil sugar, vinegar, and cinnamon twenty minutes. Dip peaches quickly in hot water, then rub off the fur with a towel. Stick each peach with four cloves. Put into syrup, and cook until soft, using one-half peaches at a time.

Chili Sauce.

12 medium-sized ripe tomatoes.
1 pepper finely chopped.
1 onion finely chopped.
2 cups vinegar.
3 tablespoons sugar.

1 tablespoon salt.
2 teaspoons clove.
2 teaspoons cinnamon.
2 teaspoons allspice.
2 teaspoons grated nutmeg.

Peel tomatoes and slice. Put in a preserving kettle with remaining ingredients. Heat gradually to boiling point, and cook slowly two and one-half hours.

Ripe Tomato Pickle.

3 pints tomatoes peeled and chopped.
1 cup chopped celery.
4 tablespoons chopped red pepper.
4 tablespoons chopped onion.

4 tablespoons salt.
6 tablespoons sugar.
6 tablespoons mustard seed.
½ teaspoon clove.
½ teaspoon cinnamon.
1 teaspoon grated nutmeg.

2 cups vinegar.

Mix ingredients in order given. Put in a stone jar and cover. This uncooked mixture must stand a week before using, but may be kept a year.

Ripe Cucumber Pickle.

Cut cucumbers in halves lengthwise. Cover with alum water, allowing two teaspoons powdered alum to each quart of water. Heat gradually to boiling point, then let stand on back of range two hours. Remove from alum water and chill in ice water. Make a syrup by boiling five minutes two pounds sugar, one pint vinegar, with two tablespoons each of whole cloves and stick cinnamon tied in a piece of muslin. Add cucumbers and cook ten minutes. Remove cucumbers to a stone jar and pour over the syrup. Scald syrup three successive mornings, and return to fruit.

Unripe Cucumber Pickles (Gherkins).

Wipe four quarts small unripe cucumbers. Put in a stone jar and add one cup salt dissolved in two quarts boiling water and let stand three days. Drain cucumbers from brine, bring brine to boiling point, pour over cucumbers, and again let stand three days; repeat. Drain, wipe cucumbers, and pour over one gallon boiling water in which one tablespoon alum has been dissolved. Let stand six hours, then drain from alum water. Cook cucumbers ten minutes, a few at a time, in one-fourth the following mixture heated to the boiling point and boiled ten minutes : —

1 gallon vinegar.	2 sticks cinnamon.
4 red peppers.	2 tablespoons allspice berries.
	2 tablespoons cloves.

Strain remaining liquor over pickles which have been put in a stone jar.

Chopped Pickles.

4 quarts chopped green tomatoes.	3 teaspoons allspice.
¾ cup salt.	3 teaspoons cloves.
2 teaspoons pepper.	½ cup white mustard seed.
3 teaspoons mustard.	4 green peppers sliced.
3 teaspoons cinnamon.	2 chopped onions.
	2 quarts vinegar.

Add salt to tomatoes, let stand twenty-four hours, and drain. Add spices to vinegar, and heat to boiling point; then add tomatoes, peppers, and onions, and cook fifteen minutes after boiling point is reached.

Spanish Pickles.

1 peck green tomatoes
    thinly sliced.
4 onions thinly sliced.
1 cup salt.
½ oz. cloves.
½ oz. allspice berries.

½ oz. peppercorns.
½ cup brown mustard seed.
1 lb. brown sugar.
4 green peppers finely
    chopped.
Cider vinegar.

Sprinkle alternate layers of tomatoes and onions with salt, and let stand over night. In the morning drain, and put in a preserving kettle, adding remaining ingredients, using enough vinegar to cover all. Heat gradually to boiling point and boil one-half hour.

Chow-Chow.

2 quarts small green tomatoes.
12 small cucumbers.
3 red peppers.
1 cauliflower.
2 bunches celery.
1 pint small onions.
2 quarts string beans.

¼ lb. mustard seed.
2 oz. turmeric.
½ oz. allspice.
½ oz. pepper.
½ oz. clove.
Salt.
1 gallon vinegar.

Prepare vegetables and cut in small pieces, cover with salt, let stand twenty-four hours, and drain. Heat vinegar and spices to boiling point, add vegetables, and cook until soft.

Pickled Onions.

Peel small white onions, cover with brine, allowing one and one-half cups salt to two quarts boiling water, and let stand two days; drain, and cover with more brine; let stand two days, and again drain. Make more brine and heat to boiling point, put in onions and boil three minutes. Put in jars, interspersing with bits of mace, white peppercorns, cloves, bits of bay leaf, and slices of red pepper. Fill jars to overflow with vinegar scalded with sugar, allowing one cup sugar to one gallon vinegar. Cork while hot.

CHAPTER XXXVII.

RECIPES ESPECIALLY PREPARED FOR THE SICK.

STATISTICS prove that two-thirds of all disease is brought about by error in diet. The correct proportions of food-principles have not been maintained, or the food has been improperly cooked. Physicians agree, with but few exceptions, that the proper preparation of food for the sick is of as great importance in the restoration to health as administration of drugs. Time and manner of serving are of equal importance.

Take especial care in setting an invalid's tray. Cover with a spotless tray-cloth or dinner napkin, folding the same, if it is larger than tray, that it may just come over edge. Avoid a fringed cloth, as the fringe is apt to prove annoying.

Select the daintiest china, finest glass, and choicest silver, making changes as often as possible. Cheer the patient with a bright blossom laid on tray, or a small vase of flowers placed in left hand corner. Place plate at front of tray, near the edge ; knife at right of plate, with sharp edge toward plate ; fork at left of plate, tines up ; spoon at head of plate. or, if more convenient for the patient, at right of knife, bowl up; cup and saucer at right of plate, with handle arranged so that cup may be easily lifted; tumbler above knife, and filled two-thirds full of freshly drawn water just before taking into the sick-room. The individual butter, or bread and butter plate, should be placed at left hand corner over fork. The napkin may be placed at right of cup. Salt should appear, but pepper never. Avoid having too many things on the tray at one time. If soup, meat, and a light dessert are to be served to a convalescent, have one course removed before another appears. Foods which are intended to be served hot should be placed in heated dishes and kept covered during transit from kitchen, that patient may receive them hot. Equal care should be taken to have cold foods served cold; never lukewarm. A glass of milk, cup of gruel, or cup of beef-tea should be on a plate covered with a doily.

Never consult the patient as to his menu. If there is anything he especially desires, you will be informed. Anticipation often creates appetite. Serve in small quantities; the sight of too much food often destroys the appetite. If liquid diet must be adhered to, give as great variety as is allowable. If patient is restricted to milk diet, and milk is somewhat objectionable, it may be tolerated by serving in different ways, — such as Koumiss, Albumenized Milk, or by addition of Apollinaris, Seltzer water, or rennet.

After the completion of a meal, the tray should be removed at once from the sick-room. If any solid food remains, it should be burned, and liquids disposed of at once.

Liquid Foods may first be considered. Barley water and rice water are known as astringent or demulcent drinks, and are generally used to reduce a laxative condition. The starch of barley is perhaps more valuable than that of rice. Toast water is often beneficial in cases of extreme nausea. A small quantity of clam water may be given when the stomach refuses to retain other foods. Clam water is also used to increase a secretion of mother's milk.

Oatmeal water is occasionally ordered for dyspeptic patients, but more frequently used for the workman on the road or the farmer in the field. In the hottest days of summer, oatmeal water may be drunk with safety where ice water would be extremely dangerous.

Fruit waters are principally used for fever patients. They are cooling, refreshing, and mildly stimulating, and are valuable for the salts and acids they contain. Lemons, being easily procured and of moderate price, are most extensively used.

Beef essence, which is the expressed juices of beef, being nutritious, is given when a condensed form of food is necessary. Many preparations of beef essence are on the market in the form of powder, paste, liquid, and tablets; some of which are valuable, but they are more expensive and not as nutritious as home-made essence, and patients are apt to quickly tire of them. One pound of beef cut from the top of the round will frequently yield four ounces of beef essence.

Beef tea contains the juices of beef diluted with water, and is given as a stimulant, rather than as a nutrient as is popularly supposed. It furnishes a pleasing variety to a liquid diet, and by its use a large quantity of water is ingested. If the color of beef is objectionable to a patient, serve in a colored glass.

Egg-nogs are recommended where it is necessary to take a large amount of nutriment daily, as is often the case when the system is much reduced by a severe illness.

Semi-solid Foods comprise the gruels. When made from corn or oatmeal they are heat-producing, and should never be given when inflammatory symptoms are present. Imperial Granum makes a delicious gruel, which has largely superseded the more common kinds. It is quickly made, and unless expense must be considered is generally to be preferred. Although containing much starch, in the process of manufacture the starch has largely been converted into dextrine; therefore it may be given even when there is inflammation. Flour and cracker gruels to many prove a pleasant variety, and often assist in reducing a laxative condition. Arrowroot makes a delicate gruel, is more easily digested than any other form of starch, and is often valuable in cases of gastric irritation. It should never be given to infants.

Solid Foods comprise the principal diet during convalescence. At this time the nurse shows her skill and judgment quite as much as during the critical part of the disease. Foods must be taken which are nutritious, easy of assimilation, and given frequently, in small quantities, and at regular intervals. The convalescent, if allowed to follow his own inclinations, often produces a relapse by improper diet.

It is often desirable to prepare water ices and ice creams quickly and in small quantities for the sick. This may be easily accomplished by putting the mixture to be frozen in a small tin box (one-pound baking-powder can), placing box in lard pail and surrounding with finely crushed ice and salt. Cover pail; as mixture begins to freeze, scrape from sides and bottom of box and beat until smooth. Continue until of the desired consistency.

Barley Water.

3 tablespoons barley.	Salt.
4 cups cold water.	Lemon juice.

Sugar.

Pick over barley and soak in water over night, or for several hours. Boil gently one and one-half hours. Strain; season with salt, lemon juice, and sugar. Reheat and serve.

Rice Water.

2 tablespoons rice.	Milk or cream.
2 cups cold water.	Salt.

Pick over rice, add to water, and boil until rice is tender; strain, and add to rice water, milk or cream as desired. Season with salt and reheat. A half-inch piece of stick cinnamon may be cooked with rice, and will assist in reducing a laxative condition.

Oatmeal Water.

1 cup fine oatmeal.	2 quarts water (which has been boiled and cooled).

Add oatmeal to water, and keep in a warm place (at temperature of 80° F.) one and one-half hours. Strain and cool.

Toast Water.

Equal measures of stale bread   Salt.
  toasted and boiling water.

Cut bread in quarter-inch slices, put in a pan, and dry
thoroughly in a slow oven until crisp and brown.   Break
in pieces, add water, and let stand one hour.   Strain
through cheese cloth, and season.   Serve hot or cold.

Apple Water.

1 large sour apple.   2 teaspoons sugar.
            1 cup boiling water.

Wipe, core, and pare apple.   Put sugar in the cavity.
Bake until tender; mash, pour over water, let stand one-
half hour, and strain.

Tamarind Water.

2 tablespoons preserved   1 cup boiling water.
      tamarinds.   Sugar.

Pour water over tamarinds; stir until well mixed.   Let
stand twenty minutes and strain.   Sweeten to taste.

Currant Water.

2 tablespoons currant juice or   ⅔ cup cold water.
2 teaspoons currant jelly.   Sugar.

Mix juice and water, then sweeten; or beat jelly with
a fork, dissolve in water, and if not sweet enough add
sugar.

Grape Juice.

1½ cups Concord grapes.   1 cup cold water.
            ½ cup sugar.

Wash, pick over, and remove stems from grapes; add
water, and cook one and one-half hours in a double boiler.
Add sugar, and cook twenty minutes.   Strain and cool.

Lemonade.

1 tablespoon lemon juice.   2 tablespoons syrup.
Water.

Make a syrup by boiling eight minutes one cup water
and one-half cup sugar. To two tablespoons syrup add
one tablespoon lemon juice and one-half cup water. Soda
water, Apollinaris, or Seltzer water may be used.

Irish Moss Lemonade.

¼ cup Irish moss.   Juice 1 lemon.
2 cups cold water.   Sugar.

Pick over and soak Irish moss in cold water to cover.
Remove moss, add two cups cold water, and cook twenty
minutes in double boiler; then strain. To one-half cup
of liquid add lemon juice, and sugar to sweeten.

Flaxseed Lemonade.

1 tablespoon whole flaxseed.   Lemon juice.
1 pint boiling water.   Sugar.

Pick over and wash flaxseed, add water, and cook two
hours, keeping just below boiling point. Strain, add
lemon juice, and sugar to taste.

Orangeade.

Juice 1 orange.   1½ tablespoons syrup.
2 tablespoons crushed ice.

To orange juice add syrup (using less if orange is
sweet), and pour over crushed ice. Make syrup as for
Lemonade.

Sterilized Milk.

Fill small-necked half-pint bottles to within one and
one-half inches of the top with milk; cork with absorbent
cotton. Stand in a steamer of cold water, having water

surround bottles to three-fourths their height. Allow water to heat gradually until nearly to boiling point, and keep at this temperature for ten minutes. When used for infants allow from a teaspoon to a tablespoon of lime water for each bottle of milk.

Albumenized Milk.

½ cup milk.   White 1 egg.

Put white of egg in a tumbler, add milk, cover tightly, and shake thoroughly until well mixed.

Koumiss.

1 quart milk   ⅓ yeast cake dissolved in
1½ tablespoons sugar.   1 tablespoon lukewarm water.

Heat milk until lukewarm; add sugar and dissolved yeast cake. Fill beer bottles within one and one-half inches of the top, cork and invert. The corks must be firmly tied down with strong twine. Let stand for six hours at a temperature of 80° F. Chill, and serve the following day.

Egg-nog I.

1 egg.   2 tablespoons wine or
⅔ cup milk.   1 tablespoon brandy.
1 tablespoon sugar.   Few grains salt.

Beat egg slightly, add salt, sugar, and wine; mix thoroughly, add milk, and strain. Wine may be omitted, and a slight grating nutmeg used.

Egg-nog II.

Yolk 1 egg.   2 tablespoons wine or
1 tablespoon sugar.   1 tablespoon brandy.
Few grains salt.   ⅔ cup milk.
                 White 1 egg.

Beat yolk of egg, add sugar, salt, wine, and milk. Strain, and add beaten white of egg. Stir well before serving.

Egg-nog III. or Hot Water Egg-nog.

Make like Egg-nog I., using one-half cup hot water in place of milk.

Wine Whey.

1 cup milk.   1 cup sherry or port wine.

Scald milk, add wine, and let stand five minutes. By this time the curd should have separated from whey. Strain and serve, or heat before serving.

Milk Punch.

½ cup milk.   Sugar.
1 tablespoon whiskey, rum, or   Few gratings nutmeg.
    brandy.

Mix ingredients, cover, and shake well.

Entire Wheat Coffee.

2 teaspoons Wheat Coffee.   1 cup boiling water.
            1 teaspoon cold water.

Add boiling water to coffee and boil three minutes, then add cold water and let stand one minute to settle. Serve with cut sugar and scalded milk.

Phillips' Cocoa.

4 teaspoons cocoa.   ½ cup boiling water.
cold water.   1 cup scalded milk.

Mix cocoa with a little cold water, add to boiling water, boil one minute, then add scalded milk and beat one minute with Dover egg-beater. The froth formed prevents the scum, which is so unsightly.

Cocoa Cordial.

1 teaspoon cocoa.	½ cup boiling water.
1 teaspoon sugar.	1½ tablespoons port wine.

Mix cocoa and sugar, add enough of the water to form a paste. Stir in remainder of water and boil one minute, then add wine. Useful in cases of chill or exhaustion.

Broiled Beef Essence.

½ lb. steak from top of round (cut ¾ inch thick).

Wipe steak, remove all fat, and place in a heated broiler. Broil three minutes over a clear fire, turning every ten seconds to prevent escape of juices. Put on a hot plate, and cut in one and one-half inch pieces; gash each piece two or three times on each side. Express the juice with a lemon squeezer and turn into a cup, set in a dish of hot water, care being taken that heat is not sufficient to coagulate juices. Season with salt.

Broiled Beef Tea.

Dilute Broiled Beef Essence with water.

Bottled Beef Essence.

1 lb. steak from top of round.

Wipe steak, remove all fat, and cut in small pieces. Place in canning jar, cover; place on trivet in kettle and surround with cold water. Allow water to heat slowly, care being taken not to have it reach a higher temperature than 130° F. Let stand two hours; strain, and press the meat to obtain all the juices. Salt to taste.

Bottled Beef Tea.

1 lb. steak from top of round.	1 pint cold water.
Salt.	

Prepare the beef as for Bottled Beef Essence. Soak fifteen minutes in the water, and cook three hours same as

Bottled Beef Essence.   Strain and season.   In reheating, care should be taken not to coagulate the juices.

Beef tea contains albuminous juices, salts, and a very small amount of fat (so intermingled with the lean meat that it cannot be removed), together with that part of the meat which gives to it flavor and color.   The fibre that remains contains much proteid in the form of insoluble albumen, which could not be extracted.   Although the meat is tasteless, it still holds much nutriment, being deprived of but little other than its stimulating properties. When the albuminous juices of beef tea are allowed to coagulate, and tea is strained, it has about the same value as a cup of hot salted water.

Frozen Beef Tea.

Freeze Beef Tea to the consistency of a mush.

Flour Gruel.

1 tablespoon flour.   2 cups milk.
Salt.

Mix flour with one-fourth cup of milk.   Scald remaining milk in double boiler, add flour paste, and cook thirty minutes.   Season.

Arrowroot Gruel.

1 cup boiling water.   Cold water.
2 teaspoons Bermuda arrowroot.   Salt.

Mix arrowroot with cold water to form a thin paste. Add to boiling water and cook ten minutes.   Season, and add cream if desired.   Arrowroot is the purest form of starch.

Farina Gruel.

2 cups boiling water.   1 cup milk.
1 tablespoon farina.   1 egg.
Cold water.   ½ teaspoon salt.

Mix farina with enough cold water to form a thin paste. Add to boiling water and boil thirty minutes; then add milk and reheat.   Beat egg, add to gruel, season, and serve.

Indian Gruel.

2 tablespoons Indian meal.	Cold water.
1 tablespoon flour.	3 cups boiling water.
½ teaspoon salt.	Milk or cream.

Mix meal, flour, and salt; add cold water to make a thin paste. Add to boiling water, and boil gently one hour. Dilute with milk or cream. A richer gruel may be made by using milk instead of water, and cooking three hours in double boiler.

Oatmeal Gruel I.

½ cup coarse oatmeal.	1 teaspoon salt.
3 cups boiling water.	Milk.

Add oatmeal and salt to boiling water and cook three hours in double boiler. Force through a strainer, dilute with milk or cream, reheat, and strain a second time.

Oatmeal Gruel II.

⅔ cup coarse oatmeal.	1 teaspoon salt.
1 pint cold water.	Milk or cream.

Pound oatmeal until mealy, add one-third of the water, stir well, let settle, and pour off the mealy water. Repeat twice, using remaining water. Boil the mealy water thirty minutes; season with salt, dilute with milk or cream, strain, and serve. A delicate gruel, but more expensive and less nutritious than Oatmeal Gruel I.

Barley Gruel.

1 cup boiling water.	Cold water.
3 teaspoons barley flour.	½ cup milk.
¼ teaspoon salt.	

Mix barley flour with cold water to form a thin paste. Add to boiling water, and boil fifteen minutes; then add milk, season, reheat, and strain.

Cracker Gruel.

½ Boston cracker.   ¼ teaspoon salt.
1 cup milk.

Scald milk, and add cracker rolled and sifted. Cook five minutes in double boiler. Season.

Imperial Granum.

1 tablespoon Imperial Granum.   ½ cup boiling water.
½ cup scalded milk.   Salt.
Cold water.

Mix Granum with cold water to form a thin paste. Add to milk and water, and cook fifteen minutes in double boiler, then season. Increase the proportion of milk to the needs of the patient.

Clam Water.

Wash and scrub one and one-half dozen clams. Cook in covered kettle with three tablespoons water until shells open. Remove clams, strain liquor through double cheese cloth. Serve hot or as a frappé.

Mutton Broth.

3 lbs. mutton (from the neck).   Few grains pepper.
2 quarts cold water.   3 tablespoons rice or
1 teaspoon salt.   3 tablespoons barley.

Wipe meat, remove skin and fat, and cut in small pieces. Put into kettle with bones, and cover with cold water. Heat gradually to boiling point, skim, then season with salt and pepper. Cook slowly until meat is tender, strain, and remove fat. Reheat to boiling point, add rice or barley, and cook until rice or barley is tender. If barley is used, soak over night in cold water. Some of the meat may be served with the broth.

Chicken Broth.

Dress and clean a chicken; remove skin and fat, disjoint, and wipe with a wet cloth.   Put into stewpan, cover with cold water, heat slowly to boiling point, skim, and cook until meat is tender.   When half done, season with one and one-half teaspoons salt and few grains pepper.   Strain, and remove fat.   There should be about three pints of stock.   Reheat to boiling point, add two tablespoons washed rice, and cook until rice is soft.

Indian Meal Mush.

½ cup Indian meal.   1 cup boiling water.
¾ cup milk.   ½ teaspoon salt.

Mix meal and salt, add milk, and stir into boiling water.   Cook three hours in double boiler.   Serve with sugar and cream.

Rye Meal Mush.

½ cup rye meal.   ½ cup cold water.
1¼ cups boiling water.   ½ teaspoon salt.

Mix meal, salt, and cold water.   Add to boiling water, and boil five minutes.   Cook one hour in double boiler. Serve with maple syrup.

Oatmeal Mush.

½ cup coarse oatmeal.   2 cups boiling water.
½ teaspoon salt.

Add salt and oatmeal to boiling water.   Cook three or four hours in double boiler.   Serve with sugar and cream.

Hominy Mush.

½ cup fine hominy.   1 pint boiling water.
½ teaspoon salt.

Prepare as for Quaker Oats Mush, cooking one hour in double boiler.

Quaker Oats Mush.

⅔ cup Quaker Rolled Oats.   1¼ cups boiling water.
½ teaspoon salt.

Add salt to boiling water; then add oats, and cook one-half hour in double boiler. Serve with sugar and cream. Any preparation of steamed rolled oats may be used.

Beef Balls.

Take a small piece of steak from top of round; wipe and cut in one-third inch strips. With a knife scrape the freshly cut surface, removing all that is possible of the soft part of meat; then turn and scrape other side. Season with salt; if pepper is desired, use sparingly. Form into small balls, using as little pressure as possible. Cook one minute in a hot omelet pan, sprinkled with salt, shaking pan to keep the balls in motion. Arrange on small pieces of buttered toast, and garnish with parsley.

Raw Beef Sandwiches.

Prepare bread as for Bread and Butter Sandwiches. Spread one-half the pieces with scraped beef, generously seasoned with salt; if pepper is desired, use sparingly. Cover with remaining pieces.

Egg Sandwiches.

Cut thin slices of stale bread in triangles, then toast. Put together in pairs, having between the pieces thoroughly cooked egg yolk, rubbed to a paste, seasoned with salt, and moistened with soft butter.

To Broil Birds in Buttered Cases.

Butter a sheet of letter paper, place a boned bird on lower half of sheet, fold upper half over bird, bringing edges of paper together. Begin at edges, and fold over lower side and ends of paper three times. Place in a wire broiler, and broil ten minutes over a slow fire, being careful that paper does not catch on fire.   Remove from case, place on slice of toast, season with salt, pepper, and butter.   Garnish with thin slices of lemon and parsley.   A breast of chicken, tenderloin of steak, or lamb chop may be cooked in the same way.

Rennet Custard (Junket).

1 cup milk.	1 tablespoon sherry wine.
2 tablespoons sugar.	1 teaspoon liquid rennet.

Heat milk until lukewarm, add sugar and wine; when sugar is dissolved, add rennet.   Turn into a small mould, and let stand in a cool place until firm.   Serve with sugar and cream.   Cinnamon or nutmeg may be used in place of wine.   Liquid rennet may be bought in bottles of any first-class grocer.

CHAPTER XXXVIII.

HELPFUL HINTS TO THE YOUNG HOUSEKEEPER.

To Scald Milk. Put in top of double boiler, having water boiling in under part. Cover, and let stand on top of range until milk around edge of double boiler has a bead-like appearance.

For Buttered Cracker Crumbs, allow from one-fourth to one-third cup melted butter to each cup of crumbs. Stir lightly with a fork in mixing, that crumbs may be evenly coated and light rather than compact.

To Cream Butter. Put in a bowl and work with a wooden spoon until soft and of creamy consistency. Should buttermilk exude from butter it should be poured off.

To Extract Juice from Onion. Cut a slice from root end of onion, draw back the skin, and press onion on a coarse grater, working with a rotary motion.

To Chop Parsley. Remove leaves from parsley. If parsley is wet, first dry in a towel. Gather parsley between thumb and fingers and press compactly. With a sharp vegetable knife cut through and through. Again gather in fingers and recut, so continuing until parsley is finely cut.

To Caramelize Sugar. Put in a smooth granite saucepan or omelet pan, place over hot part of range, and stir constantly until melted and of the color of maple syrup. Care must be taken to prevent sugar from adhering to sides of pan or spoon.

To Make Caramel. Continue the caramelization of sugar until syrup is quite brown and a whitish smoke arises from it. Add an equal quantity of boiling water, and simmer until of the consistency of a thick syrup. Of use in coloring soups, sauces, etc.

Acidulated Water is water to which vinegar or lemon juice is added. One tablespoon of the acid is allowed to one quart water.

To Blanch Almonds. Cover Jordan almonds with boiling water and let stand two minutes; drain, put into cold water, and rub off the skins. Dry between towels.

To Shred Almonds. Cut blanched almonds in thin strips lengthwise of the nut.

Macaroon Dust. Dry macaroons pounded and sifted.

To Shell Chestnuts. Cut a half-inch gash on flat sides and put in an omelet pan, allowing one-half teaspoon butter to each cup chestnuts. Shake over range until butter is melted. Put in oven and let stand five minutes. Remove from oven, and with a small knife take off shells. By this method shelling and blanching is accomplished at the same time, as skins adhere to shells.

Flavoring Extracts and Wine should be added if possible to a mixture when cold. If added while mixture is hot, much of the goodness passes off with the steam.

Meat Glaze. Four quarts stock reduced to one cup.

Mixed Mustard. Mix two tablespoons mustard and one teaspoon sugar, add hot water gradually until of the consistency of a thick paste. Vinegar may be used in place of water.

To Prevent Salt from Lumping. Mix with corn-starch, allowing one teaspoon corn-starch to six teaspoons salt.

To Wash Carafes. Half fill with hot soapsuds, to which is added one teaspoon washing soda. Put in newspaper torn in small pieces. Let stand one-half hour, occasionally shaking. Empty, rinse with hot water, drain. wipe outside, and let stand to dry inside.

After Broiling or Frying, if any fat has spattered on range, wipe surface at once with newspaper.

To Remove Fruit Stains. Pour boiling water over stained surface, having it fall from a distance of three feet. This is a much better way than dipping stain in and out of hot water; or wring articles out of cold water and hang out of doors on a frosty night.

To Remove Stains of Claret Wine. As soon as claret is spilt, cover spot with salt. Let stand a few minutes, then rinse in cold water.

To Clean Graniteware where mixtures have been cooked or burned on. Half fill with cold water, add washing soda, heat water gradually to boiling point, then empty, when dish may be easily washed. Pearline or any soap powder may be used in place of washing soda.

To Wash Mirrors and Windows. Rub over with chamois skin wrung out of warm water, then wipe with a piece of dry chamois skin. This method saves much strength.

To Remove White Spots from Furniture. Dip a cloth in hot water nearly to boiling point. Place over spot, remove quickly and rub over spot with a dry cloth. Repeat if spot is not removed. Alcohol or camphor quickly applied may be used.

Tumblers which have contained milk should be first rinsed in cold water before washing in hot water.

To keep a **Sink Drain** free from grease, pour down once a week at night one-half can Babbitt's potash dissolved in one quart water.

Should **Sink Drain** chance to get choked, pour into sink one-fourth pound copperas dissolved in two quarts boiling water. If this is not efficacious, repeat before sending for a plumber.

Never put **Knives** with ivory handles in water. Hot water causes them to crack and discolor.

To prevent **Glassware** from being easily broken, put in a kettle of cold water, heat gradually until water has reached boiling point. Set aside; when water is cold take out glass. This is a most desirable way to toughen lamp chimneys.

To Remove Grease Spots. Cold water and Ivory soap will remove grease spots from cotton and woollen fabrics. Castilian Cream is useful for black woollen goods, but leaves a light ring on delicately colored goods. Ether is always sure and safe to use.

To Remove Iron Rust. Saturate spot with lemon juice, then cover with salt. Let stand in the sun for several hours; or a solution of hydrochloric acid may be used.

Iron Rust may be removed from delicate fabrics by covering spot thickly with cream of tartar, then twisting cloth to keep cream of tartar over spot; put in a saucepan of cold water, and heat water gradually to boiling point.

To Remove Grass Stains from cotton goods, wash in alcohol.

To Remove Ink Stains. Wash in a solution of hydrochloric acid, and rinse in ammonia water. Wet the spot with warm water, put on Sapolio, rub gently between the hands, and generally the spot will disappear.

Cut Glass should be washed and rinsed in water that is not very hot and of same temperature.

In **Sweeping Carpets**, keep broom close to floor and work with the grain of the carpet. Occasionally turn broom that it may wear evenly.

Tie Strands of a New Broom closely together, put into a pail of boiling water, and soak two hours. Dry thoroughly before using.

Never wash the inside of **Tea or Coffee Pots** with soap-suds. If granite or agate ware is used, and becomes badly discolored, nearly fill pot with cold water, add one tablespoon borax, and heat gradually until water reaches the boiling point. Rinse with hot water, wipe, and keep on back of range until perfectly dry.

Never put cogs of a **Dover Egg Beater** in water.

Never wash **Bread Boards** in a sink. Scrub with grain of wood, using a small brush.

Before using a **new Iron Kettle**, grease inside and outside, and let stand forty-eight hours; then wash in hot water in which a large lump of cooking soda has been dissolved.

To clean a **Copper Boiler**, use Putz Pomade Cream. Apply with a woollen cloth when boiler is warm, not hot; then rub off with second woollen cloth and polish with flannel or chamois. If badly tarnished, use oxalic acid. Faucets and brasses are treated in the same way.

A bottle containing **Oxalic Acid** should be marked poison, and kept on a high shelf.

To keep an **Ice Chest** in good condition, wash thoroughly once a week with cold or lukewarm water in which washing soda has been dissolved. If by chance anything is spilt in an ice chest, it should be wiped off at once. Milk and butter very quickly absorb odors, and if in ice chest with other foods, should be kept closely covered.

Hard Wood Floors and Furniture may be polished by using a small quantity of kerosene oil applied with a woollen cloth, then rubbing with a clean woollen cloth. A very good furniture polish is made by using equal parts linseed oil and turpentine.

Polish for Hard Wood Floors. Use one part bees'-wax to two parts turpentine. Put in saucepan on range, and when wax is dissolved a paste will be formed.

To clean **Piano Keys**, rub over with alcohol.

To remove old **Tea and Coffee Stains**, wet spot with cold water, cover with glycerine, and let stand two or three hours. Then wash with cold water and hard soap. Repeat if necessary.

Before **Sweeping Old Carpets**, sprinkle with pieces of newspaper wrung out of water. After sweeping, wipe over with a cloth wrung out of a weak solution of ammonia water; which seems to brighten colors.

Platt's Chloride is one of the best **Disinfectants**. Chloride of lime is a valuable disinfectant, and much cheaper than Platt's Chloride.

Listerine is an excellent disinfectant to use for the mouth and throat.

To Make a Pastry Bag. Fold a twelve-inch square of rubber cloth from two opposite corners. Sew edges together, forming a triangular bag. Cut off point to make opening large enough to insert a tin pastry tube. A set comprising bag and twelve adjustable tubes may be bought for two and one-half dollars.

Smoked Ceilings may be cleaned by washing with cloths wrung out of water in which a small piece of washing soda has been dissolved.

For a Burn apply equal parts of white of egg and olive oil mixed together, then cover with a piece of old linen; if applied at once no blister will form. Or apply at once cooking soda, then cover with cloth and keep the same wet with cold water. This takes out the pain and prevents blistering.

Curtain and Portière Poles allow the hangings to slip easily if rubbed with hard soap.   This is much better than greasing.

Creaking Doors and Drawers should be treated in the same way.

To Remove Dust from Rattan Furniture use a small painter's brush.

CHAPTER XXXIX.

SUITABLE COMBINATIONS FOR SERVING.
BREAKFAST MENUS.

Oranges.
Oatmeal with Sugar and Cream.
Broiled Ham.   Creamed Potatoes.   Pop-overs or Fadges.
Coffee.

———◆———

Quaker Rolled Oats with Baked Apples, Sugar and Cream.
Creamed Fish.   Baked Potatoes.   Golden Corn Cake.
Coffee.

———◆———

Bananas.
Toasted Wheat with Sugar and Cream.
Scrambled Eggs.   Sautéd Potatoes.   Graham Gems.
Griddle Cakes.
Coffee.

———◆———

Grape Fruit.
Wheatlet with Sugar and Cream.
Beefsteak.   Lyonnaise Potatoes.   Twin Mountain Muffins.
Coffee.

———◆———

Sliced Oranges.
Wheat Germ with Sugar and Cream.
Warmed over Lamb.   French Fried Potatoes.   Raised Biscuits.
Buckwheat Cakes with Maple Syrup.
Coffee.

Strawberries.
Hominy with Sugar and Cream.
Bacon and Fried Eggs.　　Baked Potatoes.　　Rye Muffins.
Coffee.

———◆———

Raspberries.
Shredded Wheat Biscuit.
Dried Smoked Beef in Cream.　　Hashed Brown Potatoes.
Baking-Powder Biscuit.
Coffee.

———◆———

Watermelon.
Wheat Germ with Sugar and Cream.
Broiled Halibut.　　Potato Cakes.　　Sliced Cucumbers.
Quaker Biscuit.
Coffee.

———◆———

Canteloupe.
Pettijohns with Sugar and Cream.
Cecils with Tomato Sauce.　　Potato Balls.　　Rice Muffins.
Coffee.

———◆———

Peaches.
Farinose with Sugar and Cream.
Omelette.　　Potatoes à la Maître d' Hôtel.　　Berry Muffins.
Coffee.

———◆———

Blackberries.
H-O with Sugar and Cream.　　Dropped Eggs on Toast.
Waffles with Maple Syrup.
Coffee.

———◆———

Pears.
Wheatena with Sugar and Cream.
Corned Beef Hash.　　　　　　Milk Toast.
Coffee.
33

Grapes.
Cereal with Fruit.
Fried Smelts.   Baked Sweet Potatoes.   Sliced Tomatoes.
Oatmeal Muffins.
Coffee.

———◆———

Oatmeal Mush with Apples.
Hamburg Steaks.   Creamed Potatoes.   White Corn Cake.
Coffee.

———◆———

Plums and Pears.
Cracked Wheat with Sugar and Cream.
Baked Beans.   Fish Balls.   Brown Bread.
Coffee.

———◆———

Sliced Peaches.
Germea with Sugar and Cream.   Brown Bread Toast.
Cold Sliced Meat.   Sautéd Sweet Potatoes.
Coffee.

———◆———

Wheatena with Sugar and Cream.
Fish Hash.   Buttered Graham Toast.
Strawberry Short Cake.
Coffee.

———◆———

Grapes.
Wheat Germ with Sugar and Cream.
Lamb Chops.   Baked Potatoes.   Raised Muffins.
Doughnuts and Coffee.

———————

LUNCHEON MENUS.

Grilled Sardines.
Baked Apples with Cream.   Rolls.   Sponge Cake.
Cocoa.

Creamed Chicken.
Celery.   Rolls.
Grapes and Apples.
Tea.

◆

Lamb Croquettes.
Dressed Lettuce.   Baking-Powder Biscuit.
Gingerbread.   Cheese.
Tea.

◆

Split Pea Soup.   Crisp Crackers.
Egg Salad.   Entire Wheat Bread.
Oranges.
Cocoa.

◆

Cold Sliced Meat.   Cheese Fondue.
Bread and Butter.
Sliced Peaches.   Cookies.
Tea.

◆

Broiled Ham.   Scalloped Potatoes.
Brown Bread and Butter.
Sliced Oranges.   Wafers.

◆

Scalloped Oysters.   Rolls.
Dressed Celery.
Polish Tartlets.   Tea.

◆

Salmi of Lamb.   Olives.
Bread and Butter.
Cake.   Chocolate.

◆

Oyster Stew.
Oyster Crackers or Dry Toast.
Pickles.
Cream Whips.   Lady Fingers.

Scalloped Turkey.
Brown Bread Sandwiches.
Lettuce Salad.   Cheese Straws.
Tea.

———◆———

Turban of Fish.   Saratoga Potatoes.
Warmed over Muffins.
Nuts.   Crackers.   Cheese.
Tea.

———◆———

Cream of Tomato Soup.   Croûtons.
Omelette with Vegetables.
Bread and Butter.
Bananas.   Tea.

———◆———

Salad à la Russe.
Graham Bread and Butter.
Peach Sauce.   Scotch Wafers.
Tea.

———◆———

Cold Sliced Tongue.
Macaroni and Cheese.
Lettuce Salad.   Crackers.
Wafers.   Coffee.

———◆———

Salmon Croquettes.   Rolls.
Dressed Lettuce.
Strawberries and Cream.
Tea.

———◆———

Beef Stew with Dumplings.
Sliced Oranges.   Cake.
Tea.

———◆———

Lobster Salad.   Rolls.
Raspberries and Cream.   Wafers.
Russian Tea.

Cold Sliced Corned Beef.
Corn à la Southern.
Entire Wheat Bread and Butter.
Grapes and Pears.

DINNER MENUS.

Cream of Celery Soup.
Roast Beef.   Franconia Potatoes.   Yorkshire Pudding.
Macaroni with Cheese.   Tomato and Lettuce Salad.
Chocolate Cream.
Café Noir.

◆

Tomato Soup.
Baked Fish.   Hollandaise Sauce.
Shadow Potatoes.   Cole Slaw.
Fig Pudding.
Crackers.   Cheese.   Café Noir.

◆

Potato Soup.
Boiled Fowl.   Egg Sauce.   Boiled Rice.   Mashed Turnips.
Celery.   Vegetable Salad.
Bread and Butter Pudding.

◆

Macaroni Soup.
Fricassee of Lamb.   Riced Potatoes.   Stewed Tomatoes.
String Bean and Radish Salad.
Fruit and Nuts.

◆

Duchess Soup.
Fried Fillets of Halibut.   Shredded Potatoes.   Hot Slaw.
Beefsteak Pie.
Irish Moss Blanc-Mange with
Vanilla Wafers.

Kornlet Soup.
Maryland Chicken.   Baked Sweet Potatoes.
Creamed Cauliflower.   Cranberry Sauce.
Dressed Lettuce.   Polish Tartlets.
Café Noir.

◆

Vegetable Soup.
Veal Cutlets.   Horseradish.   Mashed Potatoes.
Cream of Lima Beans.   Dressed Celery.
Cerealine Pudding.

◆

St. Germain Soup.
Beefsteak with Oyster Blanket.   Stuffed Potatoes.   Spinach.
Pineapple Pudding.   Cream Sponge Cake.
Café Noir.

◆

White Soup.
Boiled Salmon.   Egg Sauce.   Boiled Potatoes.   Green Peas.
Cucumbers.
Strawberries and cream.   Cake.

◆

Tomato Soup without Stock.
Braised Beef.   Horseradish Sauce.   Scalloped Potatoes.
Squash.
Baked Indian Pudding.   Café Noir.

◆

Bisque Soup.
Broiled Shad.   Chartreuse Potatoes.   Asparagus on Toast.
Cucumber and Lettuce Salad.
Prune Whip.   Custard Sauce.

◆

Cream of Pea Soup.
Boiled Mutton.   Caper Sauce.   Mashed Potatoes.
Turkish Pilaf.
Graham Pudding.   Fruit and Nuts.

Turkish Soup.
Lamb Chops.   French Fried Potatoes.   Apple Fritters.
Beet Greens.
Caramel Custard.   Café Noir.

———◆———

Irish Stew with Dumplings.
Fish Croquettes.   Dinner Rolls.   Radishes.
Custard Soufflé.   Creamy Sauce.
Crackers.   Cheese.

———◆———

Black Bean Soup.
Halibut à la Créole.   Potatoes en Surprise.
Brussels Sprouts.
Swiss Pudding.   Café Noir.

———◆———

Cream of Clam Soup.
Fried Chicken   Boiled Potatoes.
Sliced Tomatoes.   Shell Beans.
Peach Short Cake.   Crackers and Cheese,

———◆———

Cream of Lima Bean Soup.
Roast Duck.   Mashed Sweet Potatoes.
Cauliflower au Gratin.
Rice Croquettes with Currant Jelly.
Grapes.   Pears.
Crackers.   Cheese.   Café Noir.

———◆———

Chicken Soup.
Broiled Sword Fish.   Cucumber Sauce.
Baked New Potatoes.   Sugared Beets.
Strawberry Cottage Pudding.
Iced Coffee.

MENU FOR THANKSGIVING DINNER.

Oyster Soup.   Crisp Crackers.
Celery.   Salted Almonds.
Roast Turkey.   Cranberry Jelly.
Mashed Potatoes.   Onions in Cream.   Squash.
Chicken Pie.
Fruit Pudding.   Sterling Sauce.
Mince, Apple, and Squash Pie.
Neapolitan Ice Cream.   Fancy Cakes.
Fruit.   Nuts and Raisins.   Bonbons.
Crackers.   Cheese.   Café Noir.

MENU FOR CHRISTMAS DINNER.

Consommé.   Bread Sticks.
Olives.   Celery.   Salted Pecans.
Roast Goose.   Potato Stuffing.   Apple Sauce.
Duchess Potatoes.   Cream of Lima Beans.
Chicken Croquettes with Green Peas.
Dressed Lettuce with Cheese Straws.
English Plum Pudding.   Brandy Sauce.
Frozen Pudding.   Assorted Cake.   Bonbons.
Crackers.   Cheese.   Café Noir.

A FULL COURSE DINNER.

First Course.

Little Neck Clams or Bluepoints, with brown-bread sandwiches. Sometimes canapés are used in place of either. For a gentlemen's dinner, canapés accompanied with sherry wine are frequently served before guests enter the dining-room.

Second Course.

Clear soup, with bread sticks, small rolls, or crisp crackers. Where two soups are served, one may be a cream soup. Cream soups are served with croûtons. Radishes, celery, or olives are passed after the soup. Salted almonds may be passed between any of the courses.

Third Course.

Bouchées or rissoles. The filling to be of light meat.

Fourth Course.

Fish, baked, boiled, or fried. Cole slaw, dressed cucumbers, or tomatoes accompany this course; with fried fish potatoes are often served.

Fifth Course.

Roast saddle of venison or mutton, spring lamb, or fillet of beef ; potatoes and one other vegetable.

Sixth Course.

Entrée, made of light meat or fish.

Seventh Course.

A vegetable. Such vegetables as mushrooms, cauliflower, asparagus, artichokes, are served, but not in white sauce.

Eighth Course.

Punch or cheese course. Punch, when served, always precedes the game course.

Ninth Course.

Game, with vegetable salad, usually lettuce or celery ; or cheese sticks may be served with the salad, and game omitted.

Tenth Course.

Dessert, usually cold.

Eleventh Course.

Frozen dessert and fancy cakes.   Bonbons are passed after this course.

Twelfth Course.

Crackers, cheese, and café noir.   Café noir is frequently served in the drawing and smoking rooms after the dinner.

Where wines and liquors are served, the first course is not usually accompanied by either; but if desired, Sauterne or other white wine may be used.

With soup, serve sherry; with fish, white wine; with game, claret; with roast and other courses, champagne.

After serving café noir in drawing-room, pass pony of brandy for men, sweet liqueur (Chartreuse, Benedictine, or Parfait d'Amour) for women; then Crême de Menthe to all.

After a short time Apollinaris should be passed. White wines and claret should be served cool; sherry should be thoroughly chilled by keeping in ice box. Champagne should be served very cold by allowing it to remain in salt and ice at least one-half hour before dinner time.   Claret, as it contains so small an amount of alcohol, is not good the day after opening.

For a simpler dinner, the third, seventh, eighth, and tenth courses, and the game in the ninth course may be omitted.

For a home dinner, it is always desirable to serve for first course a soup; second course, meat or fish, with potatoes and two other vegetables; third course, a vegetable salad, with French dressing; fourth course, dessert; fifth course, crackers, cheese, and café noir.

At a ladies' luncheon the courses are as many as at a small dinner.   In winter, grape fruit is sometimes served in place of oysters; in summer, selected strawberries in small Swedish Timbale cases.

MENUS FOR FULL COURSE DINNERS.

Blue Points.
Consommé à la Royal.
Olives.   Celery.   Salted Almonds.
Swedish Timbales with Chicken and Mushrooms.
Fried Smelts.   Sauce Tartare.   Dressed Cucumbers.
Saddle of Mutton.   Currant Jelly Sauce.
Potatoes Brabrant.   Brussels Sprouts.
Suprême of Chicken.
Mushrooms à la Sabine.
Canton Sherbet.
Canvasback Duck.   Olive Sauce.
Farina Cakes with Jelly.
Celery Salad.
Apricot and Wine Jelly.
Nesselrode Pudding.   Rolled Wafers.   Parisian Sweets.
Crackers.   Cheese.
Café Noir.

———◆———

Little Neck Clams.
Consommé au Parmesan.
Olives.   Salted Pecans.
Bouchées.
Fillets of Halibut à la Poulette with Mayonnaise.
Tomatoes.   Delmonico Potatoes.   String Beans.
Larded Fillet of Beef with Horseradish Sauce.
Glazed Sweetbreads.
Artichokes with Béchamel Sauce.
Sorbet.
Broiled Quail with Lettuce and Celery Salad.
Bananas.   Cantaloupes.
Sultana Roll with Claret Sauce.
Cinnamon Bars.   Lady Fingers.   Bonbons.
Crackers.   Cheese.
Café Noir.

Anchovy Canapés.

Julienne Soup.

Olives.   Celery.   Ginger Chips.

Oyster and Macaroni Croquettes.

Stuffed Fillets of Halibut.

French Hollandaise Sauce.   Tomato Jelly.

Spring Lamb.   Potato Fritters.

Asparagus Tips with Hollandaise Sauce.

Chaud-froid of Chicken.

Crême de Menthe Ice.

Larded Grouse.   Bread Sauce.   Lettuce and Radish Salad.

Mont Blanc.

Bombe Glacée. Sponge Drops. Almond Crescents. Bonbons.

Crackers.   Cheese.

Café Noir.

NECESSARY UTENSILS AND STORES FOR FITTING A SCHOOL KITCHEN FOR A CLASS OF TWENTY-FOUR.

Miss A. G. E. Hope.

AGATE WARE.

Hot water boiler (capacity fifteen gallons).
12 small dish pans.
1 large dish pan.
1 hand basin.
1 teakettle.
3 3-pint double boilers.

1 2-quart double boiler.
3 2-quart saucepans with covers.
3 3-quart saucepans with covers.
1 4-quart saucepan with cover.
5 1-pint saucepans with covers.
6 ½-pint saucepans with covers.
1 coffeepot.

TIN AND STEEL WARE.

12 measuring cups, divided in quarters.
12 measuring cups, divided in thirds.
24 round tin pans for washing vegetables.
24 tin plates.
6 medium-sized biscuit cutters.
6 small doughnut cutters.
1 2-quart milk can.
1 1-quart measure.
1 flour sifter with crank.
3 extension flour sifters.
3 gravy strainers.
1 colander.
1 large grater.
1 nutmeg grater.
1 set skewers.
1 dripping pan and rack.
1 steamer.
2 tin sheets.
3 large pans.
3 small bread pans.
3 cake pans.
3 pie plates.
1 pudding mould.

3 ½-pint moulds.
3 wire potato mashers.
12 small salt boxes.
12 pepper boxes (shakers).
1 flour dredger.
1 wire broiler.
4 soap shakers.
1 2-quart dipper.
Wire dish cloth.
2 dozen tablespoons.
4 dozen teaspoons.
1 griddle cake turner.
1 skimmer.
1 dish drainer.
1 dust pan.
1 Dover egg-beater.
3 small omelet pans.
1 large frying-pan.
2 dozen case knives.
2 dozen forks.
2 dozen vegetable knives.
1 carving knife and fork.
1 knife sharpener.
1 cleaver.

EARTHEN AND GLASS WARE.

6 2-quart yellow bowls.
6 1-quart white bowls.
6 large bowls for bread dough.
3 1-pint oval pudding dishes.
3 1-pint round yellow dishes.
2 2-quart pitchers.
1 1-quart pitcher.
1 1-pint pitcher.
1 butter jar.
1 bean pot.
7 soap dishes (for common soap).
7 soap dishes (for Sapolio).
1 small tea set: teapot, sugar bowl, creamer.

1 small dinner set with small tureen.
3 white platters (of different sizes).
6 large white plates.
6 small white plates.
24 sauce dishes (to be used for serving).
6 teacups and saucers.
12 after dinner cups and saucers.
1 glass lemon drill.
1 dozen tumblers.
6 2-quart Mason jars, }
6 1-quart Mason jars, } for keeping stores.
6 1-pint Mason jars, }

WOODEN WARE.

1 large wooden bucket for flour.
1 wooden bucket for pastry flour.
1 wooden bucket for sugar.
6 moulding boards.
3 rolling pins.
3 wooden mashers.
3 wooden mixing spoons.
12 scrubbing brushes.
1 large scrubbing brush.
6 vegetable brushes.

1 small pair steps.
2 towel racks.
1 sink scraper.
2 long-handled brushes.
2 short-handled brushes (one for stove, one for floor).
2 blacking brushes.
1 dauber.
1 large feather duster.
1 small feather duster.

LINENS, DUSTERS, ETC.

3 hand towels (for teacher).
1 dozen dish towels.
6 glass towels.
4 dish cloths.
6 oven cloths.
4 floor cloths.
4 sink cloths.
3 dozen desk cloths.

2 dozen small dusters for desks.
6 cheese cloth dusters, one yard square.
6 yards coarse flannel.
1 white tablecloth, 2½ yards long.
1 red tablecloth.
1 silence cloth.
1 dozen napkins.

MISCELLANEOUS.

3 3-quart porcelain-lined iron kettles, with tight-fitting covers.
3 sets iron gem pans.
4 match boxes.

1 inkstand.
1 pair scissors.
1 bell.

STORES.

½ barrel bread flour.
1 bag whole wheat flour.
1 bag pastry flour.
25 lbs. fine granulated sugar.
5 lbs. powdered sugar.
6 lbs. rice.
6 lbs. cornmeal.
2 1-pound packages corn-starch.
4 1-pound boxes baking powder.
12-pound bag salt.
½-pound box mustard.
1 box each cinnamon, clove, allspice, and mace.

2 oz. whole mace.
2 oz. whole cloves.
2 oz. whole peppercorns.
¼ lb. nutmegs
2 lbs. currants.
2 lbs. raisins.
½ lb. citron.
36 cakes common soap.
12 bars Ivory soap.
36 cakes Sapolio.
6 tins stove polish.
2 tins Putz Cream (for cleaning faucets and boiler).

GLOSSARY.

Accolade de perdreaux. Brace of partridge.

Agneau. Lamb.

Agra dolce (*sour sweet*). An Italian sauce served with meat.

À la, au, aux. With or dressed in a certain style.

Allemande (*à la*). In German style.

Ambrosia. Food for the gods. Often applied to a fruit salad.

Américaine (*à l'*). In American style.

Ancienne (*à l'*). In old style.

Angelica. A plant, the stalks of which are preserved and used for decorating moulds.

Asafetida. A gum resin. Its taste is bitter and sub-acrid, and by the Asiatics it is used regularly as a condiment.

Asperges. Asparagus.

Au gratin. With browned crumbs.

Aurora sauce. A white sauce to which lobster butter is added.

Avena. Oats.

Baba Cakes. Cakes baked in small moulds; made from a yeast dough mixture to which is added butter, sugar, eggs, raisins, and almonds. Served as a pudding with hot sauce.

Bain-Marie. A vessel of any kind containing heated water, in which other vessels are placed in order to keep their contents heated.

Bannocks. Scottish cakes made of barley or oatmeal, cooked on a griddle.

Bards. Slices of pork or bacon to lay on the breast of game for cooking.

Basil. A pot herb.

Bay leaves. Leaves from a species of laurel.

Béarnaise (*à la*). In Swiss style.

Béarnaise sauce. Named from Béarnaise, Swiss home of Henry VIII.

Béchamel (*à la*). With sauce made of chicken stock and milk or cream.

Beignet. Fritter.

Beurre noir. Black butter.

Biscuit Glacé. Small cakes of ice cream.

Bisque. A soup usually made from shellfish; or an ice cream to which is added finely chopped nuts.

Blanch (*to*). To whiten.

Blanquette. White meat in cream sauce.

Bœuf braisé. Braised beef.

Bœuf à la jardinière. Braised beef with vegetables.

Bombe glacée. Moulded ice cream and ice, or two kinds of ice cream. Outside of one kind, filling of another.

Bouchées. Literally, mouthful. Small patties.

Bouquet of herbs. A sprig each of thyme, savory, marjoram, and parsley.

Bourgeoise (*à la*). In family style.

Bretonne sauce. A stock sauce in which chopped parsley is served.

Café noir. Black coffee.

Cervelles de veau. Calf's brains.

Chartreuse. A mould of aspic in which there are vegetables; a meat preparation filling the centre of the mould. Used to denote anything concealed.

Chateaubriand. A cut from the centre of a fillet of beef.

Chaud-froid. Literally hot cold. In cookery a jellied sauce.

Chou-fleur. Cauliflower.

Chutney. An East India sweet pickle.
Civet. A game stew.
Compotes. Fruits stewed in syrup and kept in original shape.
Consommé de volaille. Chicken soup.
Côtelettes. Cutlets.
Court bouillon. A highly seasoned liquor in which to cook fish.
Créole (à la). With tomatoes.
Croûte au pot. A brown soup poured over small pieces of toast.
Curry powder. A yellow powder of which the principal ingredient is turmeric. Used largely in India.

De, d'. Of.
Devilled. Highly seasoned.
Dinde farcie. Stuffed turkey.
Dinde, sauce céleri. Turkey with celery sauce.

Écossaise (à l'). In Scottish style.
En bellevue. In aspic jelly. Applied to meats.
En coquilles. In shells.
En papillotes. In papers.
Éperlans frits. Fried smelts.
Espagnole sauce. A rich brown sauce.

Farci-e. Stuffed.
Fillet de bœuf piqué. Larded fillet of beef.
Flamande (à la). In Holland style.
Foie de veau grillé. Broiled liver.
Fondue A dish prepared of cheese and eggs.
Fraises. Strawberries.
Frappé. Semi-frozen.
Fricassée de poulet. Fricassee of chicken.
Fromage. Cheese.

Gâteau. Cake.
Gelée. Jelly.
Génevoise (à la). In Swiss style.
Glacé. Iced or glossed over.
Grilled. Broiled.

Hachis de bœuf. Beef hash.
Hoe cakes. Cakes made of white corn-meal, salt, and boiling water; cooked on a griddle.
Homard. Lobster.
Hors-d'œuvres. Side dishes.
Huîtres en coquille. Oysters in shell.
Huîtres frites. Fried oysters.

Italienne (à l'). In Italian style.

Jambon froid. Cold ham.
Jardinière. Mixed vegetables.

Kirschwasser. Liqueur made from cherry juice.
Kuchen. German for cake.
Kümmel. Liqueur flavored with cumin and caraway seed.

Lait. Milk.
Laitue. Lettuce.
Langue de bœuf à l'écarlate. Pickled tongue.

Macaroni au fromage. Macaroni with cheese.
Macédoine. A mixture of several kinds of vegetables.
Maigre. A vegetable soup without stock.
Maître d'hôtel. Head steward.
Mango. A fruit of the West Indies, Florida, and Mexico.
Mango pickles. Stuffed and pickled young melons and cucumbers.
Maraschino. A cordial.
Marrons. Chestnuts.
Menu. A bill of fare.
Morue. Salt cod.

Noël. Christmas.
Noir. Black.
Nouilles. Noodles.
Noyau. A cordial.

Œufs farcis. Stuffed eggs.
Œufs pochés. Poached eggs.
Omelette aux fines herbes. Omelette with fine herbs.
Omelette aux champignons. Omelette with mushrooms.

Pain. Bread.
Panade. Bread and milk cooked to a paste.
Paté de biftecks. Beefsteak pie.
Paté de foie gras. A paste made of fatted geese livers.
Pigeonneaux. Squabs.
Pois. Peas.
Pommes. Apples.
Pommes de terre. Potatoes.
Pommes de terre à la Lyonnaise. Lyonnaise potatoes.

Pone cakes. A cake made in the South, baked in the oven.

Potage. Soup.

Poulets sautés. Fried chicken.

Queues de bœuf. Ox-tails.

Ragoût. A highly seasoned meat dish.

Réchauffés. Warmed over dishes.

Removes. The roasts or principal dishes.

Ris de veau. Sweetbreads.

Salade de laitue. Lettuce salad.

Salade de légumes. Vegetable salad.

Salpicon. Highly seasoned minced meat mixed with a thick sauce.

Selle de venaison. Saddle of venison.

Sippets. English for croûtons.

Soufflé. Literally, puffed up.

Soupe à l'ognon. Onion soup.

Sucres. Sweets.

Tarte aux pommes. Apple pie.

Tourte A tart.

Truite saumonée. Salmon trout.

COURSE OF INSTRUCTION

AS GIVEN AT THE

BOSTON COOKING SCHOOL,

174 TREMONT STREET.

PRACTICE LESSONS.

ONE lesson a week, from 9 to 12.30. Eight Pupils constitute a full class. Pupils may enter one or more classes. After the lesson the food prepared is served to the pupils. Applications to enter classes may be made from October to February. Classes for cooks in Second and Third Courses on Thursday and Friday at 2 P. M.

No extra charge for materials in Cooks' Classes.

FIRST COURSE. — PLAIN COOKING.

Twelve Lessons for $12.00. Materials, $3.00.

First Lesson.	*Second Lesson.*
The Making and Care of a Fire.	Baking Bread.
Coffee.	Potato Soup.
Mixing Water Bread.	Broiled Fish.
Tomato Soup (without stock).	Mashed Potatoes.
Croûtons.	Boiled Eggs.
Boiled Potatoes.	Hash.
Mutton Chops.	Scalloped Eggs.
German Toast.	Blanc-Mange.

Third Lesson.

Brown Soup Stock.
Mixing Milk Bread.
Griddle Cakes.
Boiled Fish.
Drawn Butter or Egg Sauce.
Steamed Potatoes.
Tapioca Cream.

Fourth Lesson.

Vegetable Soup.
To Clarify Fat and Try out Lard.
Baking Milk Bread.
Baked Potatoes.
Broiled Steak.
Broiled Meat Cakes.
Baked Custards.
Cookies or Ginger Snaps.

Fifth Lesson.

Beef Stew with Dumplings.
Graham Bread.
Scalloped Fish.
White Sauce.
Poached Eggs on Toast.
Short Cakes.
Gingerbread.
Tea.

Sixth Lesson.

Golden Corn Cake.
Fish Balls.
Fried Fish.
Fried Potatoes.
Omelet.
Chocolate.
Harvard Pudding.
Apple and Hard Sauce.

Seventh Lesson.

Fish Chowder.
Stuffed Eggs.
Bread Omelet.
Bacon.
Creamed Potatoes.
Graham Gems.
Chocolate Bread Pudding.
Hard Sauce.
Parker House Rolls.

Eighth Lesson.

Pea Soup.
Crisp Crackers.
Baked Beans.
Veal Cutlets.
Doughnuts.
Brown Bread.
Steamed Squash.
Apple Pie.

Ninth Lesson.

Scotch Broth.
Corn Fritters.
Tomato Salad.
Milk Toast.
Sweet Sandwiches.
Cake.
Eggs in Batter.
Sherbet.

Tenth Lesson.

Roast Beef.
Potato Croquettes.
Macaroni.
Scalloped Cabbage.
Cereal with Fruit.
Rye Muffins.
Prune Pudding.
Custard Sauce.

Eleventh Lesson.

Oyster Soup or Stew.
Broiled Oysters.
Veal Birds.
Cole Slaw.
Twin Mountain Muffins.
Peach Tapioca Pudding.
Coffee Cake.
Sandwiches.

Twelfth Lesson.

Roast or Fricassee Chicken.
Rice with Cheese.
Creamed Turnips.
Hominy Cakes.
Plain Lobster.
French Dressing.
Custard Soufflé.
Creamy Sauce.

SECOND COURSE. — RICHER COOKING.

Twelve Lessons for $15.00.   Materials, $3.00.

First Lesson.

Coffee.
Baked Apples.
Lyonnaise Potatoes.
Broiled Beefsteak with Maître
    d'Hôtel Butter.
Eggs à la Goldenrod.
Rice Griddle Cakes.
Soda Biscuit.
Frizzled Beef.

Second Lesson.

Mutton Cutlets Breaded, with To-
    mato Sauce.
French Fried Potatoes.
Parisienne Potatoes.
Baked Eggs.
Rye Drop Cakes.
Waffles.
Lemon Syrup.
Chocolate.

Third Lesson.

Spanish Omelet.
Parker House Rolls.
Scalloped Oysters.
Smothered Oysters.
Oysters Sautéd.
Eggs in Baskets.
Breakfast Bacon.
Moulded Snow.
Foamy Sauce.

Fourth Lesson.

Stock for Clear Soup.
Broiled Fish.
Tartar Sauce.
Potato Croquettes.
Fish Balls.
Macaroni or Spaghetti.
Fried Oysters or Scallops.
Thanksgiving Pudding.
Brandy Sauce.

Fifth Lesson.

Clear Soup.
Egg Balls.
Shadow Potatoes.
Baked Fish, Sauce Hollandaise.
Sticks and Rolls.
Cabbage Salad.
Boiled Dressing.
Caramel Custard.
Caramel Sauce.

Sixth Lesson.

Cream of Tomato Soup.
Braised Chicken.
Potato Balls.
Lima Beans.
Farina Cakes with Jelly.
Raised Muffins.
Custard Soufflé.
Creamy Sauce.
Cold Cabinet Pudding.

Seventh Lesson.

Purée of Fish.
Cusk à la Crême.
White Sauce.
Curried Lobster.
Potato Salad.
Apple or Lemon Pie.
Cream Cakes.
Quaker Bread.

Eighth Lesson.

Black Bean Soup.
Croûtons.
Roast Beef.
Franconia Potatoes.
Yorkshire Pudding.
Parsnip Fritters.
Spinach.
Coffee Cream.
Rice Croquettes.

Ninth Lesson.

Swiss Potato Soup.
Stuffed Leg of Mutton.
Currant Jelly Sauce.
Turkish Pilaf.
Turnips in White Sauce.
Tea Rolls.
Scalloped Apple.
Cream Pies.

Tenth Lesson.

Cream of Celery Soup.
Roast Chicken or
Fricassee.
Boiled Rice.
Cranberry Sauce.
Mashed Potatoes.
Spider Corn Cake.
Cake.
Frosting.
Snow Pudding.

Eleventh Lesson.

White Soup.
Chicken Croquettes.
Broiled Squabs.
Apple Fritters.
Pinwheel Biscuits.
Lady Fingers.
Sponge Drops.
Charlotte Russe.
Orange or
Wine Jelly.

Twelfth Lesson.

Puff Paste.
Oyster Patties.
Raspberry Tarts.
Creamed Oysters.
Lobster Salad.
Mayonnaise Dressing.
Salted Almonds.
Ice Cream or
Sherbet.

DINNER COURSE.

Twelve Lessons for $18.00.   Materials, $6:00.

First Lesson.	*Second Lesson.*

Oyster Soup.

Halibut à la Créole.

Chicken Sauté.

Creamed Cauliflower.

Rolls.

Almond Wafers.

Orange Trifle.

Café Noir.

St. Germain Soup.

Broiled Fillet of Beef.

Mushroom Sauce.

Mashed Sweet Potato.

Egg Salad.

Fig Pudding.

Yellow Sauce.

Coffee.

Third Lesson.   *Fourth Lesson.*

Oyster Gumbo Soup.

Baked Fish with Oysters.

French Hollandaise Sauce.

Hot Slaw.

Chicken Salad.

Cream Dressing.

Chocolate Nougat.

Boiled Frosting.

Ginger Cream.

Purée of Spinach.

Lobster Cream.

Boned Birds.

Creamed Celery.

Oysters à la D'Uxelles.

Potato Salad.

Burnt Almond Charlotte.

Fifth Lesson.   *Sixth Lesson.*

Bisque of Lobster.

Fillet of Beef.

Horseradish Sauce.

Potatoes au Gratin.

Banana Fritters.

Shrimp Salad.

Pudding à la Macédoine.

Potage à la Reine.

Puff Paste.

Patties.

Cream Horns.

Cheese Straws.

Pineapple Cream.

Seventh Lesson.   *Eighth Lesson.*

Cream of Asparagus Soup.

Lobster à la Newburg.

Chicken à la Providence.

Chocolate Cream Fritters.

Nut Sandwiches.

Victoria Punch.

Peanut Cookies.

Duchess Soup.

Halibut à la Poulette.

Queen of Muffins.

Larded Grouse.

Bread Sauce.

Ornamental Frosting.

Orange Ice.

Ninth Lesson.

Clam Soup with Poached Eggs.
Chicken Timbales.
Béchamel Sauce.
Beefsteak with Oyster Blanket.
Delmonico Potatoes.
Sponge Cake.
Baked Alaska.

Tenth Lesson.

Consommé.
Lobster Cutlets.
Chicken Soufflé.
Mushroom Sauce.
Brussels Sprouts.
Lemon Queens.
Bombe Glacée.
Parisian Sweets.

Eleventh Lesson.

Cream of Lettuce Soup.
Fillet of Sole.
Sauce Tartare.
Stewed Mushrooms.
Shredded Potatoes.
Lobster Salad.
Marshmallow Cake.
Café Parfait.

Twelfth Lesson.

Cream of Cauliflower Soup.
Swedish Timbales.
Creamed Sweetbreads.
Roast Duck.
Olive Sauce.
Fruit Punch.
Sand Tarts.
Frozen Pudding.

SPECIAL LESSONS IN COOKING, by previous appointment, price, $2.00 each. Materials extra.

SPECIAL LESSONS IN LAUNDRY WORK, by previous appointment, price, $2.00 each. Attention given to the doing up of shirts, silk and woollen underwear, colored clothes, table linen, laces, and chiffons.

Afternoon lessons given to Classes in Sick-room Cookery from 2 to 4.30 o'clock. Six lessons for $5.00. Materials, $1.00.

THE NORMAL COURSE extends from January to July. Tuition, $125. For circular and information, apply to the Principal.

DEMONSTRATION LECTURES given during the winter every Wednesday at 10 o'clock A. M. Tickets for course of 12 lectures, with reserved seat, $5.00. Single admission, 50 cents.

DEMONSTRATION LECTURES for Cooks, Wednesday and Friday evenings at 7.45 o'clock. Admission, 25 cents.

ROOMS OPEN DAILY, from 9 A. M. to 5 P. M.

INDEX.

FOSS'

EXTRACTS

IN ANY OF THE VALUABLE RECEIPTS IN THIS BOOK WHERE
FRUIT FLAVORING IS CALLED FOR, THE VERY BEST
RESULTS WILL BE OBTAINED BY USING

Foss' Pure Flavoring Extracts

Why?

Because OF THEIR ABSOLUTE PURITY

Because OF THEIR UNUSUAL STRENGTH

Because OF THEIR DELICATE FLAVOR

THEY ARE USED BY MANY OF THE LEADING TEACHERS
OF COOKERY, AND ARE ALSO USED AT THE **BOSTON
COOKING SCHOOL**, WHERE THE AIM IS ALWAYS TO
SECURE THE *PUREST* AND *BEST* ARTICLES OF FOOD

These Extracts are preferred and used by Mrs. D. A. Lincoln

Awarded the Gold Medal (Highest Award)
by the Massachusetts Charitable Mechanic
Association, 1892, for Purity and Superiority

KINGSFORD'S
OSWEGO STARCH

THE STANDARD OF EXCELLENCE

Kingsford's Corn Starch

The
Original

For Over
50 Years

SOLD ALL AROUND THE WORLD

For the Laundry ❧ ❧ ❧

Silver Gloss Starch

A GIANT IN STRENGTH
MATCHLESS IN PURITY

Kingsford's "Pure" Starch

FOR ECONOMY AND GOOD QUALITY

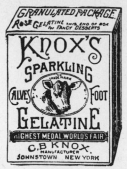

Old Grist Mill Entire Wheat Coffee ✢ ✢ ✢ ✢ ✢ ✢

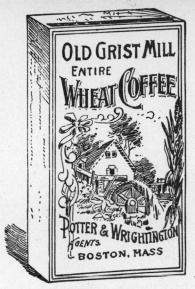

A PERFECT HYGIENIC SUBSTITUTE FOR COF-FEE, CONTAINING THE ENTIRE WHEAT KERNEL ROASTED AND GROUND

It has all the delicate flavor of Moca and Java, but unlike these Coffees it does not produce biliousness or irritate the nerves.

It aids digestion, is easily assimilated by the weakest stomach, and assists nature in preserving the complexion clear and fresh.

BEWARE OF IMITATIONS OR OTHER COFFEE SUBSTITUTES SAID TO BE AS GOOD.

Sold only in 1-lb. Cartons, 20 cents. Never in Bulk.

SOMETHING NEW FOR BREAKFAST.

Old Grist Mill Toasted Wheat.

THE TOASTED WHEAT IS A PERFECT HYGIENIC FOOD.

As fresh bread becomes more easily digested by toasting, so in our process of preparing and toasting the Wheat the same chemical change takes place, which renders it easier of assimilation, at the same time giving it that delightful flavor which is so palatable, making the **TOASTED WHEAT** a delight to the robust and healthy, and a boon to the invalids and convalescents.

Give it freely to the children; they thrive on it, as it is not heating like Oat Meals and other Cereals.

It contains all the health-giving qualities of the wheat; the phosphates, nitrates, and fat-producing qualities are fully retained, which are the necessary qualities for strengthening the bones, muscles, and nerves.

An introduction of this remarkable Health Food to your family will demonstrate its wholesome and nutritious qualities, and render it an indispensable necessity of the breakfast table.

Ask your grocer for a sample. If he does not carry it in stock, insist on his obtaining it for you. We will furnish the samples free.

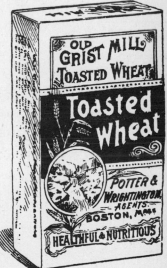

POTTER & WRIGHTINGTON,

Manufacturers of OLD GRIST MILL HEALTH FOODS,

60 COMMERCE STREET, BOSTON, MASS., U. S. A.

Choice
House Furnishings

FOREIGN AND DOMESTIC.

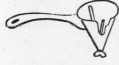

NO other house in this country can show such a variety. French Fry Pans; Jelly Sieves; Enamelled, Tin, and Copper Moulds — more than 1200 patterns and different sizes; Soufflé Dishes; Coffee Mills; Pepper Mills; Table Coffee Roasters; Coffee Pots and Machines; Pot au feu; Shirred Egg Dishes; Casseroles; Marmites; Salad Forks and Spoons; Salad Washers; Cook's Knives; Hateletts; Vegetable Cutters; Paste Cutters; Ramikins; Parisien Potato Cutters; Wood Cooking-School Spoons; also, a large variety of English and German Culinary Goods.

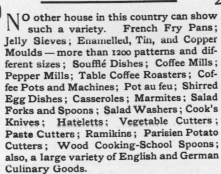

We call special attention to our Plate Warmers, to use with charcoal and for register.

English Knife Machines clean from two to eight knives at a time. Also Knife Boards, Fireplace Fittings, Andirons, Fenders, Fire Sets, Brushes, and Bellows.

We have imported a line of latest **COOK BOOKS**, elegantly illustrated in colors, with all information as to purchasing market supplies; cutlery and carving; setting the most elaborate tables, from the simplest to the most elegant entertainments. These are at the disposal of customers. **FREE FOR ONE WEEK**; after that, 2 cents a day, till returned.

F. A. WALKER & CO.
House Furnishers

Importers ∴ Wholesalers ∴ Retailers
Established, 1839.

Catalogues with 3,000 illustrations at Store, or mailed on receipt of 10 cents for mailing.

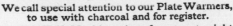
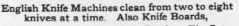
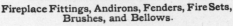

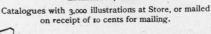

Crimped Crust Quaker Bread

Is the sweetest and best that can be turned out — dainty of crust, rich and moist inside.

It is common-sense bread ; it is scientific bread.

Every virtue of the flour, every aroma of the bread, is held as you never saw it before.

It is more nutritious, and will keep longer than any other bread without becoming stale.

The great secret is in the pan. Simple as a clothespin. It steams as well as bakes the bread, and never burns it.

Quaker Crimped Crust Bread

is especially recommended by Miss Fannie Merritt Farmer.

Witchkloth
The Magic Polisher

SAVES Work and Worry.
SAVES Wear and Tear.
SAVES Time and Trouble.

And it Saves Money.

The simplest and best of all the polishers. The cleanest and quickest. Try it on the silverware, the bicycle, the piano, the harness, the glassware — on any polished thing that has lost its shine, and you'll be astounded and delighted with the result. Like a piece of cotton cloth to look at. Used as you'd use a wiping rag.

It hurts nothing. It costs next to nothing.

All dealers, or send 15 cents for sample piece to
Asbury=Paine Mfg. Co., Wayne Junction, Phila., Pa.

Perfection.

If you are interested in having a varied, a dainty and a wholesome home bill of fare, use the perfect shortening—

COTTOLENE

Makes every dish it enters wholesome and delicious.

Genuine Cottolene is sold everywhere with trade-marks—
"Cottolene" and *steer's head in cotton-plant wreath*—on every tin.

MADE ONLY BY

THE N. K. FAIRBANK COMPANY,

Chicago, St. Louis, New York, Boston, Philadelphia,
San Francisco, New Orleans, Montreal.

GRANITE IRONWARE.

OVER ONE THOUSAND SHAPES AND SIZES HAVE BEEN THE

STANDARD 20 YEARS

Manufactured only by ST. LOUIS STAMPING CO

ST. LOUIS, and For Sale Everywhere.

BRANCHES:

96 Beekman Street, NEW YORK.   143 & 145 Lake St., CHICAGO

BOSTON : Nos. 93, 95, 97, 99, and 101 NORTH STREET

With the use of **King Arthur Flour** comes a better understanding concerning **quality in** bread.

Absolute Purity ∴ **Delicate Flavor**

Amount of Nutrition

possessed by the **King Arthur Brand**, together with he good qualities usually found in first-class flour, nakes **King Arthur** perfection.

Sands, Taylor & Wood,

Wholesale Distributors,
172 State Street, Boston.